Deltora Quest

デルトラクエスト

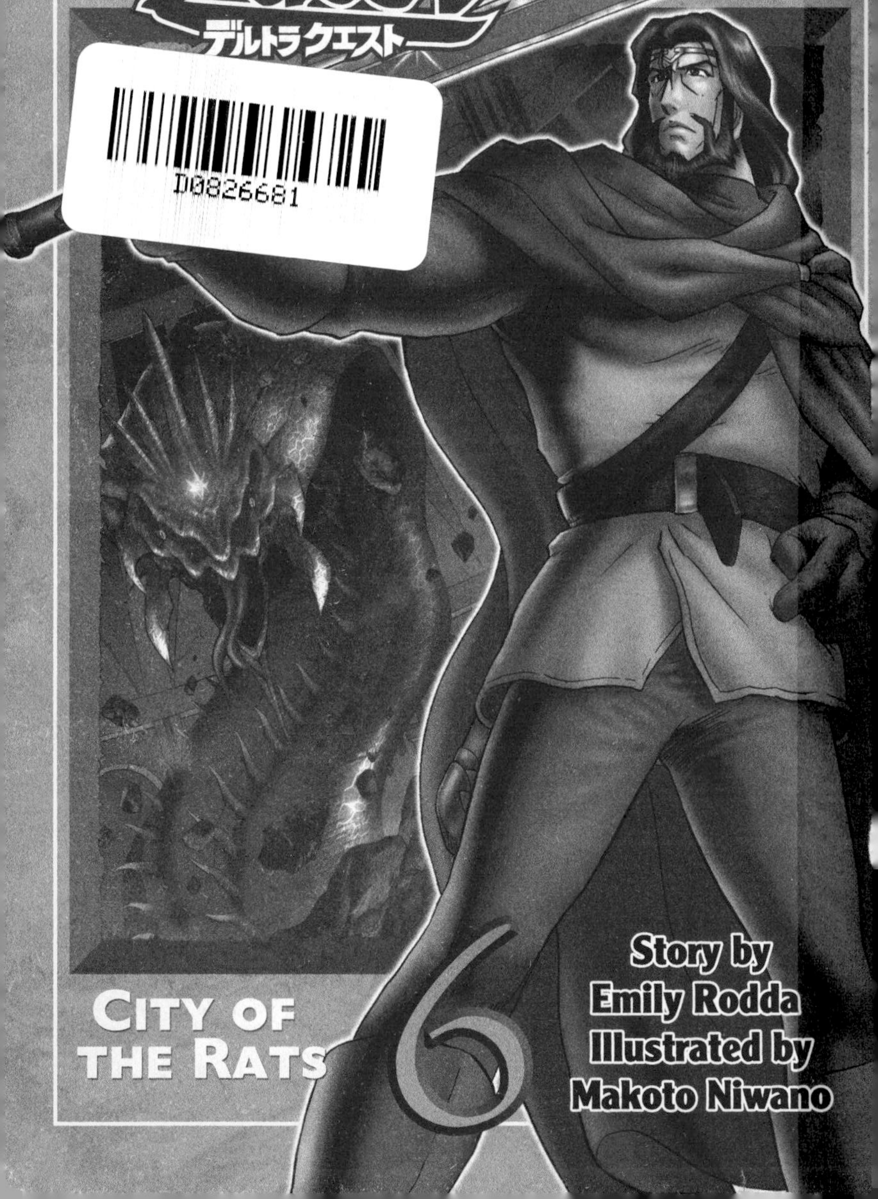

City of the Rats

6

Story by
Emily Rodda
Illustrated by
Makoto Niwano

DELTORA QUEST
デルトラ クエスト
Volume 6: Character Introductions

Lief
The only son of Jarred, the Hero of Deltora. He sets out on a journey to find the Seven Gems and restore peace to the Kingdom of Deltora, which has fallen into the hands of the Shadow Lord.

Filli
A strange creature who is always with Jasmine.

Jasmine
Formerly a resident of the Forests of Silence. At the request of her mother's spirit, she agrees to help Lief and Barda on their quest.

The Ra-Kacharz
The keepers of cleanliness, who rule the immaculate city of Noradz. There are nine of them in all.

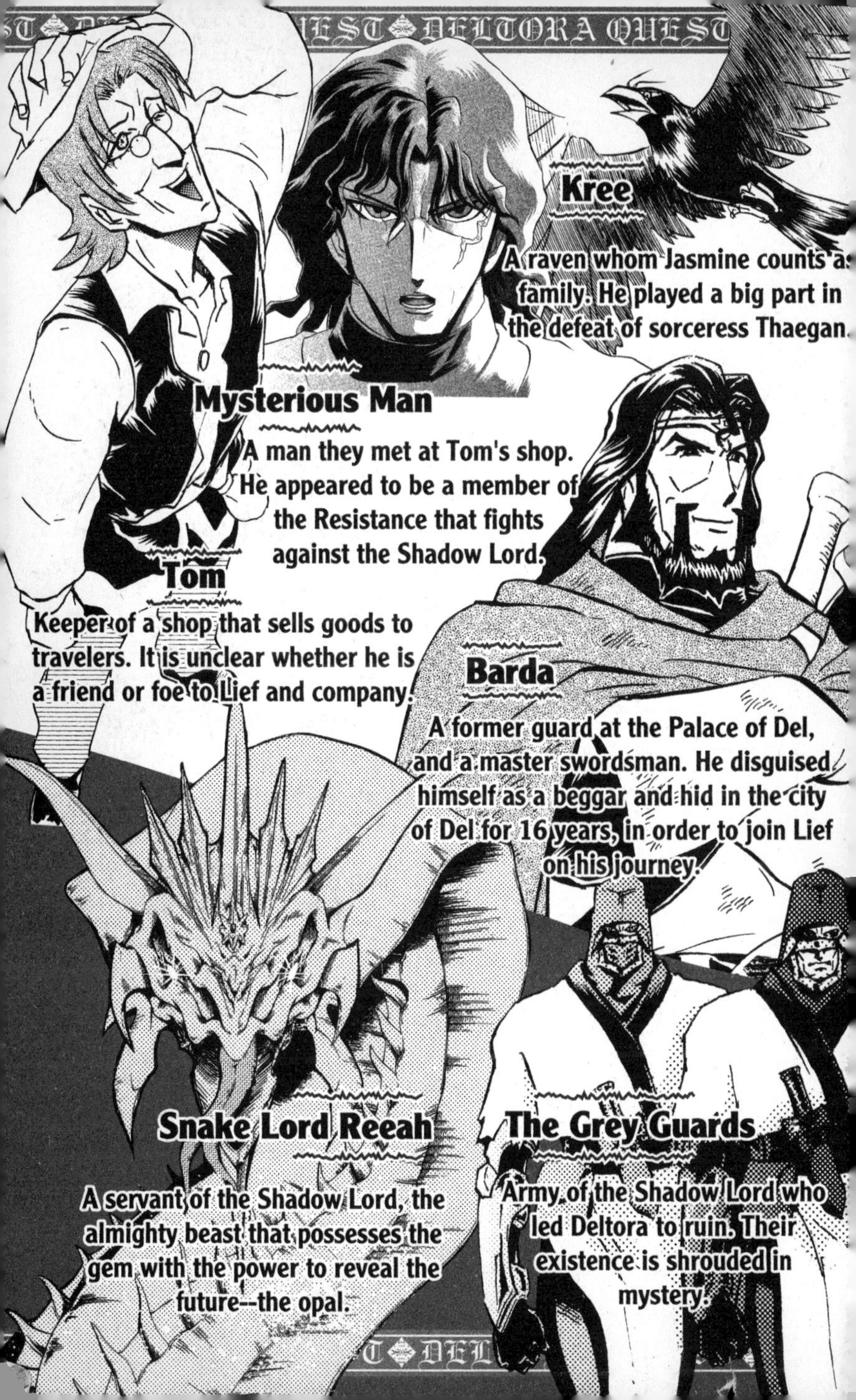
DELTORA QUEST
Kree
A raven whom Jasmine counts as family. He played a big part in the defeat of sorceress Thaegan.
Mysterious Man
A man they met at Tom's shop. He appeared to be a member of the Resistance that fights against the Shadow Lord.
Tom
Keeper of a shop that sells goods to travelers. It is unclear whether he is a friend or foe to Lief and company.
Barda
A former guard at the Palace of Del, and a master swordsman. He disguised himself as a beggar and hid in the city of Del for 16 years, in order to join Lief on his journey.
The Grey Guards
Army of the Shadow Lord who led Deltora to ruin. Their existence is shrouded in mystery.
Snake Lord Reeah
A servant of the Shadow Lord, the almighty beast that possesses the gem with the power to reveal the future--the opal.

Synopsis

Lief, Barda and Jasmine are on a quest to find the Seven Gems and restore peace to Deltora. After overcoming numerous hardships, they obtain the topaz and the ruby.

THANK YOU.

NOW WE HAVE TWO!

LET US OUT!

BAM

GRR! WHAT ARE THEY GOING TO DO WITH US?

Lief and company head for the City of the Rats to find the next gem, but on the way, they are taken prisoner at Noradz, a city ruled by nine keepers of cleanliness known as the Ra-Kacharz.

BOOOOM

HOW DID YOU ES-CAPE THE DUN-GEON ?!

The three escape the dungeon with the help of the servant girl Tira, but Reece, head of the Ra-Kacharz, catches them and our heroes almost lose their lives.

YOU WERE GIVEN A LIFE SENTENCE, BUT YOU HAVE ADDED TO YOUR CRIMES!

SWOOSH!

NOW YOU MUST BE EXECUTED !!

I WILL CARRY OUT YOUR SENTENCE IMMEDIATELY !!

CRRRACK!!

RAAAGH!

KAPOW!

In the nick of time, Tira risks her life to save them, and Barda defeats Reece. But there is no time to relax...

WHY YOU --!!

WHAT ?!

YOU WON'T LEAVE HERE ALIVE!

...as Reece's minion Ra-Kacharz are close on their heels!

WE'RE LEAVING!! NO MATTER WHAT IT TAKES!!

BLAST IT! THEY'RE HERE!

DELTORA QUEST
デルトラ クエスト

Volume 6: Table of Contents

Deltora Quest

デルトラクエスト

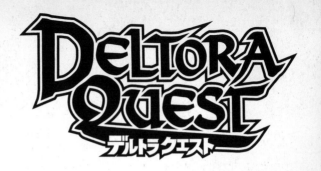

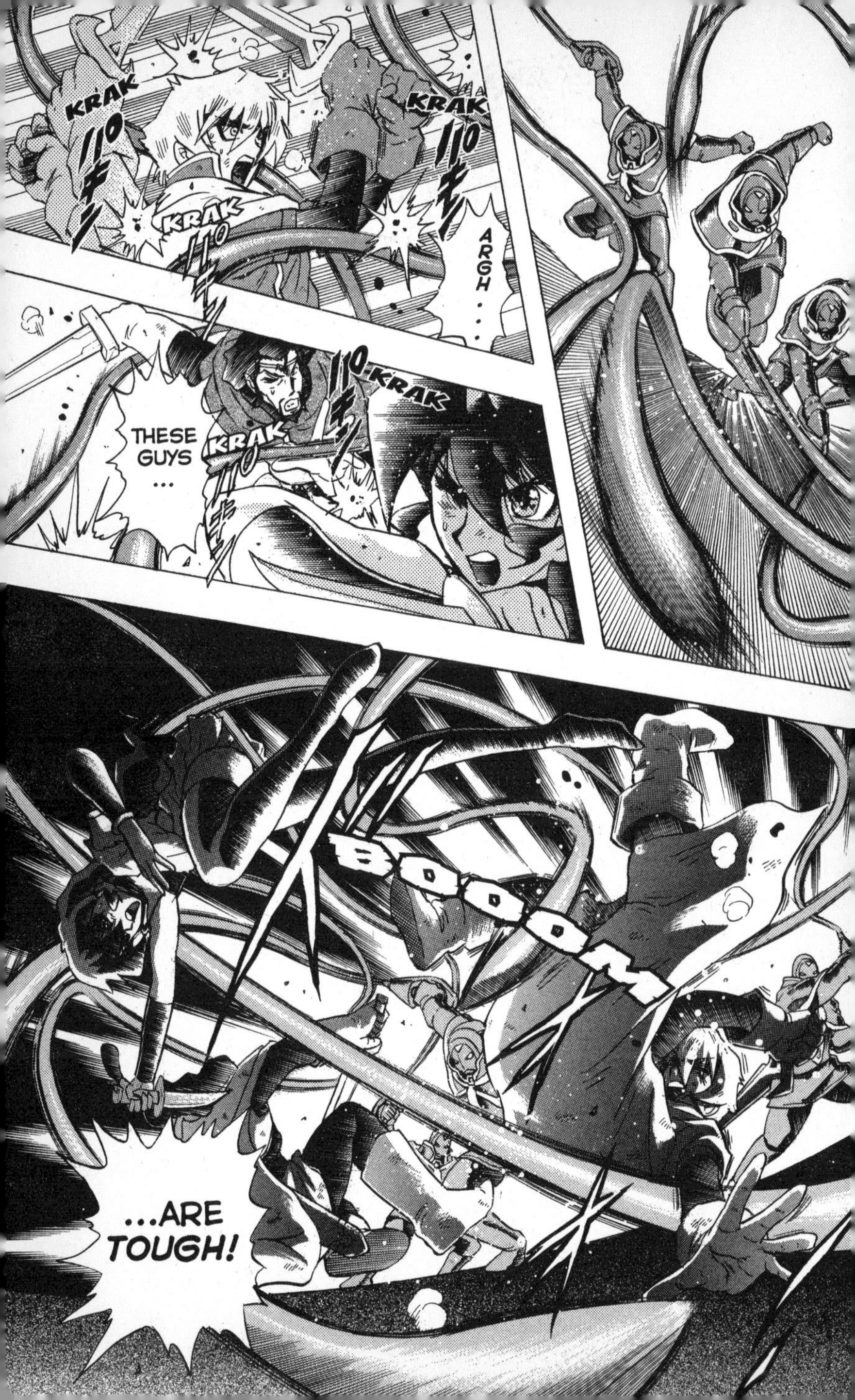
KRAK
ARGH...
KRAK
KRAK
O-KRAK
KRAK
THESE GUYS...
BOOOOM
...ARE TOUGH!

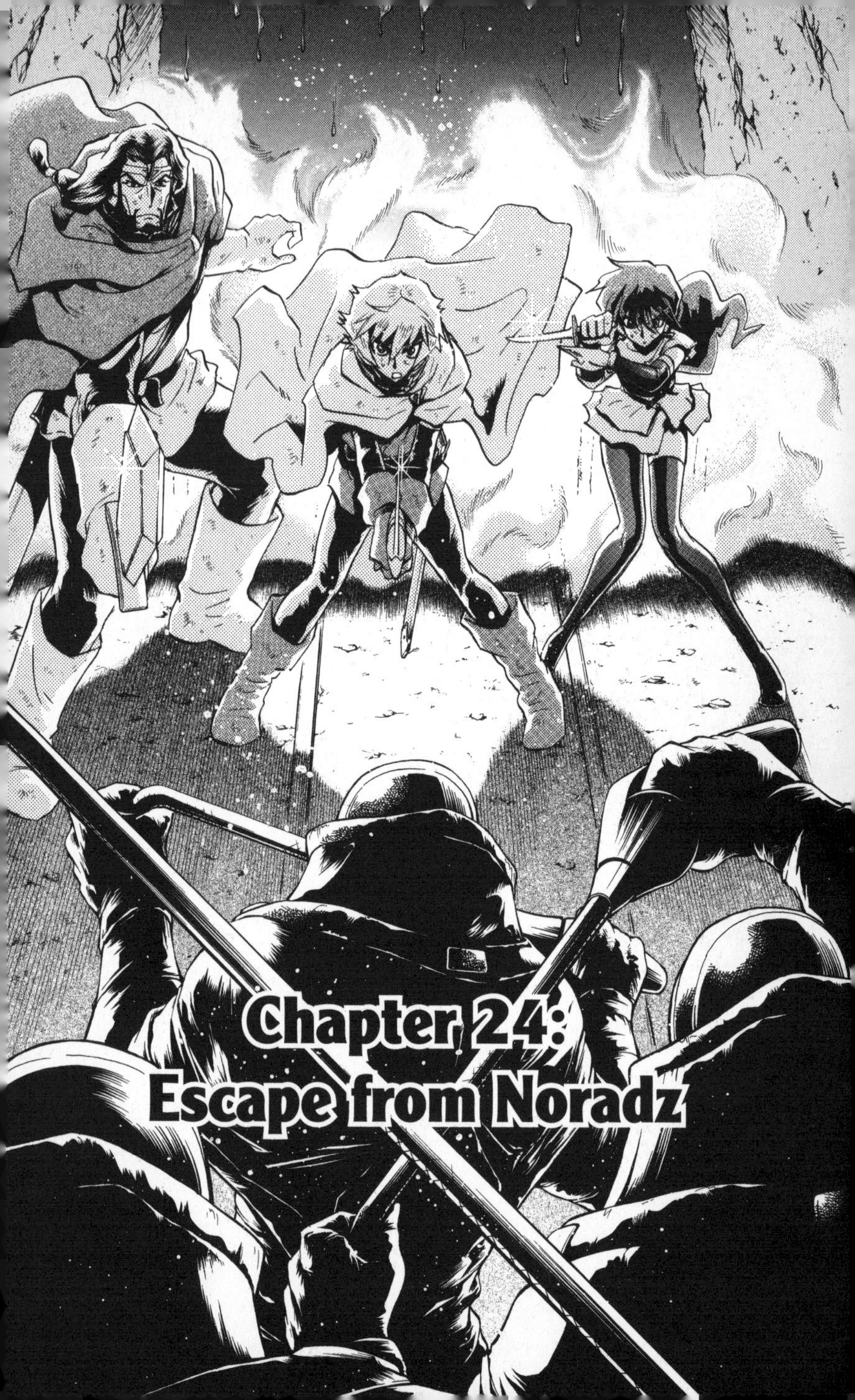
Chapter 24:
Escape from Noradz

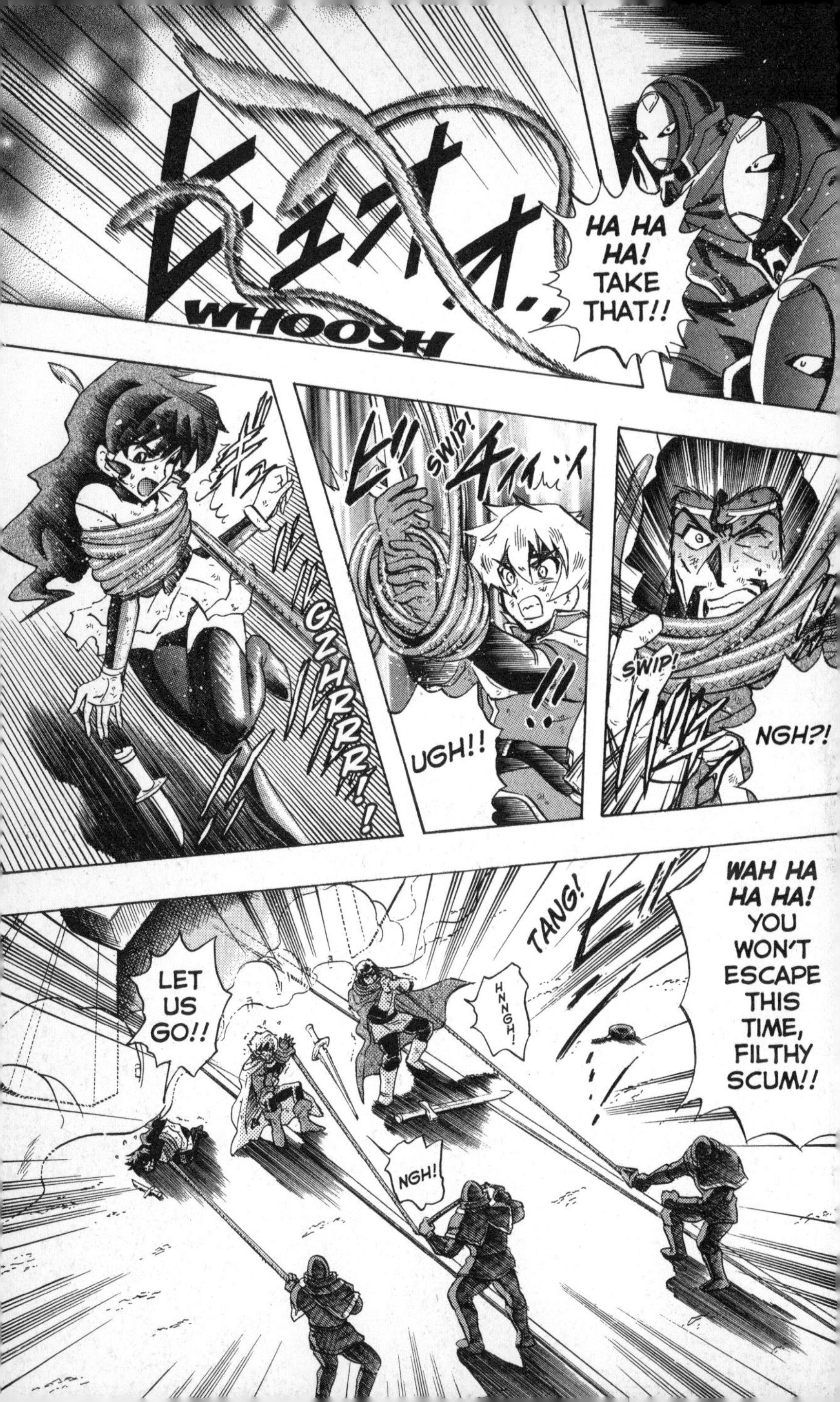
WHOOSH
HA HA HA! TAKE THAT!!
SWIP!
NGH?!
SWIP!
UGH!!
GZHRRR!!
WAH HA HA HA! YOU WON'T ESCAPE THIS TIME, FILTHY SCUM!!
TANG!
HNNGH!
NGH!
LET US GO!!

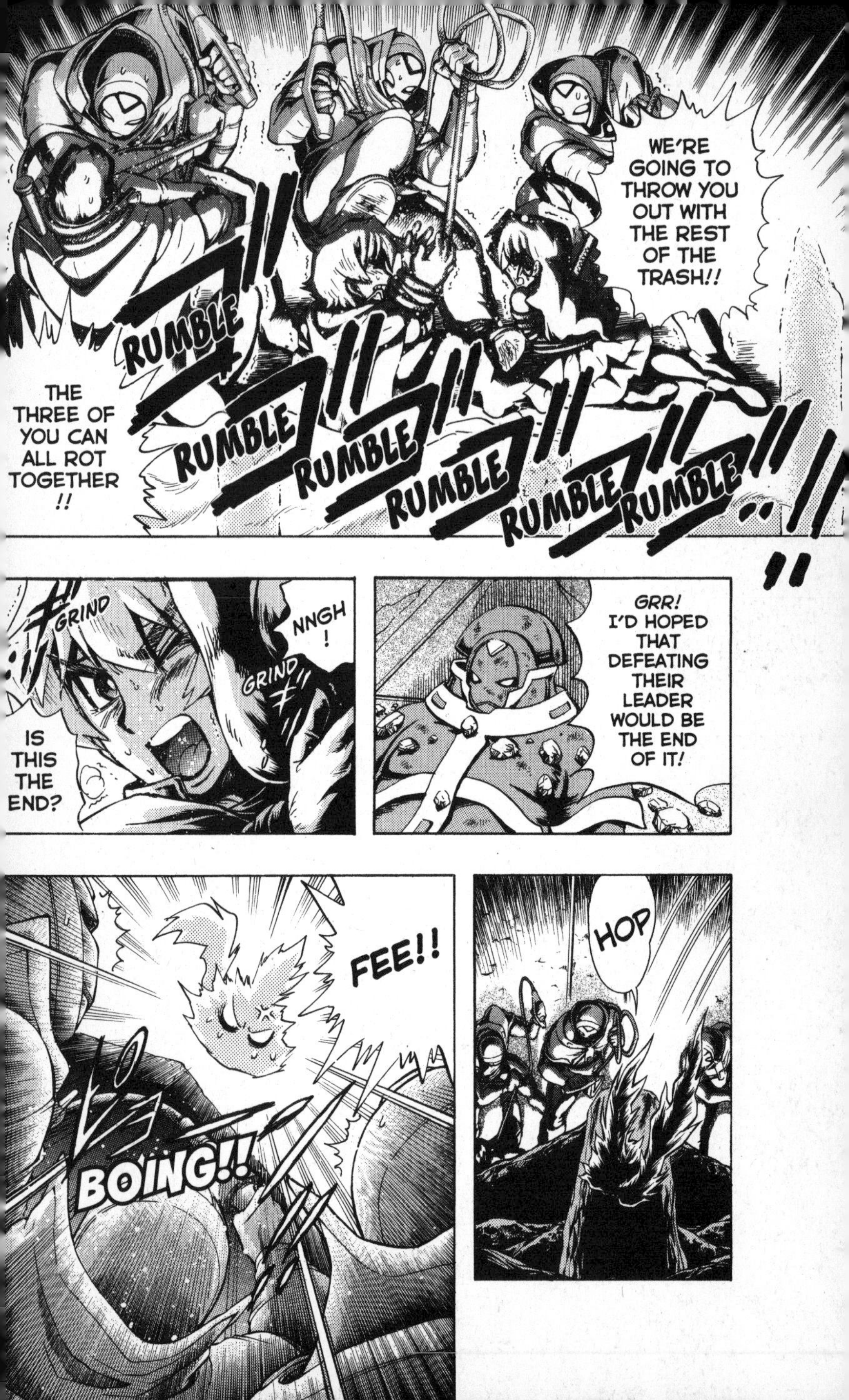
WE'RE GOING TO THROW YOU OUT WITH THE REST OF THE TRASH!!
RUMBLE RUMBLE RUMBLE RUMBLE RUMBLE RUMBLE!!
THE THREE OF YOU CAN ALL ROT TOGETHER!!
GRR! I'D HOPED THAT DEFEATING THEIR LEADER WOULD BE THE END OF IT!
GRIND
NNGH!
GRIND
IS THIS THE END?
HOP
FEE!!
BOING!!

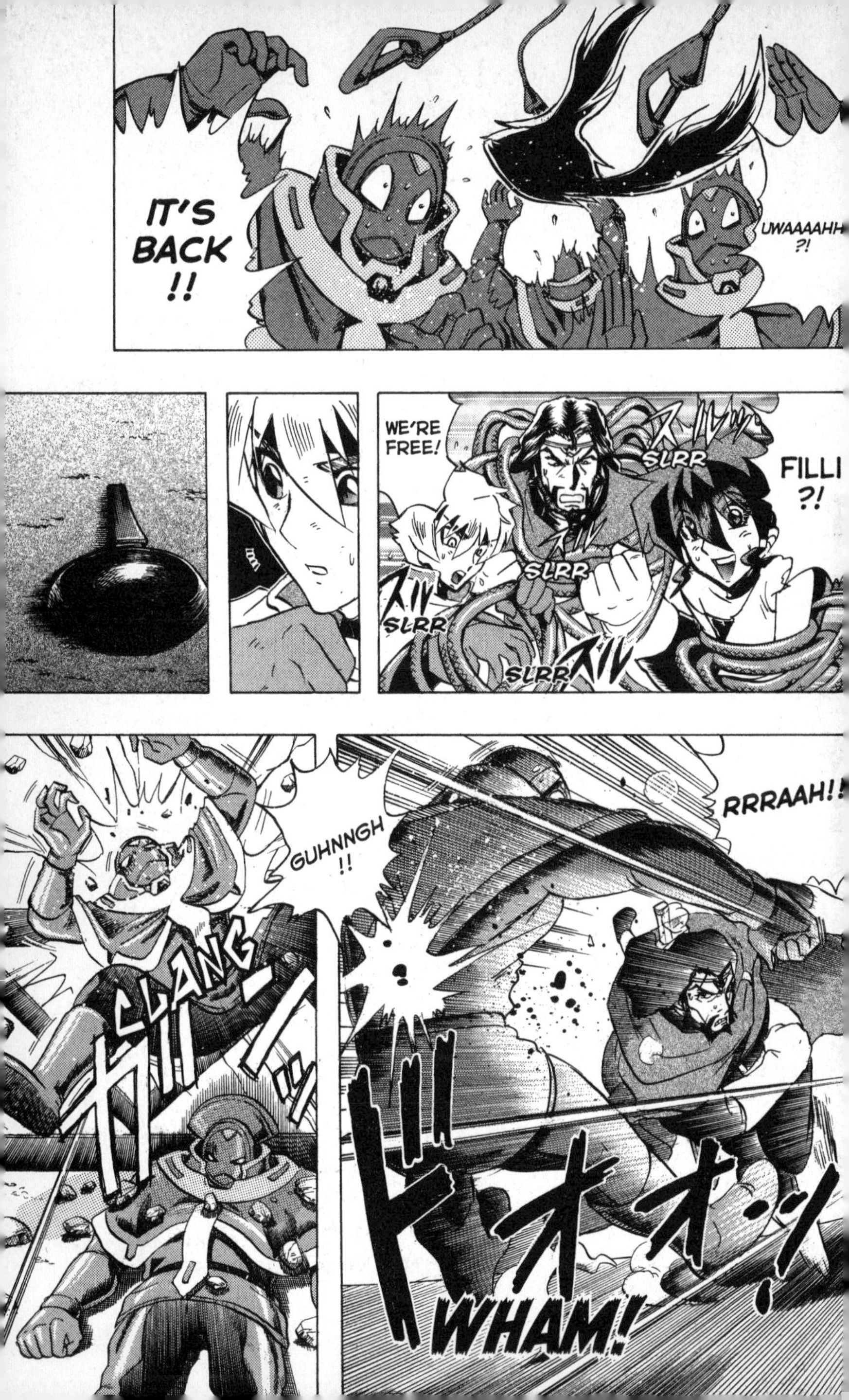
UWAAAAHH ?!
IT'S BACK !!
FILLI ?!
SLRR
WE'RE FREE!
SLRR
SLRR
SLRR
RRRAAH!!
GUHNNGH !!
WHAM!
CLANG

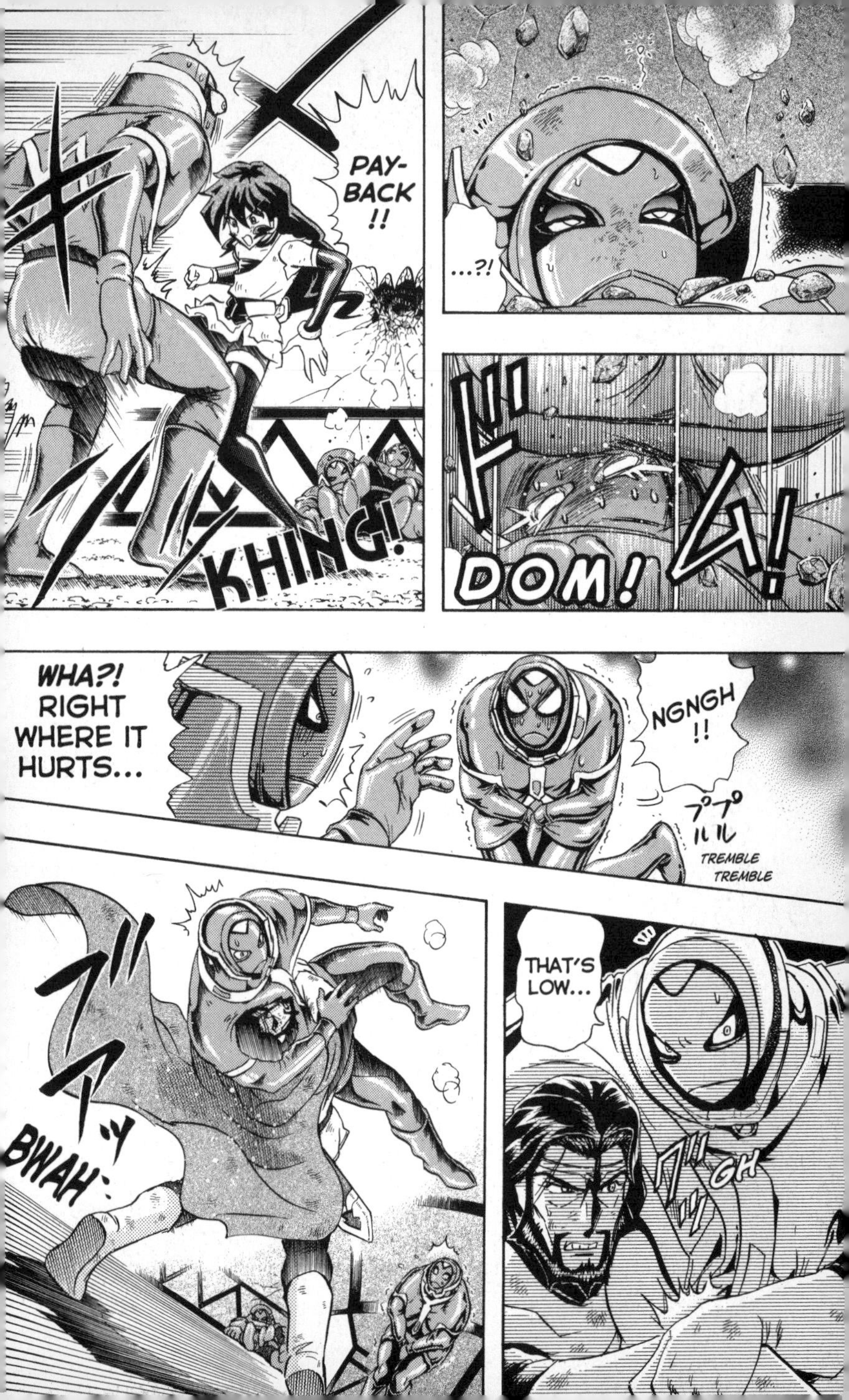

...?!
ドム!
DOM!
PAY-BACK!!
KHING!
NGNGH!!
プルプル
TREMBLE TREMBLE
WHA?! RIGHT WHERE IT HURTS...
THAT'S LOW...
グッ
GH
ブァッ
BWAH

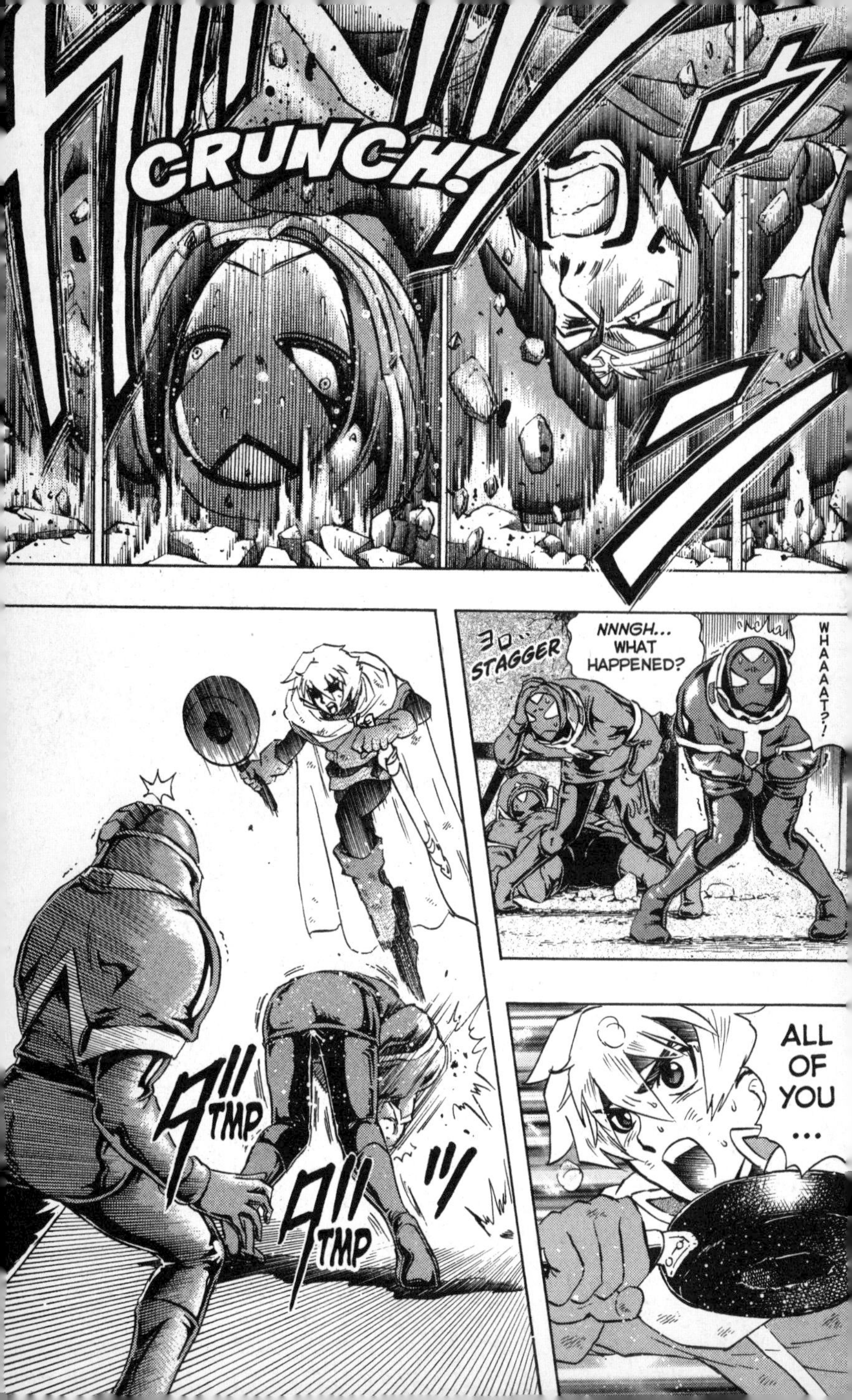
CRUNCH!
ヨロ… STAGGER
NNNGH... WHAT HAPPENED?
WHAAAAAT?!
ALL OF YOU ...
TMP
TMP

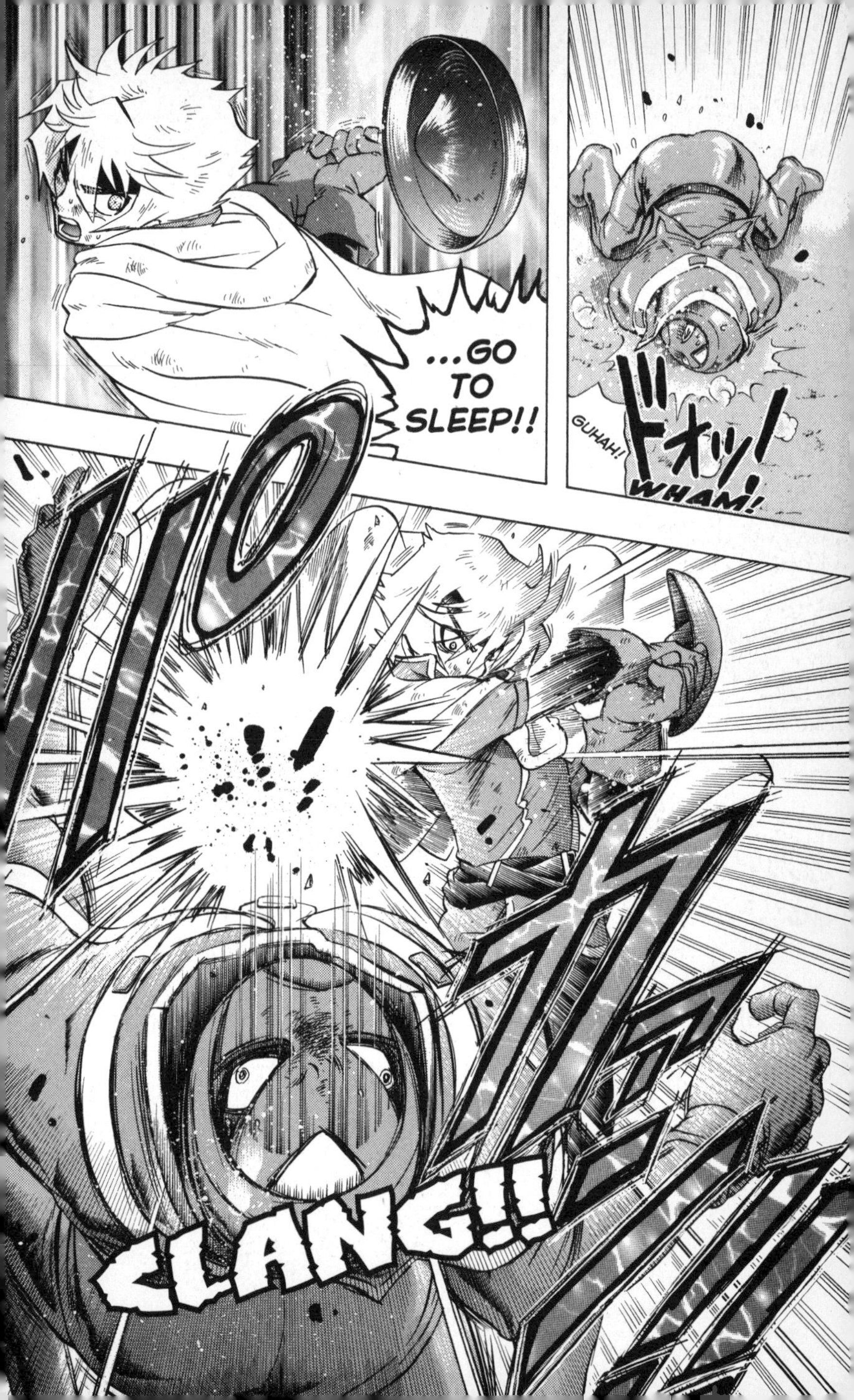
GUHAH!
ドオッ!
WHAM!
...GO TO SLEEP!!
CLANG!!

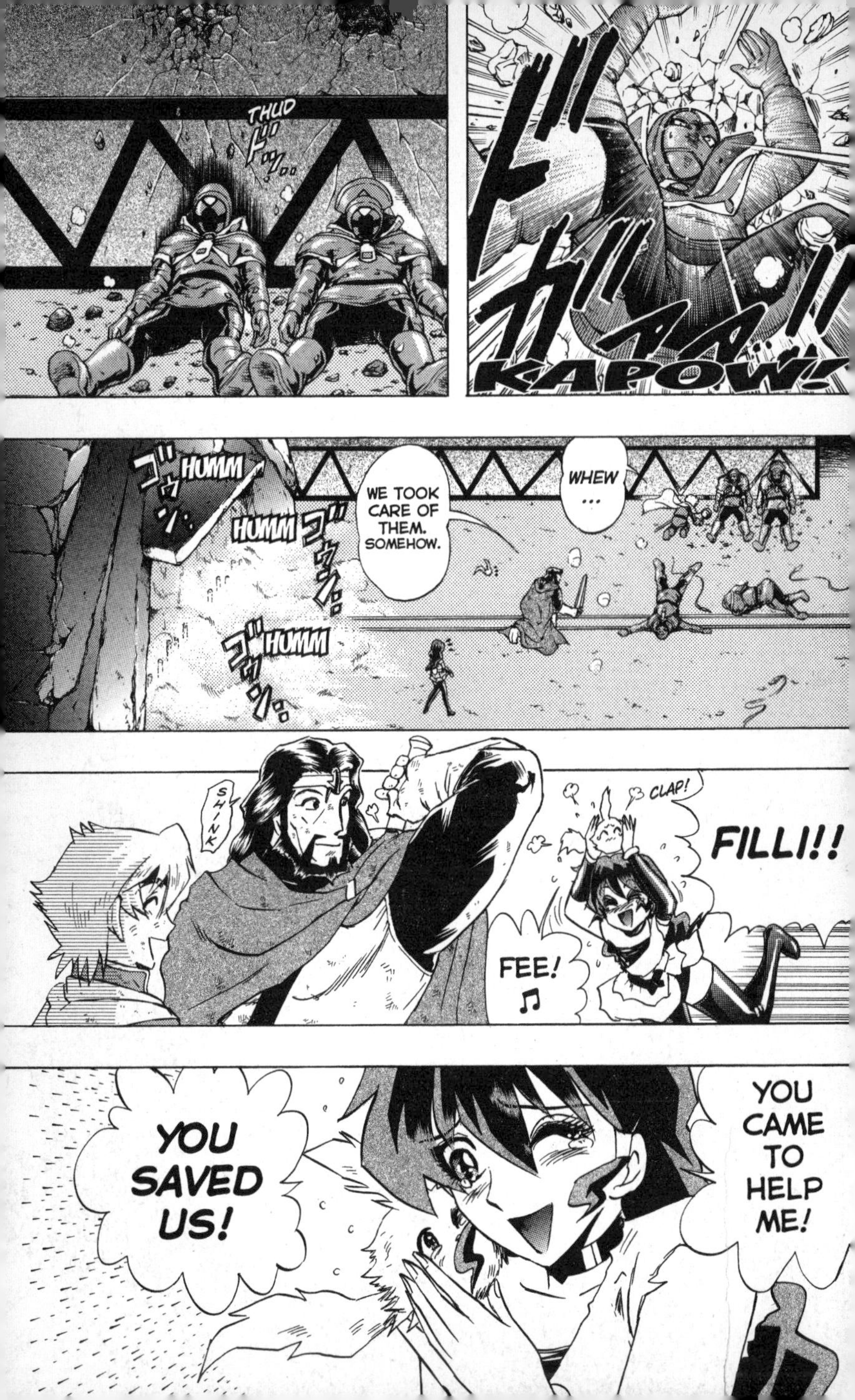
KAPOW!
THUD
WHEW ...
WE TOOK CARE OF THEM. SOMEHOW.
HUMM
HUMM
HUMM
FILLI!!
CLAP!
FEE! ♫
SHINK
YOU CAME TO HELP ME!
YOU SAVED US!

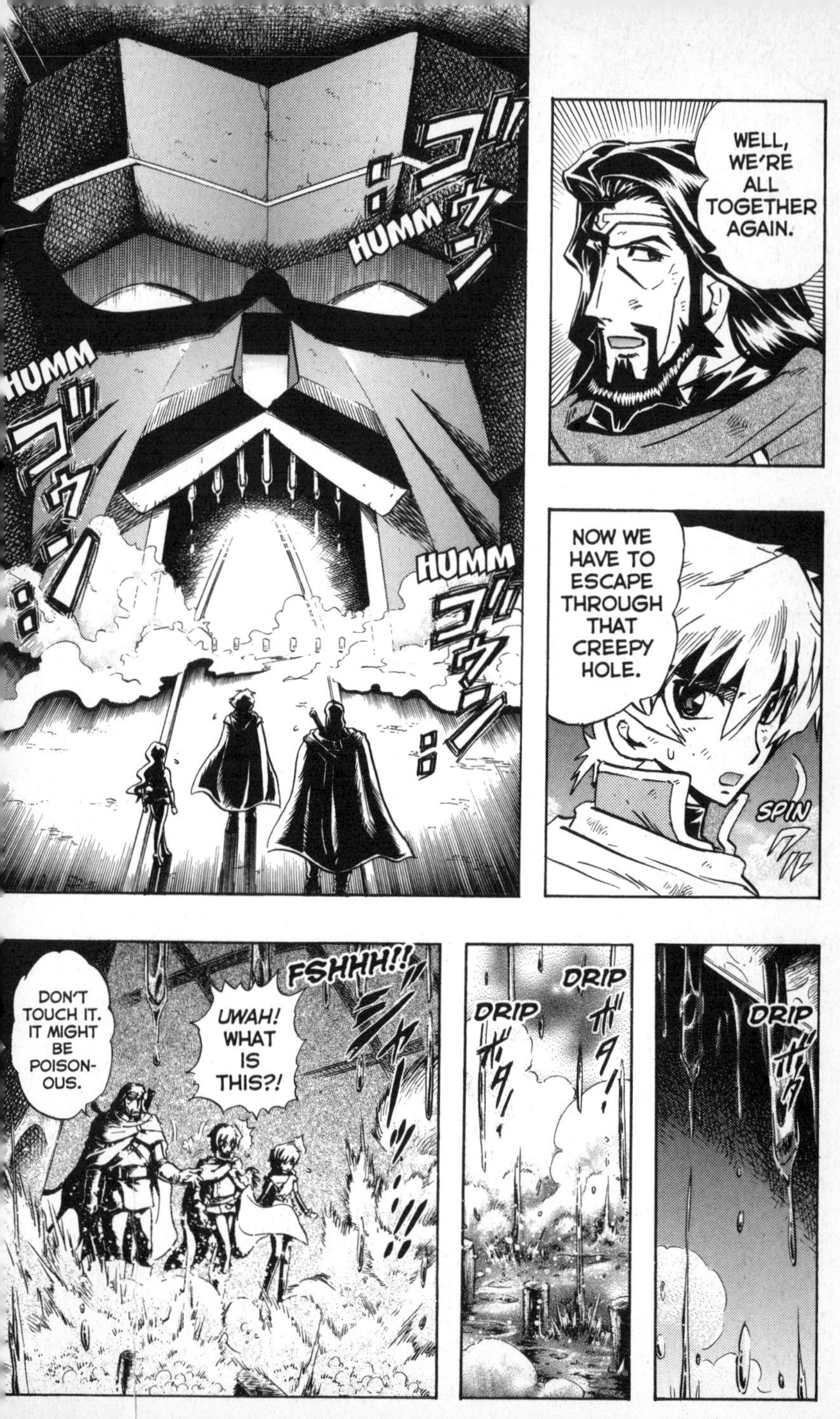

WELL, WE'RE ALL TOGETHER AGAIN.
NOW WE HAVE TO ESCAPE THROUGH THAT CREEPY HOLE.
SPIN
HUMM
HUMM
HUMM
DRIP
DRIP
DRIP
FSHHH!!
UWAH! WHAT IS THIS?!
DON'T TOUCH IT. IT MIGHT BE POISON-OUS.

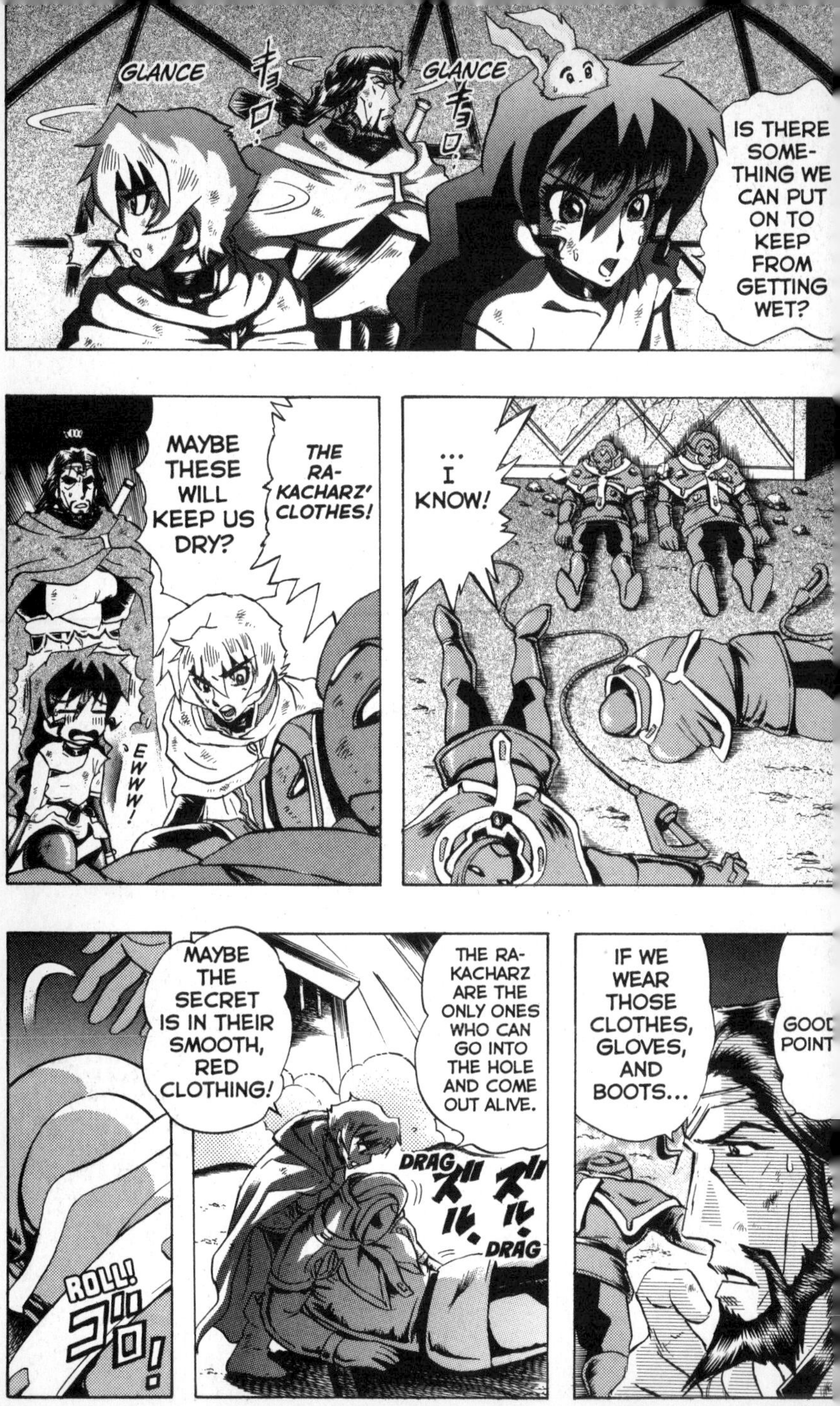
IS THERE SOMETHING WE CAN PUT ON TO KEEP FROM GETTING WET?
GLANCE
キョロ
GLANCE
キョロ
... I KNOW!
THE RA-KACHARZ' CLOTHES!
MAYBE THESE WILL KEEP US DRY?
EWWW!
GOOD POINT
IF WE WEAR THOSE CLOTHES, GLOVES, AND BOOTS...
THE RA-KACHARZ ARE THE ONLY ONES WHO CAN GO INTO THE HOLE AND COME OUT ALIVE.
DRAG
ズル
ズル
DRAG
MAYBE THE SECRET IS IN THEIR SMOOTH, RED CLOTHING!
ROLL!
ゴロ!

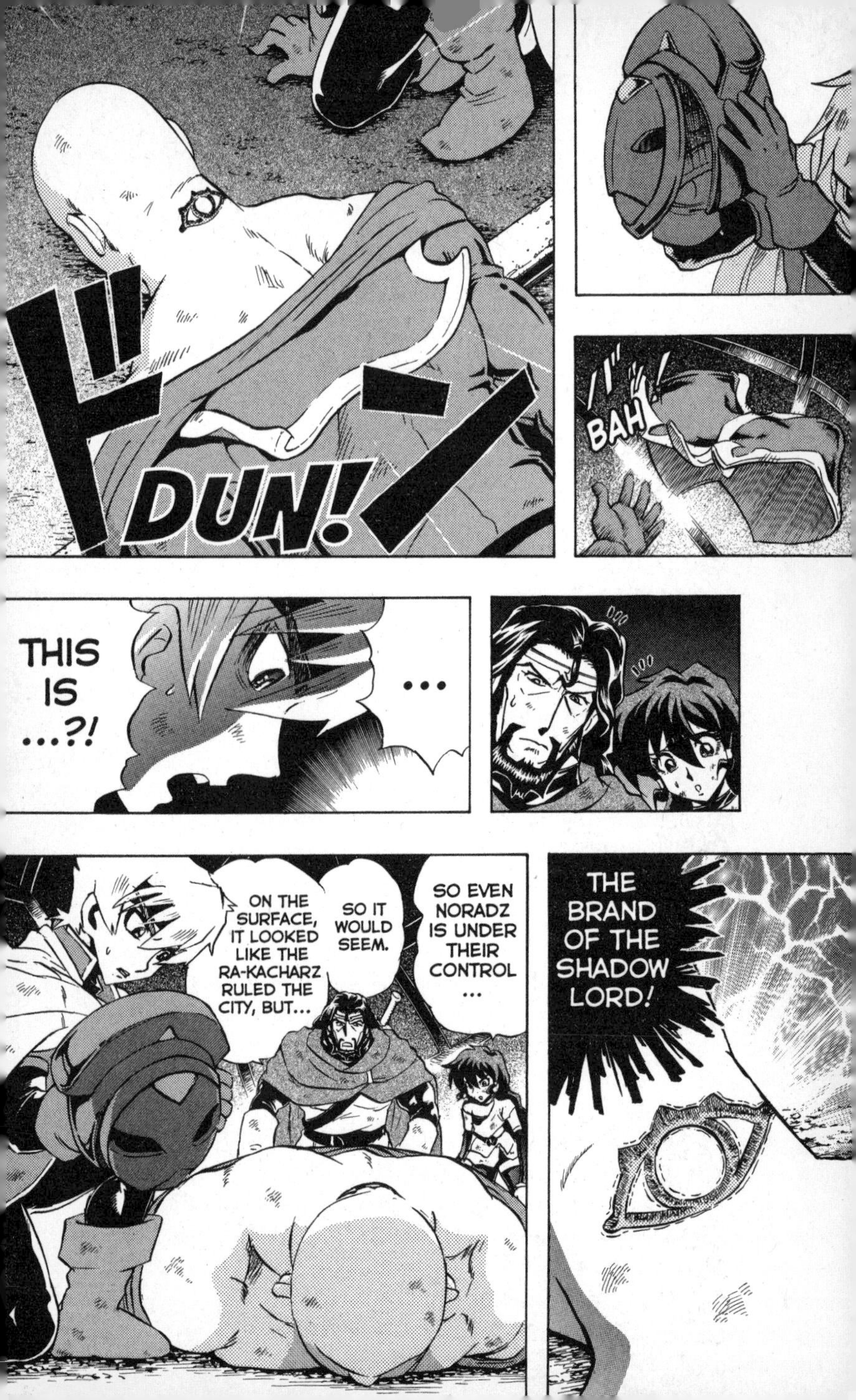
BAH
DUN!
...
THIS IS ...?!
THE BRAND OF THE SHADOW LORD!
SO EVEN NORADZ IS UNDER THEIR CONTROL ...
SO IT WOULD SEEM.
ON THE SURFACE, IT LOOKED LIKE THE RA-KACHARZ RULED THE CITY, BUT...

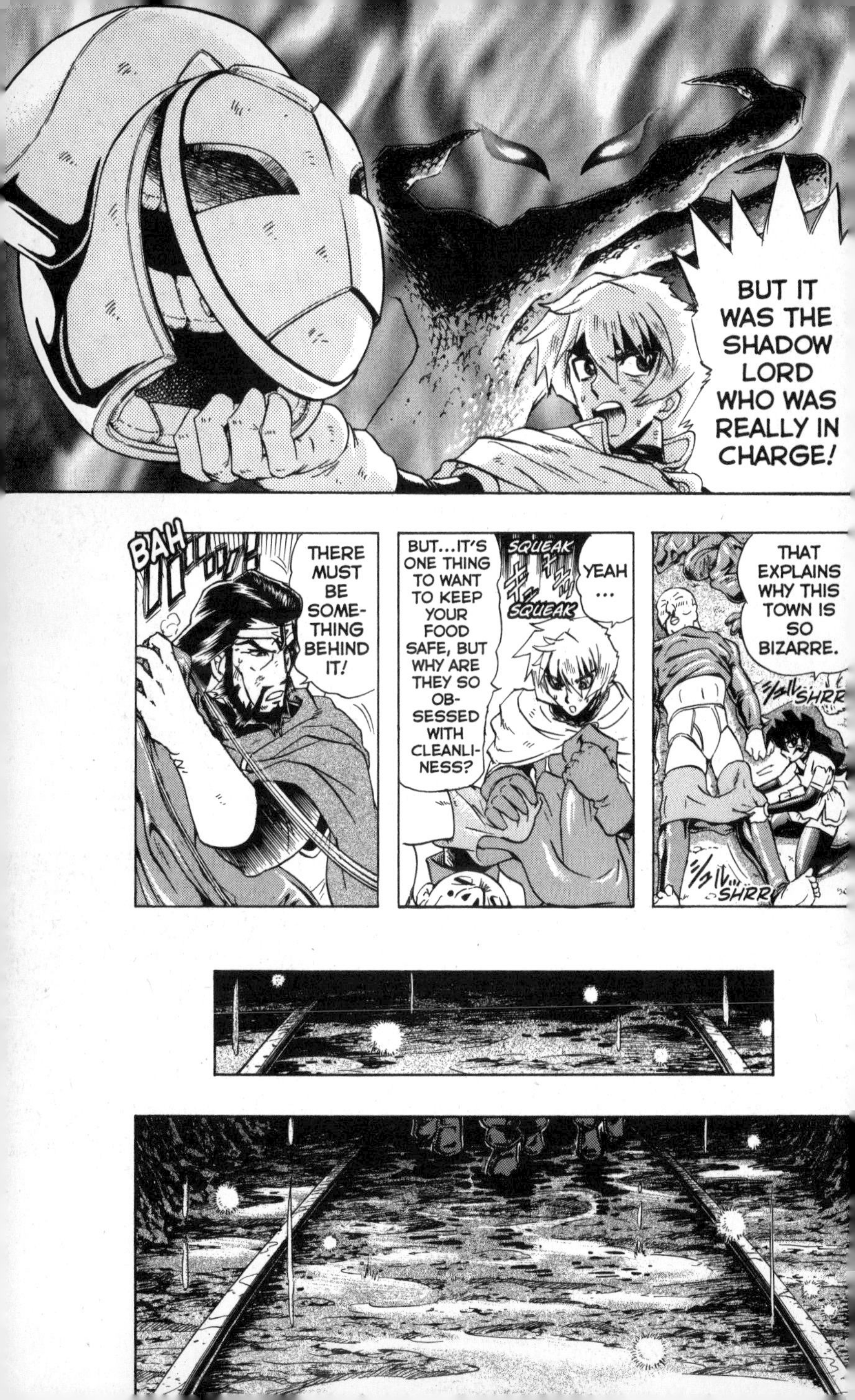
BUT IT WAS THE SHADOW LORD WHO WAS REALLY IN CHARGE!
THAT EXPLAINS WHY THIS TOWN IS SO BIZARRE.
SHRR
SHRR
YEAH ...
SQUEAK
SQUEAK
BUT...IT'S ONE THING TO WANT TO KEEP YOUR FOOD SAFE, BUT WHY ARE THEY SO OB-SESSED WITH CLEANLI-NESS?
BAH
THERE MUST BE SOME-THING BEHIND IT!

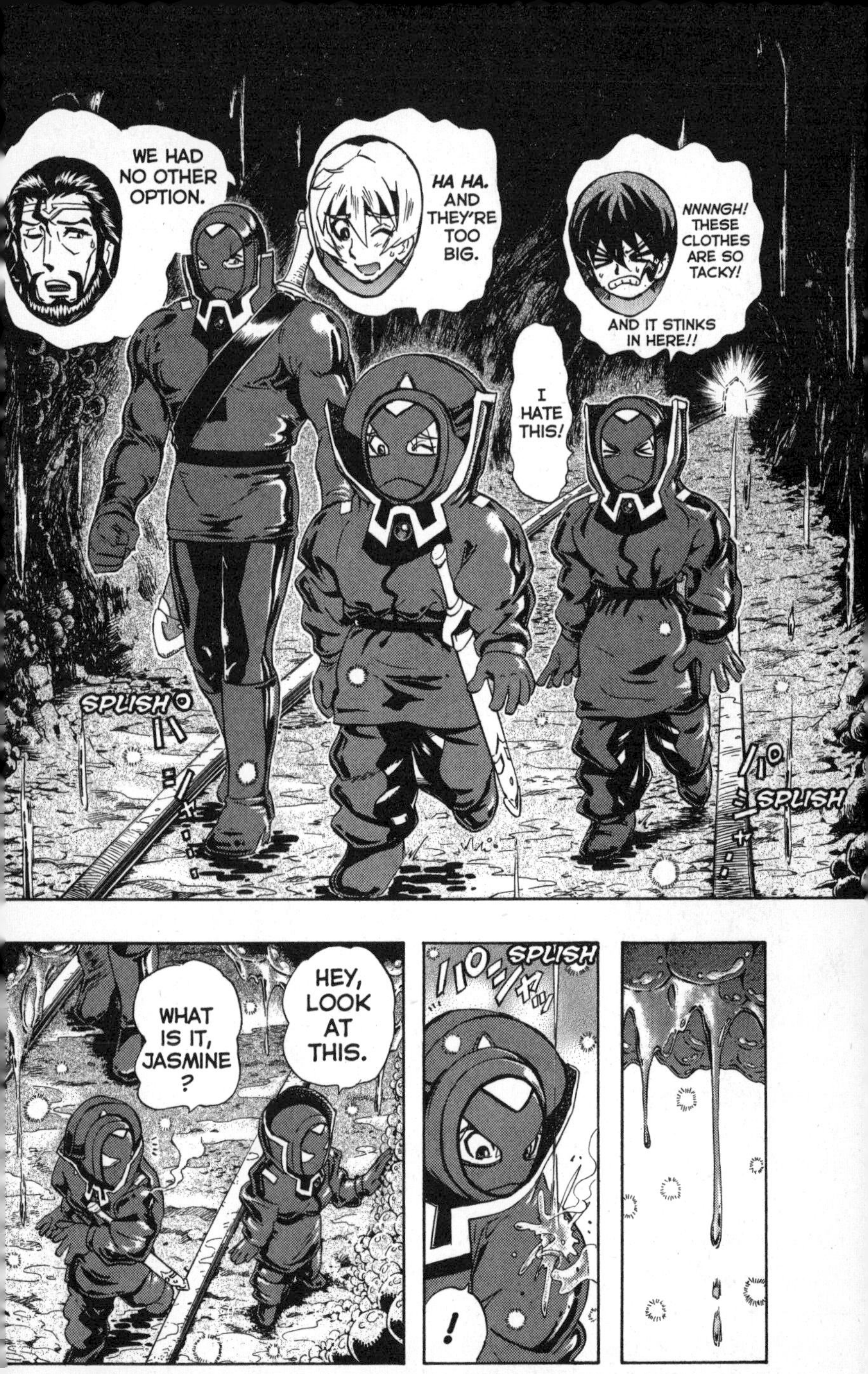
NNNNGH! THESE CLOTHES ARE SO TACKY!
AND IT STINKS IN HERE!!
I HATE THIS!
HA HA. AND THEY'RE TOO BIG.
WE HAD NO OTHER OPTION.
SPLISH
SPLISH
SPLISH
!
HEY, LOOK AT THIS.
WHAT IS IT, JASMINE?

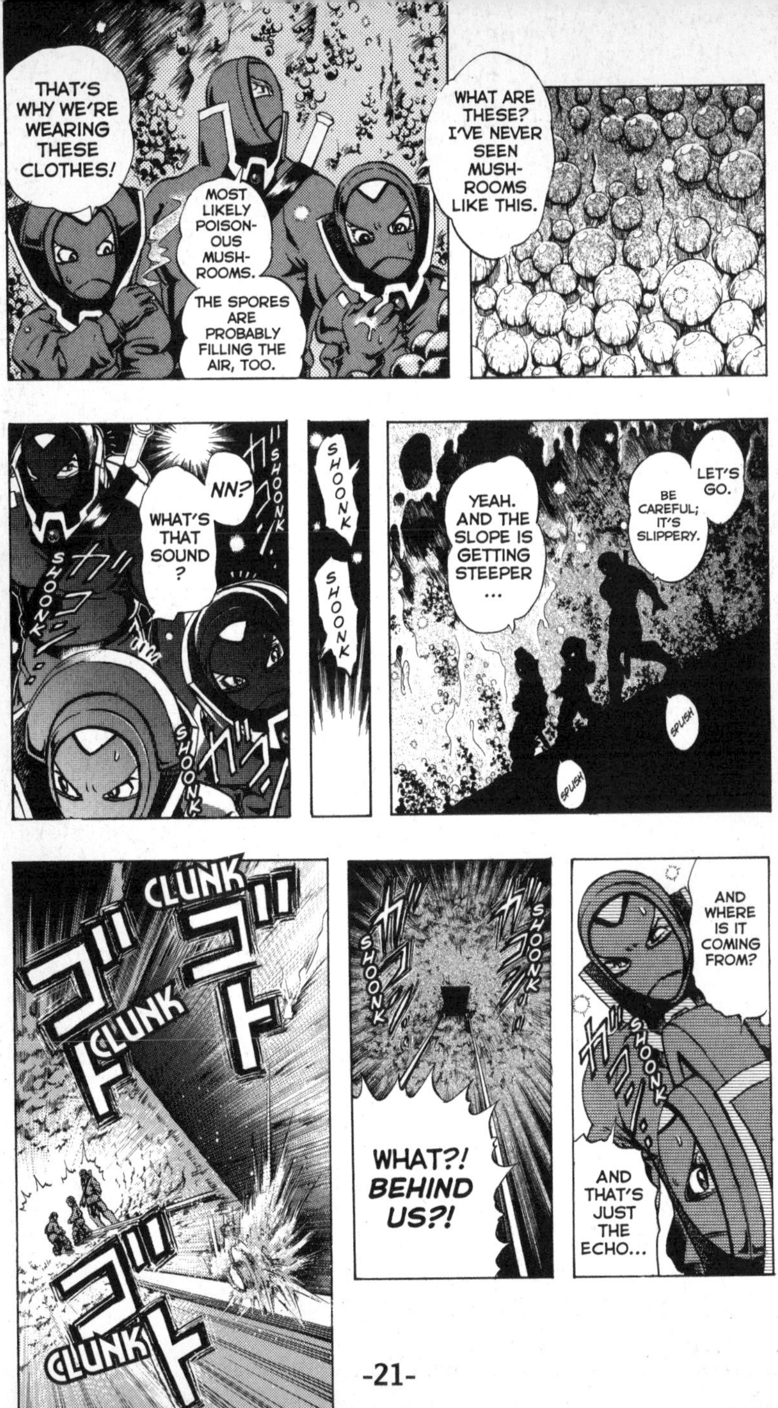
WHAT ARE THESE? I'VE NEVER SEEN MUSH-ROOMS LIKE THIS.
MOST LIKELY POISON-OUS MUSH-ROOMS.
THE SPORES ARE PROBABLY FILLING THE AIR, TOO.
THAT'S WHY WE'RE WEARING THESE CLOTHES!
LET'S GO.
BE CAREFUL; IT'S SLIPPERY.
YEAH. AND THE SLOPE IS GETTING STEEPER ...
SPUSH
SPUSH
SHOONK
SHOONK
SHOONK
NN?
WHAT'S THAT SOUND ?
SHOONK
SHOONK
AND WHERE IS IT COMING FROM?
SHOONK
AND THAT'S JUST THE ECHO...
SHOONK
SHOONK
WHAT?! BEHIND US?!
CLUNK
CLUNK
CLUNK

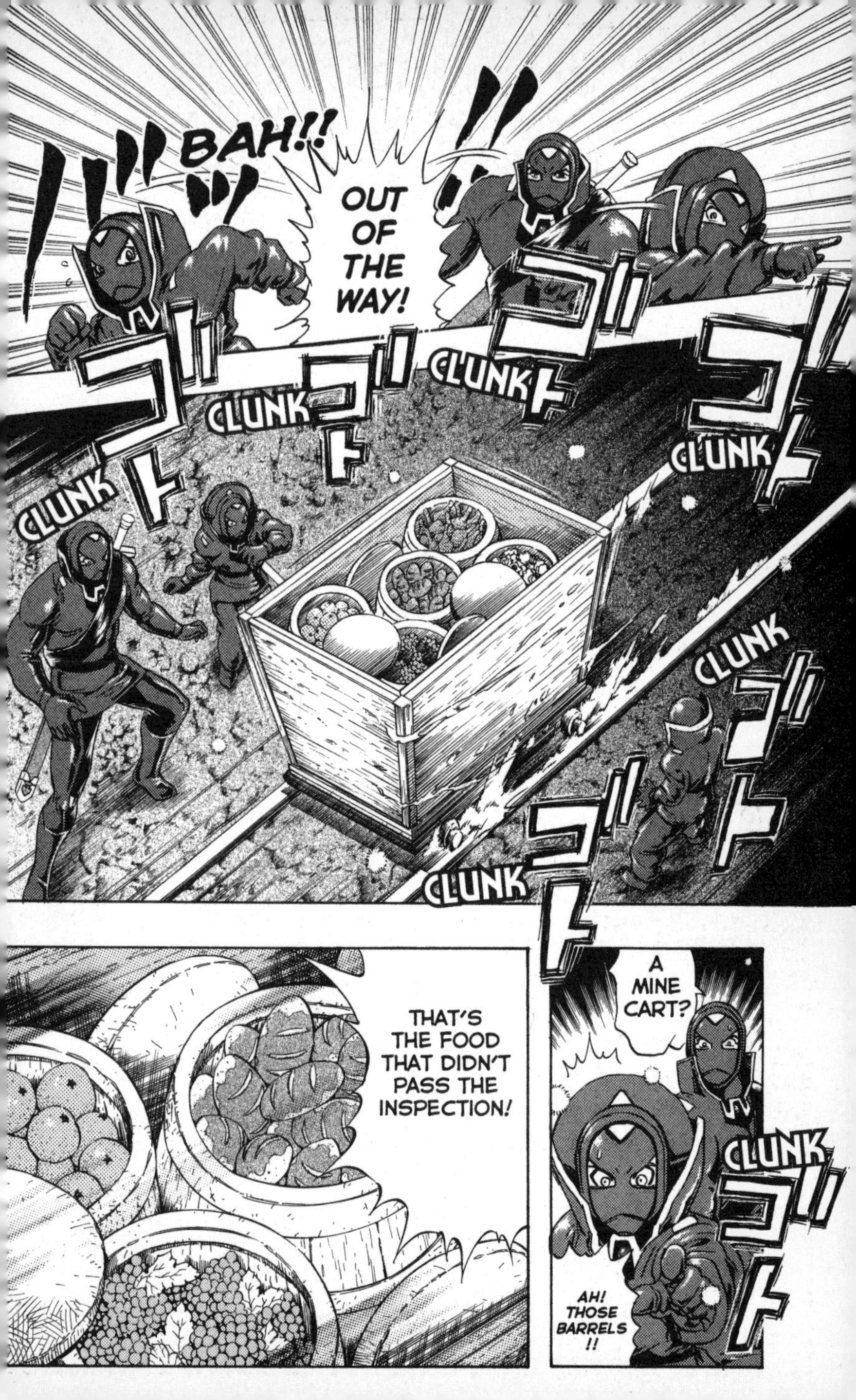

OUT OF THE WAY!
BAH!!
CLUNK
CLUNK
CLUNK
CLUNK
CLUNK
CLUNK
A MINE CART?
CLUNK
AH! THOSE BARRELS!!
THAT'S THE FOOD THAT DIDN'T PASS THE INSPECTION!

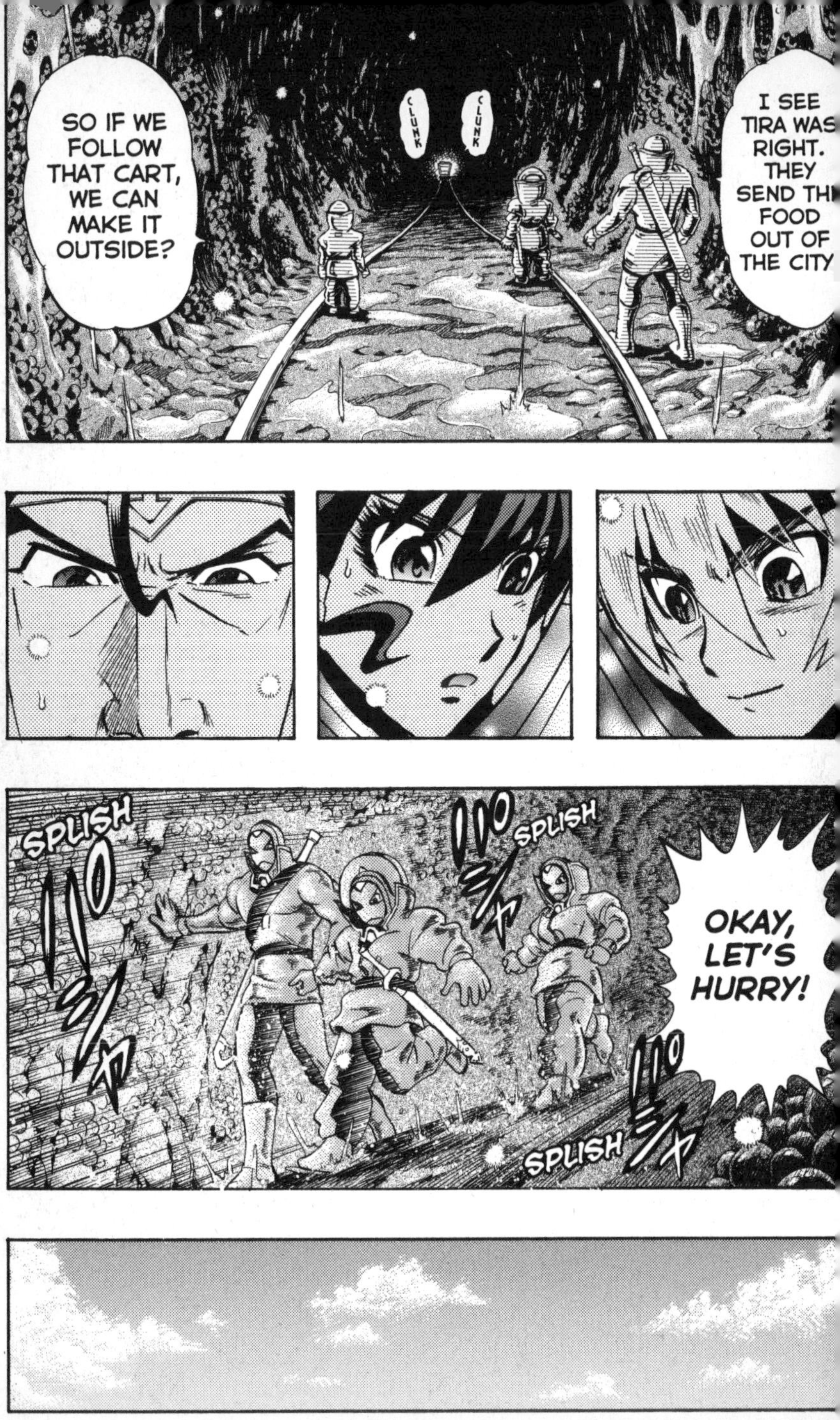
I SEE TIRA WAS RIGHT. THEY SEND TH FOOD OUT OF THE CITY
CLUNK
CLUNK
SO IF WE FOLLOW THAT CART, WE CAN MAKE IT OUTSIDE?
OKAY, LET'S HURRY!
SPLISH
SPLISH
SPLISH

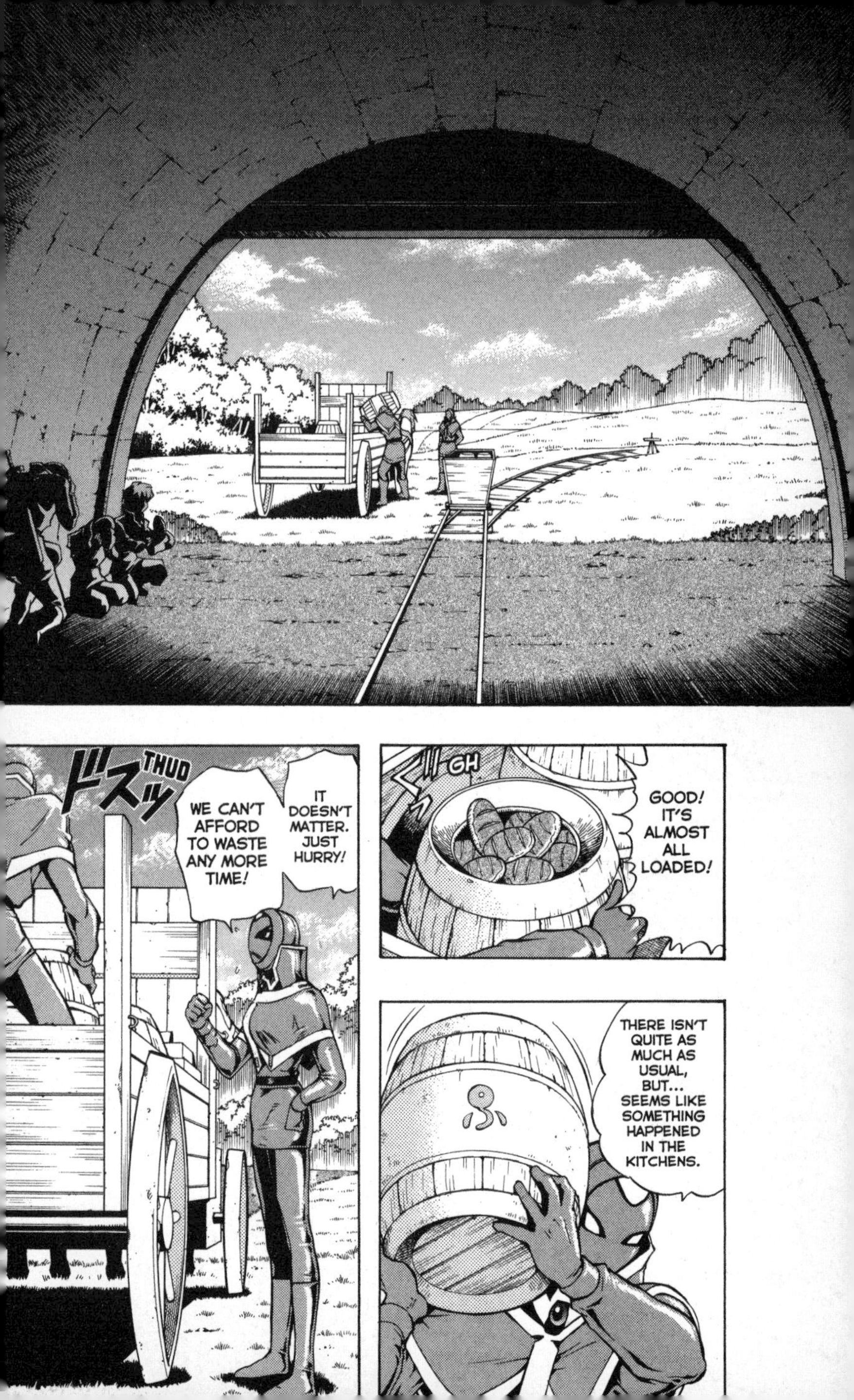

GH
GOOD! IT'S ALMOST ALL LOADED!
THERE ISN'T QUITE AS MUCH AS USUAL, BUT... SEEMS LIKE SOMETHING HAPPENED IN THE KITCHENS.
ドスッ
THUD
IT DOESN'T MATTER. JUST HURRY!
WE CAN'T AFFORD TO WASTE ANY MORE TIME!

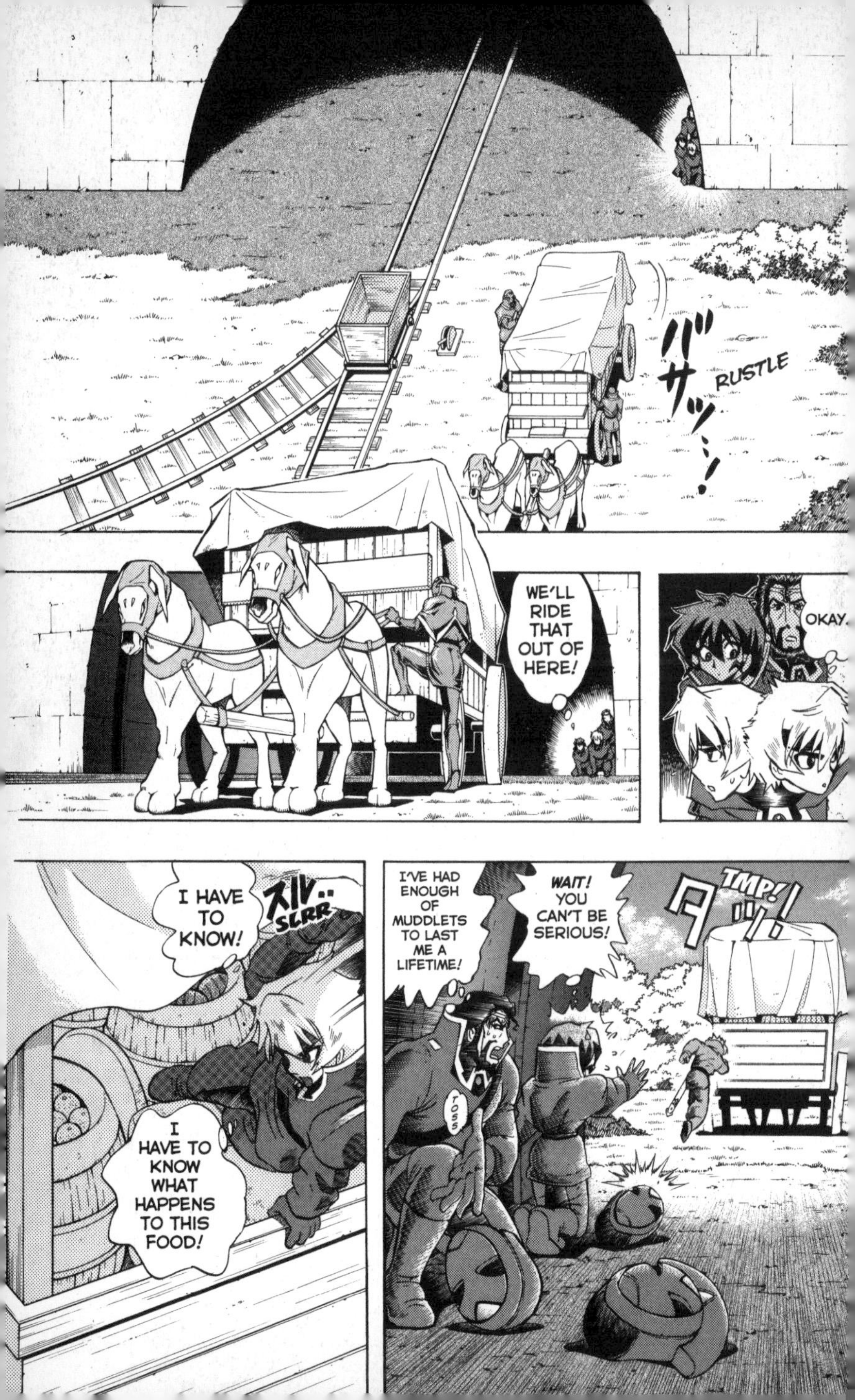
バサッ
RUSTLE
OKAY.
WE'LL RIDE THAT OUT OF HERE!
タ
TMP!
WAIT! YOU CAN'T BE SERIOUS!
I'VE HAD ENOUGH OF MUDDLETS TO LAST ME A LIFETIME!
TOSS
I HAVE TO KNOW!
スル
SLRR
I HAVE TO KNOW WHAT HAPPENS TO THIS FOOD!

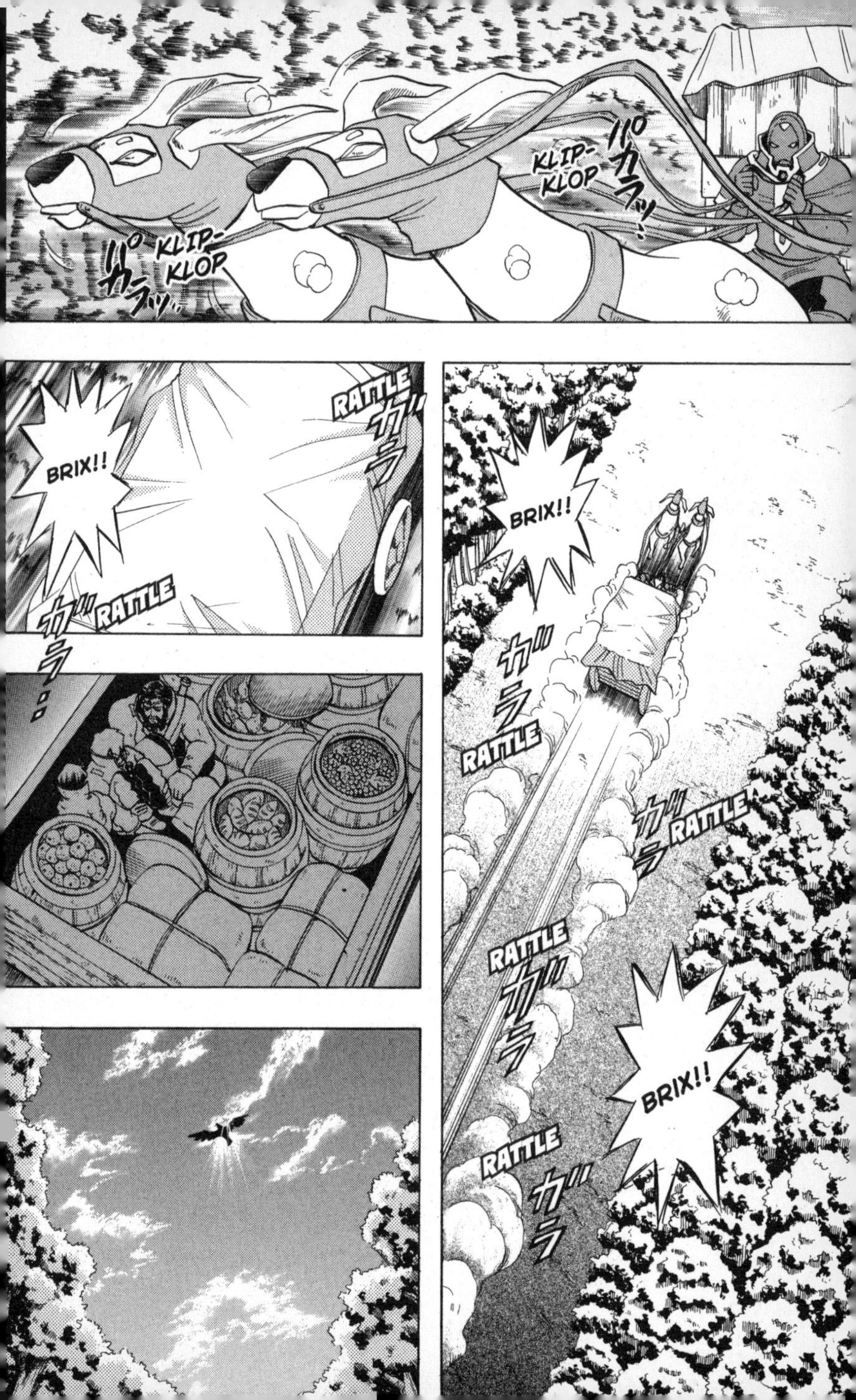
パカラッ!
KLIP-KLOP
パカラッ...
KLIP-KLOP
BRIX!!
ガラ
RATTLE
ガラ
RATTLE
RATTLE
ガラ
BRIX!!
RATTLE
ガラ
RATTLE
ガラ
BRIX!!
ガラ
RATTLE
ガラ...

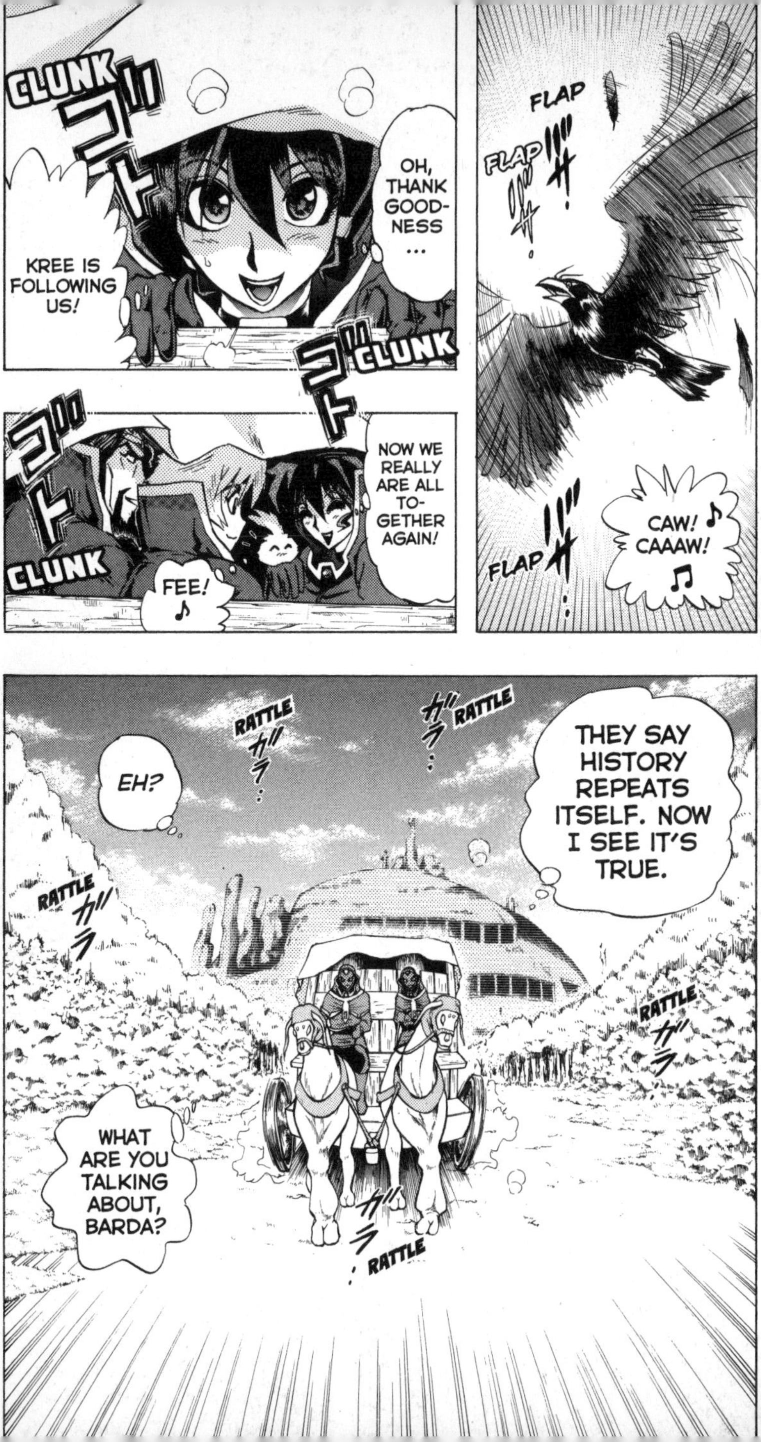
FLAP
FLAP
FLAP
CAW! ♪ CAAAW! ♫
CLUNK
OH, THANK GOOD-NESS ...
KREE IS FOLLOWING US!
CLUNK
NOW WE REALLY ARE ALL TO-GETHER AGAIN!
CLUNK
FEE! ♪
THEY SAY HISTORY REPEATS ITSELF. NOW I SEE IT'S TRUE.
RATTLE
RATTLE
EH?
RATTLE
RATTLE
WHAT ARE YOU TALKING ABOUT, BARDA?
RATTLE

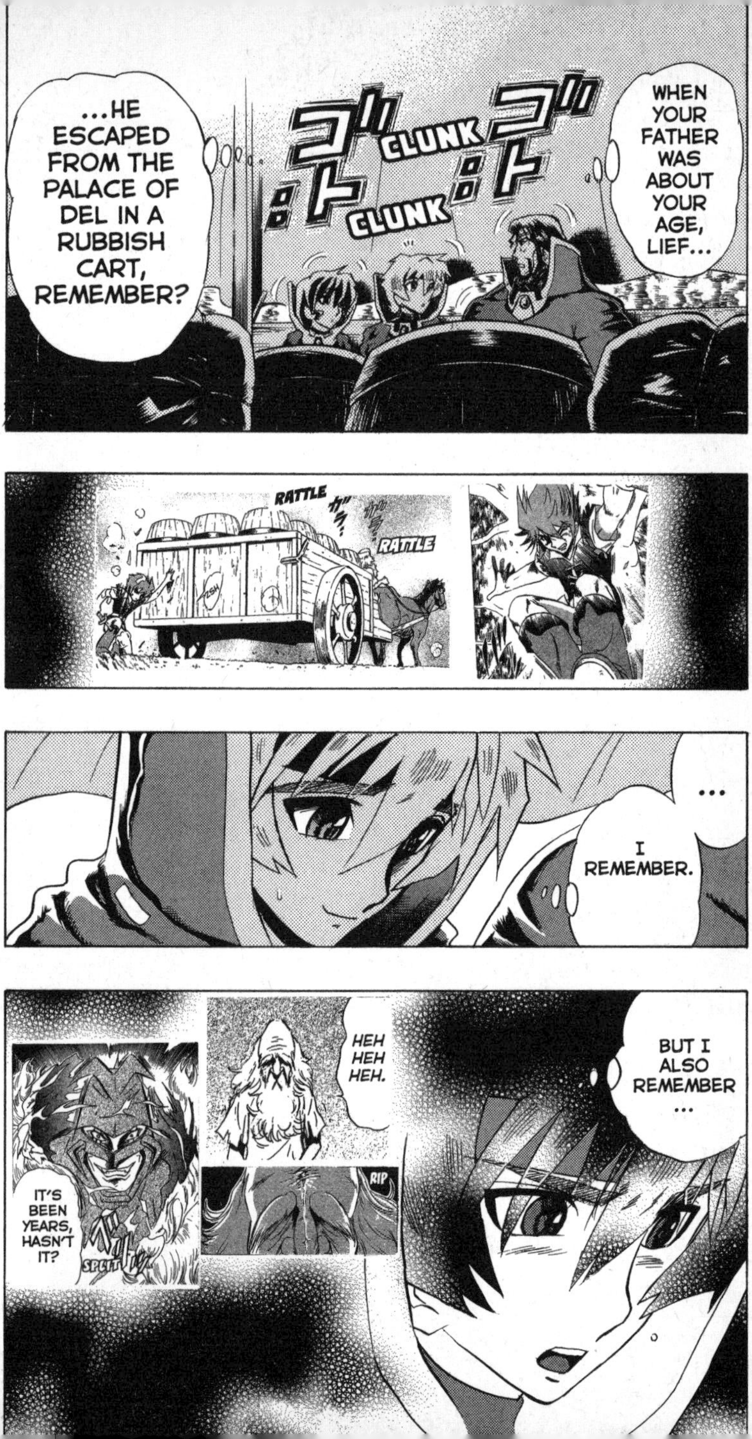
WHEN YOUR FATHER WAS ABOUT YOUR AGE, LIEF...
CLUNK
CLUNK
...HE ESCAPED FROM THE PALACE OF DEL IN A RUBBISH CART, REMEMBER?
RATTLE
RATTLE
...
I REMEMBER.
BUT I ALSO REMEMBER ...
HEH HEH HEH.
RIP
IT'S BEEN YEARS, HASN'T IT?
SPLIT

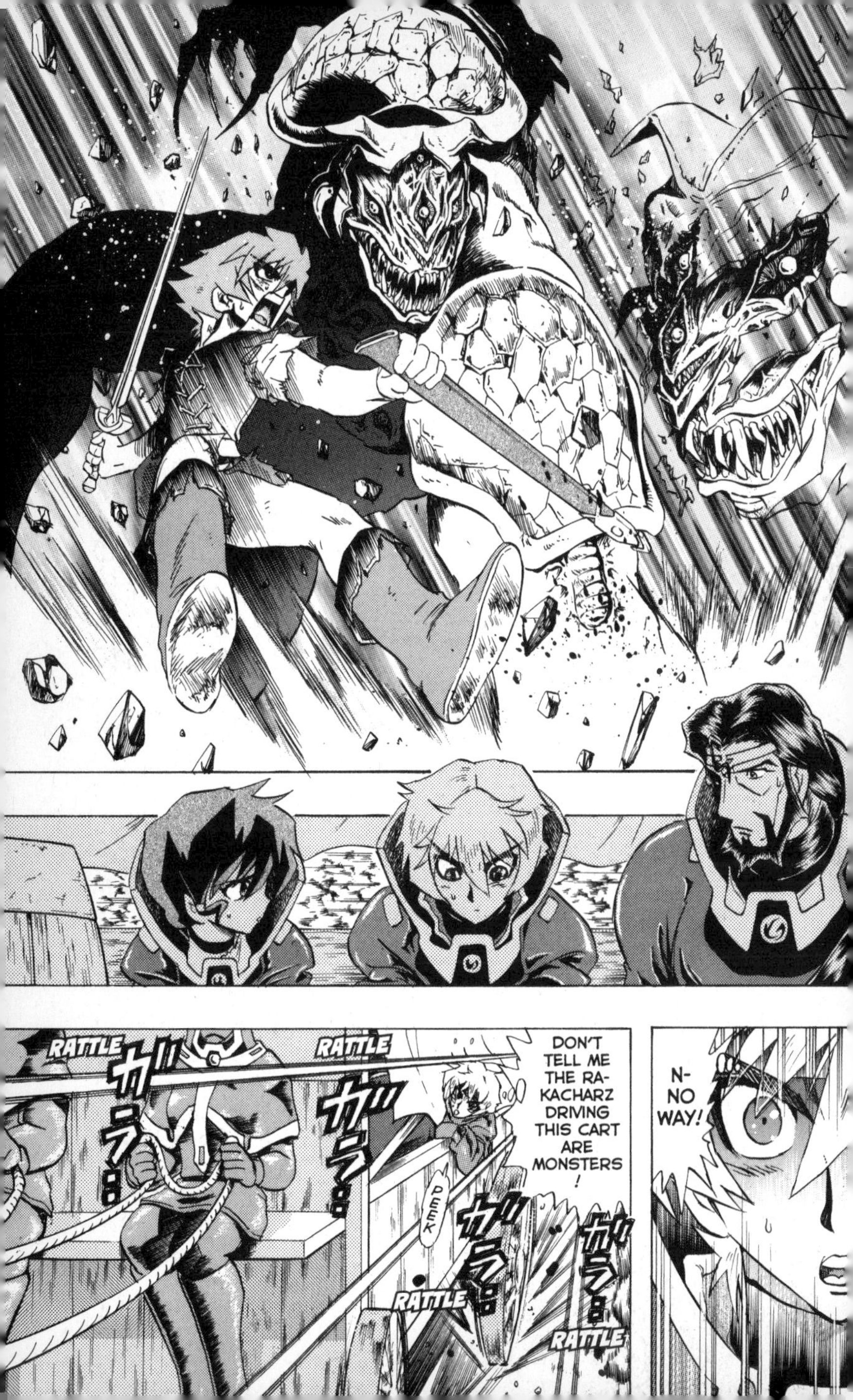
N-
NO
WAY!
DON'T TELL ME THE RA-KACHARZ DRIVING THIS CART ARE MONSTERS!
PEEK
RATTLE
RATTLE
RATTLE
RATTLE

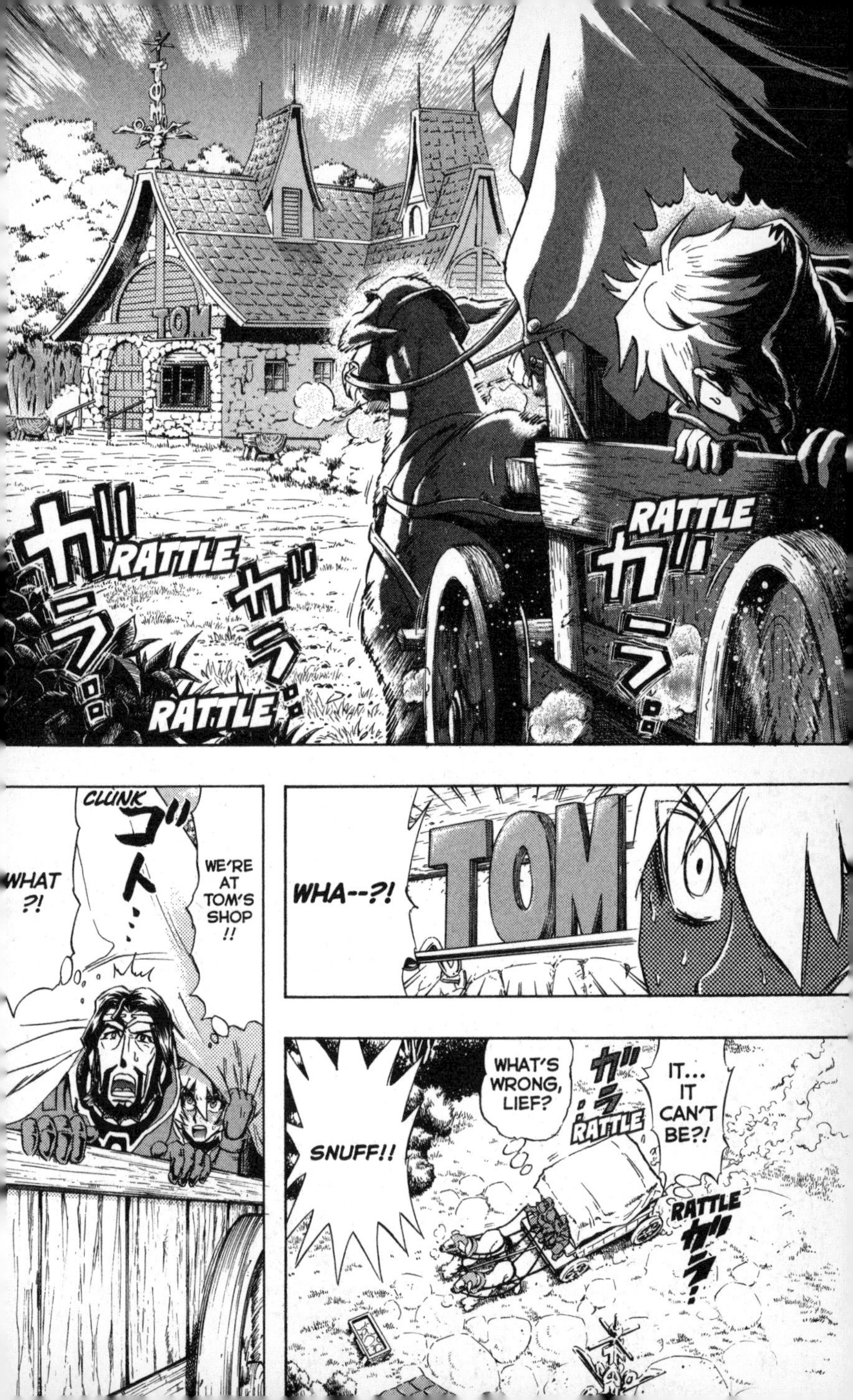
RATTLE
RATTLE
RATTLE
TOM
WHA--?!
IT... IT CAN'T BE?!
RATTLE
WHAT'S WRONG, LIEF?
RATTLE
SNUFF!!
CLUNK
WE'RE AT TOM'S SHOP!!
WHAT?!

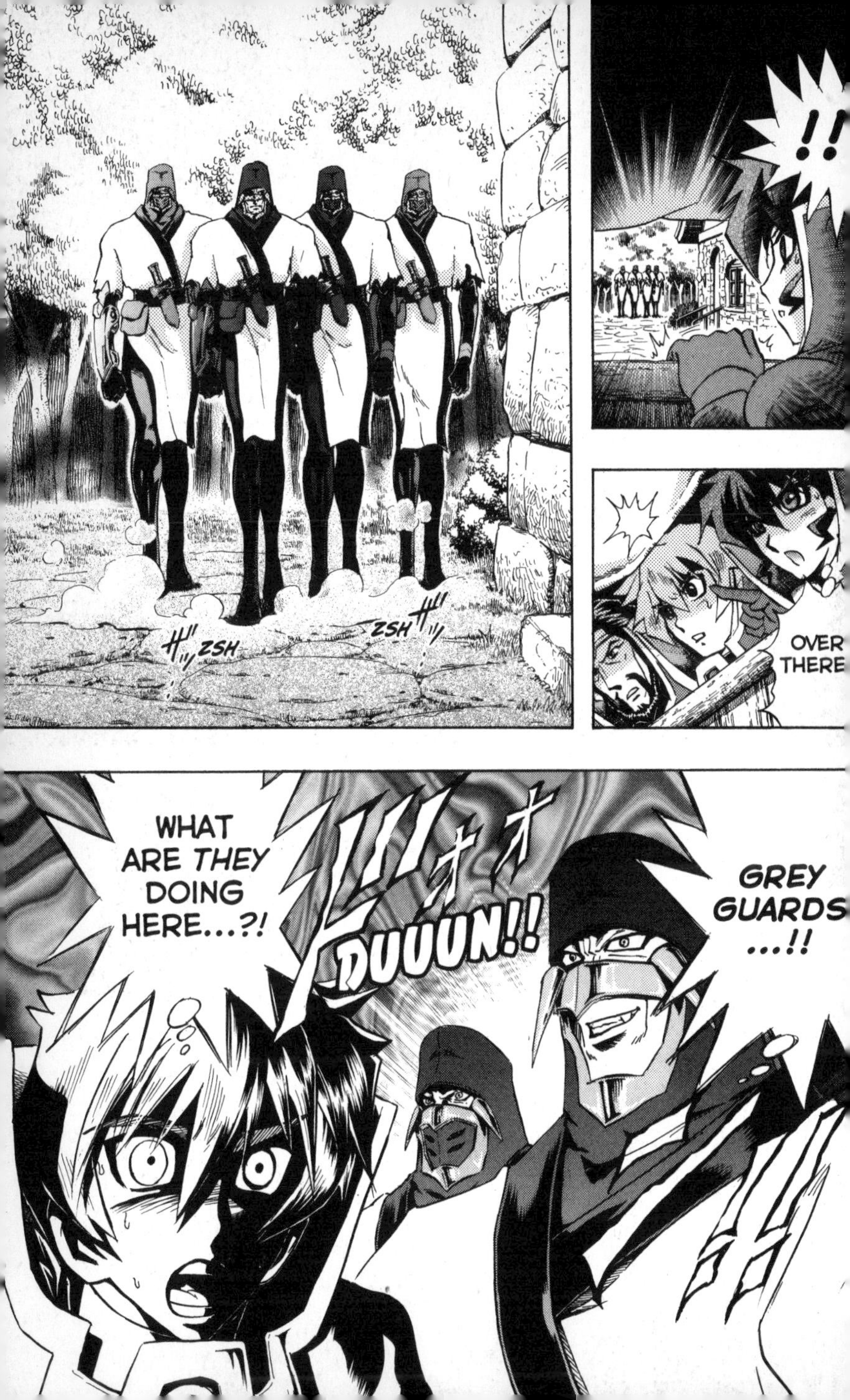
!!
OVER THERE
ZSH
ZSH
GREY GUARDS ...!!
DUUUN!!
WHAT ARE THEY DOING HERE...?!

DELTORA QUEST
デルトラクエスト

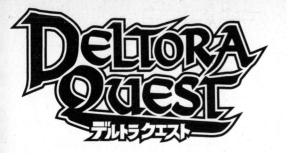

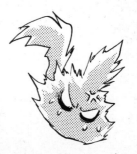

Chapter 25 Across the Broad-River!!

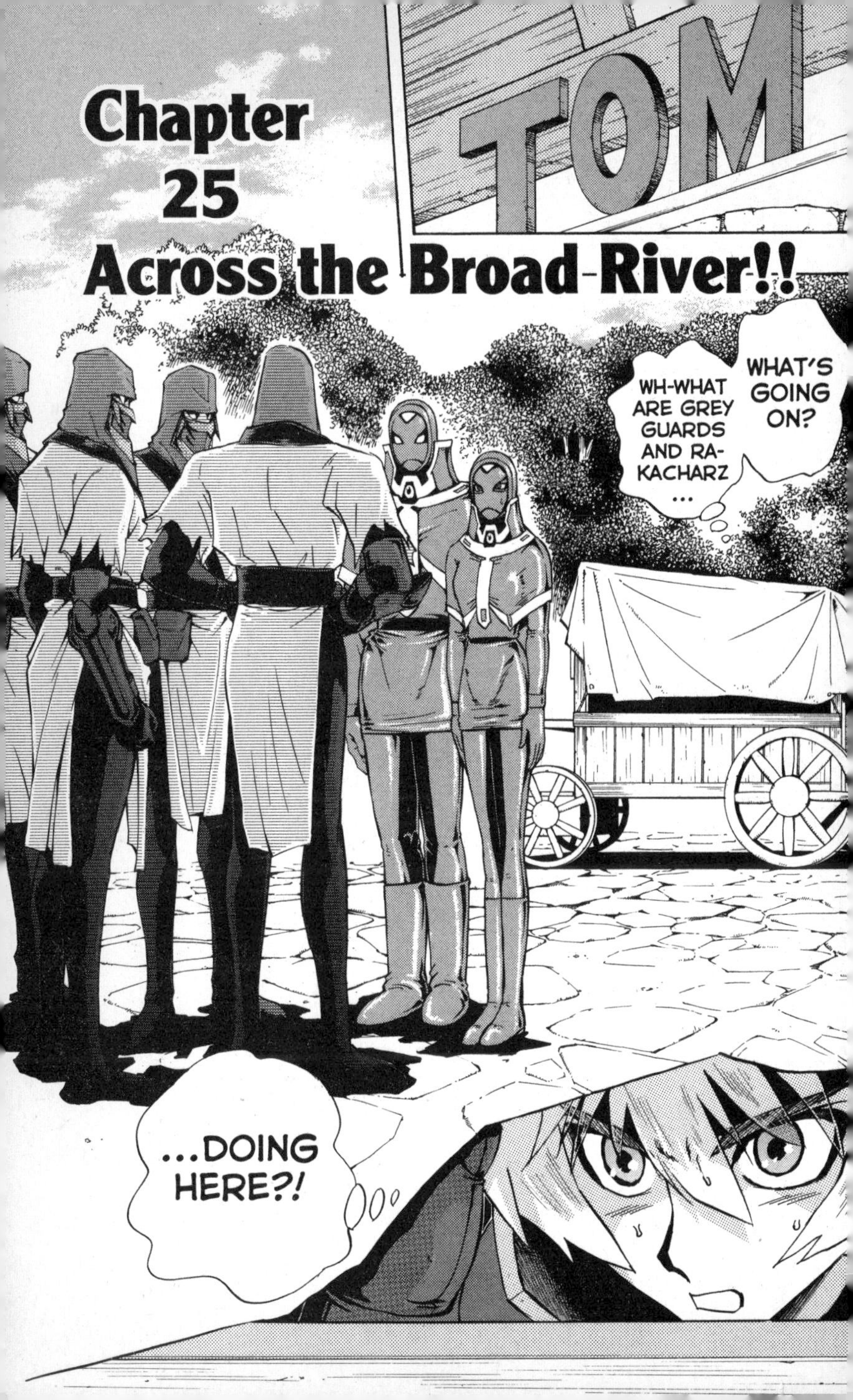
TOM
WHAT'S GOING ON?
WH-WHAT ARE GREY GUARDS AND RA-KACHARZ ...
...DOING HERE?!

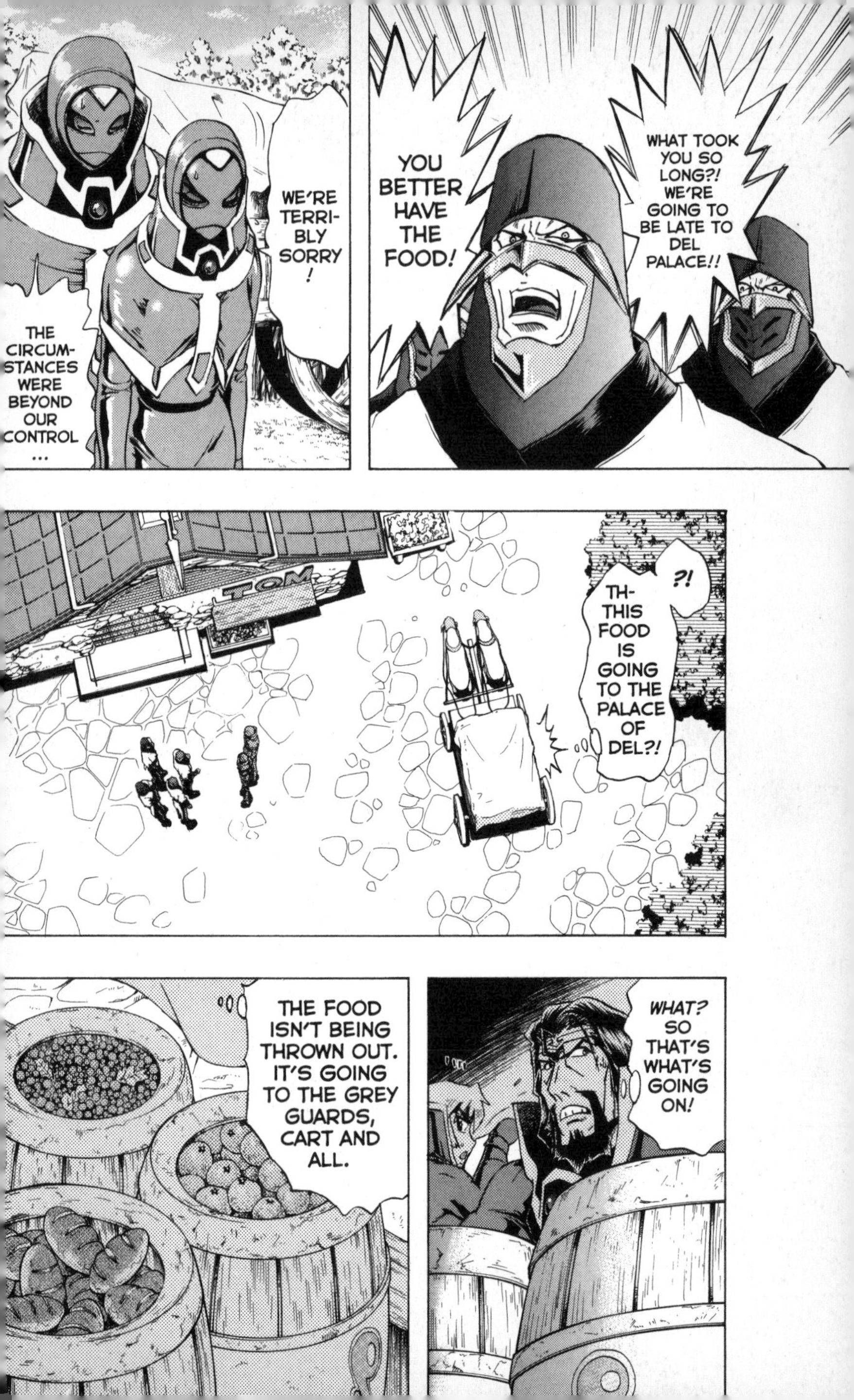
WHAT TOOK YOU SO LONG?! WE'RE GOING TO BE LATE TO DEL PALACE!!
YOU BETTER HAVE THE FOOD!
WE'RE TERRIBLY SORRY!
THE CIRCUMSTANCES WERE BEYOND OUR CONTROL...
?!
TH- THIS FOOD IS GOING TO THE PALACE OF DEL?!
TOM
WHAT? SO THAT'S WHAT'S GOING ON!
THE FOOD ISN'T BEING THROWN OUT. IT'S GOING TO THE GREY GUARDS, CART AND ALL.

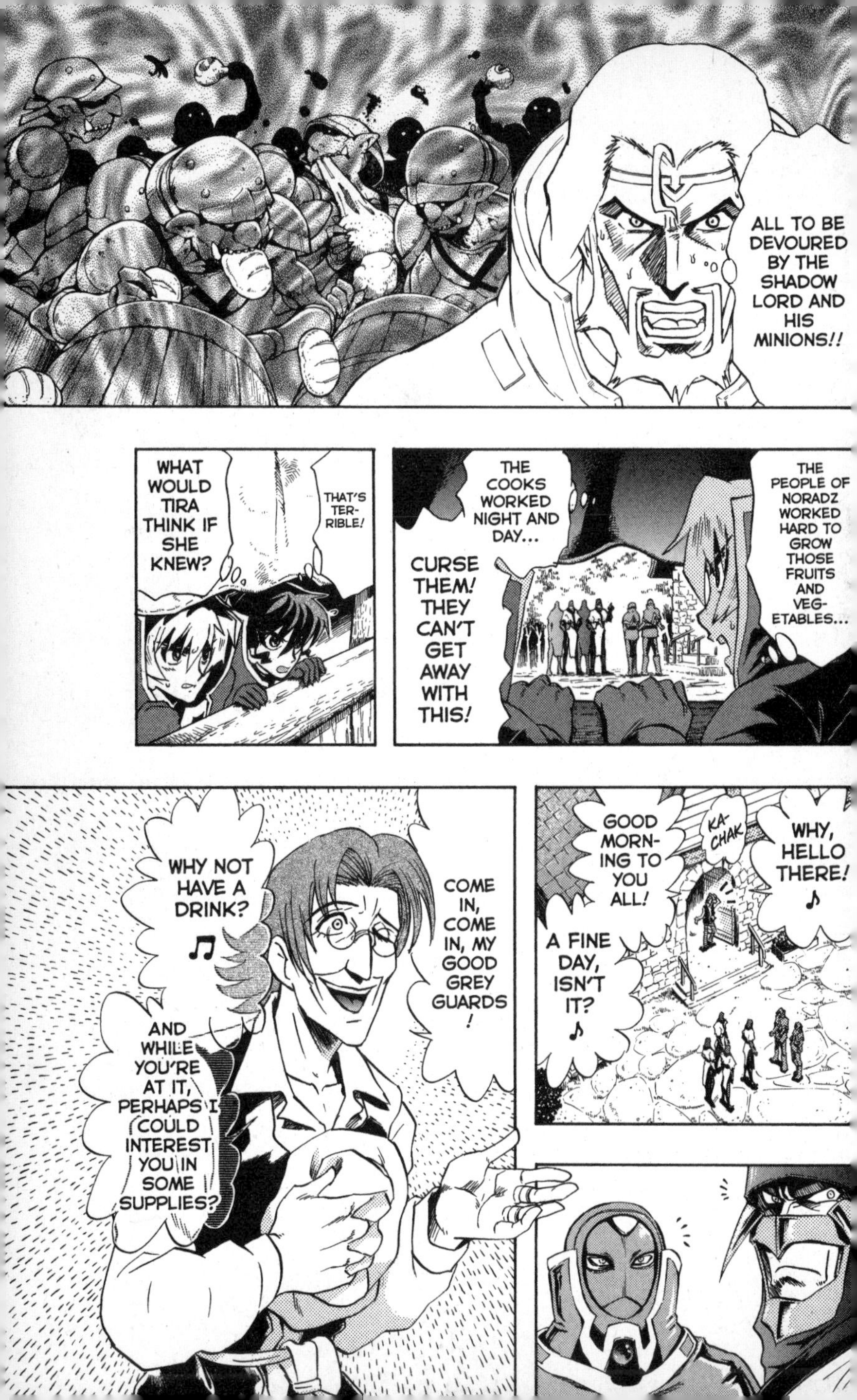
ALL TO BE DEVOURED BY THE SHADOW LORD AND HIS MINIONS!!
THE PEOPLE OF NORADZ WORKED HARD TO GROW THOSE FRUITS AND VEG-ETABLES...
THE COOKS WORKED NIGHT AND DAY...
CURSE THEM! THEY CAN'T GET AWAY WITH THIS!
THAT'S TER-RIBLE!
WHAT WOULD TIRA THINK IF SHE KNEW?
WHY, HELLO THERE! ♪
KA-CHAK
GOOD MORN-ING TO YOU ALL!
A FINE DAY, ISN'T IT? ♪
COME IN, COME IN, MY GOOD GREY GUARDS!
WHY NOT HAVE A DRINK? ♫
AND WHILE YOU'RE AT IT, PERHAPS I COULD INTEREST YOU IN SOME SUPPLIES?

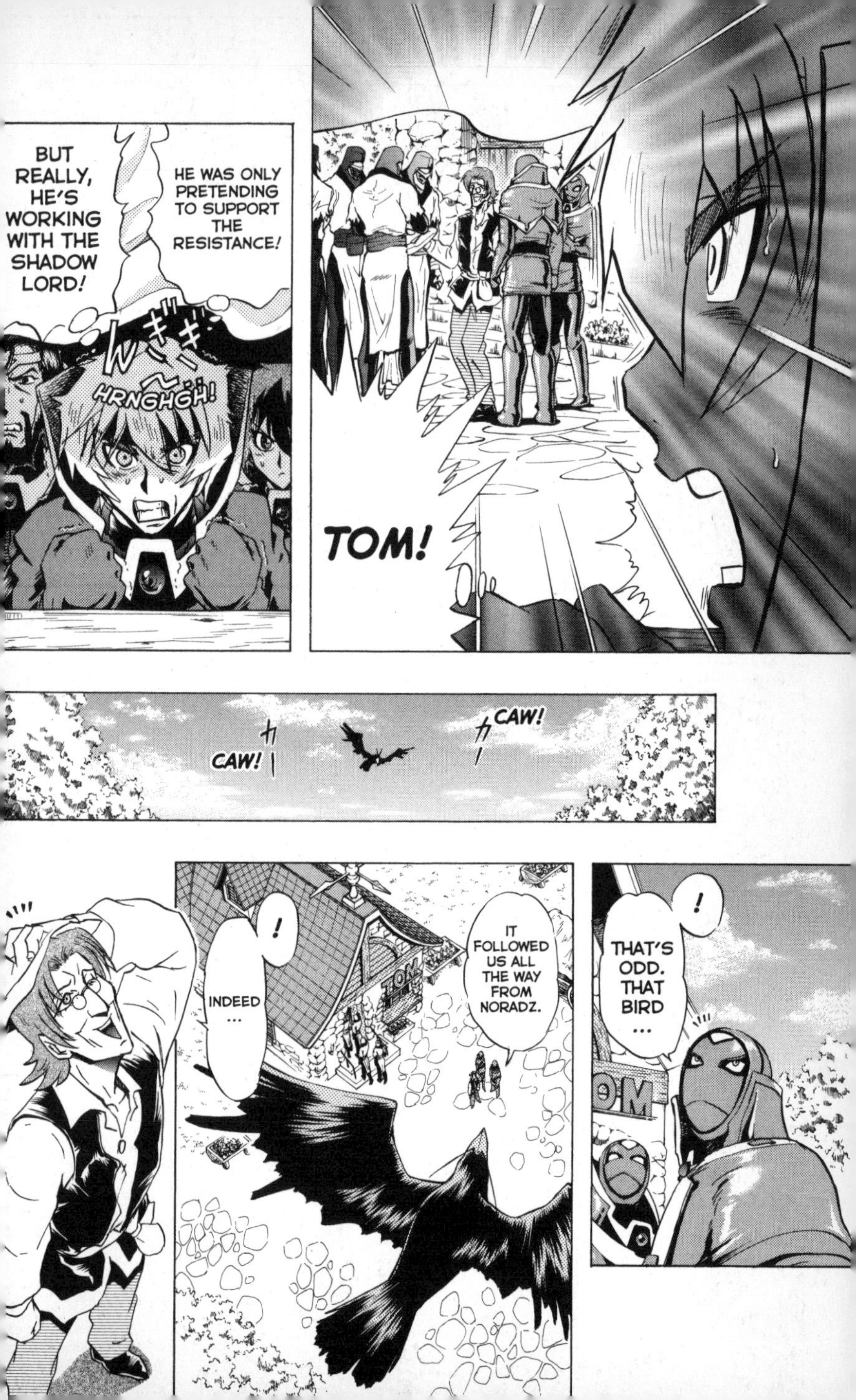
TOM!
HE WAS ONLY PRETENDING TO SUPPORT THE RESISTANCE!
BUT REALLY, HE'S WORKING WITH THE SHADOW LORD!
HRNGHGH!
CAW!
CAW!
!
THAT'S ODD. THAT BIRD ...
TOM
IT FOLLOWED US ALL THE WAY FROM NORADZ.
!
INDEED ...

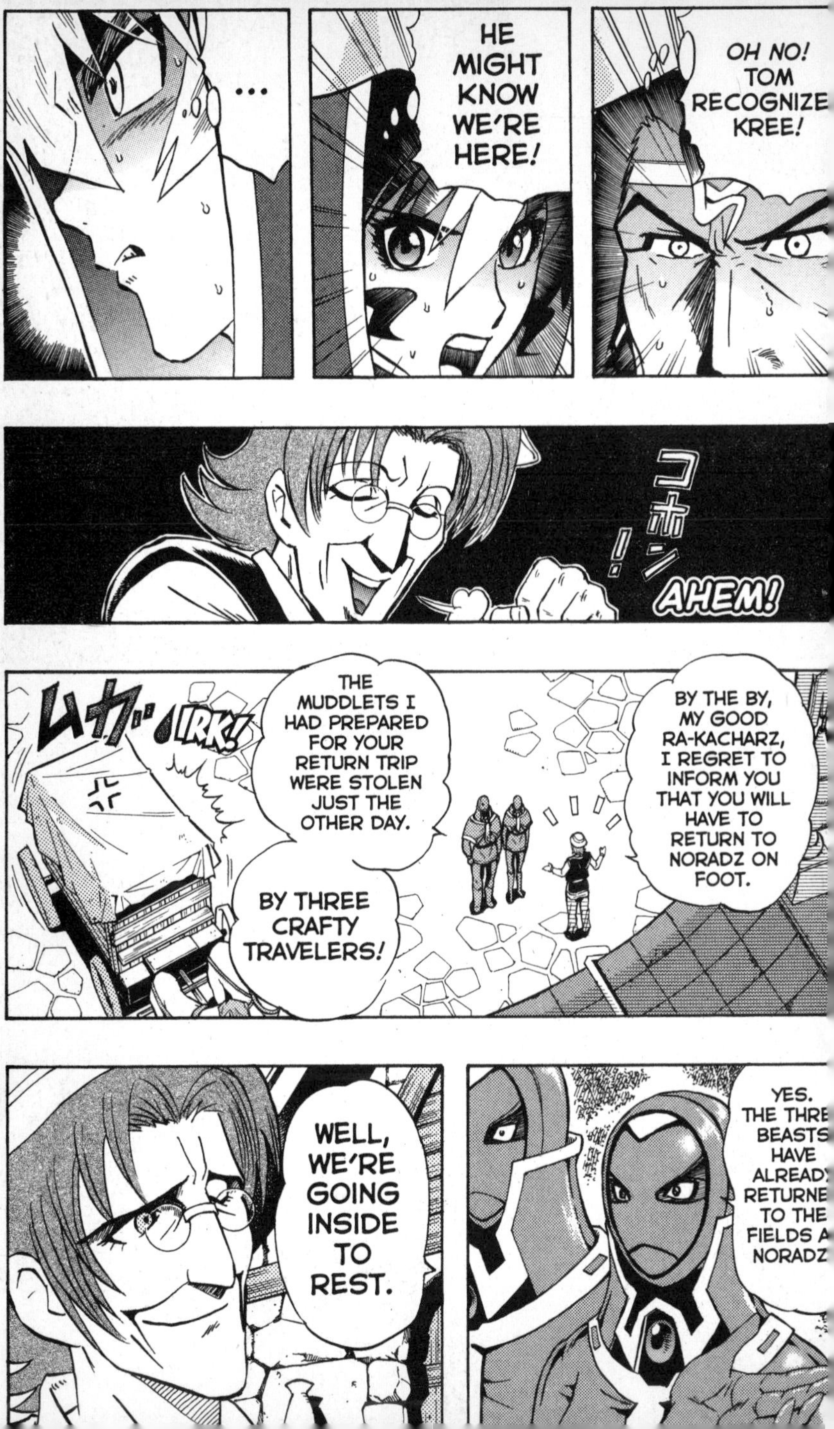
OH NO! TOM RECOGNIZE KREE!
HE MIGHT KNOW WE'RE HERE!
...
コホン!!
AHEM!
BY THE BY, MY GOOD RA-KACHARZ, I REGRET TO INFORM YOU THAT YOU WILL HAVE TO RETURN TO NORADZ ON FOOT.
THE MUDDLETS I HAD PREPARED FOR YOUR RETURN TRIP WERE STOLEN JUST THE OTHER DAY.
BY THREE CRAFTY TRAVELERS!
ムカッ
IRK!
YES. THE THRE BEASTS HAVE ALREADY RETURNE TO THE FIELDS A NORADZ
WELL, WE'RE GOING INSIDE TO REST.

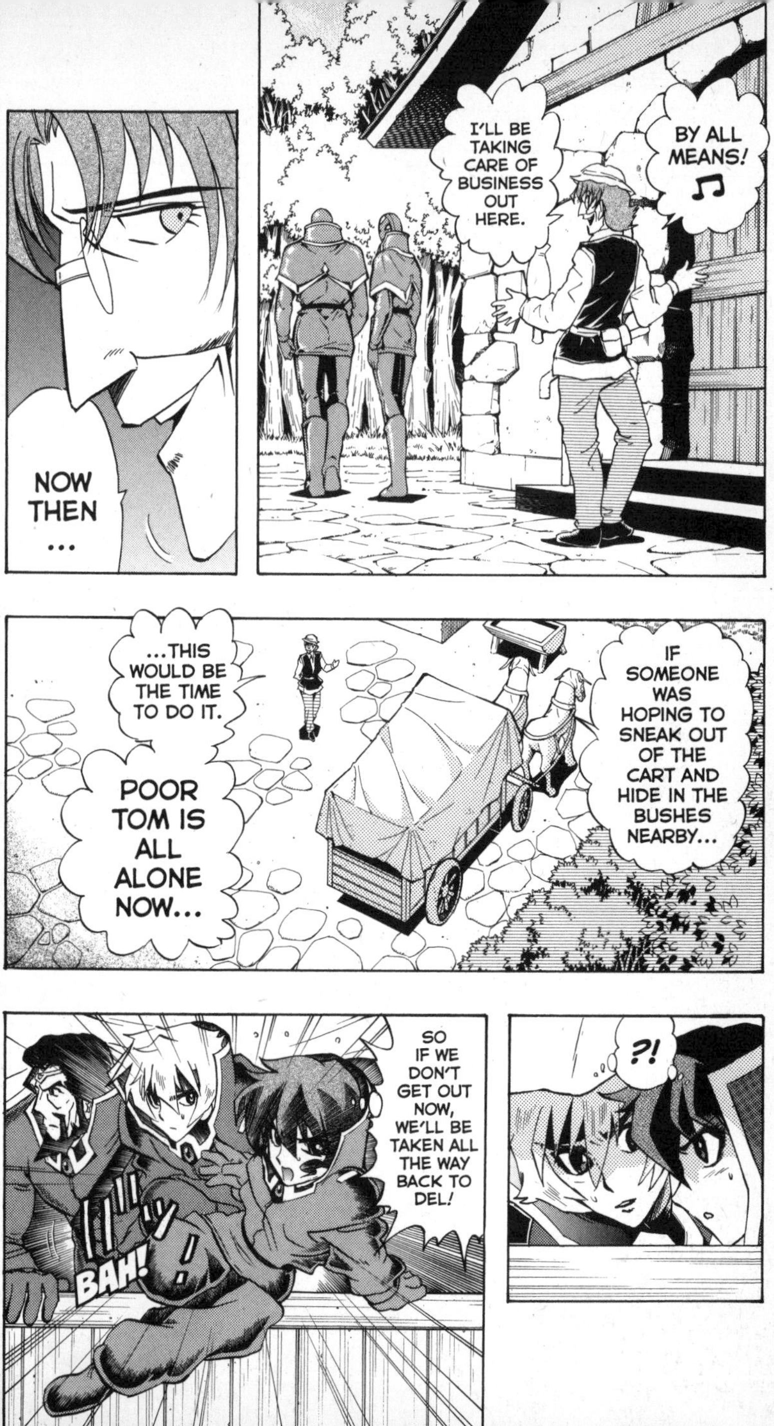
BY ALL MEANS! ♫
I'LL BE TAKING CARE OF BUSINESS OUT HERE.
NOW THEN ...
IF SOMEONE WAS HOPING TO SNEAK OUT OF THE CART AND HIDE IN THE BUSHES NEARBY...
...THIS WOULD BE THE TIME TO DO IT.
POOR TOM IS ALL ALONE NOW...
?!
SO IF WE DON'T GET OUT NOW, WE'LL BE TAKEN ALL THE WAY BACK TO DEL!
BAH!

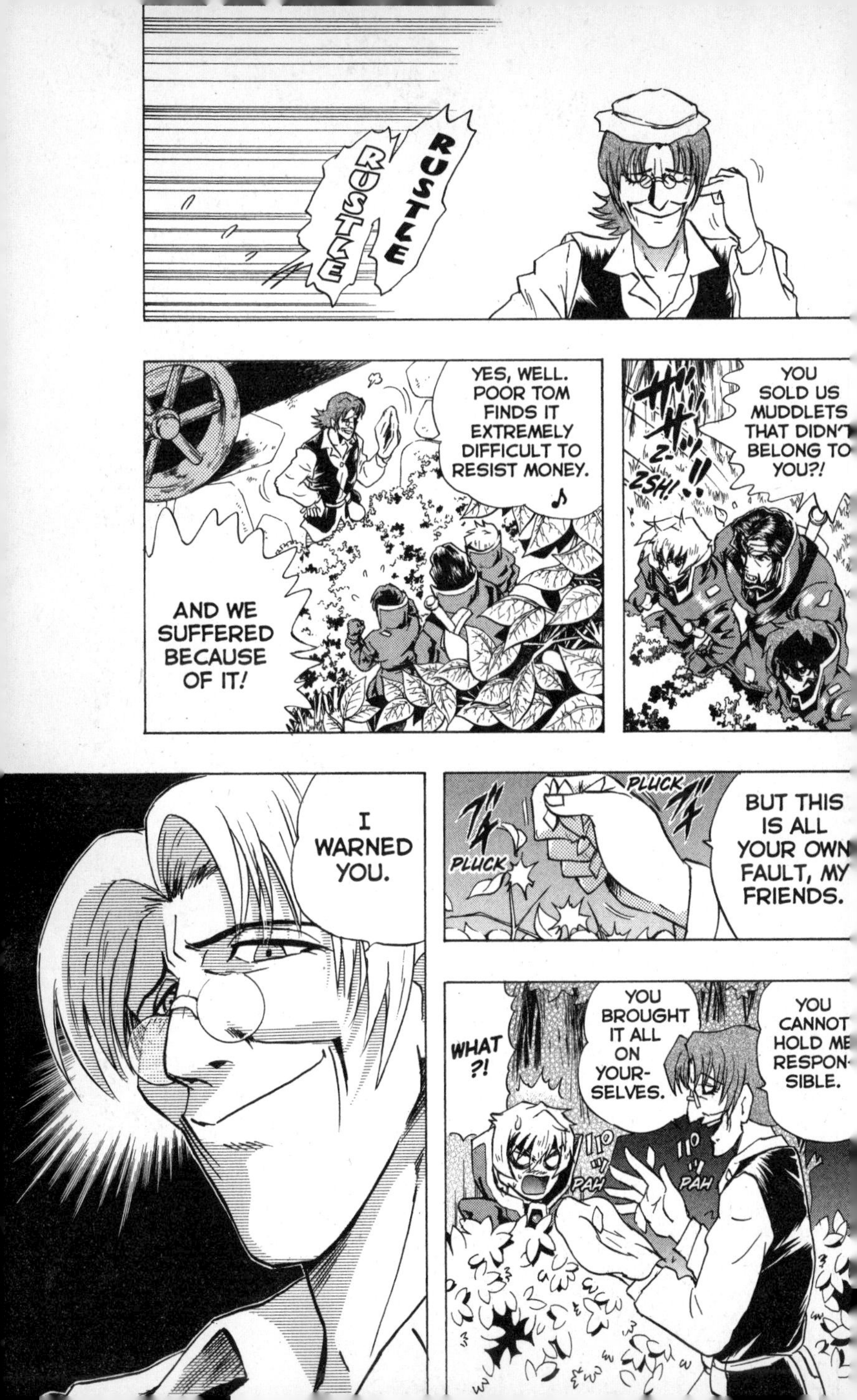
RUSTLE
RUSTLE
YOU SOLD US MUDDLETS THAT DIDN'T BELONG TO YOU?!
Z-ZSH!!
YES, WELL. POOR TOM FINDS IT EXTREMELY DIFFICULT TO RESIST MONEY. ♪
AND WE SUFFERED BECAUSE OF IT!
BUT THIS IS ALL YOUR OWN FAULT, MY FRIENDS.
PLUCK
PLUCK
YOU CANNOT HOLD ME RESPONSIBLE.
YOU BROUGHT IT ALL ON YOURSELVES.
WHAT?!
PAH
PAH
I WARNED YOU.

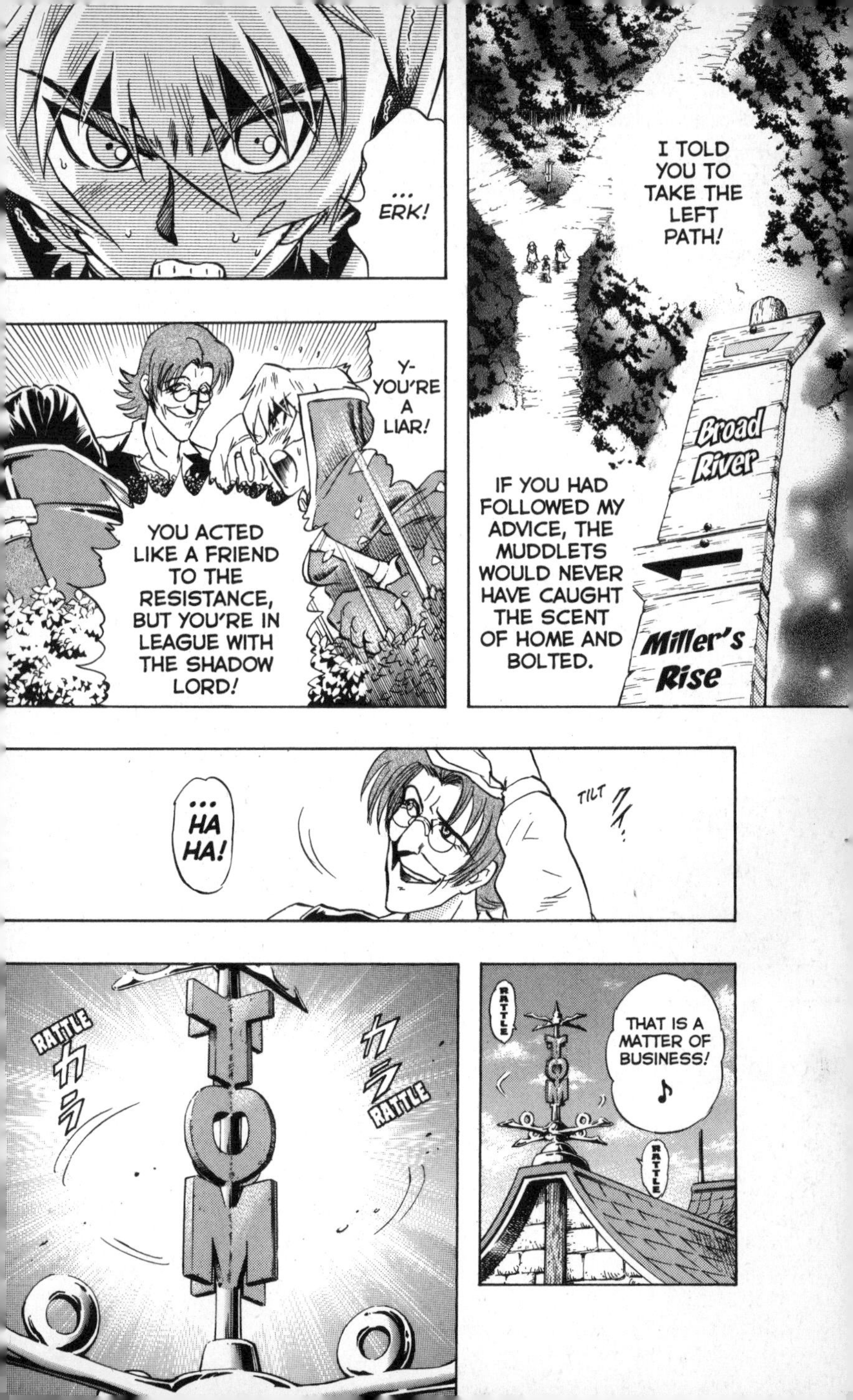
I TOLD YOU TO TAKE THE LEFT PATH!
Broad River
IF YOU HAD FOLLOWED MY ADVICE, THE MUDDLETS WOULD NEVER HAVE CAUGHT THE SCENT OF HOME AND BOLTED.
Miller's Rise
... ERK!
Y-YOU'RE A LIAR!
YOU ACTED LIKE A FRIEND TO THE RESISTANCE, BUT YOU'RE IN LEAGUE WITH THE SHADOW LORD!
TILT
... HA HA!
THAT IS A MATTER OF BUSINESS! ♪
RATTLE
RATTLE
カラ RATTLE
RATTLE カラ

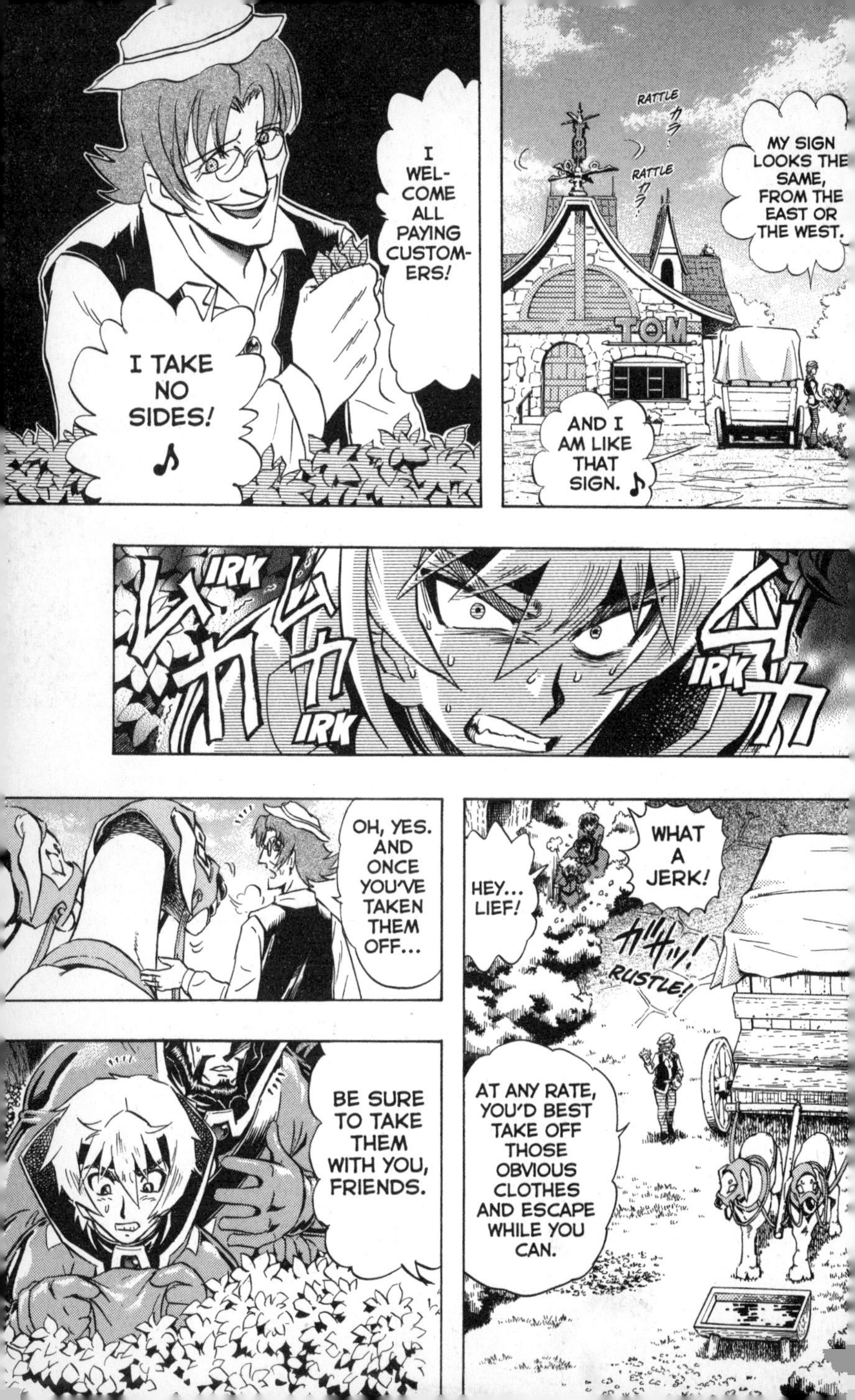
RATTLE
RATTLE
MY SIGN LOOKS THE SAME, FROM THE EAST OR THE WEST.
AND I AM LIKE THAT SIGN. ♪
I WEL-COME ALL PAYING CUSTOM-ERS!
I TAKE NO SIDES! ♪
IRK
IRK
IRK
WHAT A JERK!
HEY... LIEF!
RUSTLE!
AT ANY RATE, YOU'D BEST TAKE OFF THOSE OBVIOUS CLOTHES AND ESCAPE WHILE YOU CAN.
OH, YES. AND ONCE YOU'VE TAKEN THEM OFF...
BE SURE TO TAKE THEM WITH YOU, FRIENDS.

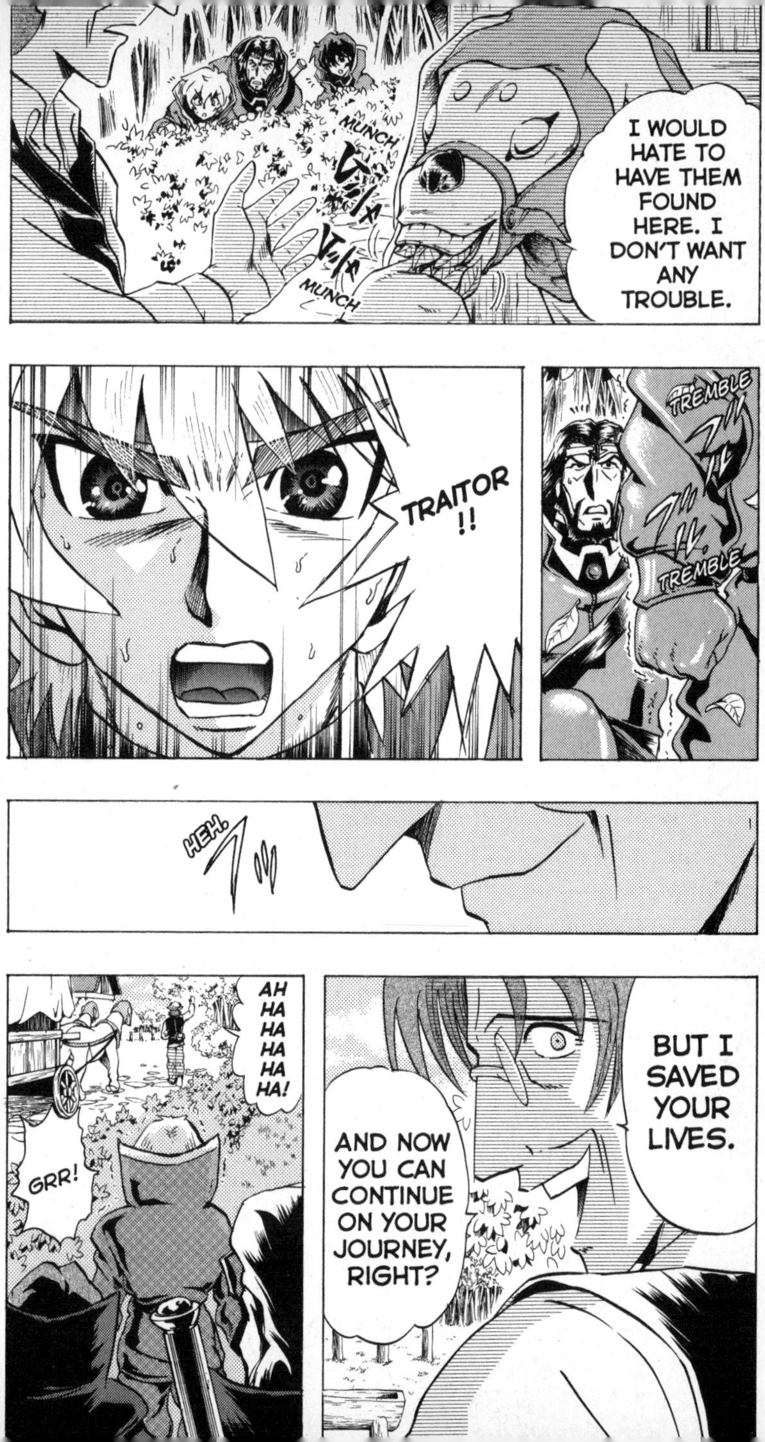
I WOULD HATE TO HAVE THEM FOUND HERE. I DON'T WANT ANY TROUBLE.
MUNCH
MUNCH
TREMBLE
TREMBLE
TRAITOR !!
HEH.
BUT I SAVED YOUR LIVES.
AND NOW YOU CAN CONTINUE ON YOUR JOURNEY, RIGHT?
AH HA HA HA HA HA!
GRR!

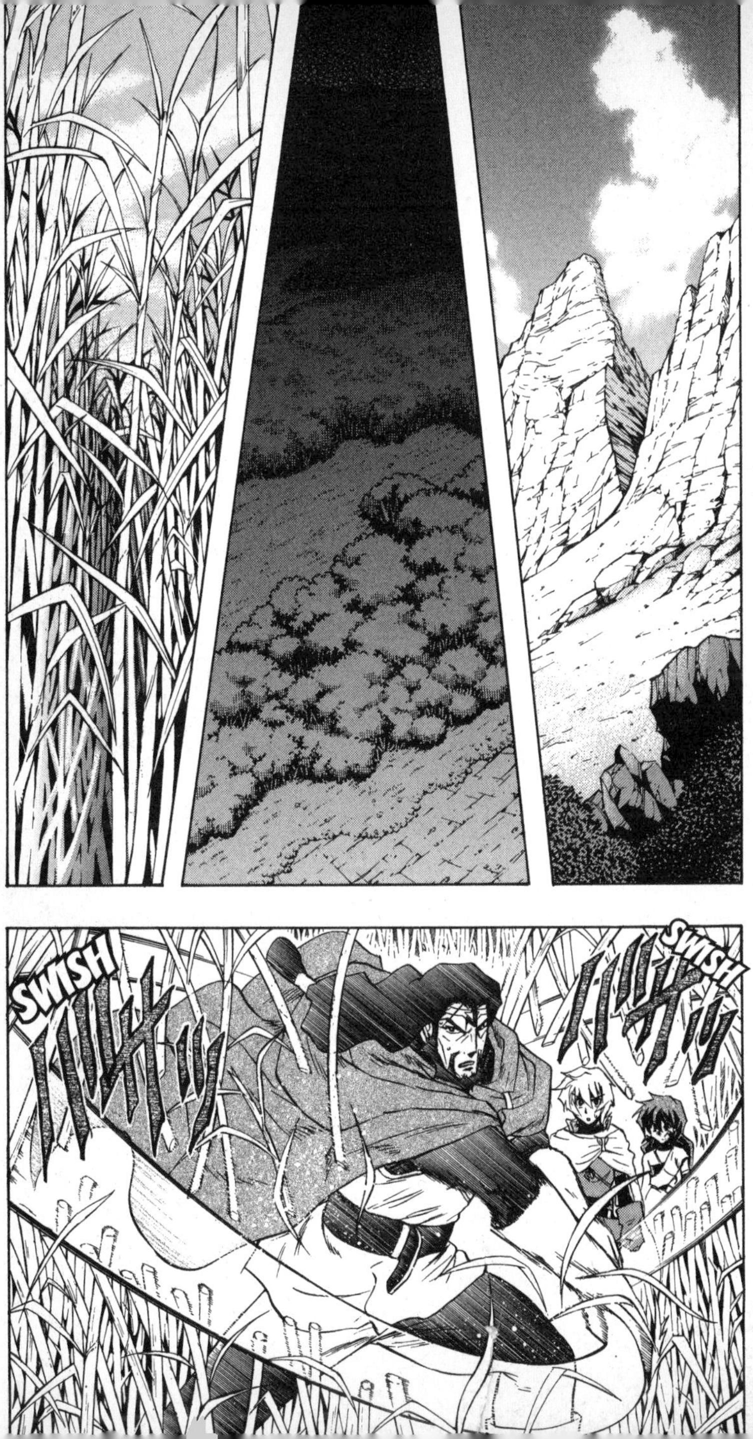
SWISH
SWISH

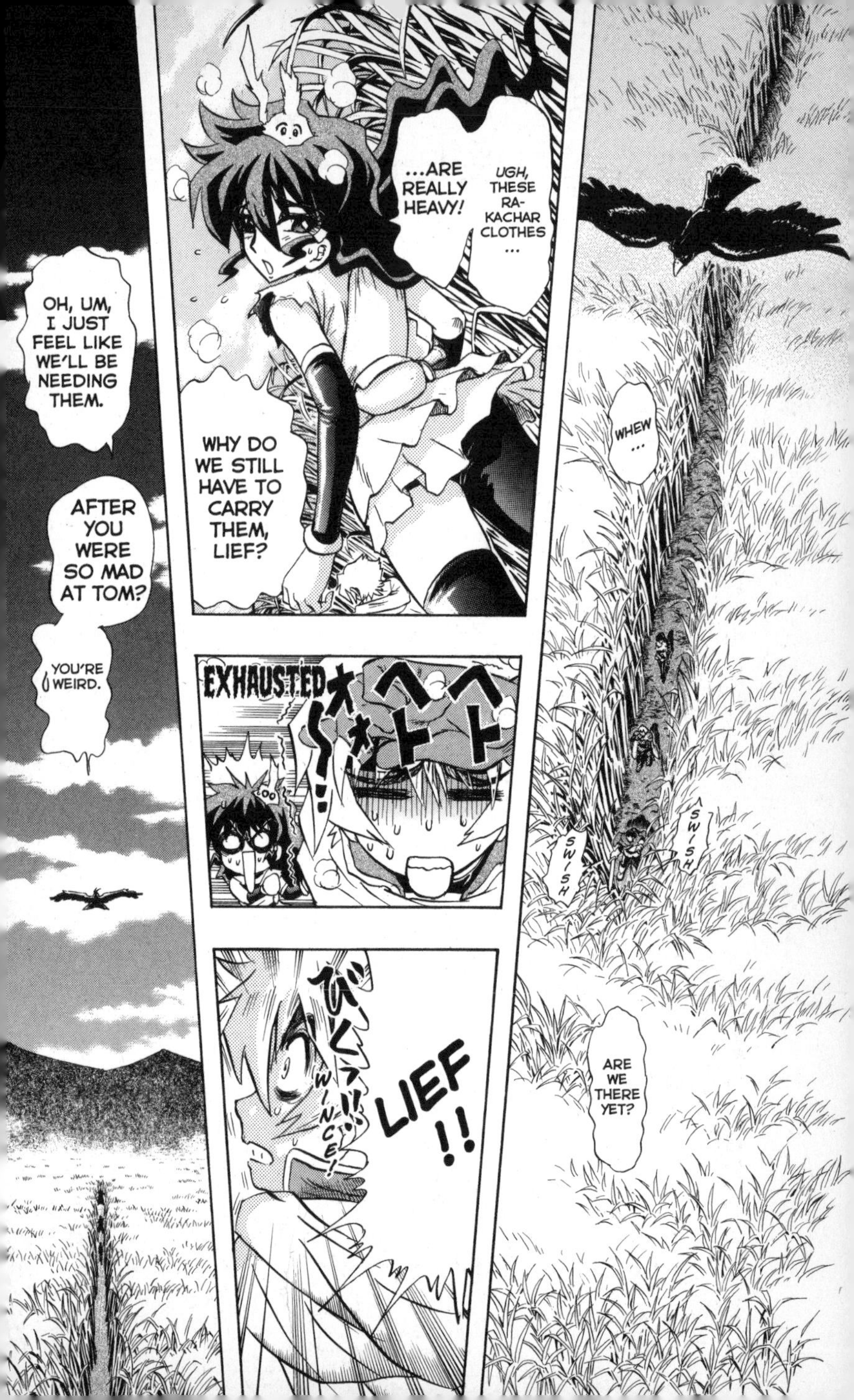
WHEW...
SWISH
SWISH
ARE WE THERE YET?
UGH, THESE RA-KACHAR CLOTHES...
...ARE REALLY HEAVY!
WHY DO WE STILL HAVE TO CARRY THEM, LIEF?
EXHAUSTED
LIEF!!
WINCE!
AFTER YOU WERE SO MAD AT TOM?
OH, UM, I JUST FEEL LIKE WE'LL BE NEEDING THEM.
YOU'RE WEIRD.

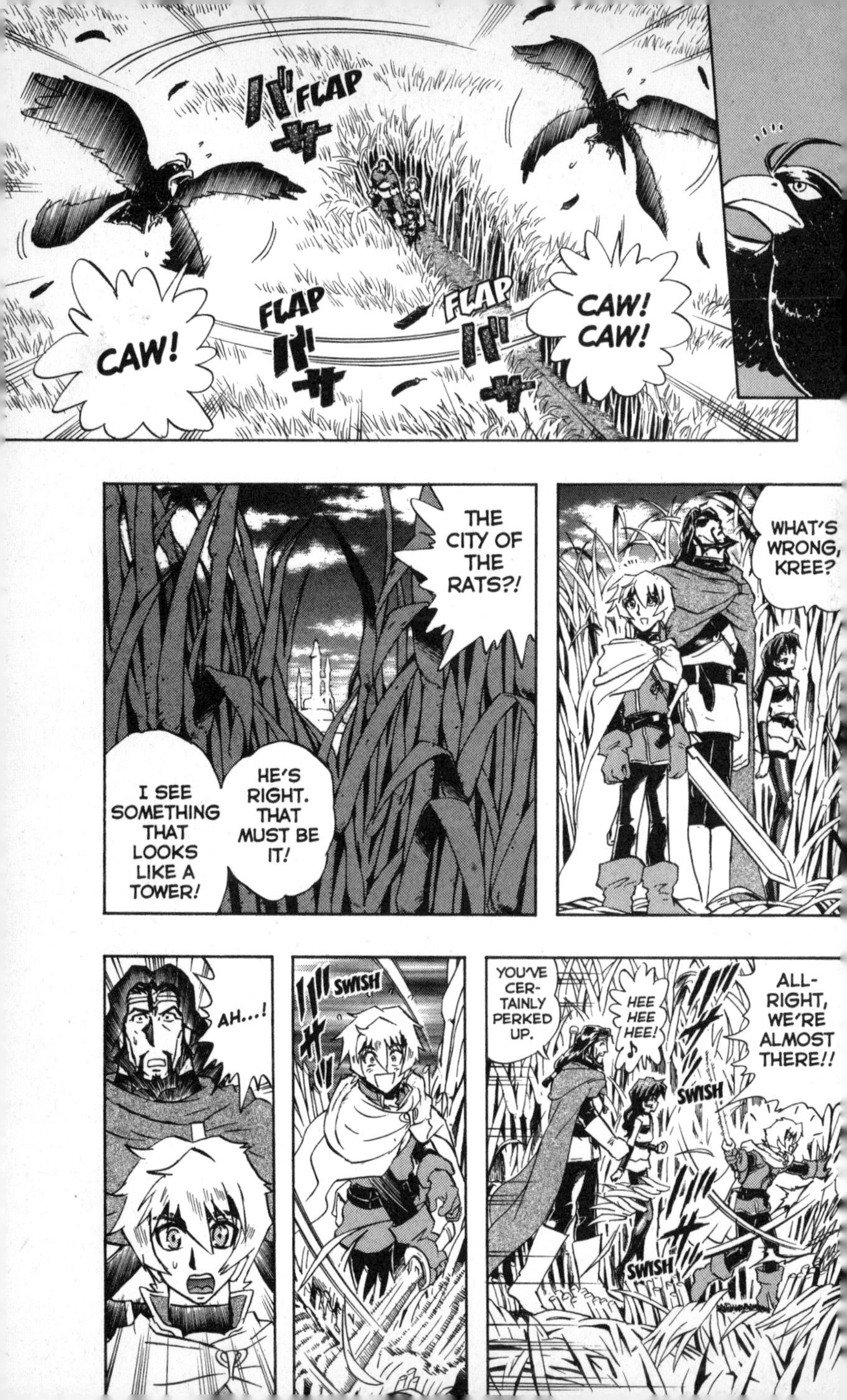
FLAP
CAW! CAW!
FLAP
FLAP
CAW!
WHAT'S WRONG, KREE?
THE CITY OF THE RATS?!
HE'S RIGHT. THAT MUST BE IT!
I SEE SOMETHING THAT LOOKS LIKE A TOWER!
ALL-RIGHT, WE'RE ALMOST THERE!!
HEE HEE HEE! ♪
YOU'VE CER-TAINLY PERKED UP.
SWISH
SWISH
SWISH
AH...!

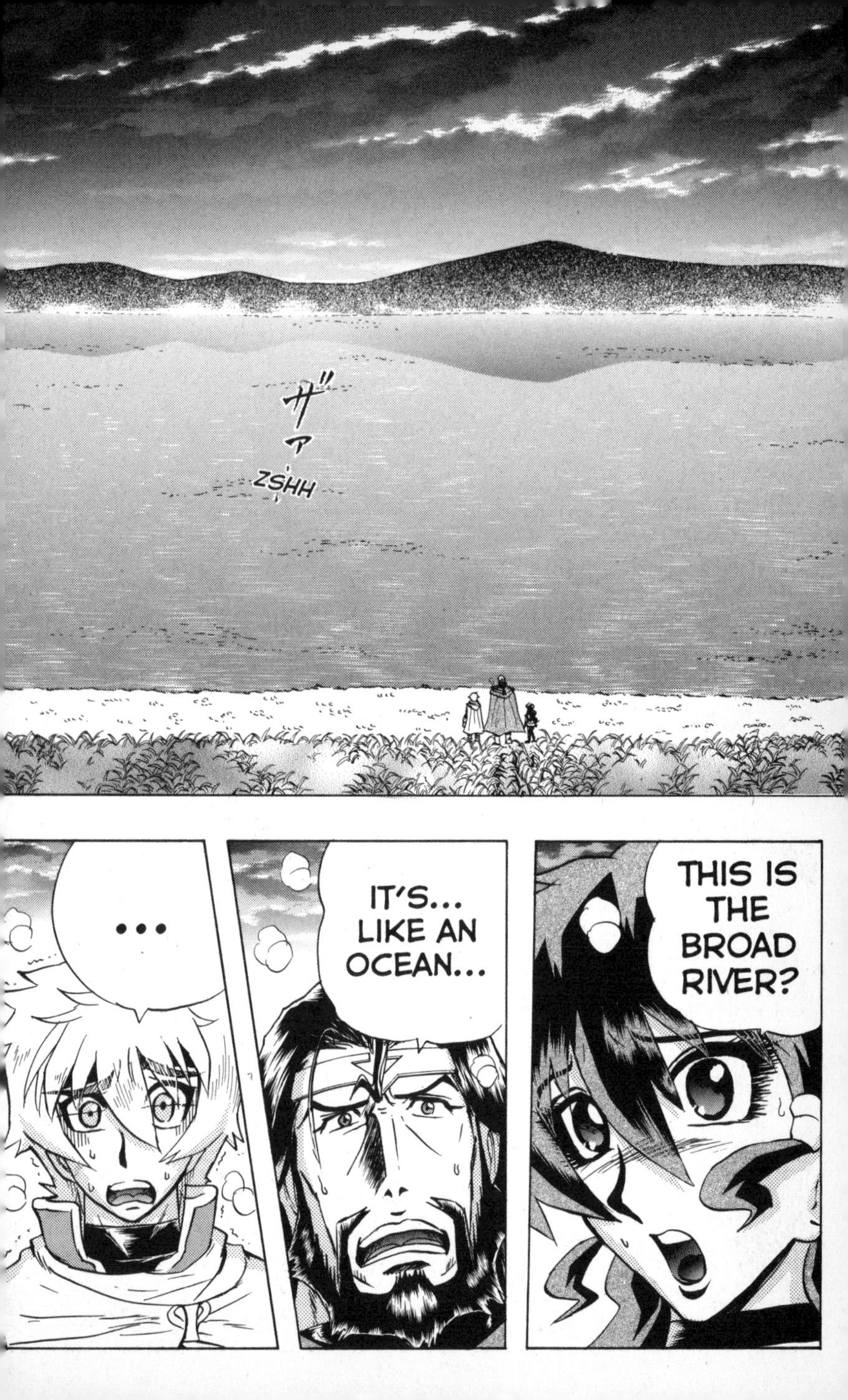
ザァ
ZSHH
THIS IS THE BROAD RIVER?
IT'S... LIKE AN OCEAN...
...

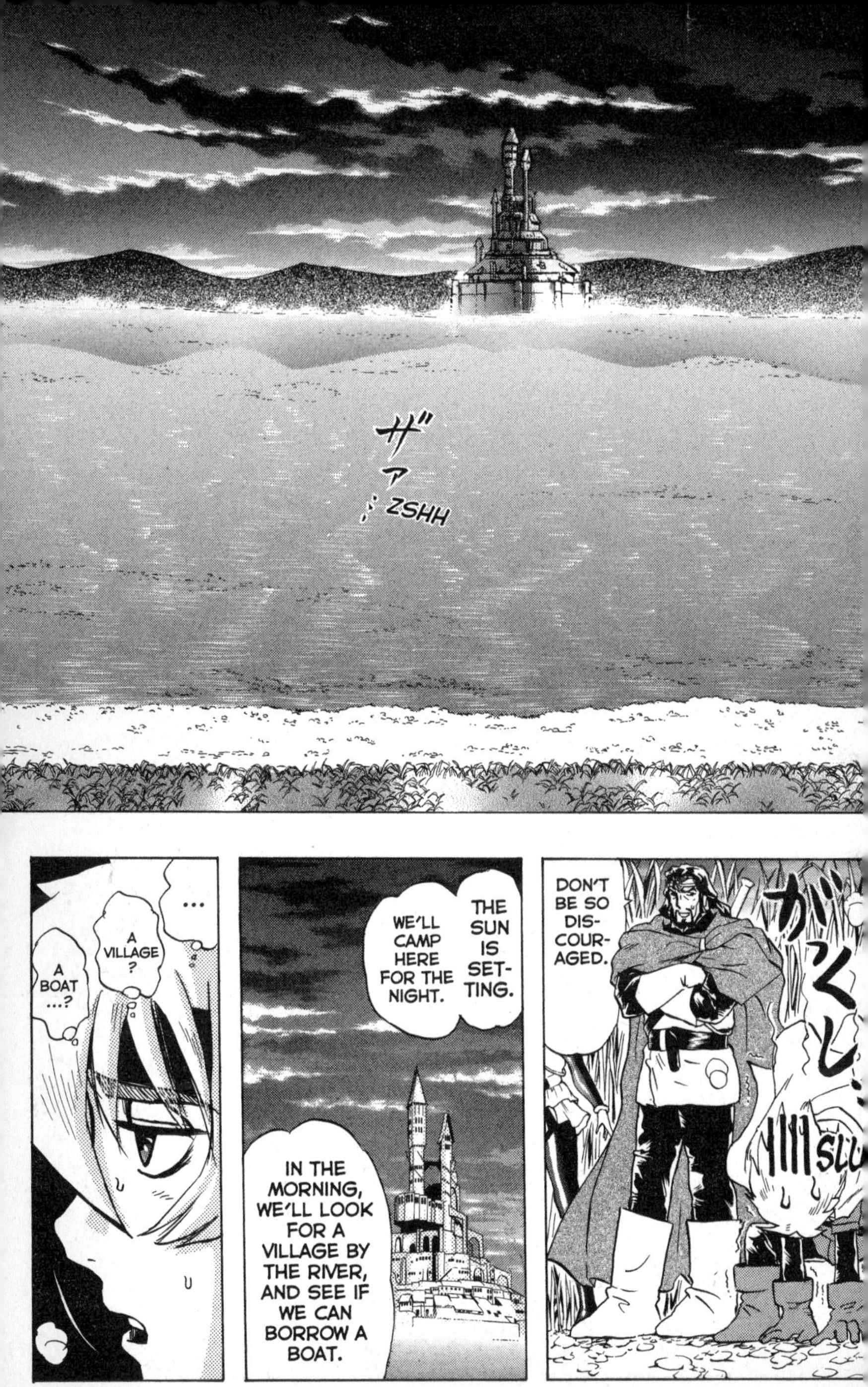
ザア…
ZSHH
がっくし…
SLU
DON'T BE SO DISCOURAGED.
THE SUN IS SETTING.
WE'LL CAMP HERE FOR THE NIGHT.
IN THE MORNING, WE'LL LOOK FOR A VILLAGE BY THE RIVER, AND SEE IF WE CAN BORROW A BOAT.
...
A VILLAGE?
A BOAT...?

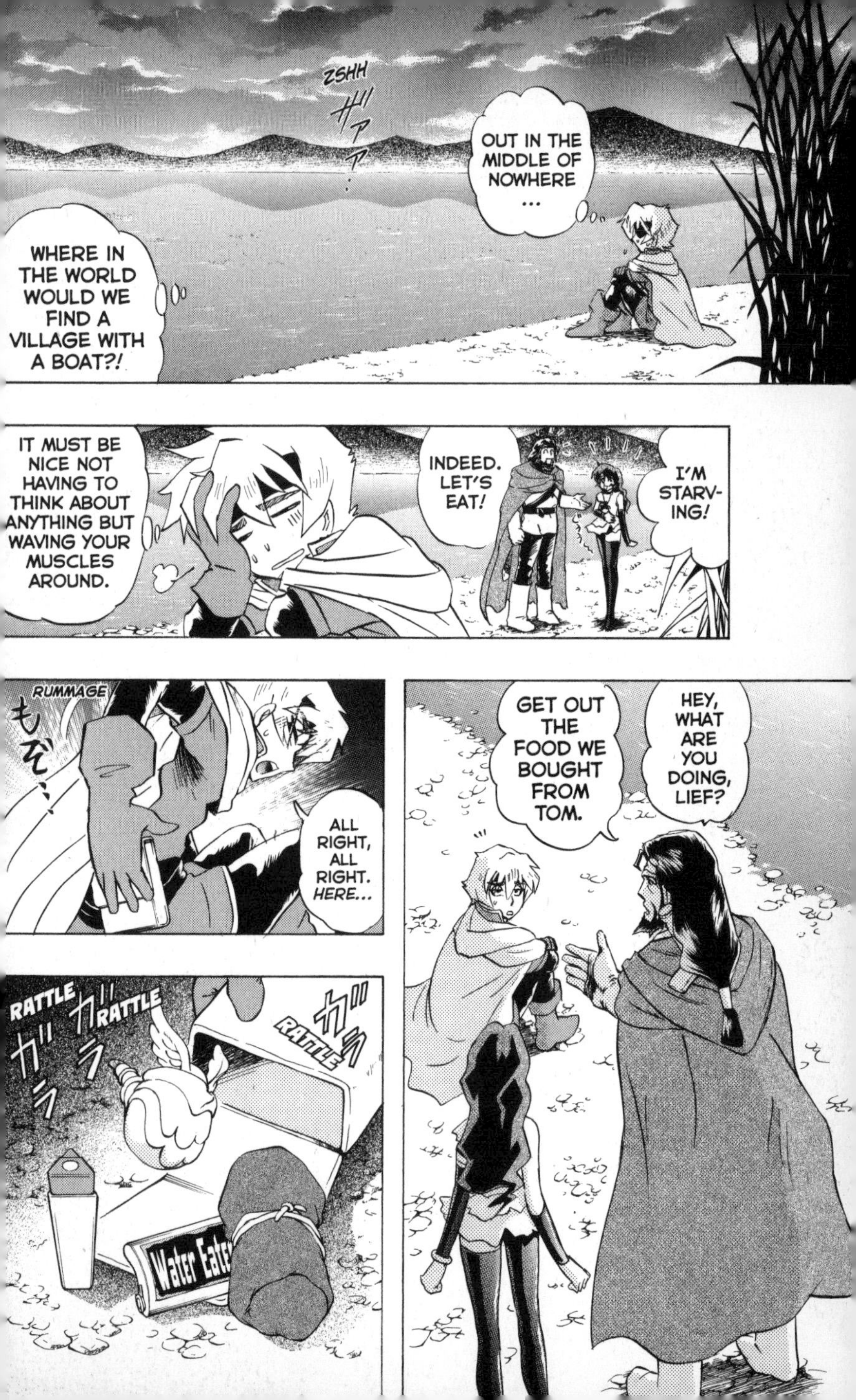
OUT IN THE MIDDLE OF NOWHERE ...
ZSHH
ザァァ...
WHERE IN THE WORLD WOULD WE FIND A VILLAGE WITH A BOAT?!
I'M STARVING!
INDEED. LET'S EAT!
IT MUST BE NICE NOT HAVING TO THINK ABOUT ANYTHING BUT WAVING YOUR MUSCLES AROUND.
HEY, WHAT ARE YOU DOING, LIEF?
GET OUT THE FOOD WE BOUGHT FROM TOM.
RUMMAGE
もぞ...
ALL RIGHT, ALL RIGHT. HERE...
RATTLE
ガラ
RATTLE
カラ
RATTLE
ガラ
Water Eater

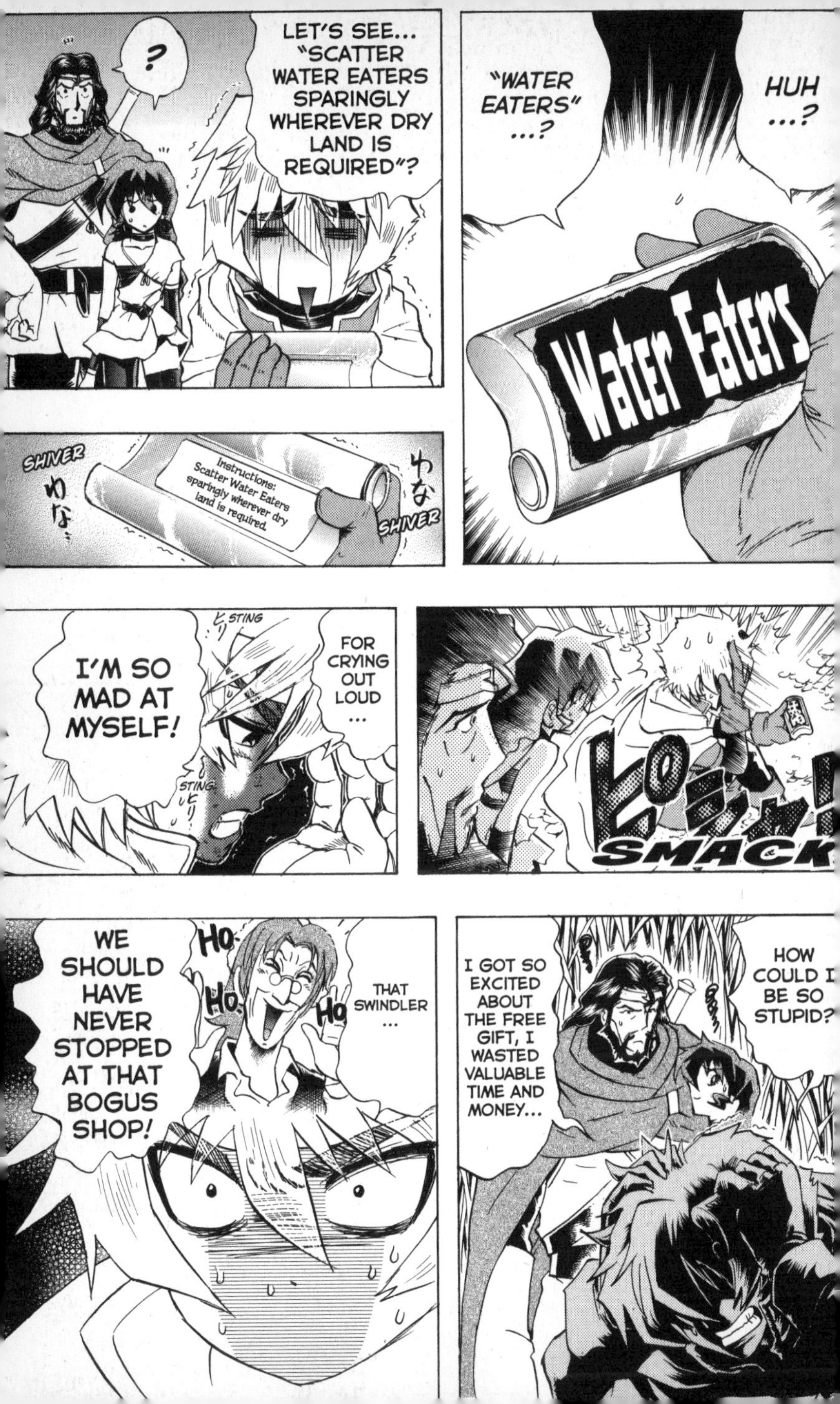
HUH ...?
"WATER EATERS" ...?
Water Eaters
LET'S SEE... "SCATTER WATER EATERS SPARINGLY WHEREVER DRY LAND IS REQUIRED"?
?
SHIVER
Instructions: Scatter Water Eaters sparingly wherever dry land is required.
SHIVER
SMACK
FOR CRYING OUT LOUD ...
STING
I'M SO MAD AT MYSELF!
STING
HOW COULD I BE SO STUPID?
I GOT SO EXCITED ABOUT THE FREE GIFT, I WASTED VALUABLE TIME AND MONEY...
THAT SWINDLER ...
HO HO HO
WE SHOULD HAVE NEVER STOPPED AT THAT BOGUS SHOP!

BAH!

THIS WORTHLESS JUNK!

SHALLAH

DAMN IT!

STOMP STOMP STOMP STOMP STOMP

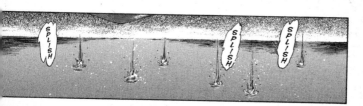

SPLISH SPLISH SPLISH

SPLISH SPLISH SPLISH SPLISH SPLISH

I HATE YOU, STUPID TOM!!

BAH!

I HATE YOU, STUPID, STUPID LIEF!!

BAH!!!

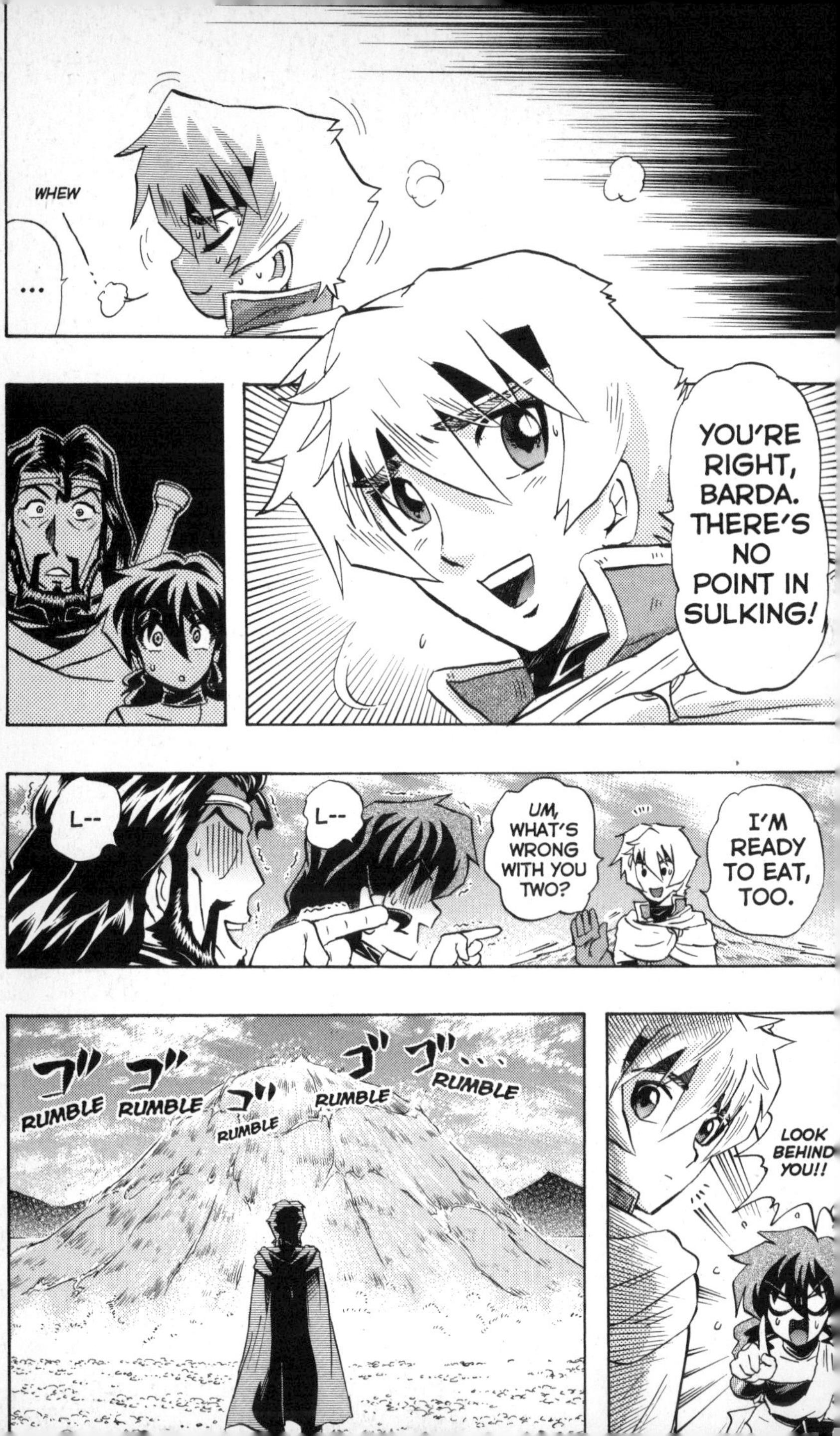
WHEW
...
YOU'RE RIGHT, BARDA. THERE'S NO POINT IN SULKING!
I'M READY TO EAT, TOO.
UM, WHAT'S WRONG WITH YOU TWO?
L--
L--
LOOK BEHIND YOU!!
ゴゴ… RUMBLE
ゴ RUMBLE
ゴ RUMBLE
ゴ RUMBLE
ゴ RUMBLE

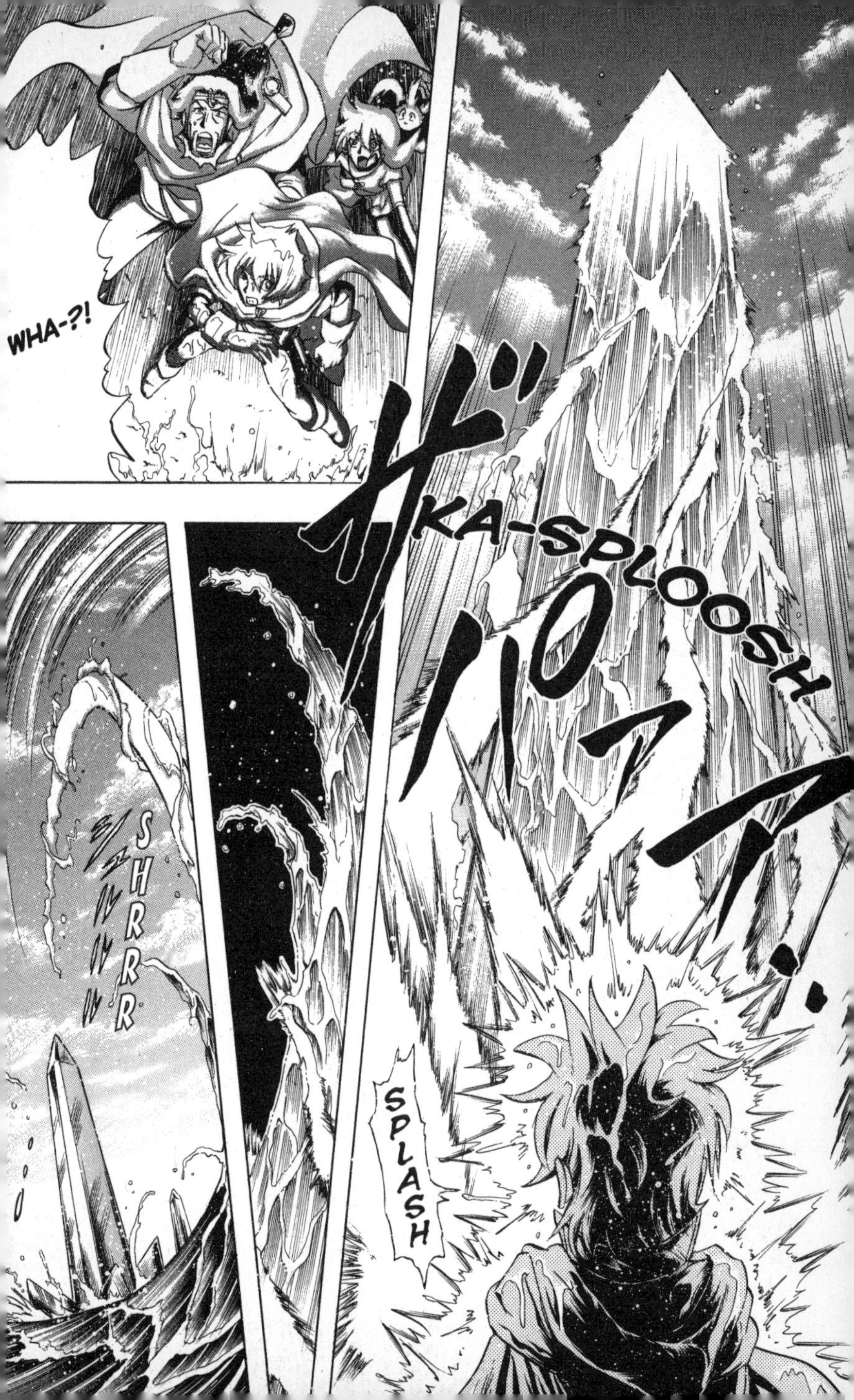
KA-SPLOOSH
WHA-?!
SPLASH
SHRRR

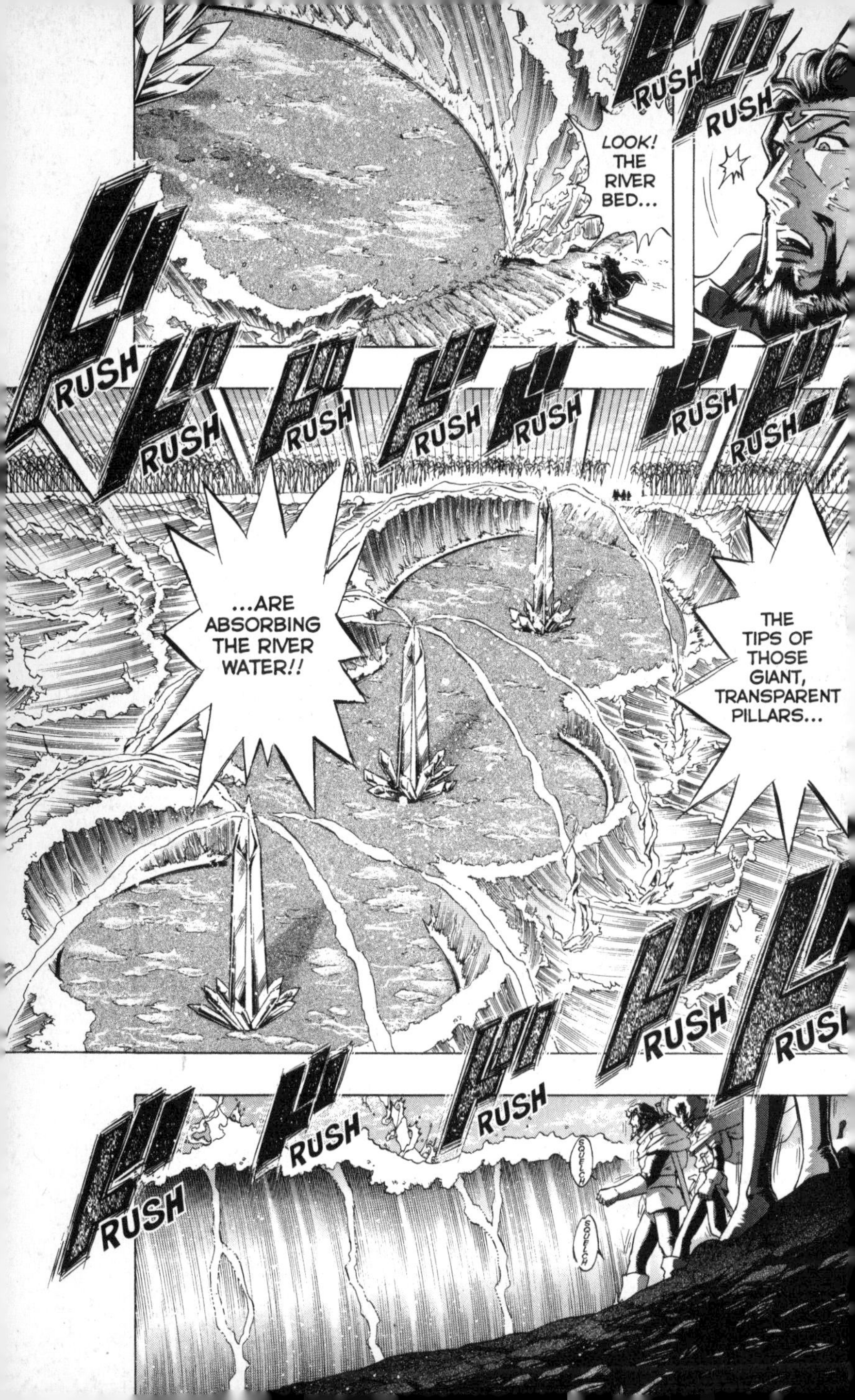
RUSH
RUSH
LOOK! THE RIVER BED...
RUSH
RUSH
RUSH
RUSH
RUSH
RUSH
RUSH
THE TIPS OF THOSE GIANT, TRANSPARENT PILLARS...
...ARE ABSORBING THE RIVER WATER!!
RUSH
RUSH
RUSH
RUSH
RUSH
SQUELCH
SQUELCH

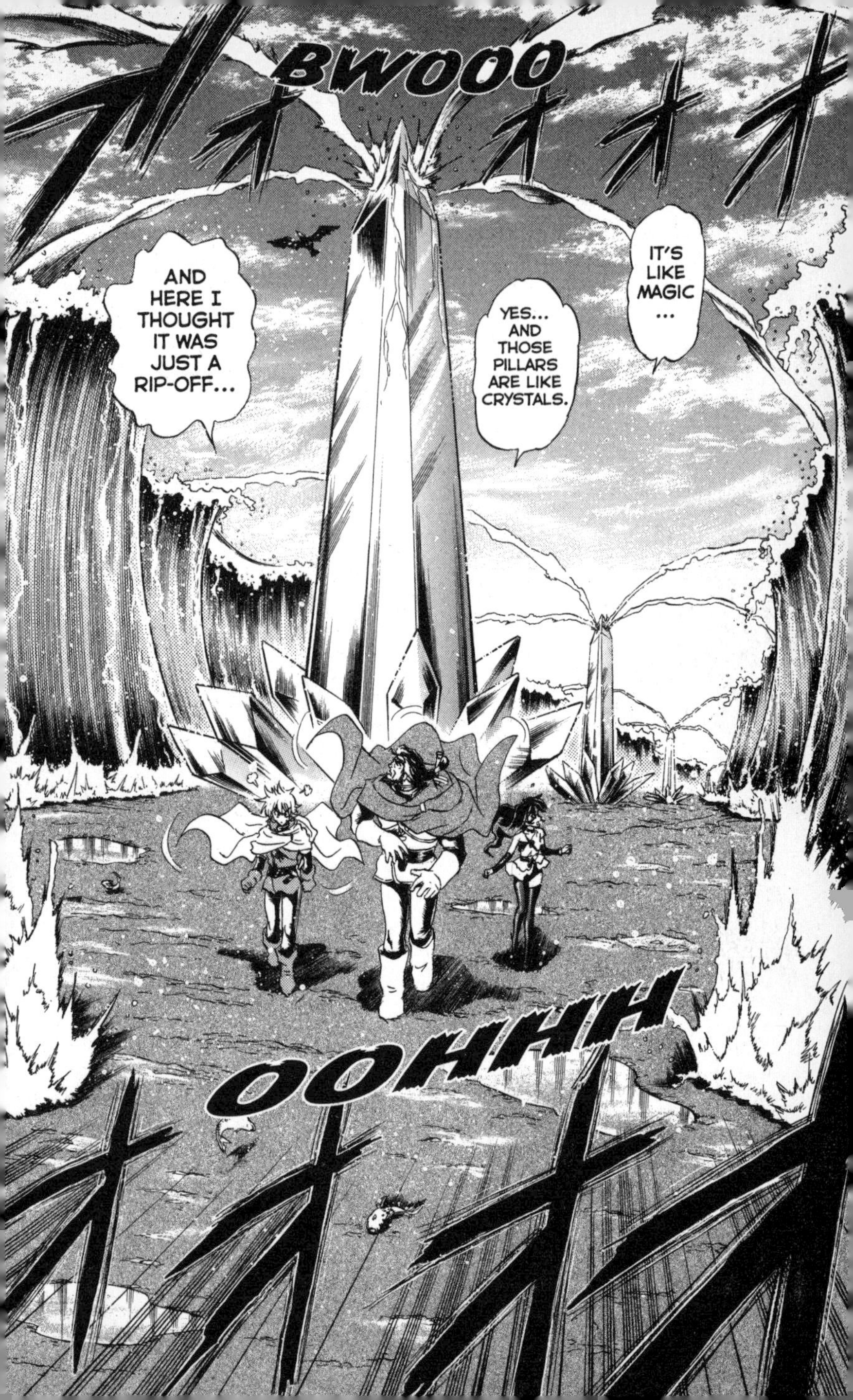
BWOOO
IT'S LIKE MAGIC...
YES... AND THOSE PILLARS ARE LIKE CRYSTALS.
AND HERE I THOUGHT IT WAS JUST A RIP-OFF...
OOHHH

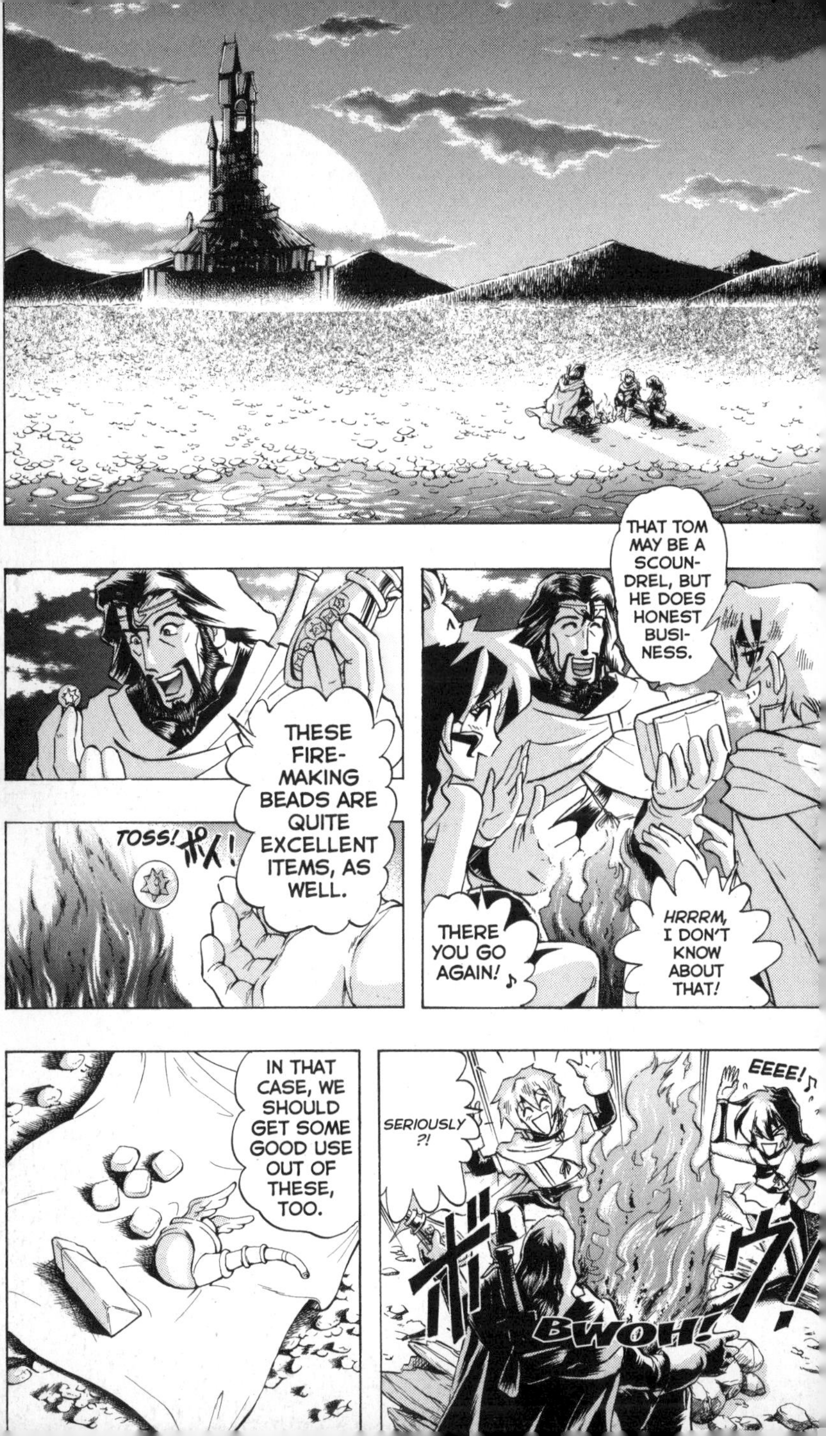
THAT TOM MAY BE A SCOUNDREL, BUT HE DOES HONEST BUSINESS.
HRRRM, I DON'T KNOW ABOUT THAT!
THERE YOU GO AGAIN! ♪
THESE FIRE-MAKING BEADS ARE QUITE EXCELLENT ITEMS, AS WELL.
TOSS! ポイ!
EEEE! ♪
SERIOUSLY?!
BWOH! ボウ!
IN THAT CASE, WE SHOULD GET SOME GOOD USE OUT OF THESE, TOO.

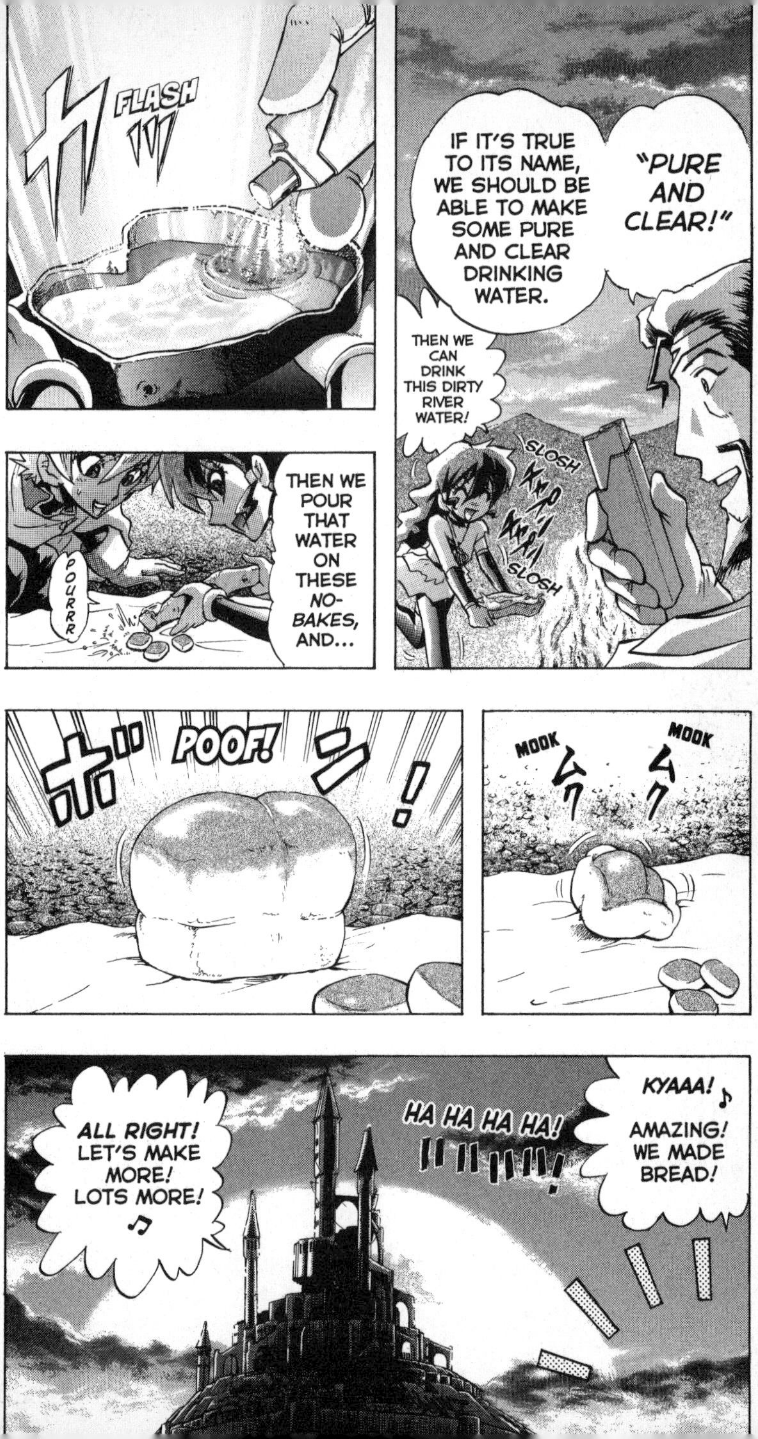
"PURE AND CLEAR!"
IF IT'S TRUE TO ITS NAME, WE SHOULD BE ABLE TO MAKE SOME PURE AND CLEAR DRINKING WATER.
THEN WE CAN DRINK THIS DIRTY RIVER WATER!
SLOSH
SLOSH
FLASH
THEN WE POUR THAT WATER ON THESE NO-BAKES, AND...
POURRR
MOOK
MOOK
POOF!
KYAAA! ♪
AMAZING! WE MADE BREAD!
HA HA HA HA!
ALL RIGHT! LET'S MAKE MORE! LOTS MORE! ♪

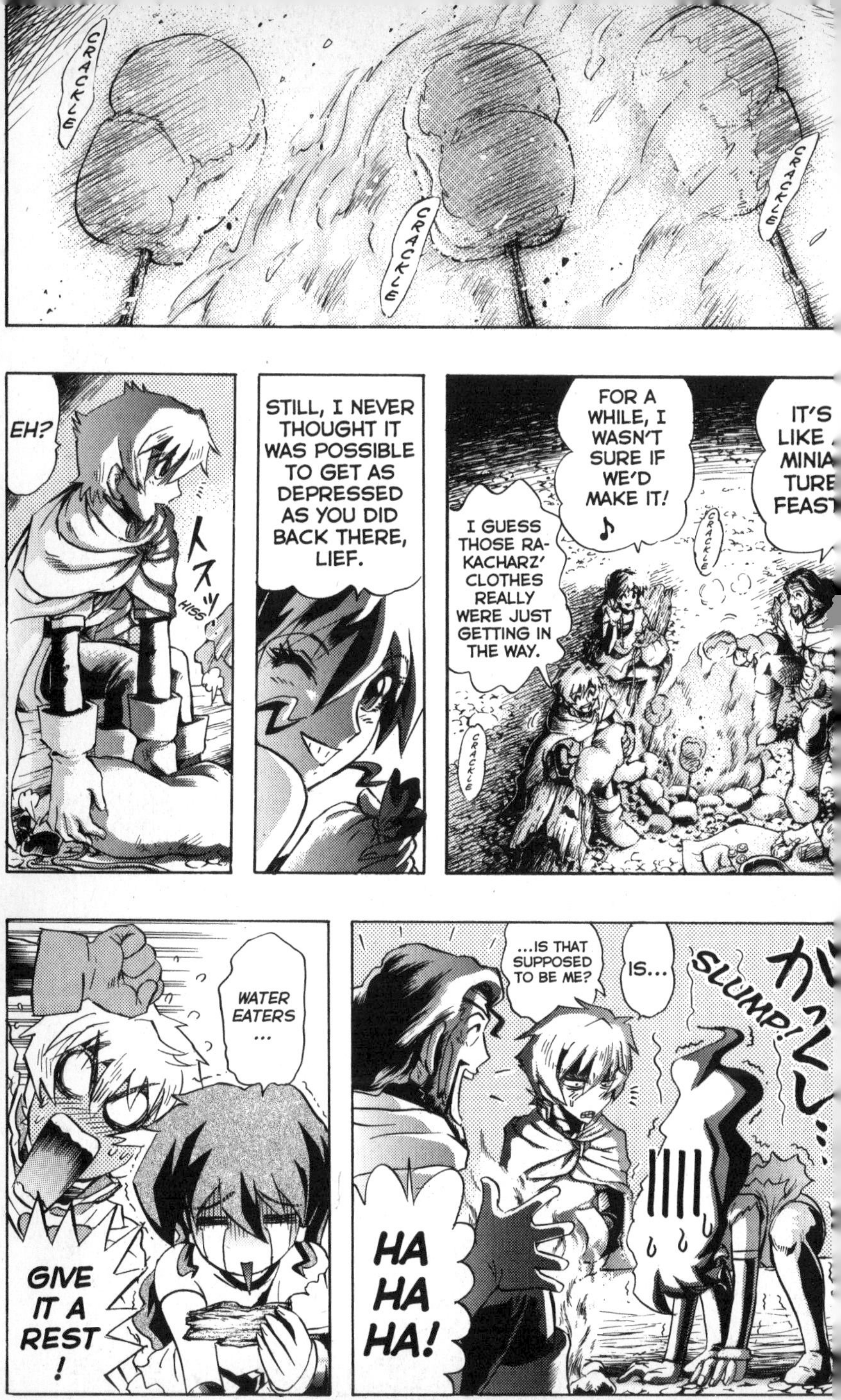
CRACKLE
CRACKLE
CRACKLE
IT'S LIKE MINIA TURE FEAST
FOR A WHILE, I WASN'T SURE IF WE'D MAKE IT! ♪
I GUESS THOSE RA-KACHARZ' CLOTHES REALLY WERE JUST GETTING IN THE WAY.
CRACKLE
CRACKLE
STILL, I NEVER THOUGHT IT WAS POSSIBLE TO GET AS DEPRESSED AS YOU DID BACK THERE, LIEF.
EH?
トスッ
HISS
がっくし…
SLUMP!
IS...
...IS THAT SUPPOSED TO BE ME?
HA HA HA!
WATER EATERS ...
GIVE IT A REST!

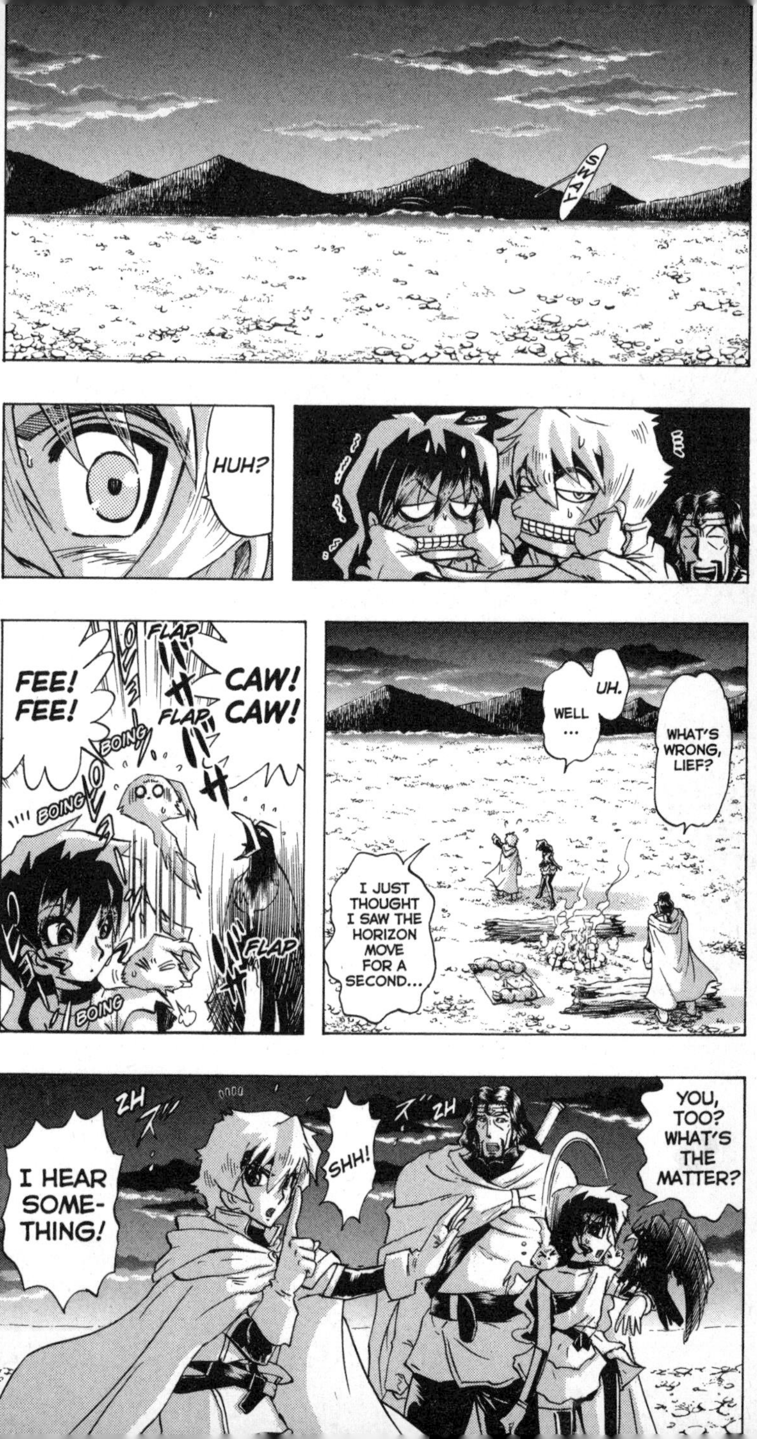
SWAY
HUH?
WHAT'S WRONG, LIEF?
UH.
WELL ...
I JUST THOUGHT I SAW THE HORIZON MOVE FOR A SECOND...
CAW! CAW!
FLAP
FLAP
FEE! FEE!
BOING
BOING
FLAP
BOING
YOU, TOO? WHAT'S THE MATTER?
ZH
SHH!
ZH
I HEAR SOME-THING!

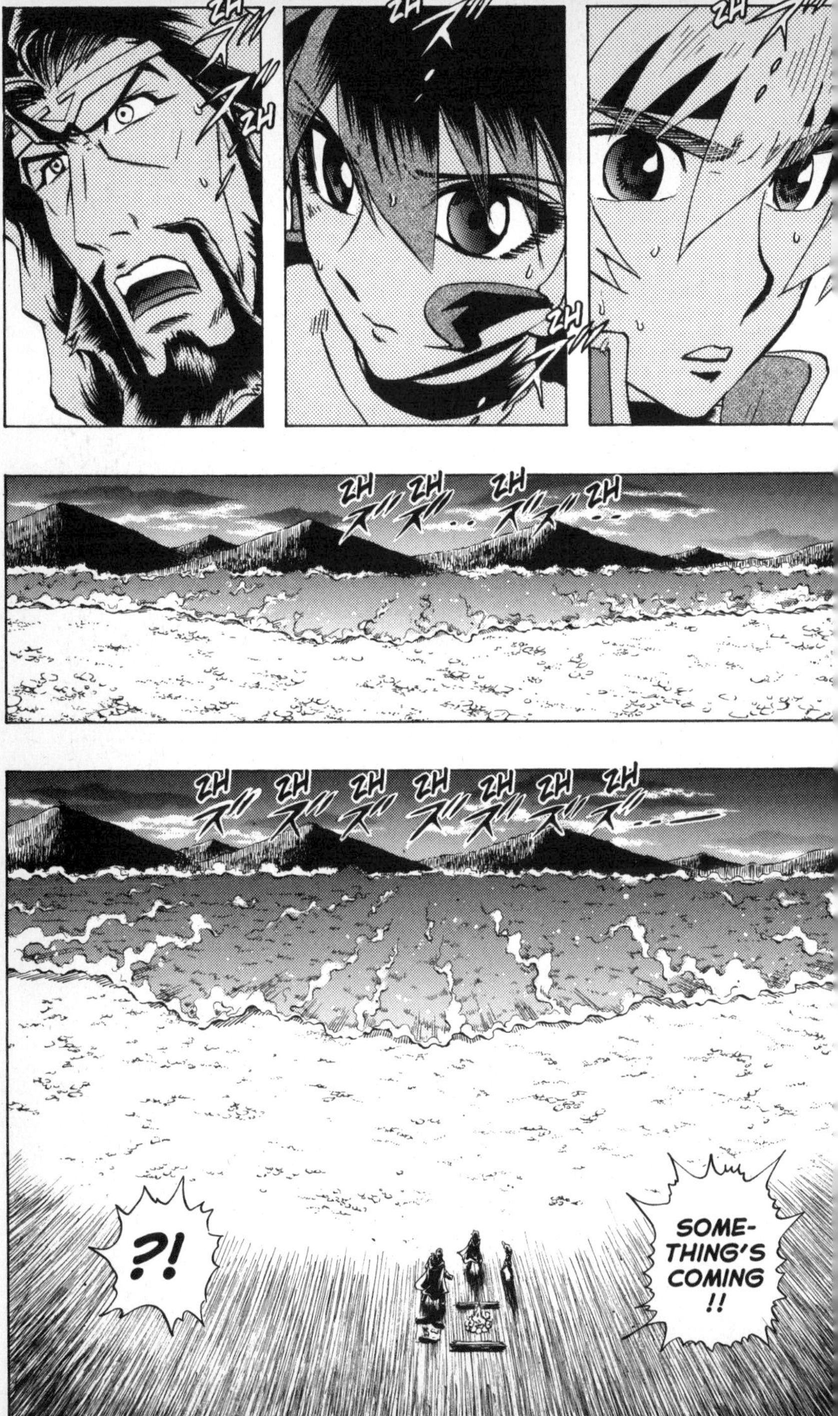
ZAH
ZAH ZAH
ZAH ZAH
ZAH ZAH ZAH ZAH
ZAH ZAH ZAH ZAH ZAH ZAH ZAH
SOME-THING'S COMING!!
?!

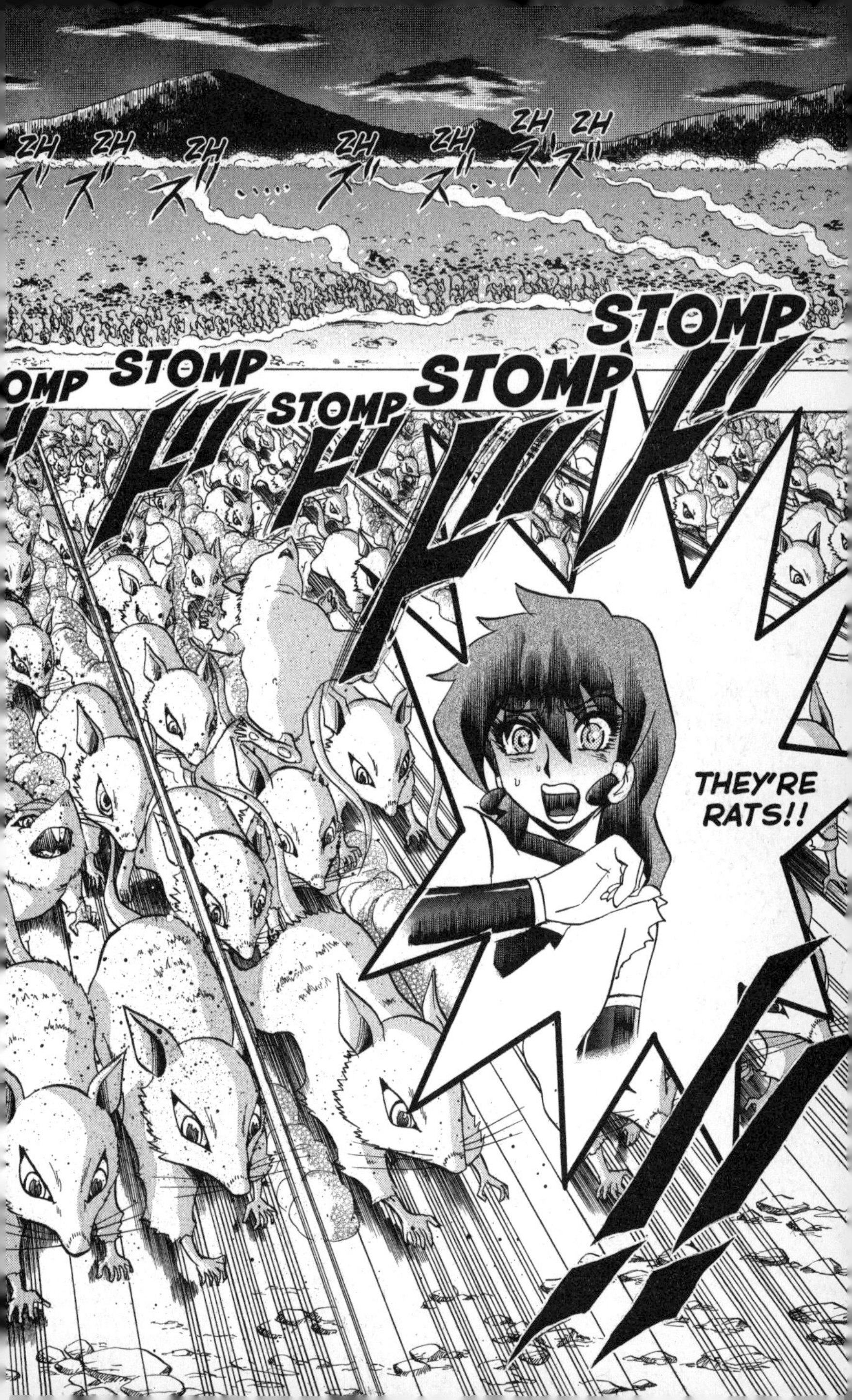
ZH
ZH
ZH
ZH
ZH
ZH
ZH
STOMP
STOMP
STOMP
STOMP
OMP
THEY'RE RATS!!

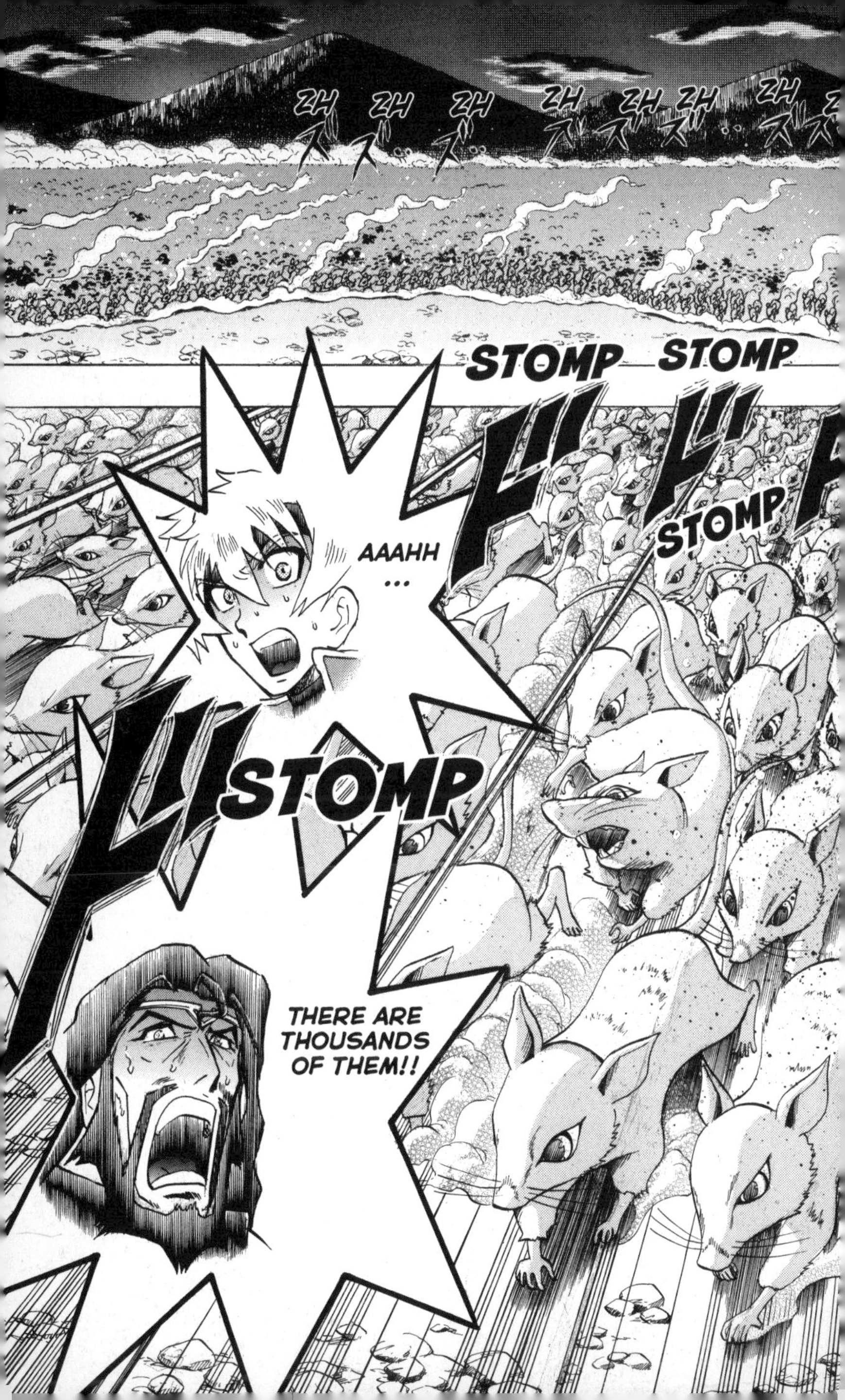
STOMP STOMP
STOMP
AAAHH ...
STOMP
THERE ARE THOUSANDS OF THEM!!

DELTORA QUEST
デルトラクエスト

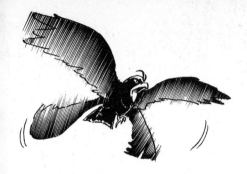

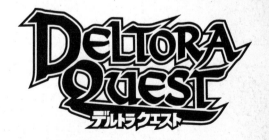

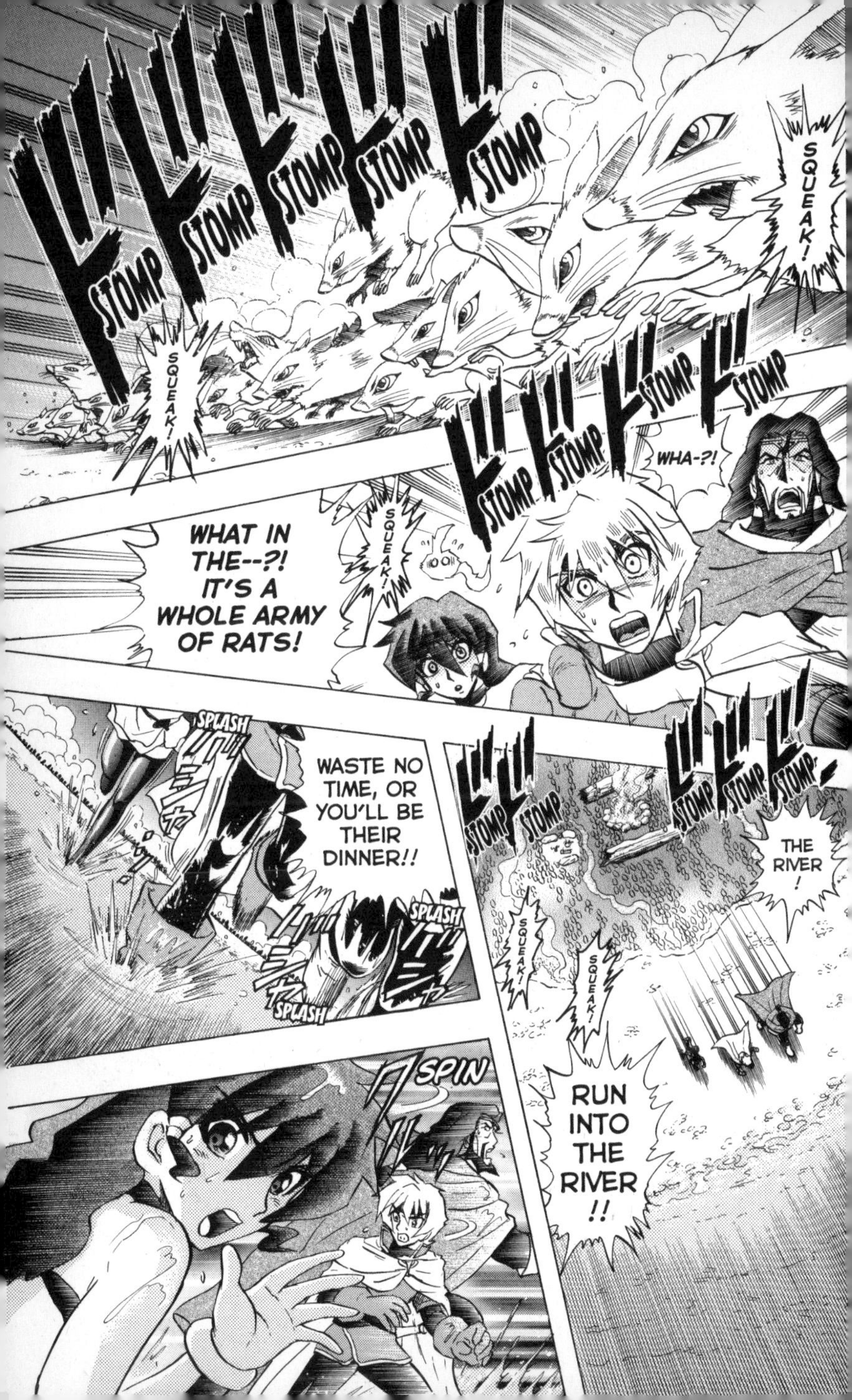

SQUEAK!
STOMP STOMP STOMP STOMP STOMP
SQUEAK!
STOMP STOMP STOMP STOMP STOMP
WHA-?!
SQUEAK!
WHAT IN THE--?! IT'S A WHOLE ARMY OF RATS!
STOMP STOMP STOMP
THE RIVER!
STOMP STOMP
SQUEAK!
SQUEAK!
RUN INTO THE RIVER!!
SPLASH
WASTE NO TIME, OR YOU'LL BE THEIR DINNER!!
SPLASH
SPLASH
SPIN

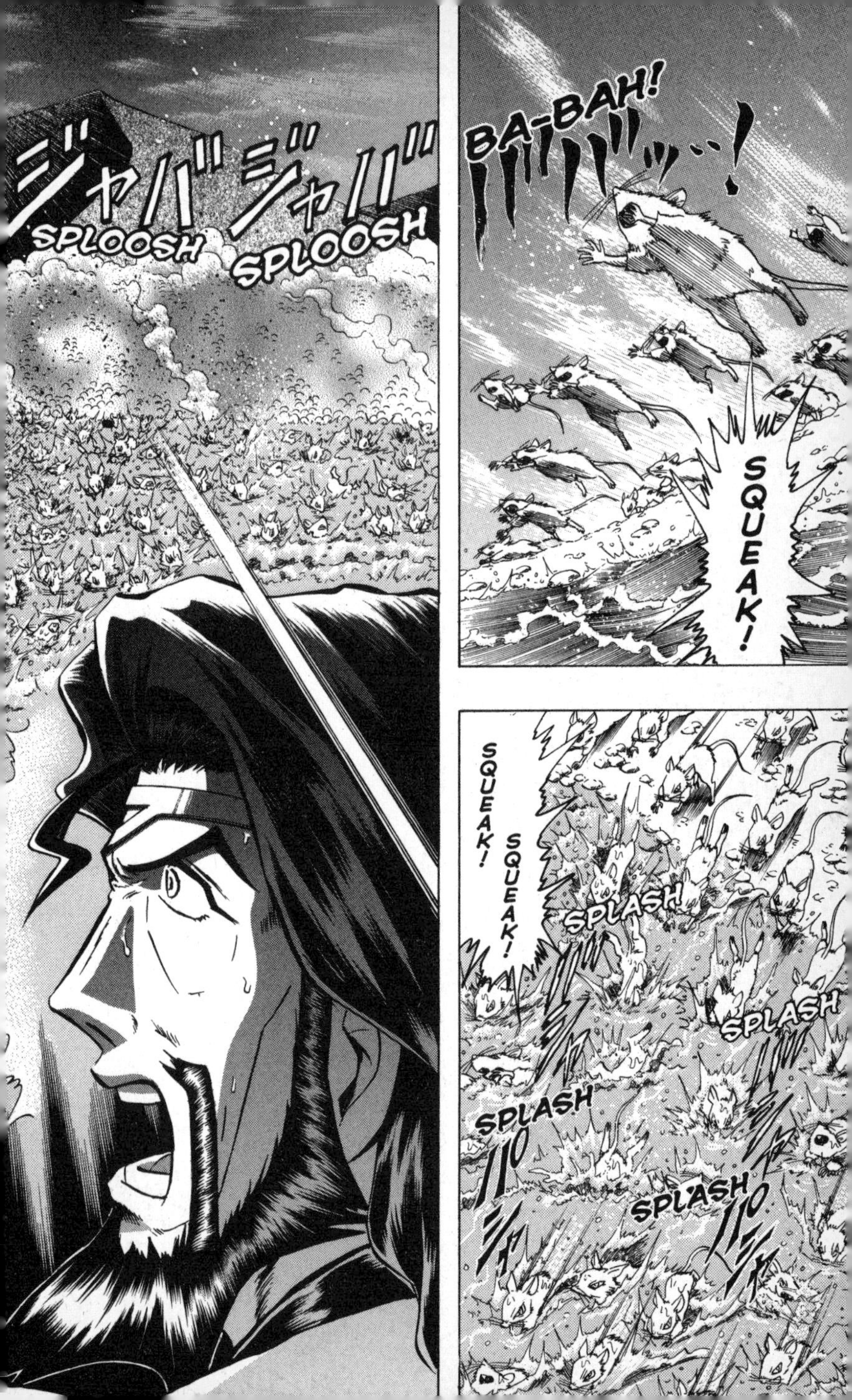
BA-BAH!
SQUEAK!
SQUEAK!
SQUEAK!
SPLASH
SPLASH
SPLASH
SPLASH
ジャバ
SPLOOSH
ジャバ
SPLOOSH

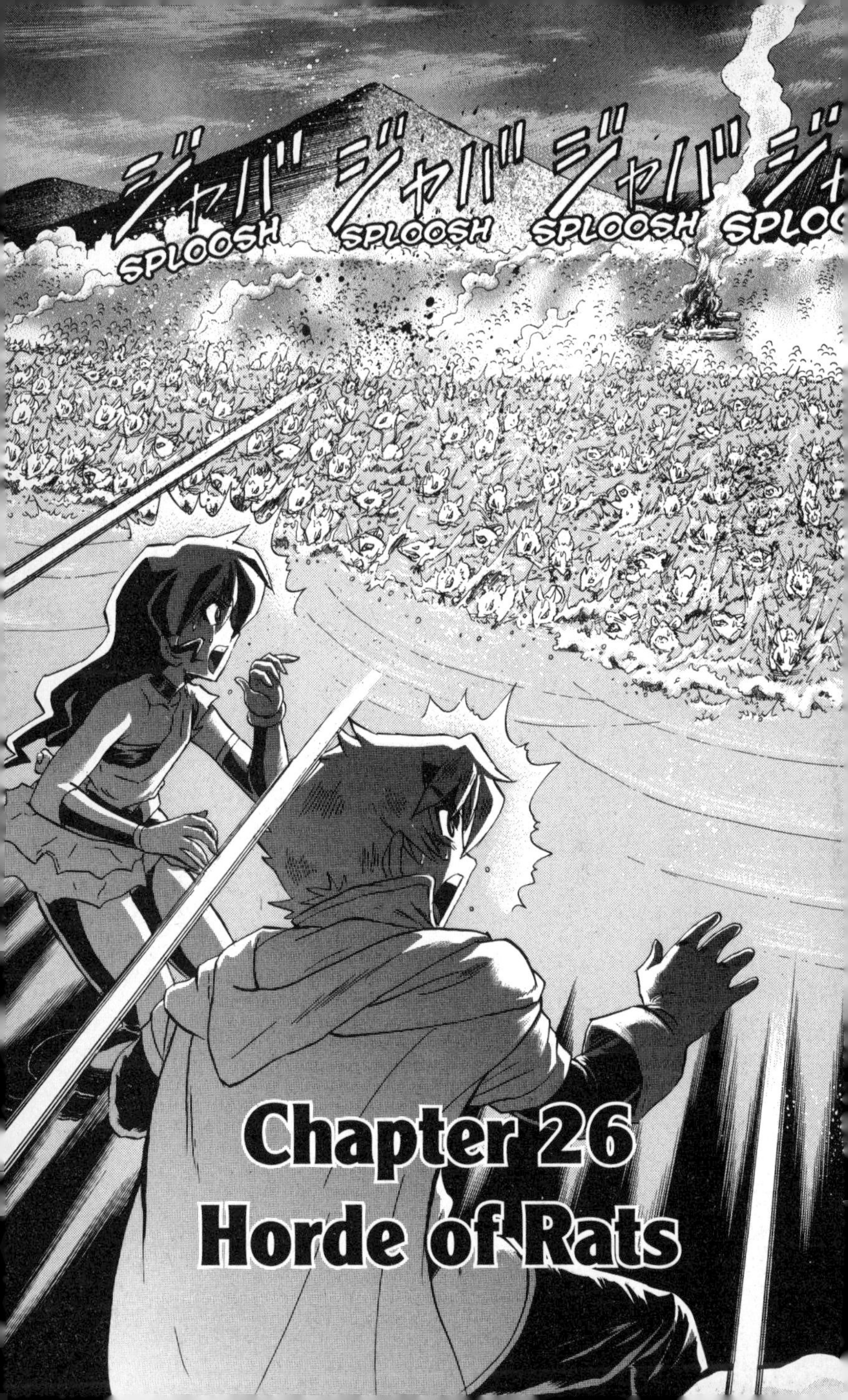
ジャバ
SPLOOSH
ジャバ
SPLOOSH
ジャバ
SPLOOSH
ジャバ
SPLOOSH

Chapter 26
Horde of Rats

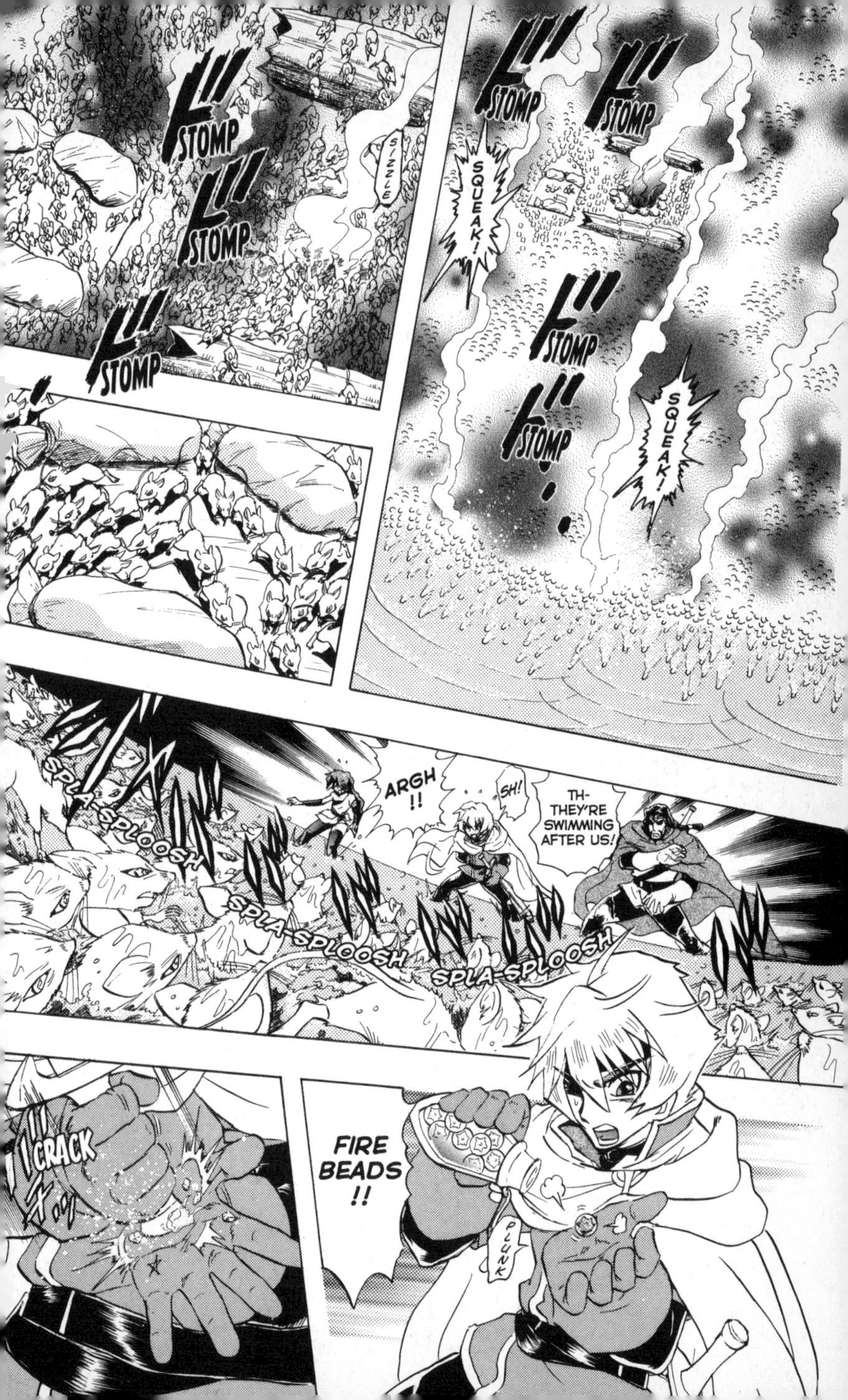
STOMP
STOMP
SQUEAK!
STOMP
STOMP
SQUEAK!
SIZZLE
STOMP
STOMP
STOMP
TH- THEY'RE SWIMMING AFTER US!
SH!
ARGH !!
SPLA-SPLOOSH
SPLA-SPLOOSH
SPLA-SPLOOSH
FIRE BEADS !!
PLUNK
CRACK

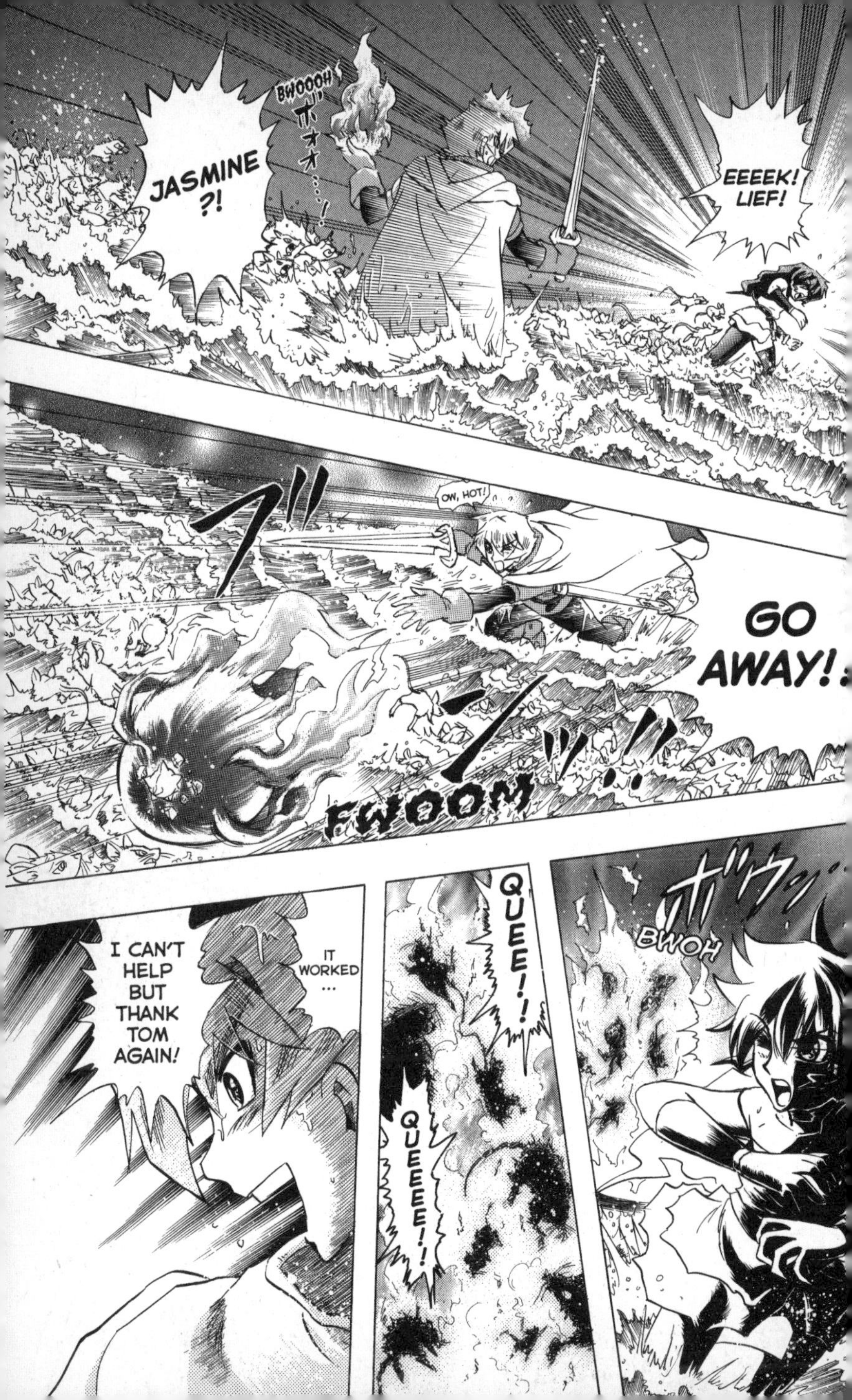
EEEEK! LIEF!
BWOOOH
JASMINE ?!
GO AWAY!
OW, HOT!
FWOOM
BWOH
QUEEE!!
QUEEEE!!
IT WORKED...
I CAN'T HELP BUT THANK TOM AGAIN!

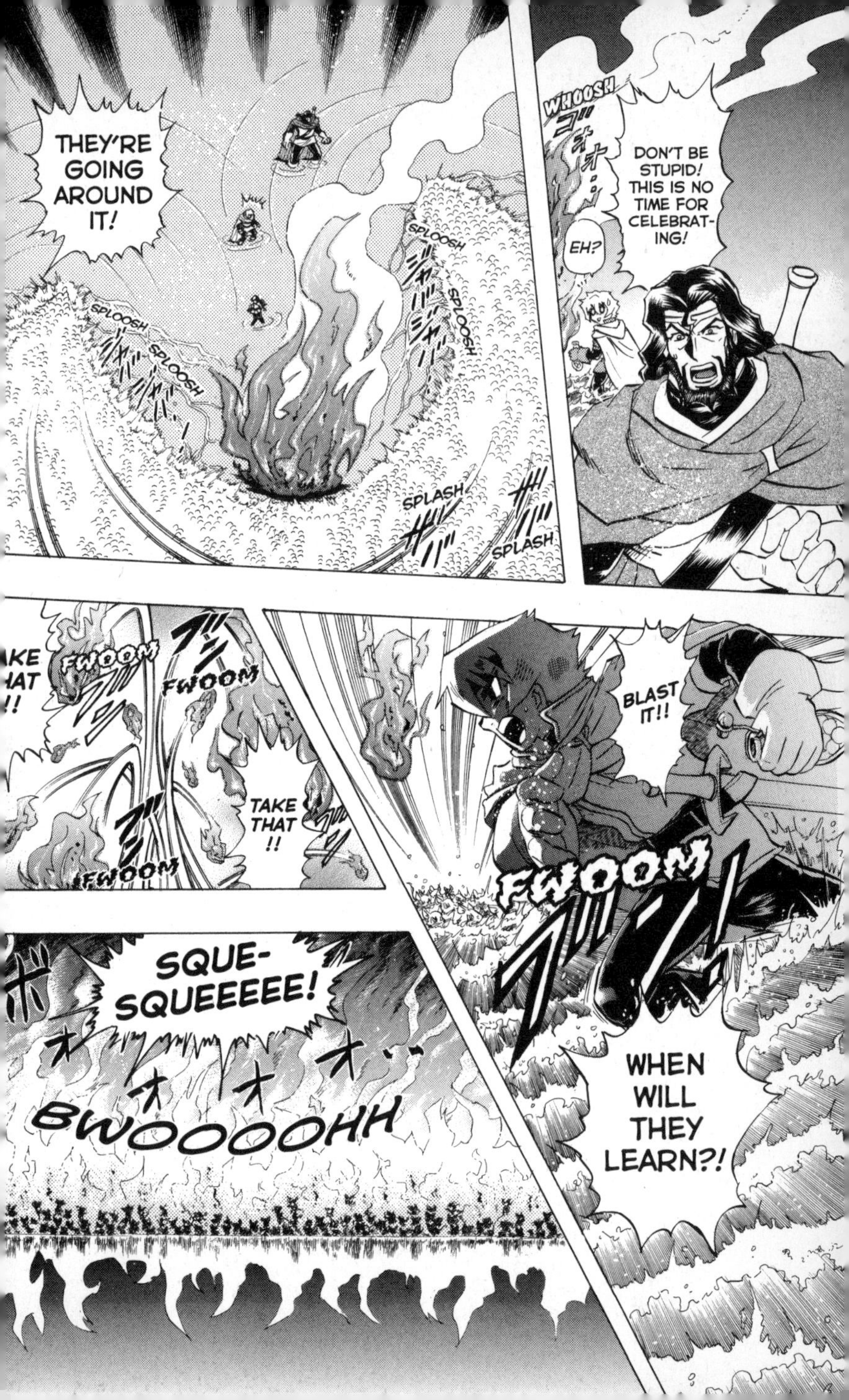
WHOOSH
EH?
DON'T BE STUPID! THIS IS NO TIME FOR CELEBRAT-ING!
THEY'RE GOING AROUND IT!
SPLOOSH
SPLOOSH
SPLOOSH
SPLOOSH
SPLASH
SPLASH
BLAST IT!!
FWOOM
WHEN WILL THEY LEARN?!
FWOOM
FWOOM
TAKE THAT!!
TAKE THAT!!
FWOOM
SQUE-SQUEEEEEE!
BWOOOOOHH

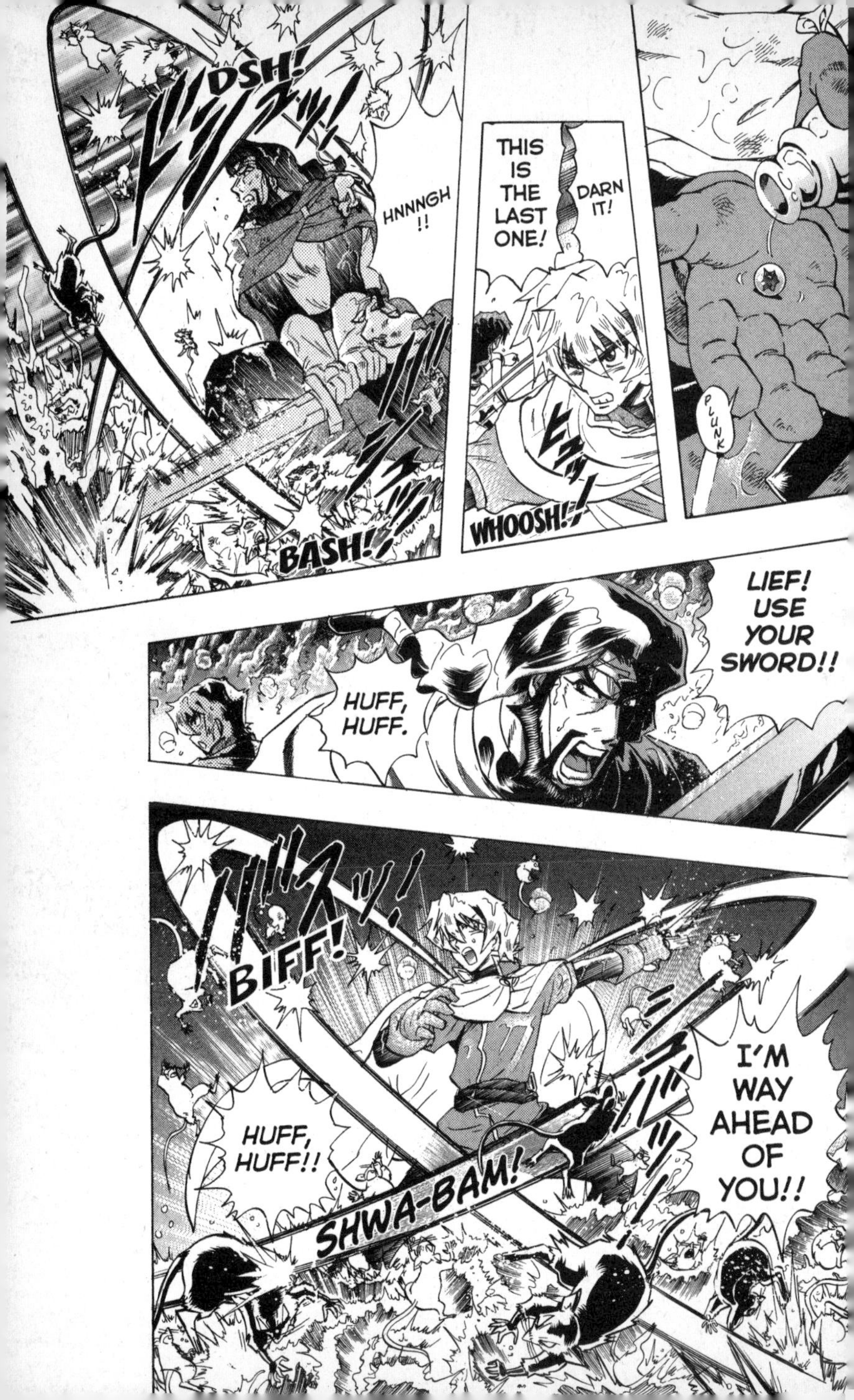
PLUNK
DARN IT!
THIS IS THE LAST ONE!
WHOOSH!!
DSH!
HNNNGH!!
BASH!!
LIEF! USE YOUR SWORD!!
HUFF, HUFF.
I'M WAY AHEAD OF YOU!!
BIFF!
HUFF, HUFF!!
SHWA-BAM!

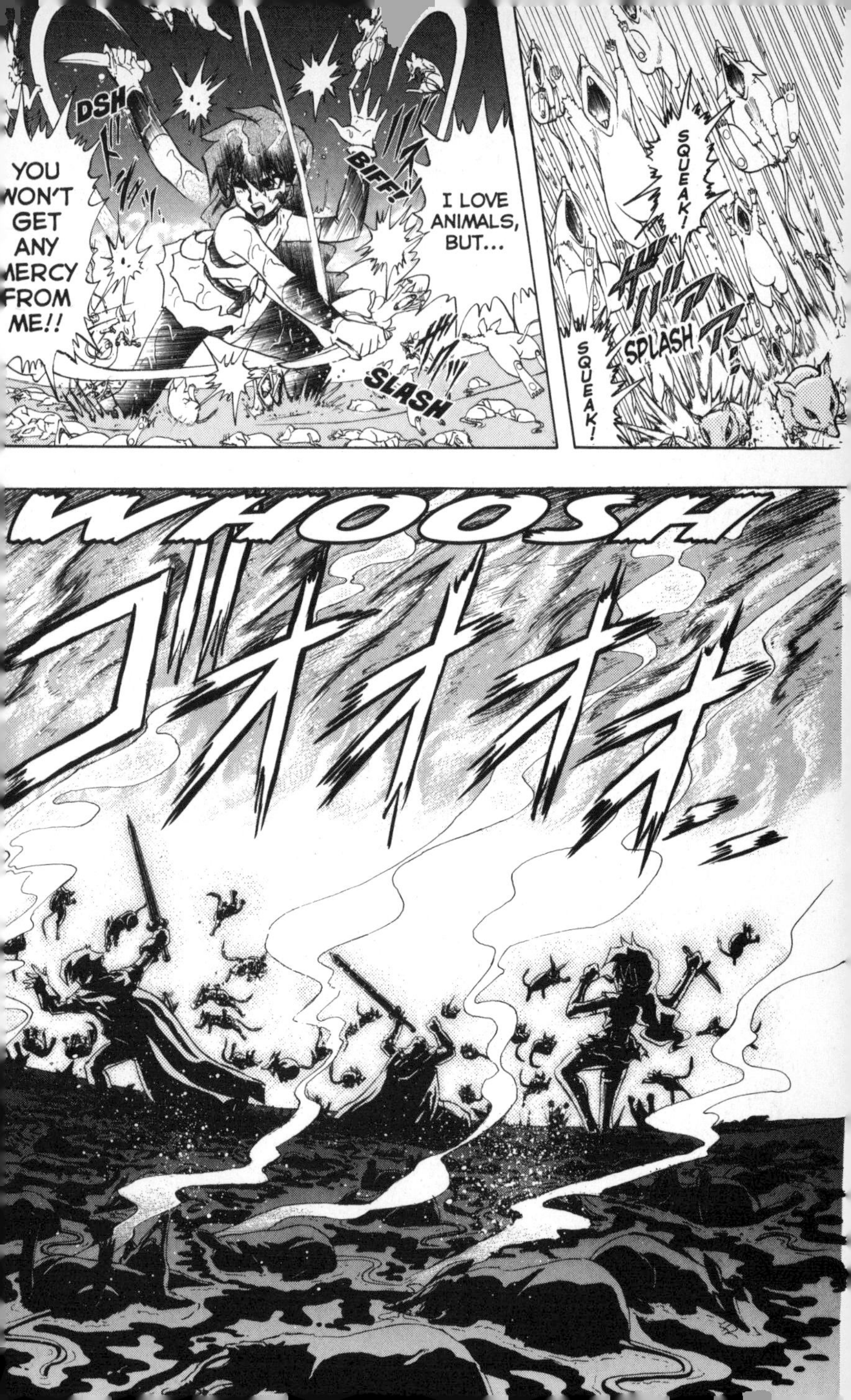
SQUEAK!
SQUEAK!
SPLASH
I LOVE ANIMALS, BUT...
YOU WON'T GET ANY MERCY FROM ME!!
DSH
BIFF!
SLASH
WHOOSH
ゴオオオ

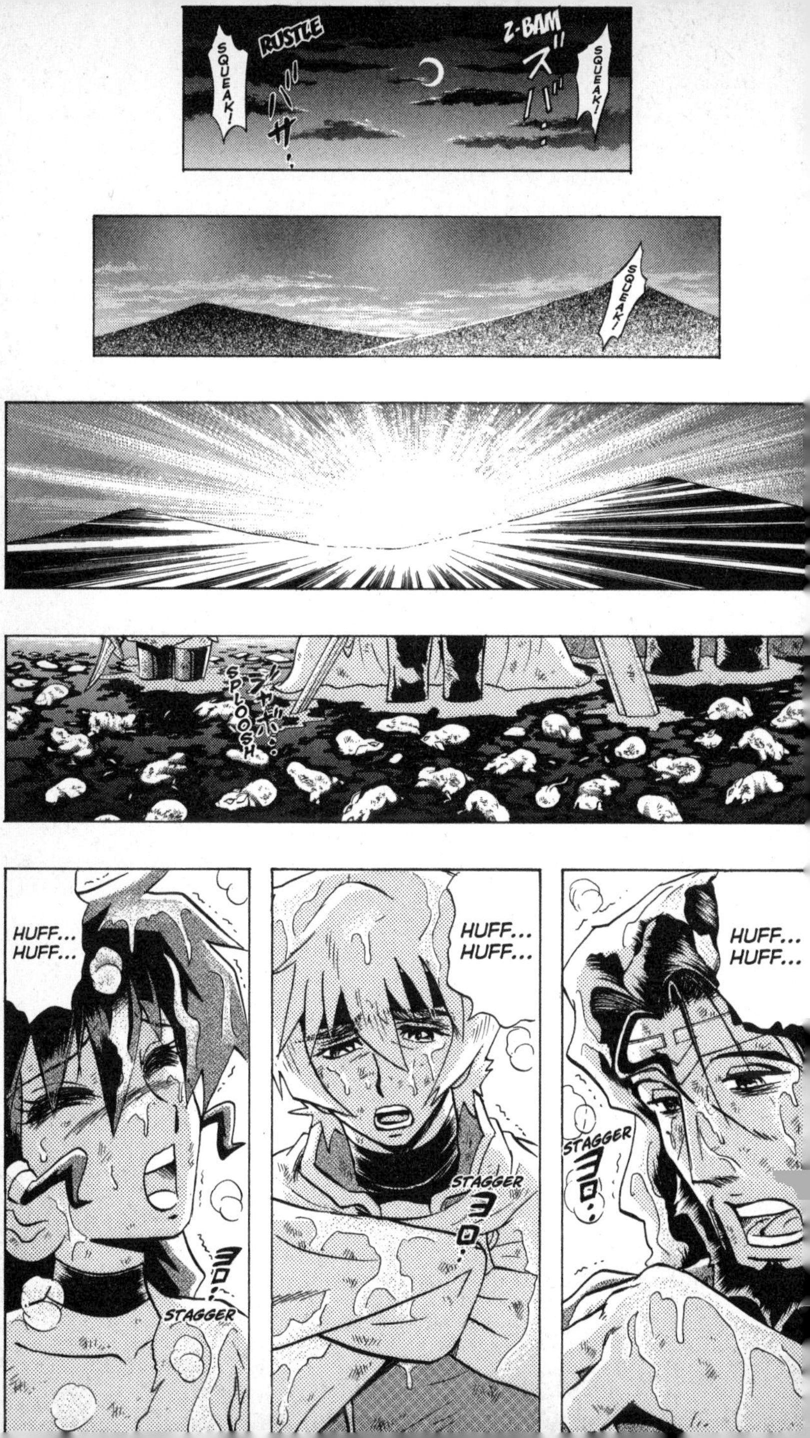
SQUEAK!
Z-BAM
RUSTLE
SQUEAK!
SQUEAK!
SPLOOSH
HUFF... HUFF...
STAGGER
HUFF... HUFF...
STAGGER
HUFF... HUFF...
STAGGER

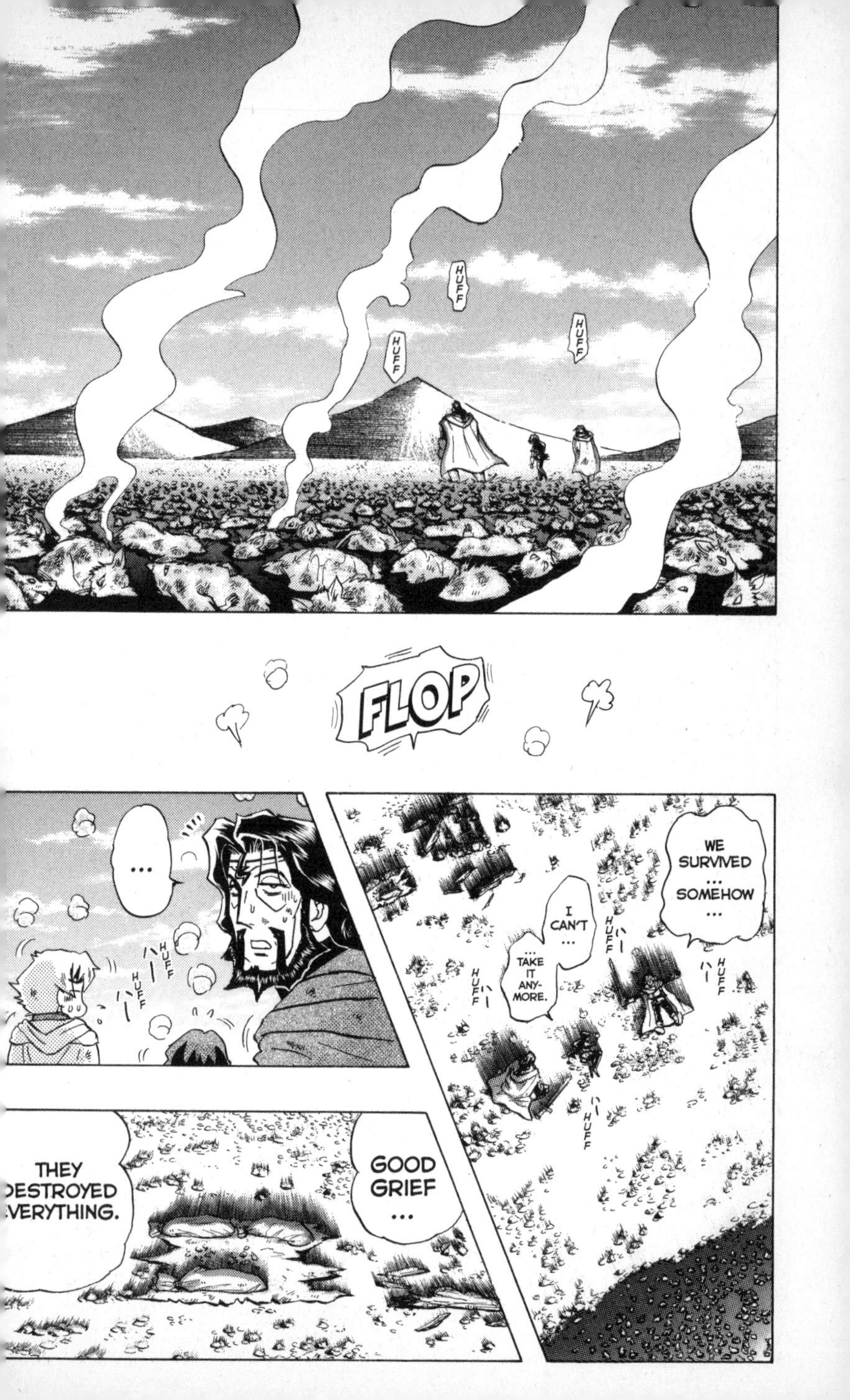
HUFF
HUFF
HUFF
FLOP
WE SURVIVED ... SOMEHOW ...
I CAN'T ...
... TAKE IT ANYMORE.
HUFF
HUFF
HUFF
HUFF
...
HUFF
HUFF
GOOD GRIEF ...
THEY DESTROYED EVERYTHING.

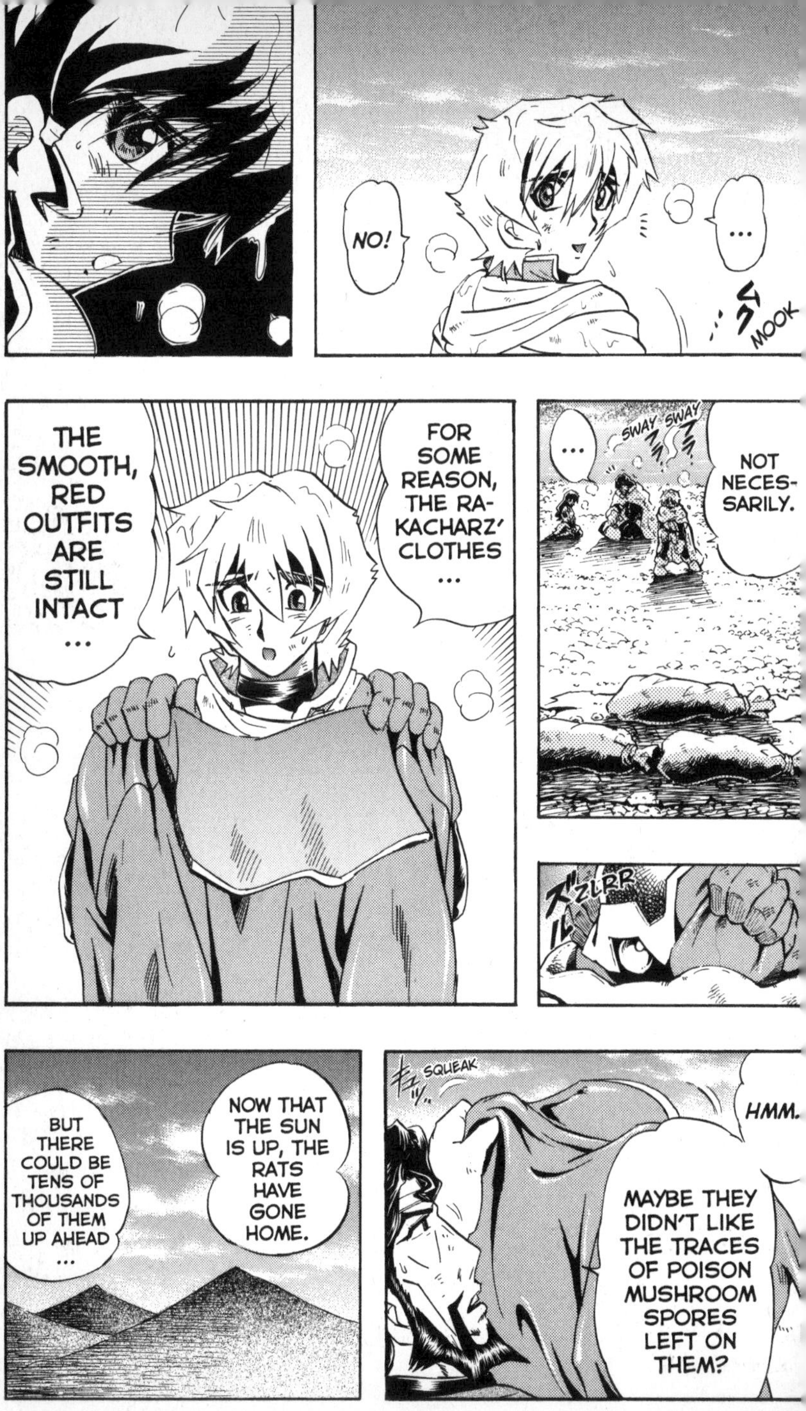
...
NO!
MOOK
NOT NECES-SARILY.
SWAY SWAY
...
ZLRR
FOR SOME REASON, THE RA-KACHARZ' CLOTHES ...
THE SMOOTH, RED OUTFITS ARE STILL INTACT ...
HMM.
SQUEAK
MAYBE THEY DIDN'T LIKE THE TRACES OF POISON MUSHROOM SPORES LEFT ON THEM?
NOW THAT THE SUN IS UP, THE RATS HAVE GONE HOME.
BUT THERE COULD BE TENS OF THOUSANDS OF THEM UP AHEAD ...

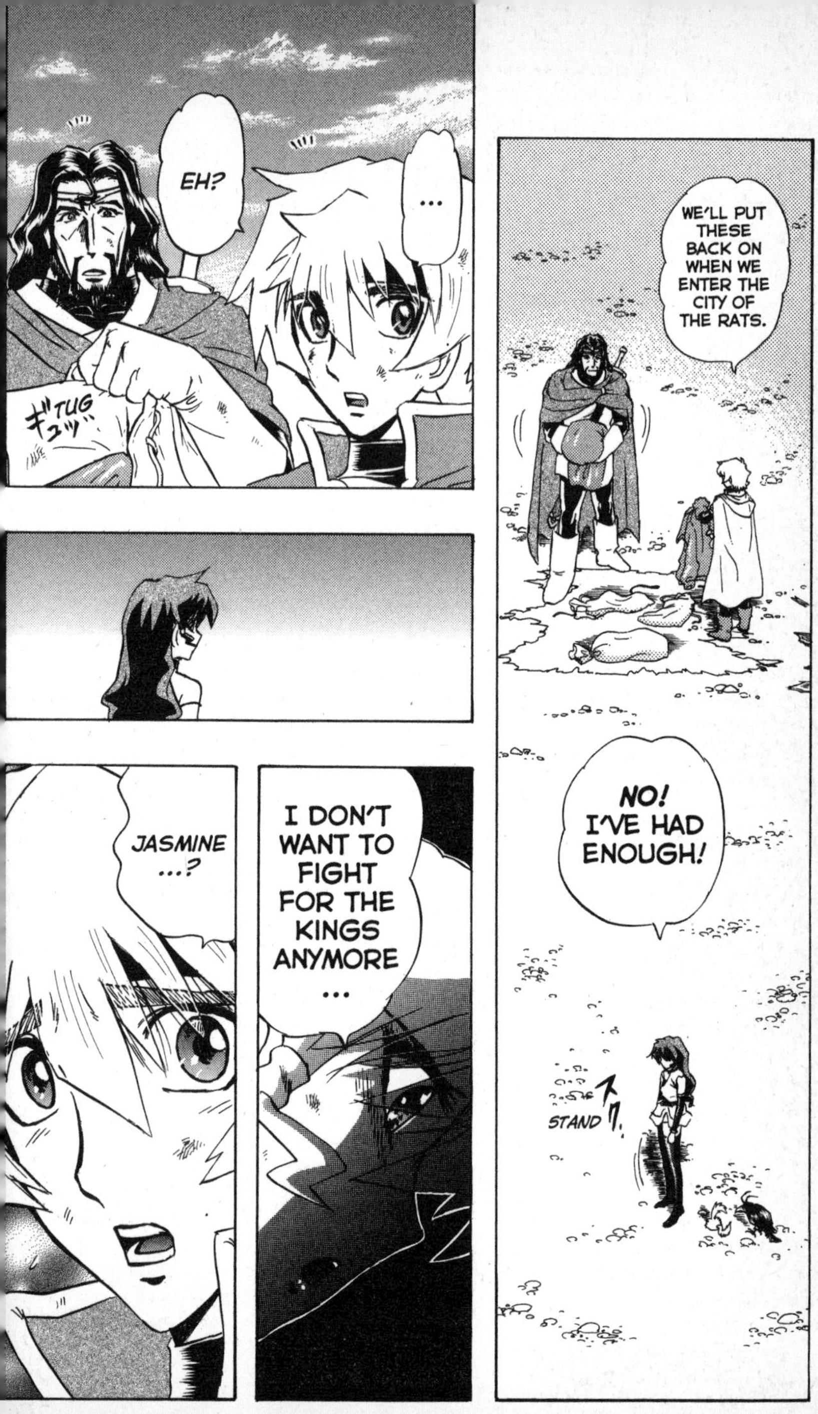

WE'LL PUT THESE BACK ON WHEN WE ENTER THE CITY OF THE RATS.
NO! I'VE HAD ENOUGH!
STAND
...
EH?
TUG
I DON'T WANT TO FIGHT FOR THE KINGS ANYMORE ...
JASMINE ...?

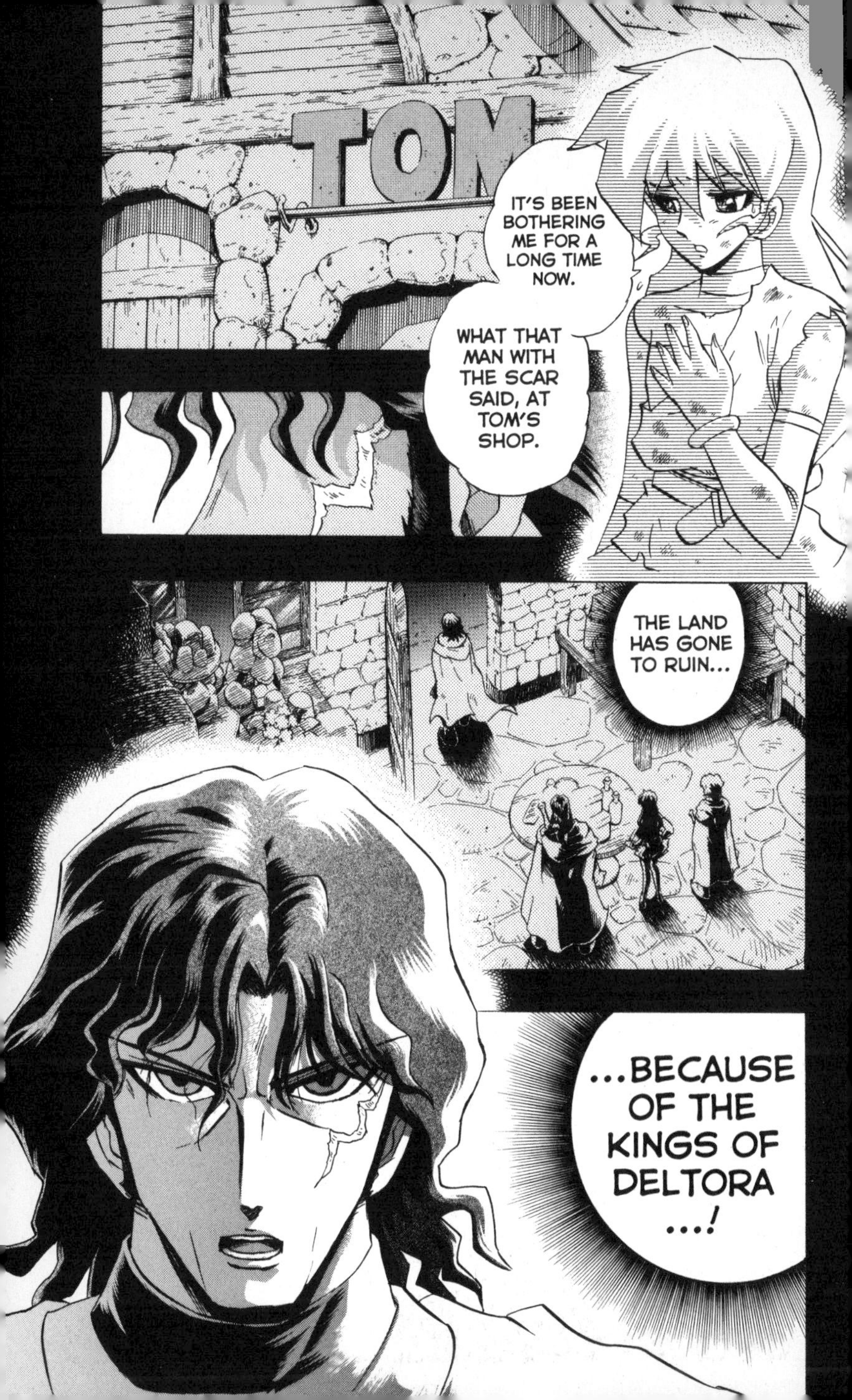

IT'S BEEN BOTHERING ME FOR A LONG TIME NOW.
WHAT THAT MAN WITH THE SCAR SAID, AT TOM'S SHOP.
TOM
THE LAND HAS GONE TO RUIN...
...BECAUSE OF THE KINGS OF DELTORA ...!

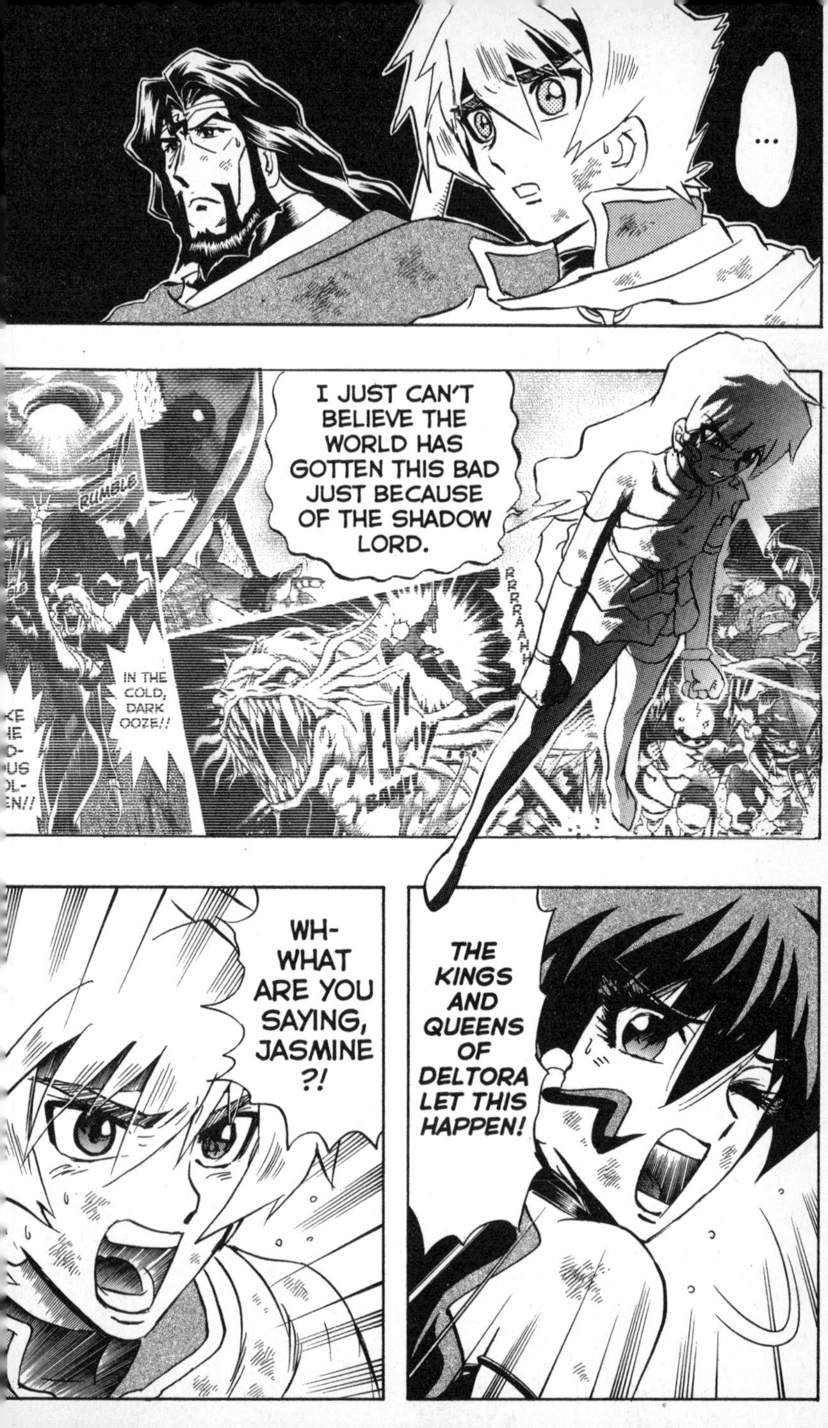
...
I JUST CAN'T BELIEVE THE WORLD HAS GOTTEN THIS BAD JUST BECAUSE OF THE SHADOW LORD.
RRRRAAHH
BAM!!
RUMBLE
IN THE COLD, DARK OOZE!!
THE KINGS AND QUEENS OF DELTORA LET THIS HAPPEN!
WH-WHAT ARE YOU SAYING, JASMINE?!

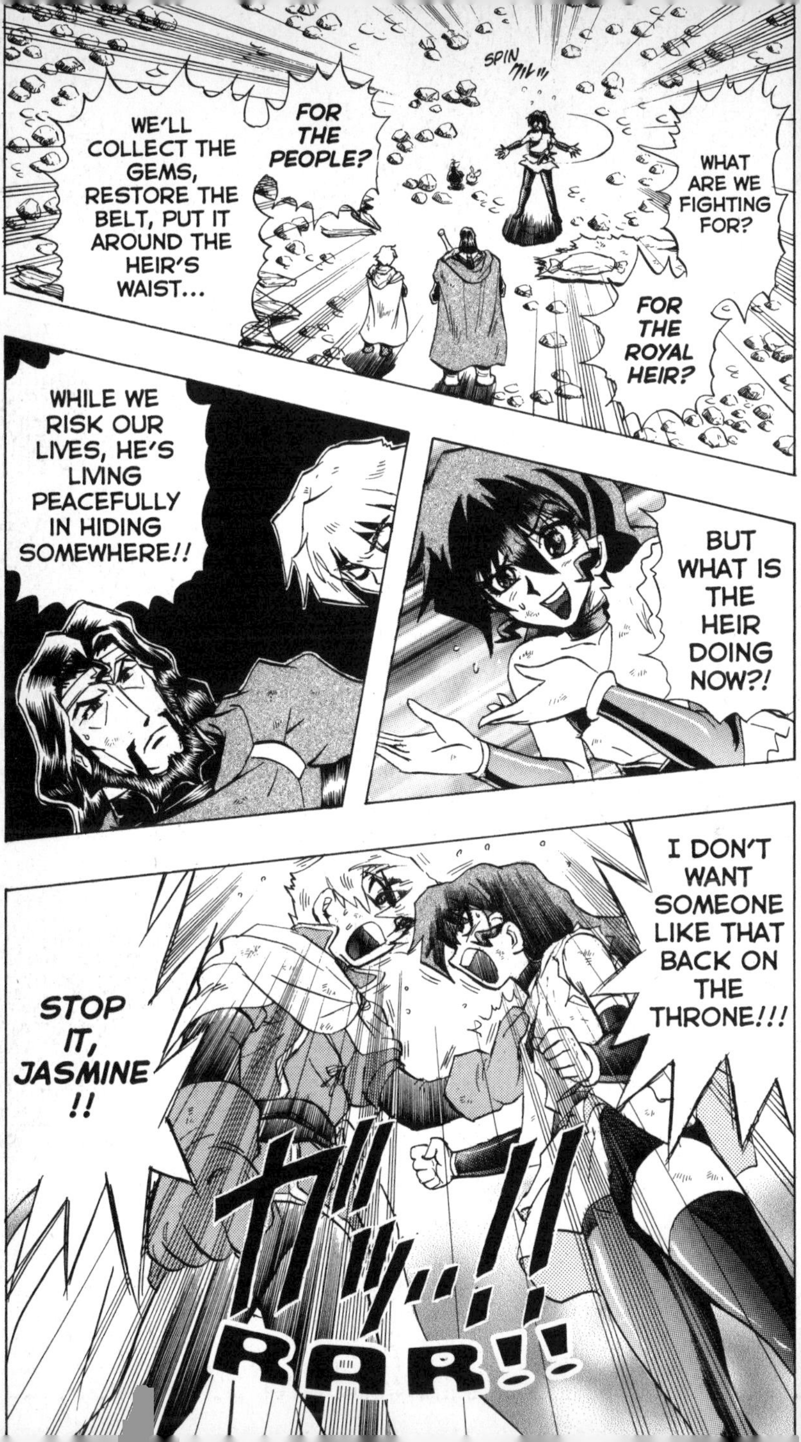
SPIN
WHAT ARE WE FIGHTING FOR?
FOR THE PEOPLE?
WE'LL COLLECT THE GEMS, RESTORE THE BELT, PUT IT AROUND THE HEIR'S WAIST...
FOR THE ROYAL HEIR?
BUT WHAT IS THE HEIR DOING NOW?!
WHILE WE RISK OUR LIVES, HE'S LIVING PEACEFULLY IN HIDING SOMEWHERE!!
I DON'T WANT SOMEONE LIKE THAT BACK ON THE THRONE!!!
STOP IT, JASMINE!!
RAR!!

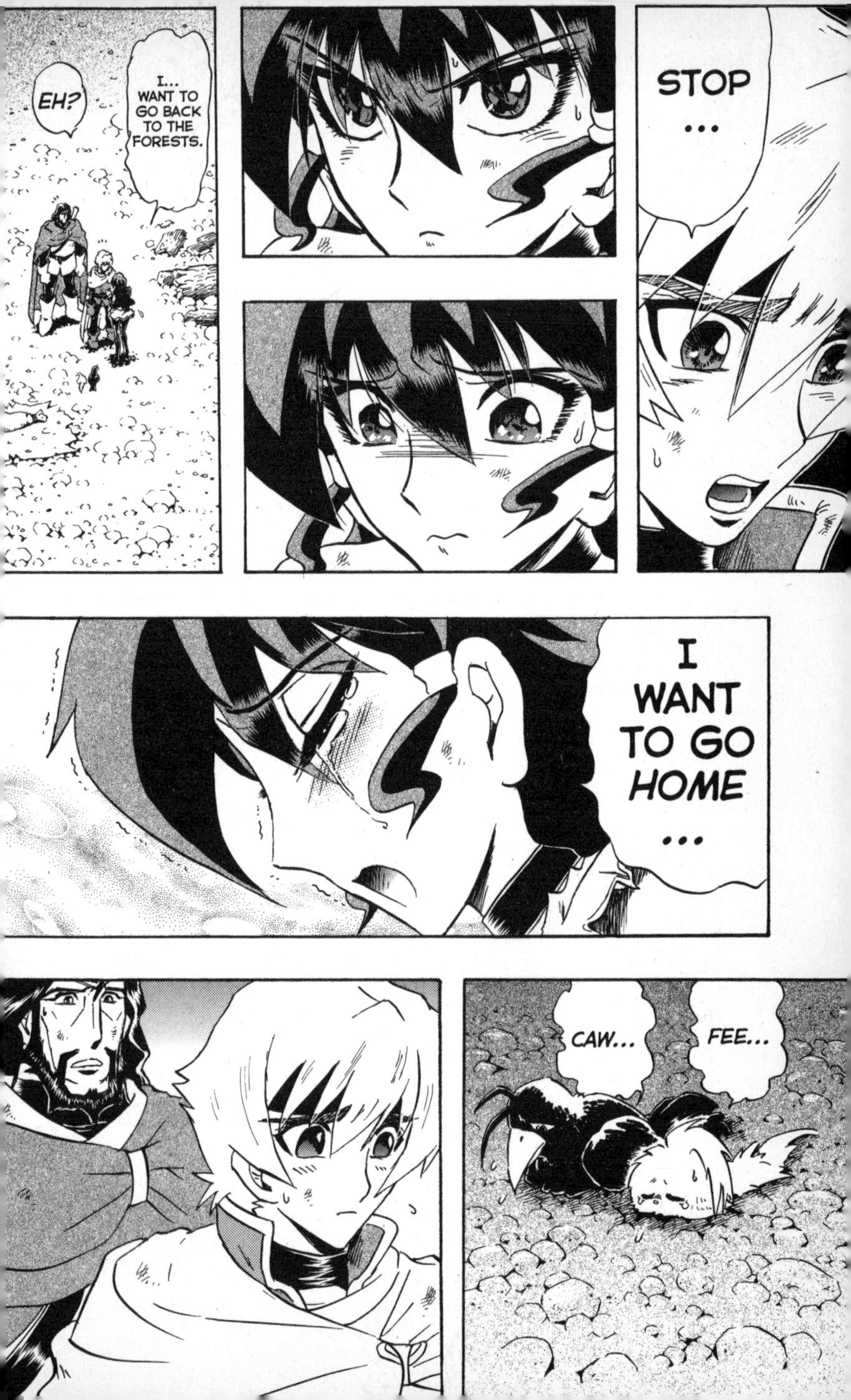
STOP ...
I... WANT TO GO BACK TO THE FORESTS.
EH?
I WANT TO GO HOME ...
FEE...
CAW...

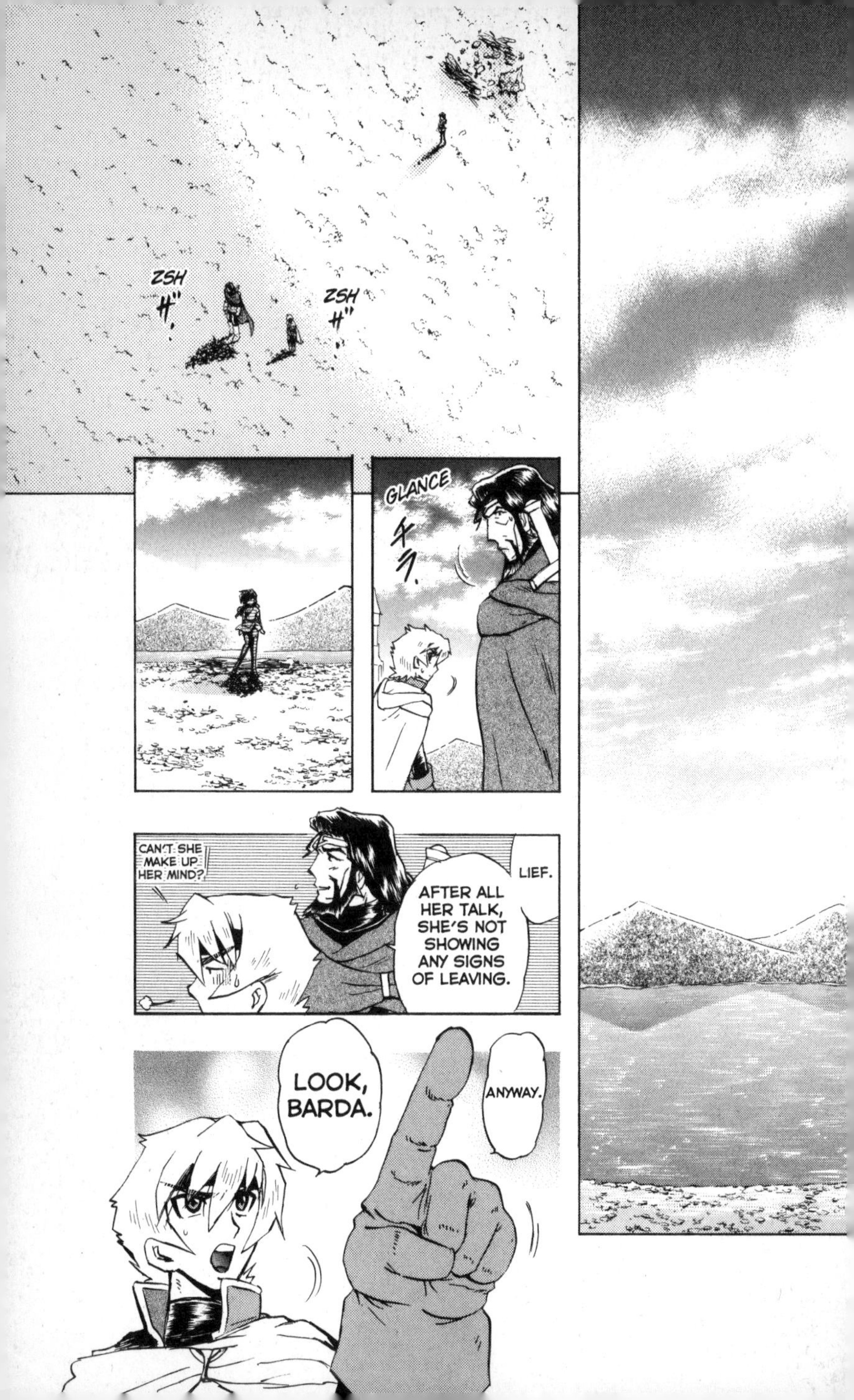
ZSH
ザッ
ZSH
ザッ
GLANCE
チラ
LIEF.
AFTER ALL HER TALK, SHE'S NOT SHOWING ANY SIGNS OF LEAVING.
CAN'T SHE MAKE UP HER MIND?
ANYWAY.
LOOK, BARDA.

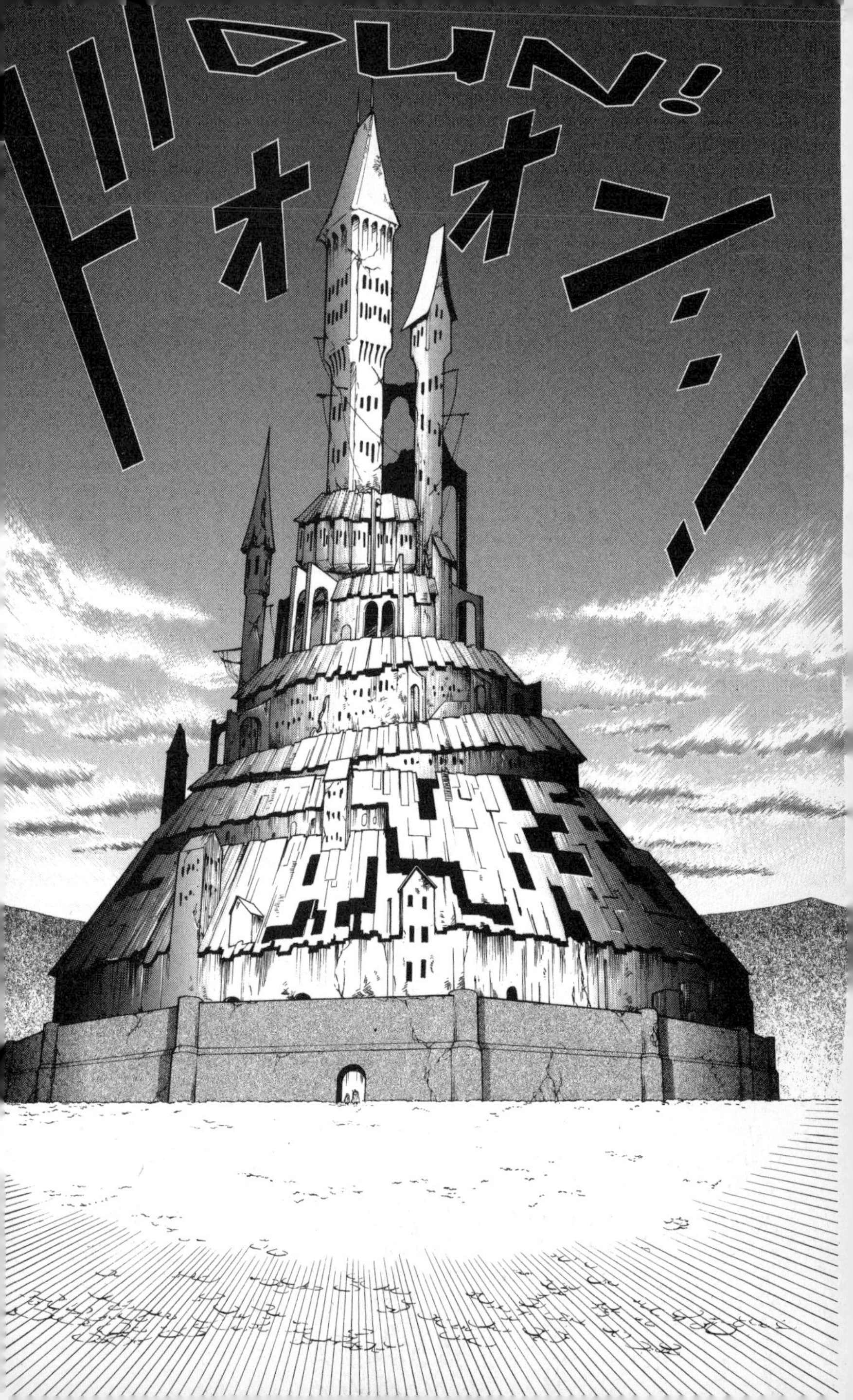
DUN!
ドオオーン!!

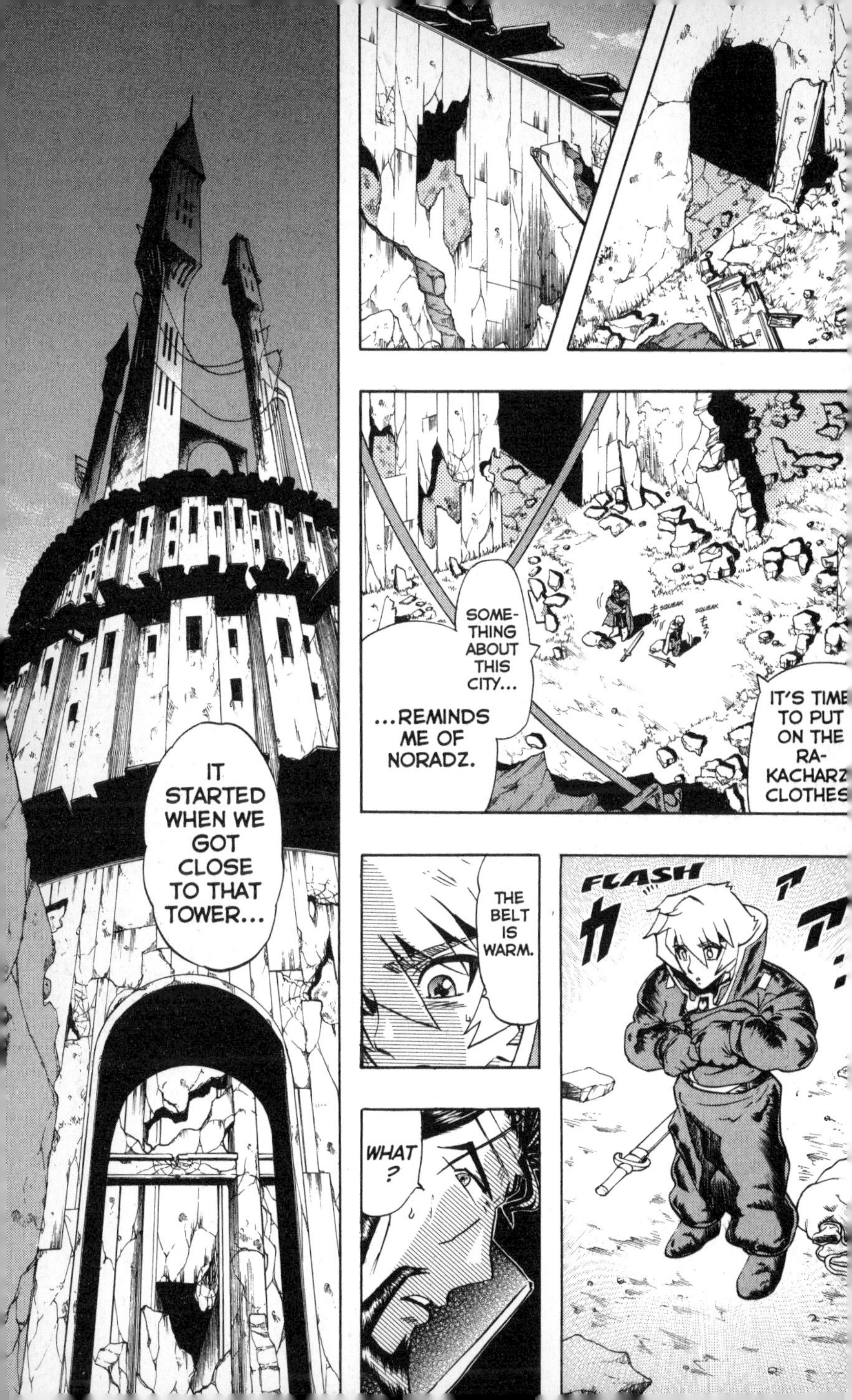

SQUEAK SQUEAK
IT'S TIME TO PUT ON THE RA-KACHARZ CLOTHES
SOME-THING ABOUT THIS CITY...
...REMINDS ME OF NORADZ.
FLASH
THE BELT IS WARM.
WHAT ?
IT STARTED WHEN WE GOT CLOSE TO THAT TOWER...

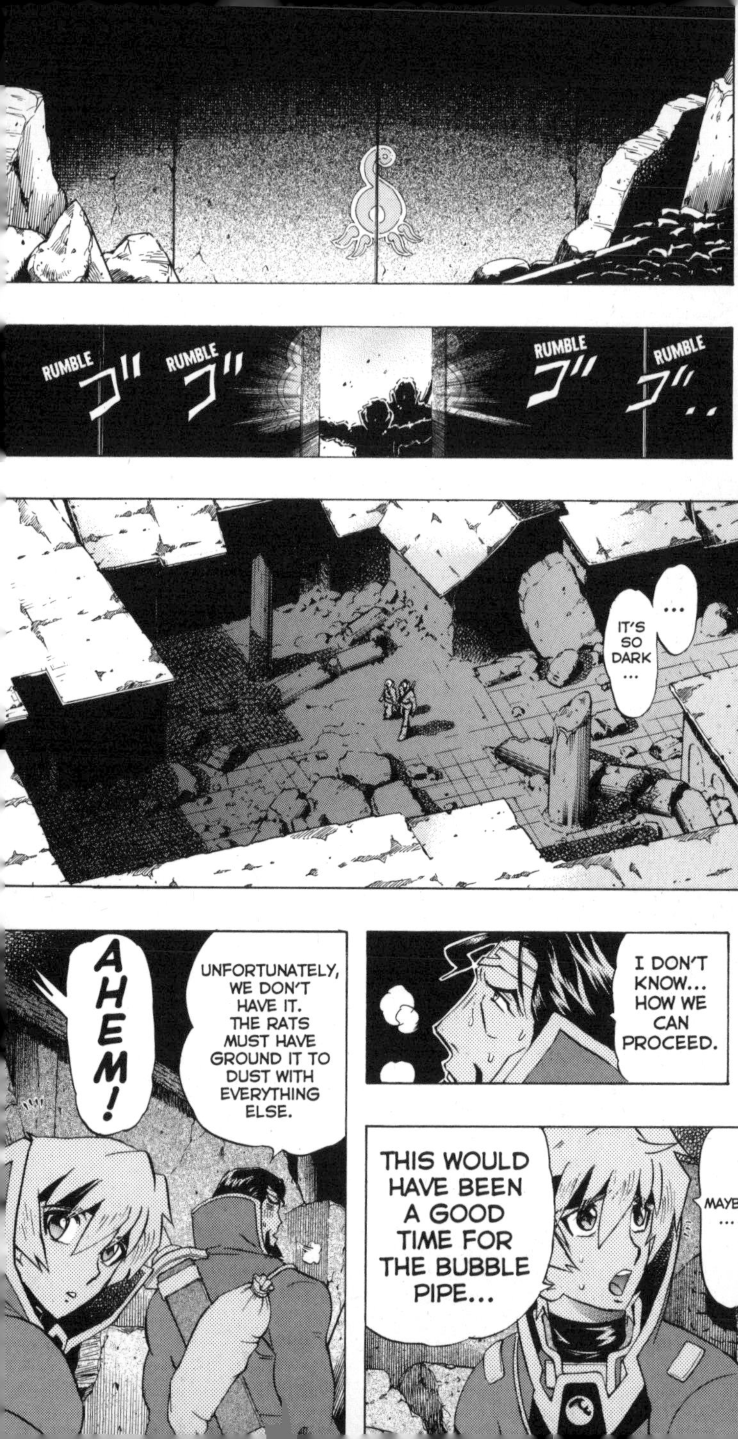

RUMBLE
RUMBLE
RUMBLE
RUMBLE
...
IT'S SO DARK...
I DON'T KNOW... HOW WE CAN PROCEED.
MAYBE...
THIS WOULD HAVE BEEN A GOOD TIME FOR THE BUBBLE PIPE...
AHEM!
UNFORTUNATELY, WE DON'T HAVE IT. THE RATS MUST HAVE GROUND IT TO DUST WITH EVERYTHING ELSE.

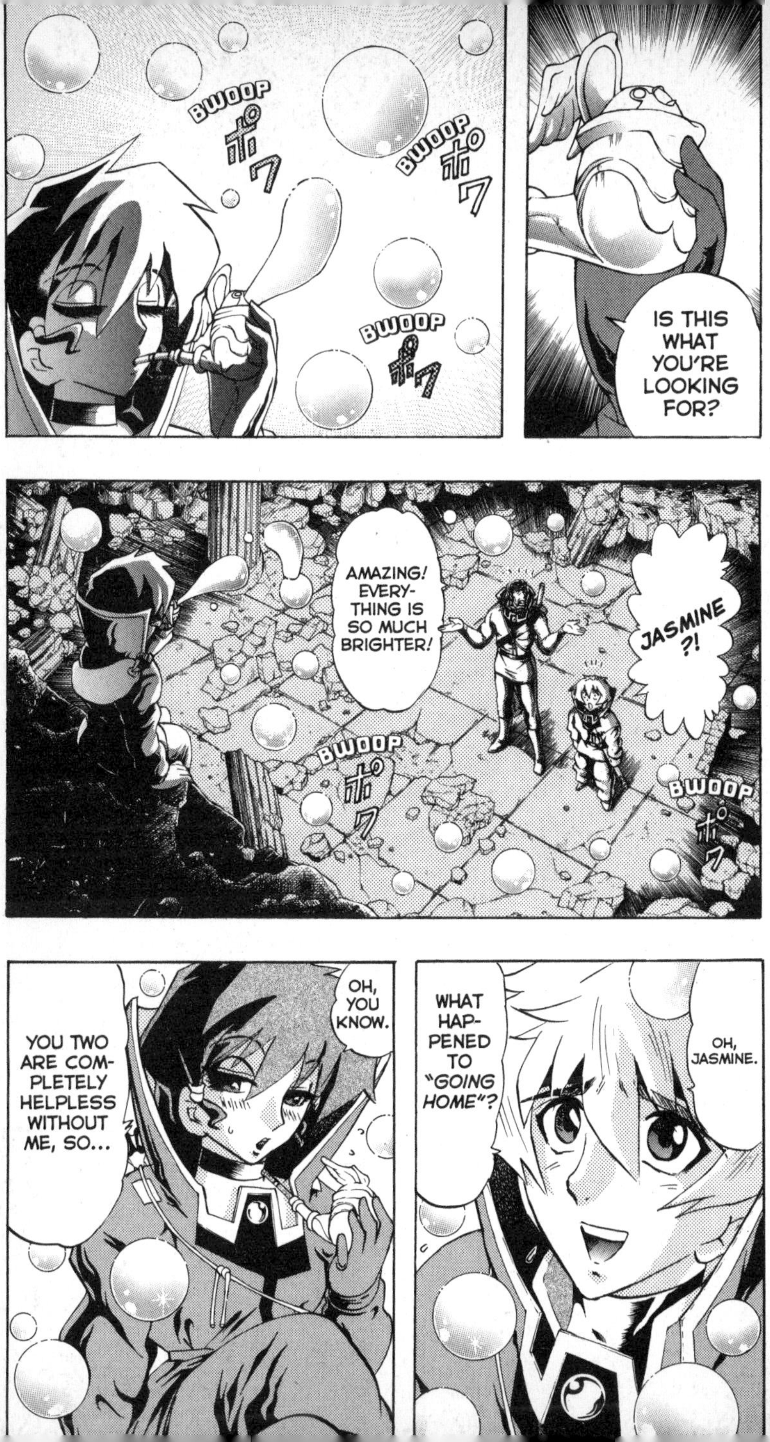
IS THIS WHAT YOU'RE LOOKING FOR?
BWOOP
ポワ
BWOOP
ポワ
BWOOP
ポワ
JASMINE?!
AMAZING! EVERYTHING IS SO MUCH BRIGHTER!
BWOOP
ポワ
BWOOP
ポワ
OH, JASMINE.
WHAT HAPPENED TO "GOING HOME"?
OH, YOU KNOW.
YOU TWO ARE COMPLETELY HELPLESS WITHOUT ME, SO...

WHERE DO YOU THINK WE ARE NOW?

WHEW...

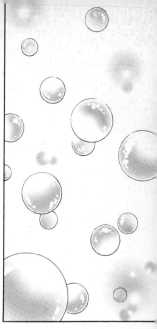

THIS PLACE IS LIKE A MAZE.

ZH

UWAH?!

KABOOM

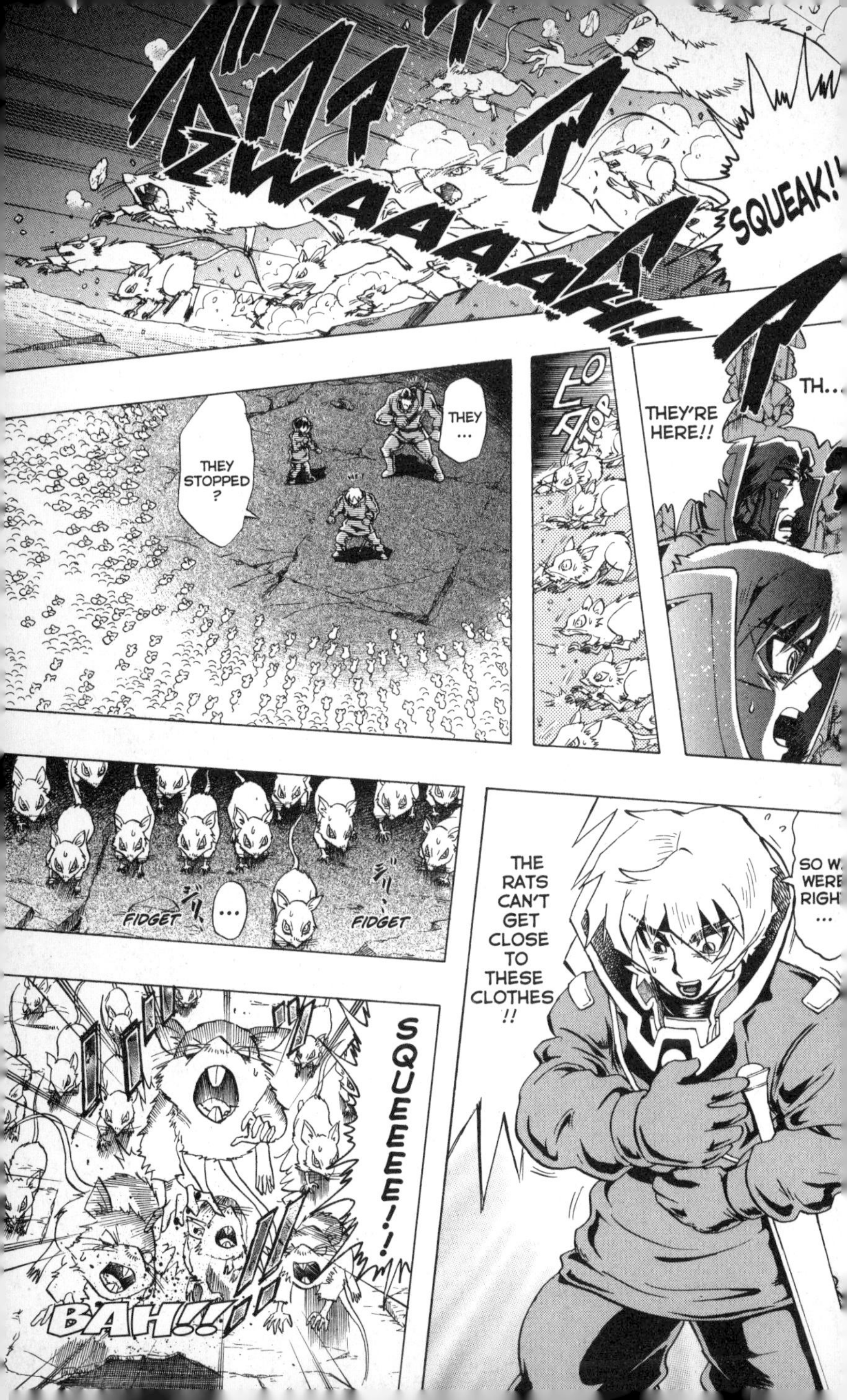
ZWAAAAAH!!
SQUEAK!!
TH...
THEY'RE HERE!!
STOP
THEY ...
THEY STOPPED ?
SO W. WERE RIGH ...
THE RATS CAN'T GET CLOSE TO THESE CLOTHES !!
FIDGET
...
FIDGET
SQUEEEEE!!
BAH!!

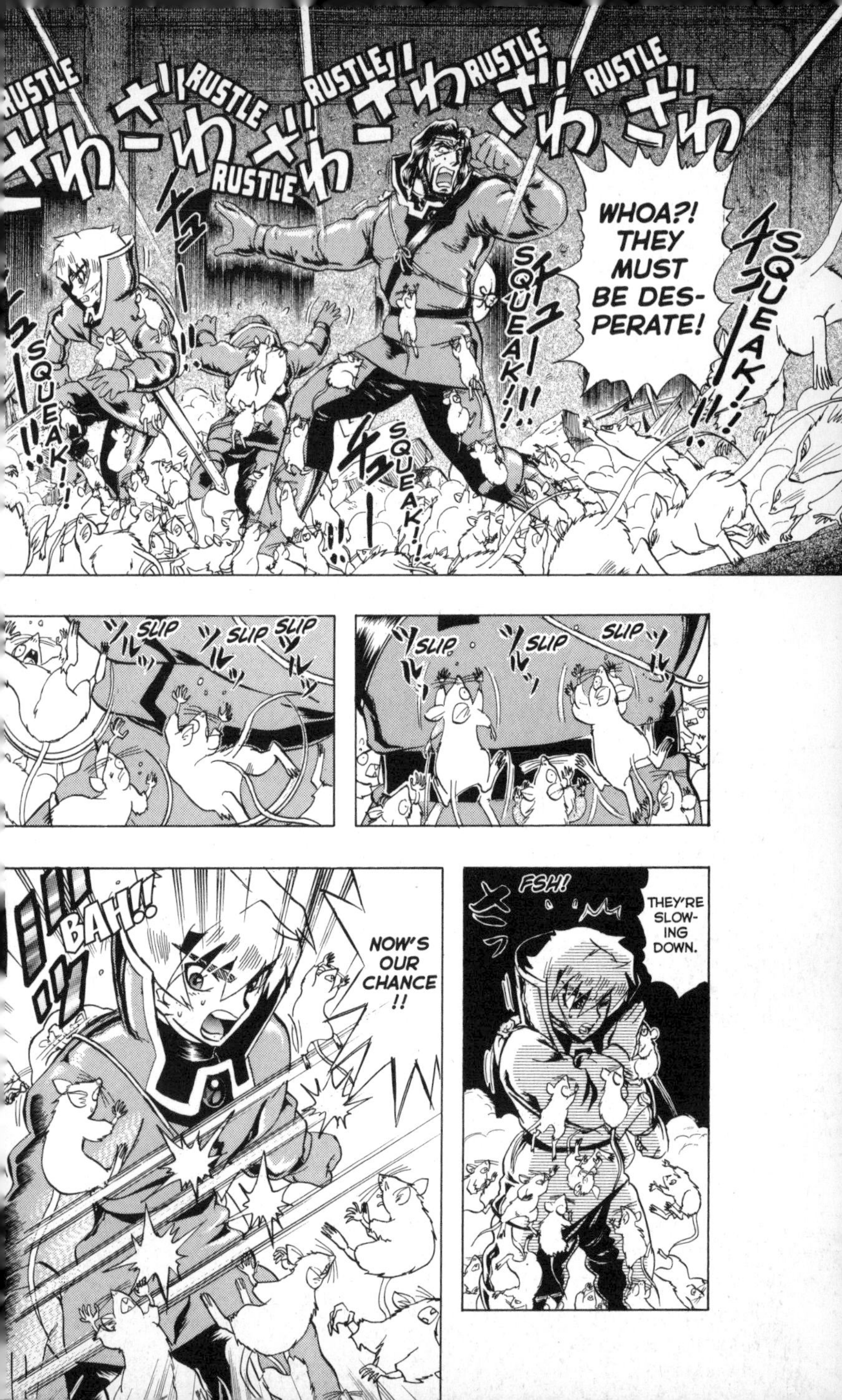
RUSTLE
RUSTLE
RUSTLE
RUSTLE
RUSTLE
RUSTLE
RUSTLE
WHOA?! THEY MUST BE DES-PERATE!
SQUEAK!!
SQUEAK!!
SQUEAK!!
SQUEAK!!
SLIP
SLIP
SLIP
SLIP
SLIP
SLIP
FSH!
THEY'RE SLOW-ING DOWN.
BAH!!
NOW'S OUR CHANCE !!

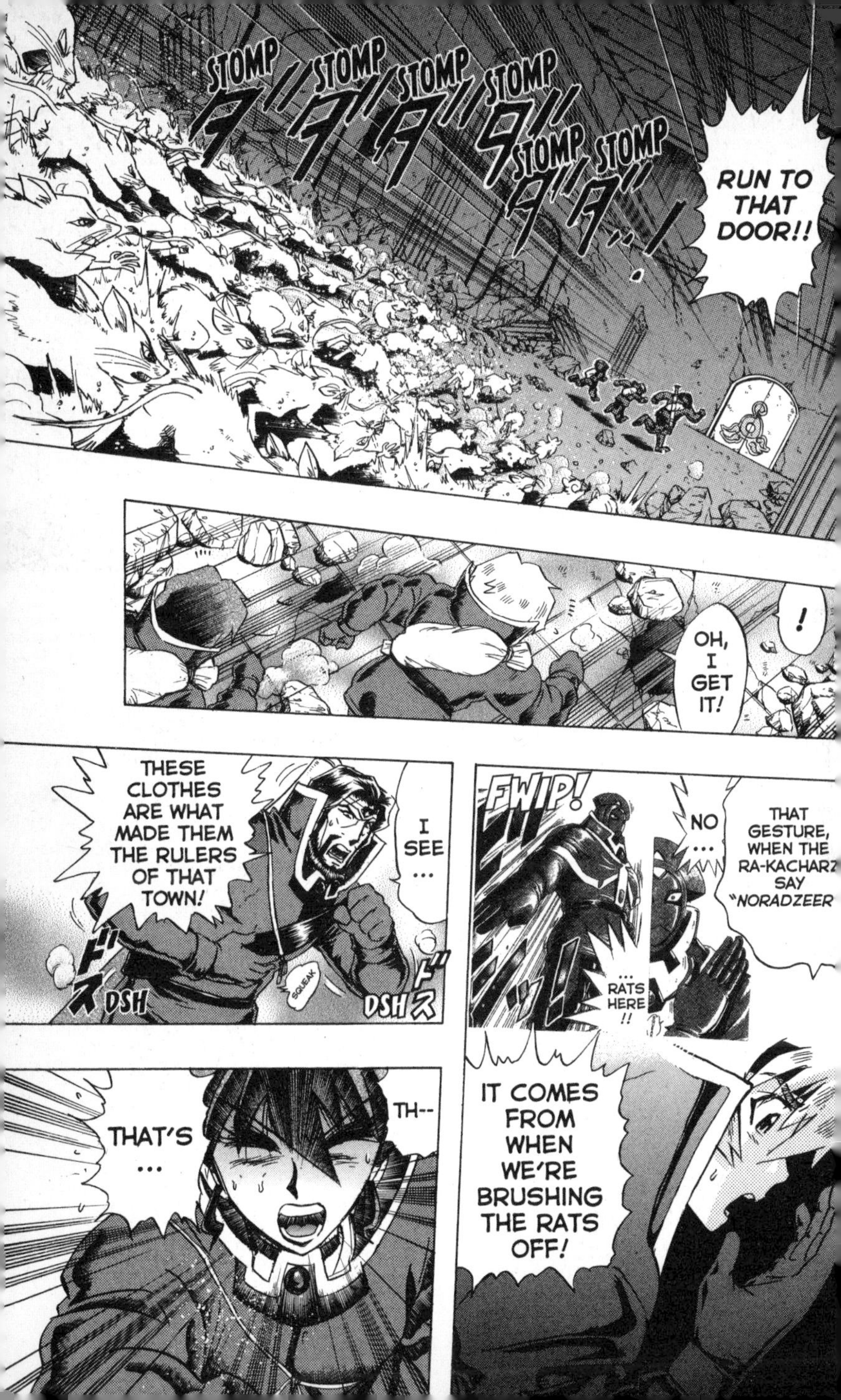
STOMP
STOMP
STOMP
STOMP
STOMP
STOMP
RUN TO THAT DOOR!!
!
OH, I GET IT!
FWIP!
THAT GESTURE, WHEN THE RA-KACHARZ SAY "NORADZEER
NO ...
... RATS HERE !!
I SEE ...
THESE CLOTHES ARE WHAT MADE THEM THE RULERS OF THAT TOWN!
ドス
DSH
SQUEAK
ドス
DSH
IT COMES FROM WHEN WE'RE BRUSHING THE RATS OFF!
TH--
THAT'S ...

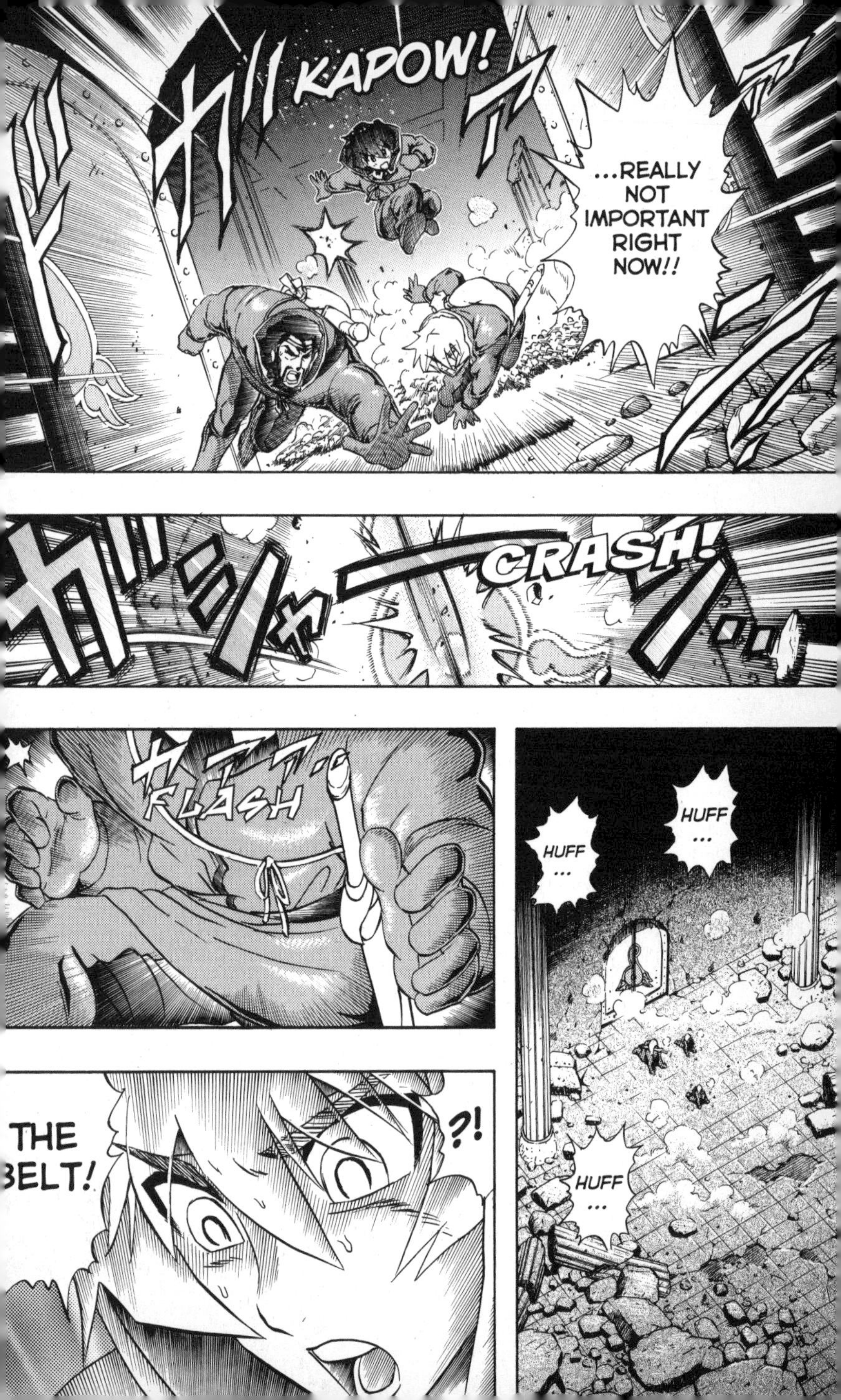
KAPOW!
...REALLY NOT IMPORTANT RIGHT NOW!!
CRASH!
HUFF ...
HUFF ...
HUFF ...
FLASH
?!
THE BELT!

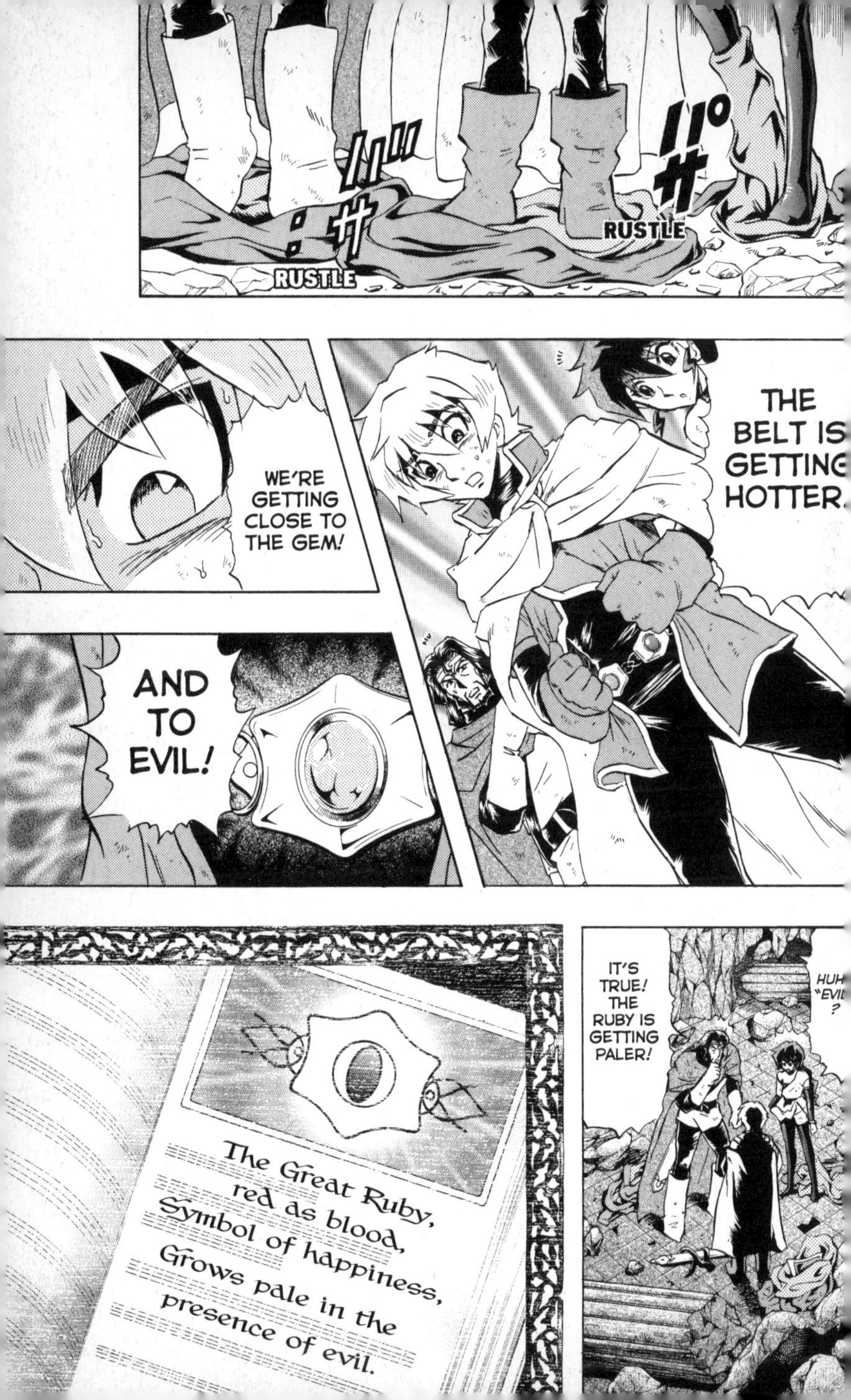
RUSTLE
RUSTLE
THE BELT IS GETTING HOTTER.
WE'RE GETTING CLOSE TO THE GEM!
AND TO EVIL!
HUH "EVIL ?
IT'S TRUE! THE RUBY IS GETTING PALER!
The Great Ruby, red as blood, Symbol of happiness, Grows pale in the presence of evil.

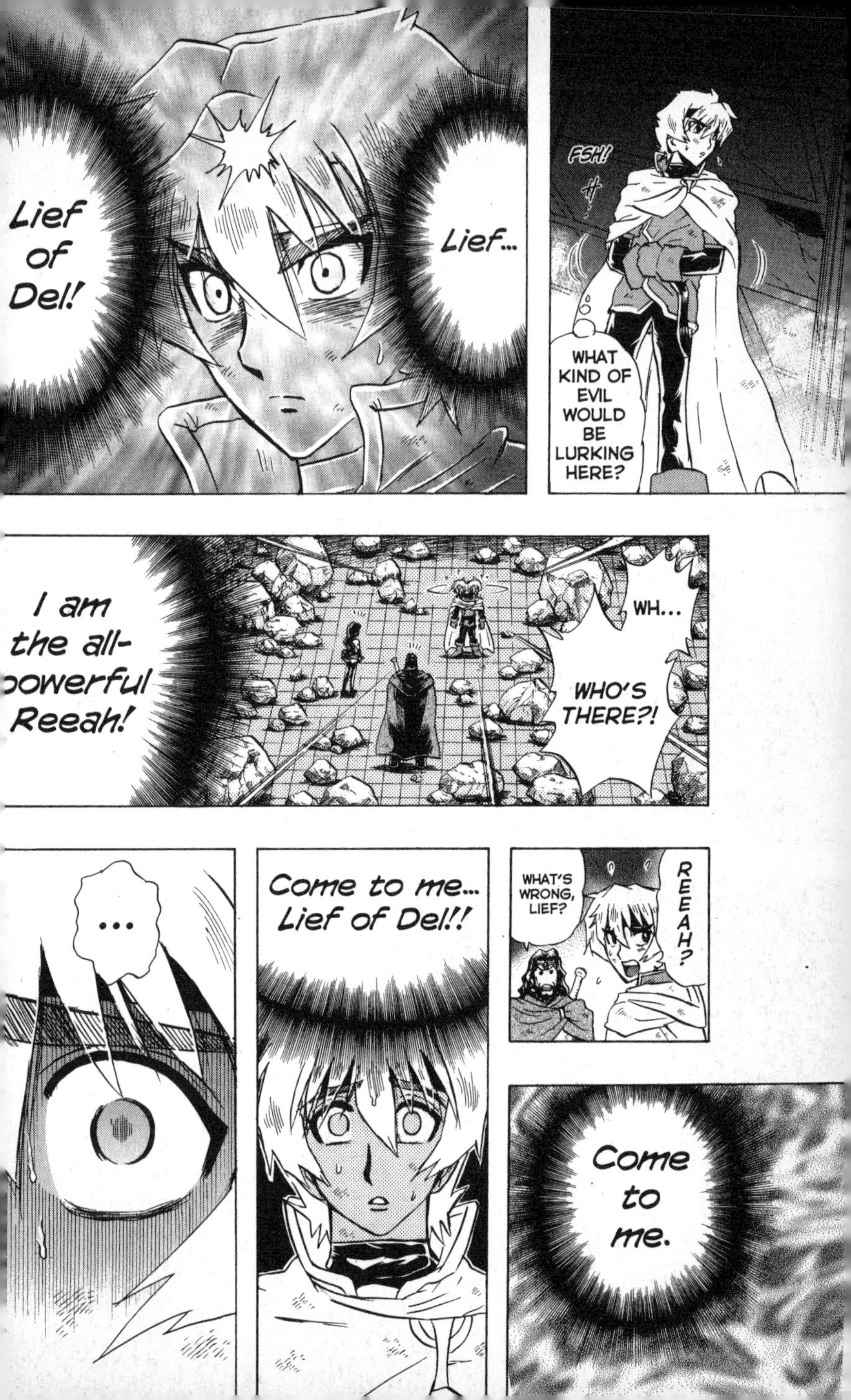
FSH!
WHAT KIND OF EVIL WOULD BE LURKING HERE?
Lief...
Lief of Del!
WH...
WHO'S THERE?!
I am the all-powerful Reeah!
REEAH?
WHAT'S WRONG, LIEF?
Come to me.
Come to me... Lief of Del!!
...

HEY, WHERE ARE YOU GOING ?!

LIEF ?

SWAY

SWAY

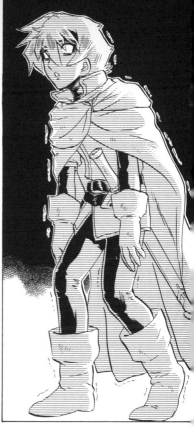

DASH!

HEY! WAIT! STOP!

WHA ....?

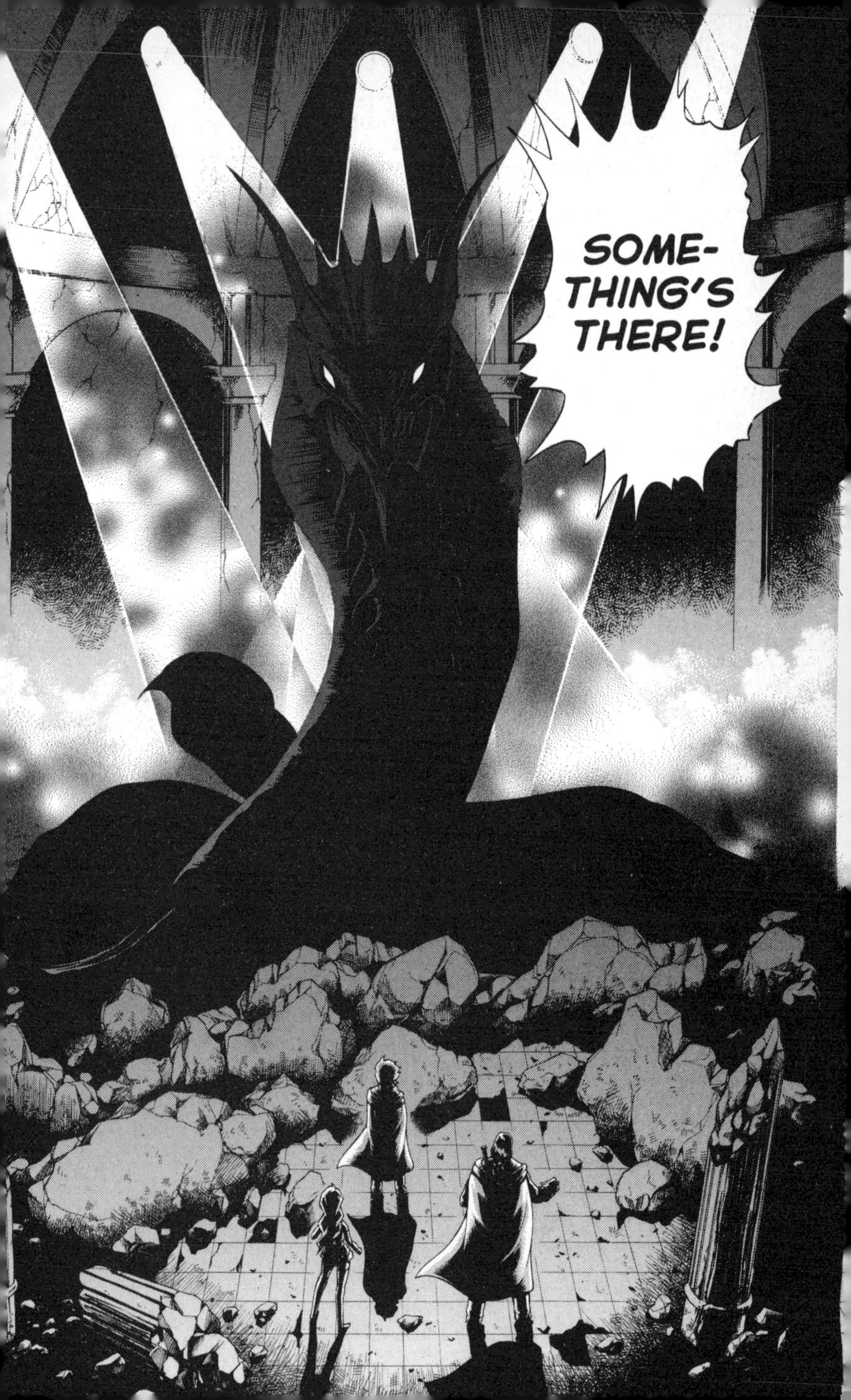
SOME-
THING'S
THERE!

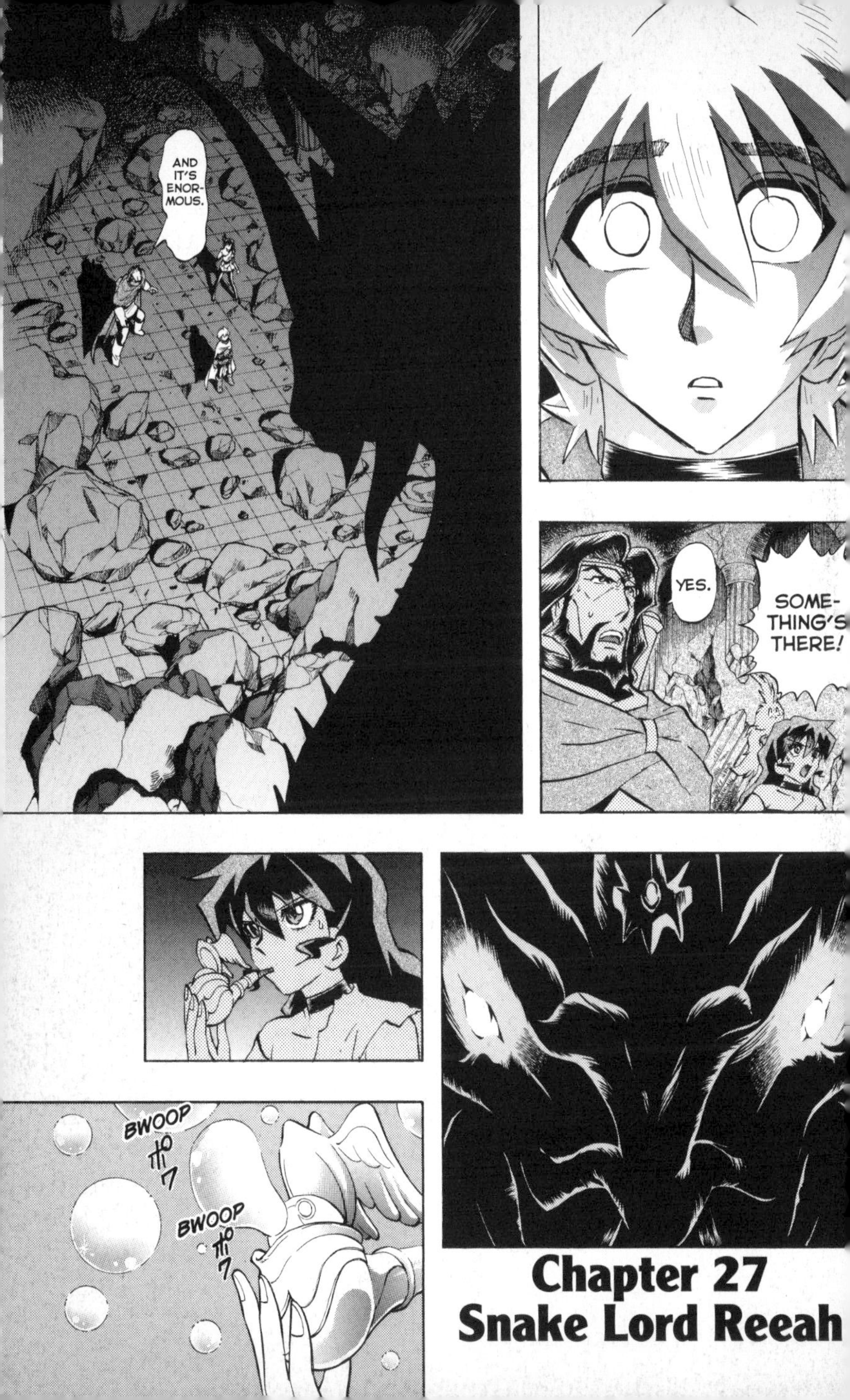
SOME-THING'S THERE!
YES.
AND IT'S ENORMOUS.
BWOOP
ポワ
BWOOP
ポワ

Chapter 27
Snake Lord Reeah

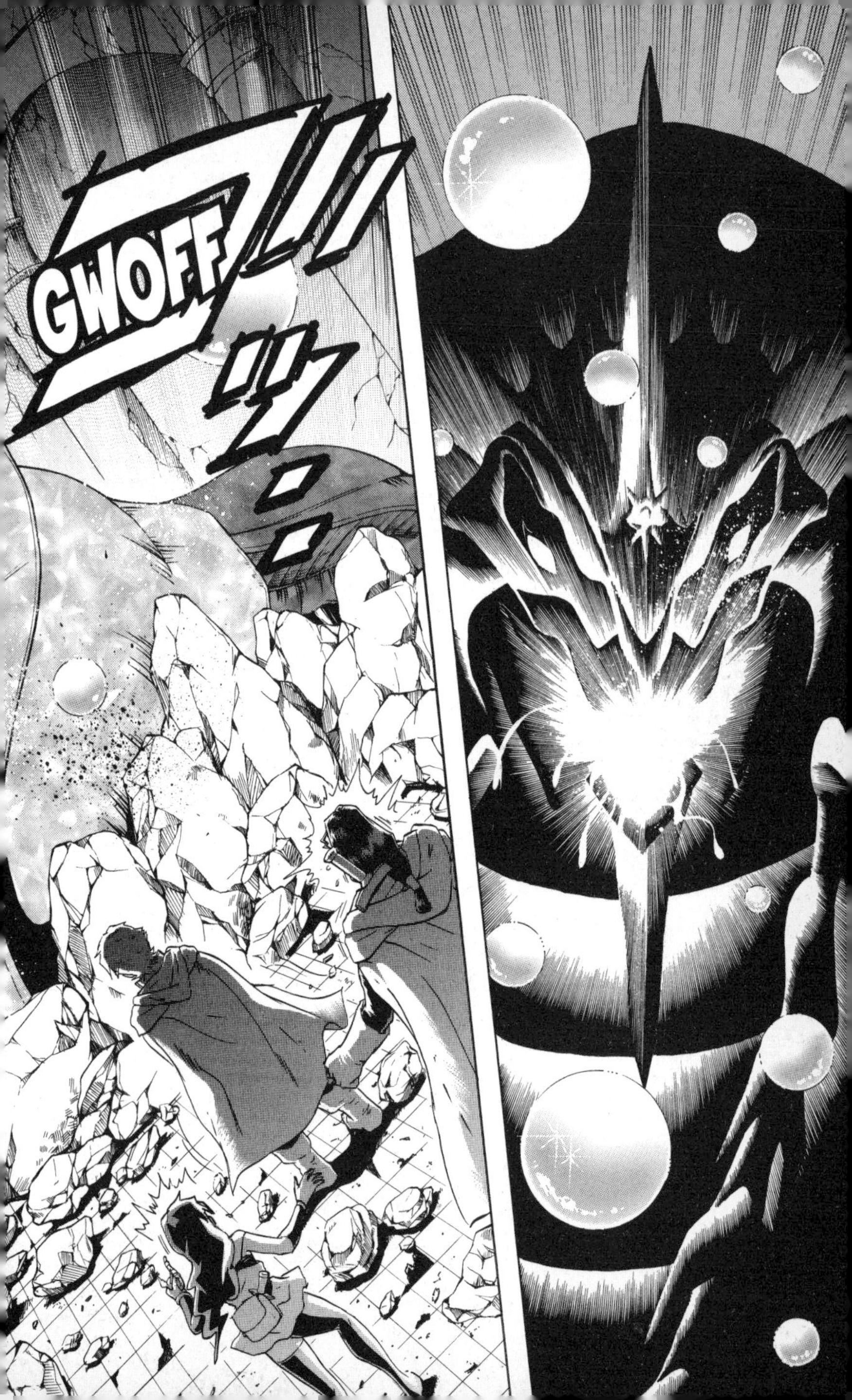
GWOFF

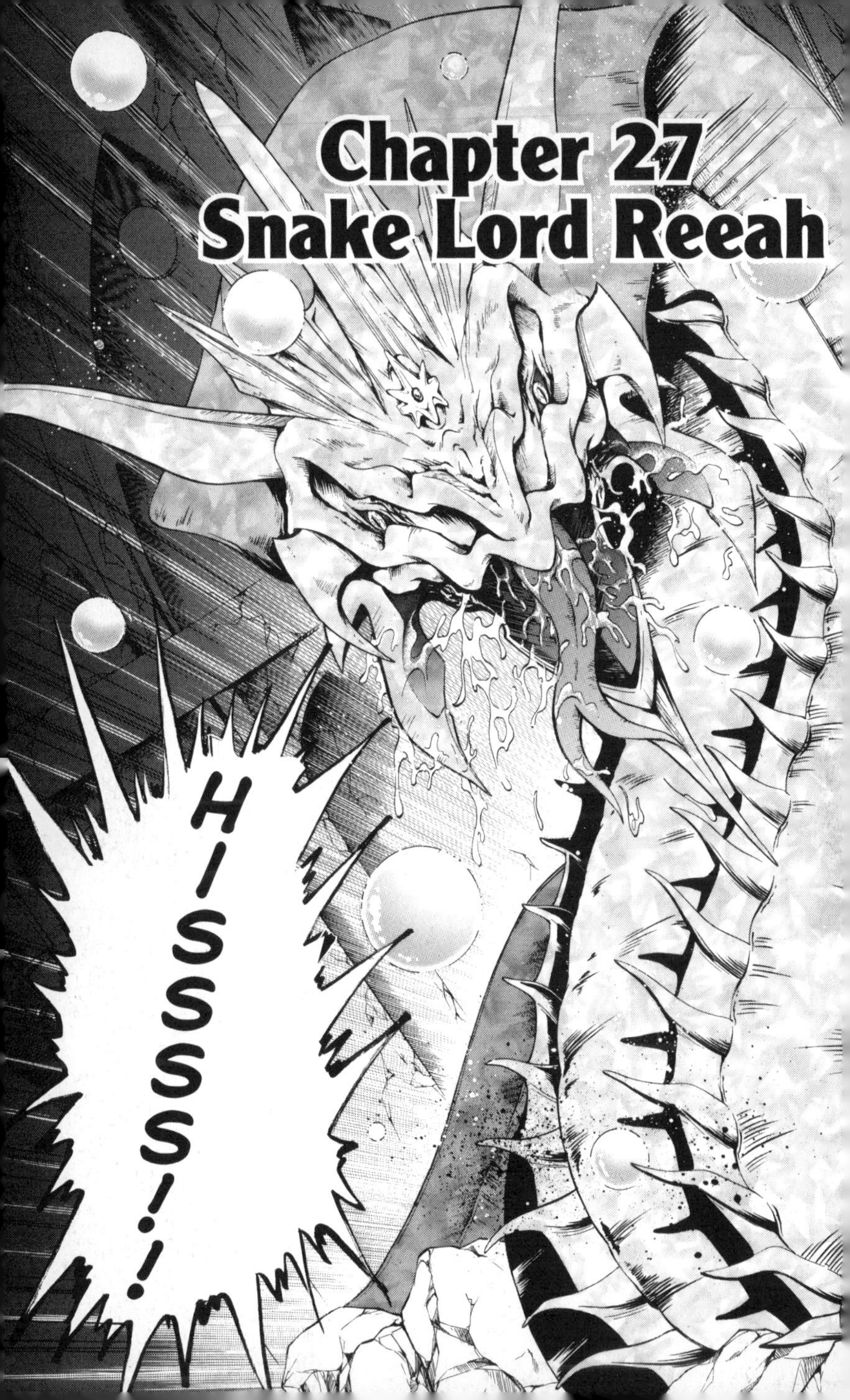
Chapter 27
Snake Lord Reeah
HISSSS!!

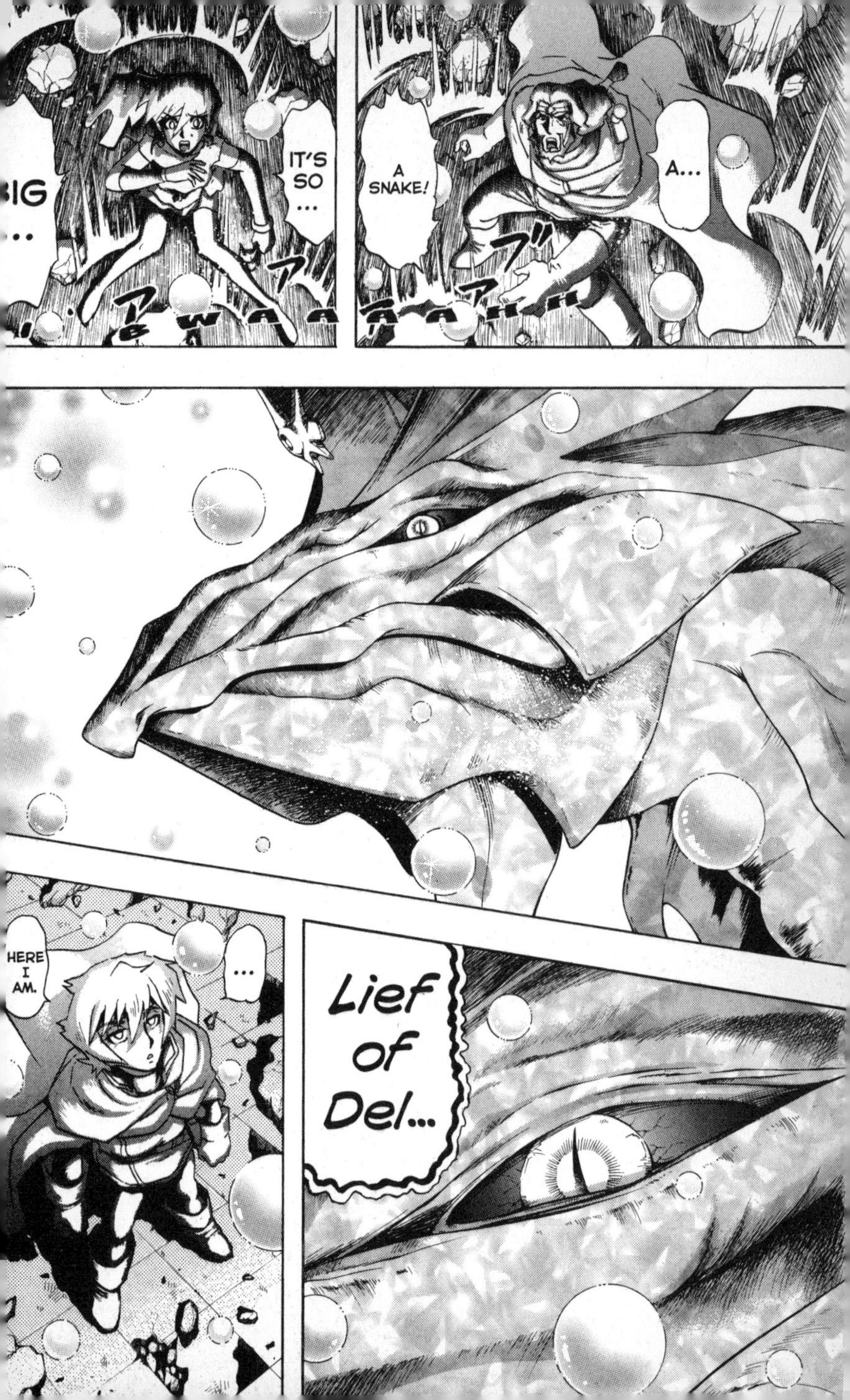
A...
A SNAKE!
IT'S SO ...
BIG ...
BWAAAAAHH
Lief of Del...
...
HERE I AM.

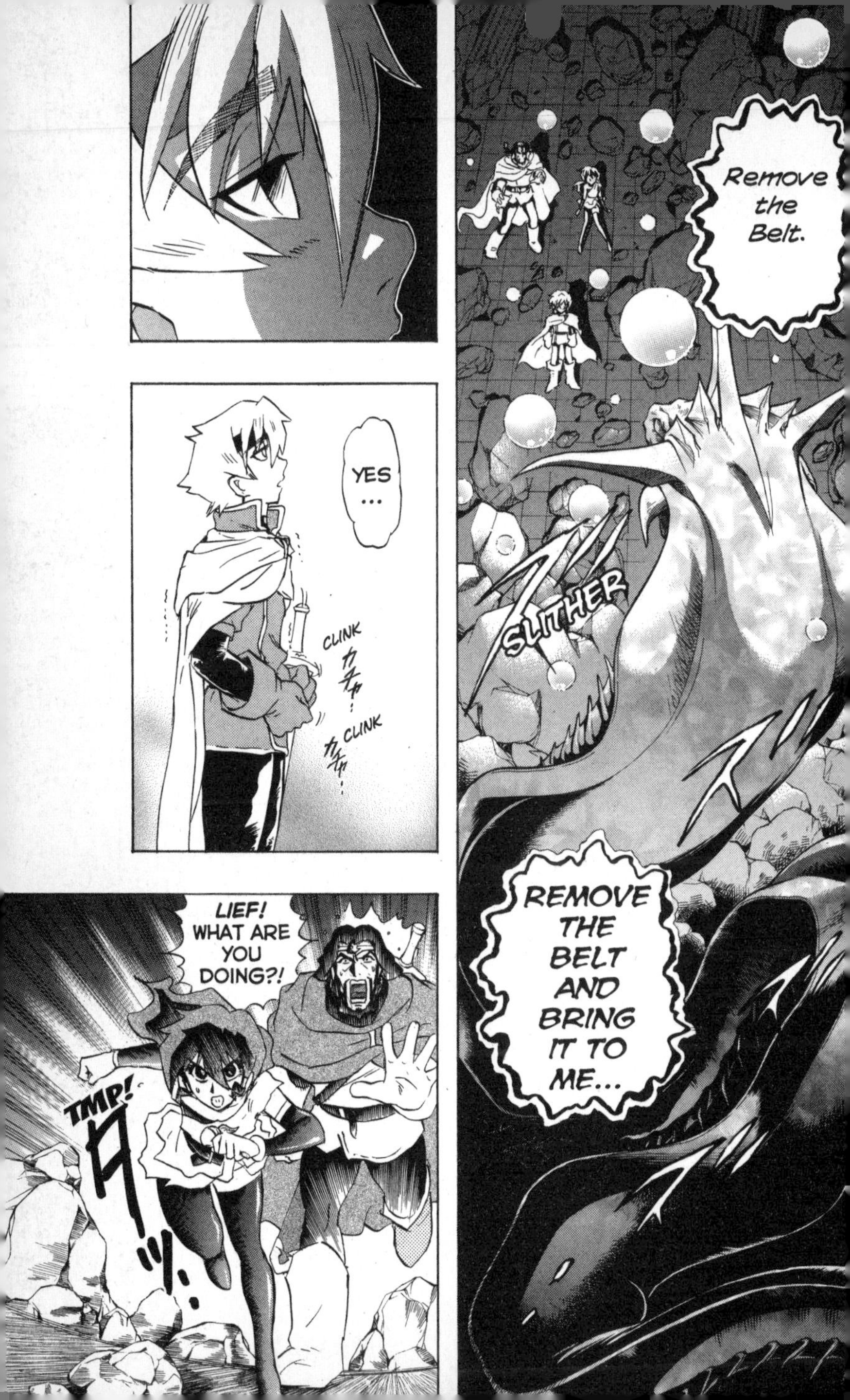
Remove the Belt.
SLITHER
REMOVE THE BELT AND BRING IT TO ME...
YES ...
CLINK
CLINK
LIEF! WHAT ARE YOU DOING?!
TMP!

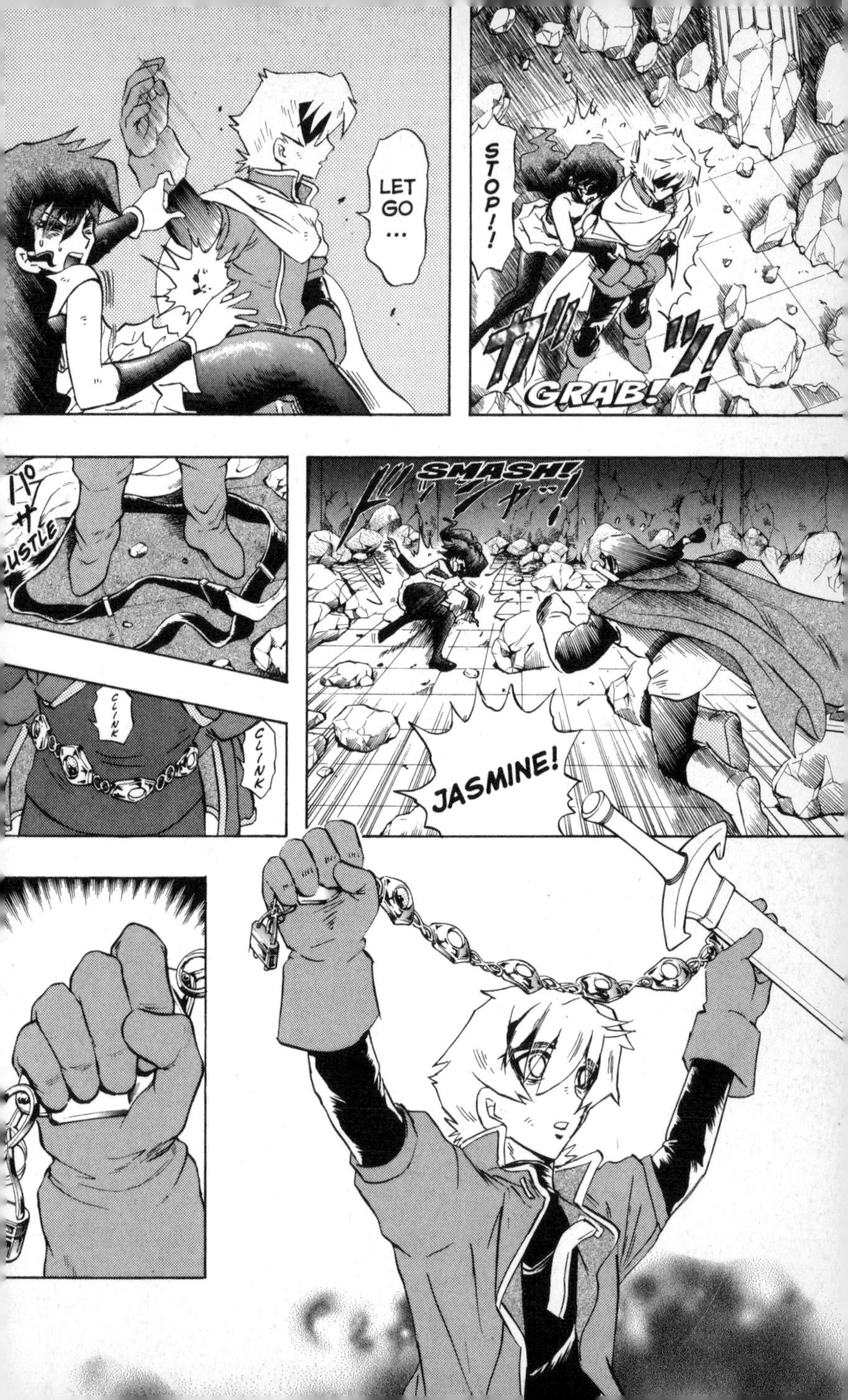
STOP!!
GRAB!
LET GO ...
SMASH!
JASMINE!
RUSTLE
CLINK
CLINK

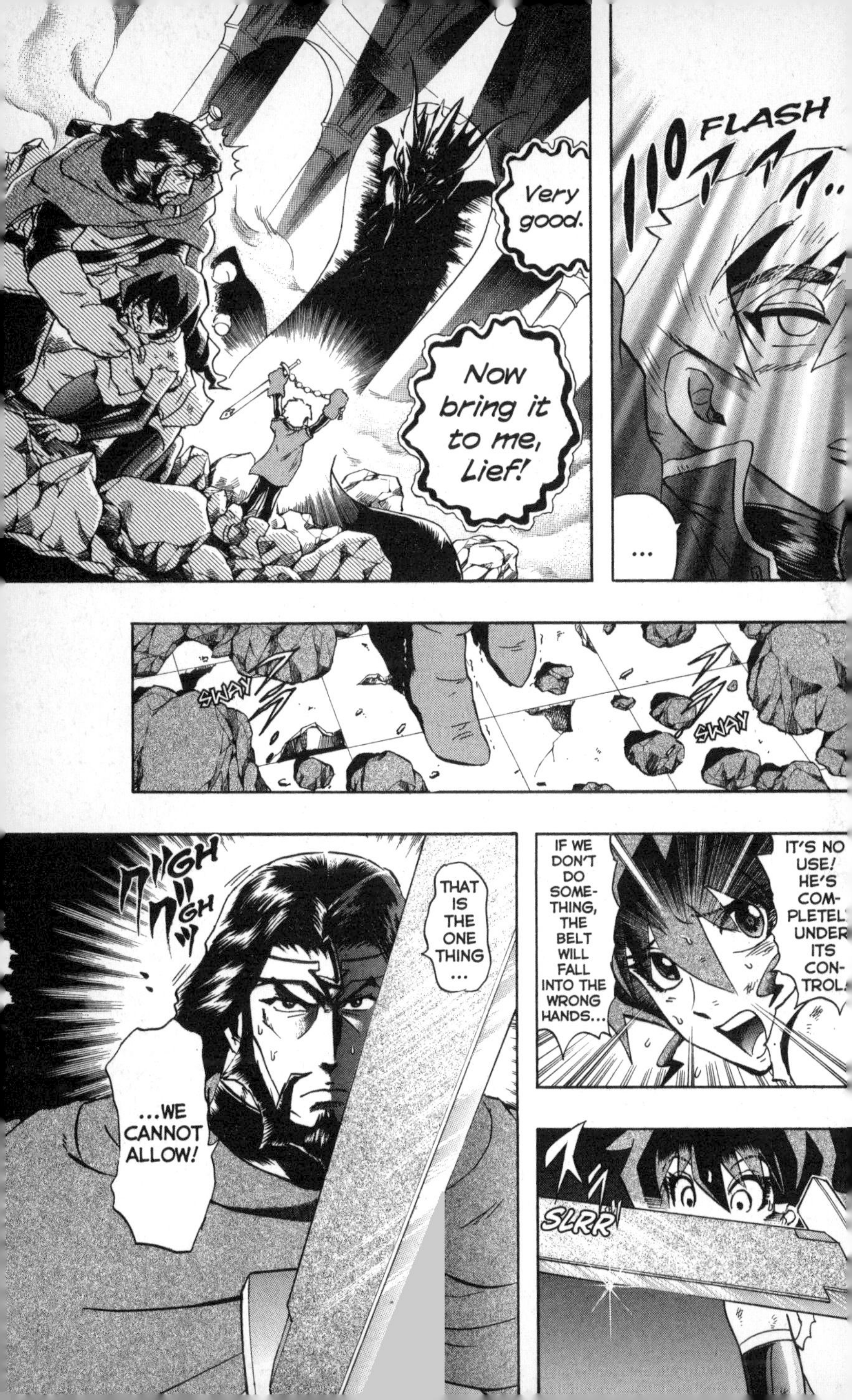
FLASH
...
Very good.
Now bring it to me, Lief!
SWAY
SWAY
IT'S NO USE! HE'S COMPLETEL UNDER ITS CONTROL
IF WE DON'T DO SOMETHING, THE BELT WILL FALL INTO THE WRONG HANDS...
SLRR
NGH
NGH
THAT IS THE ONE THING...
...WE CANNOT ALLOW!

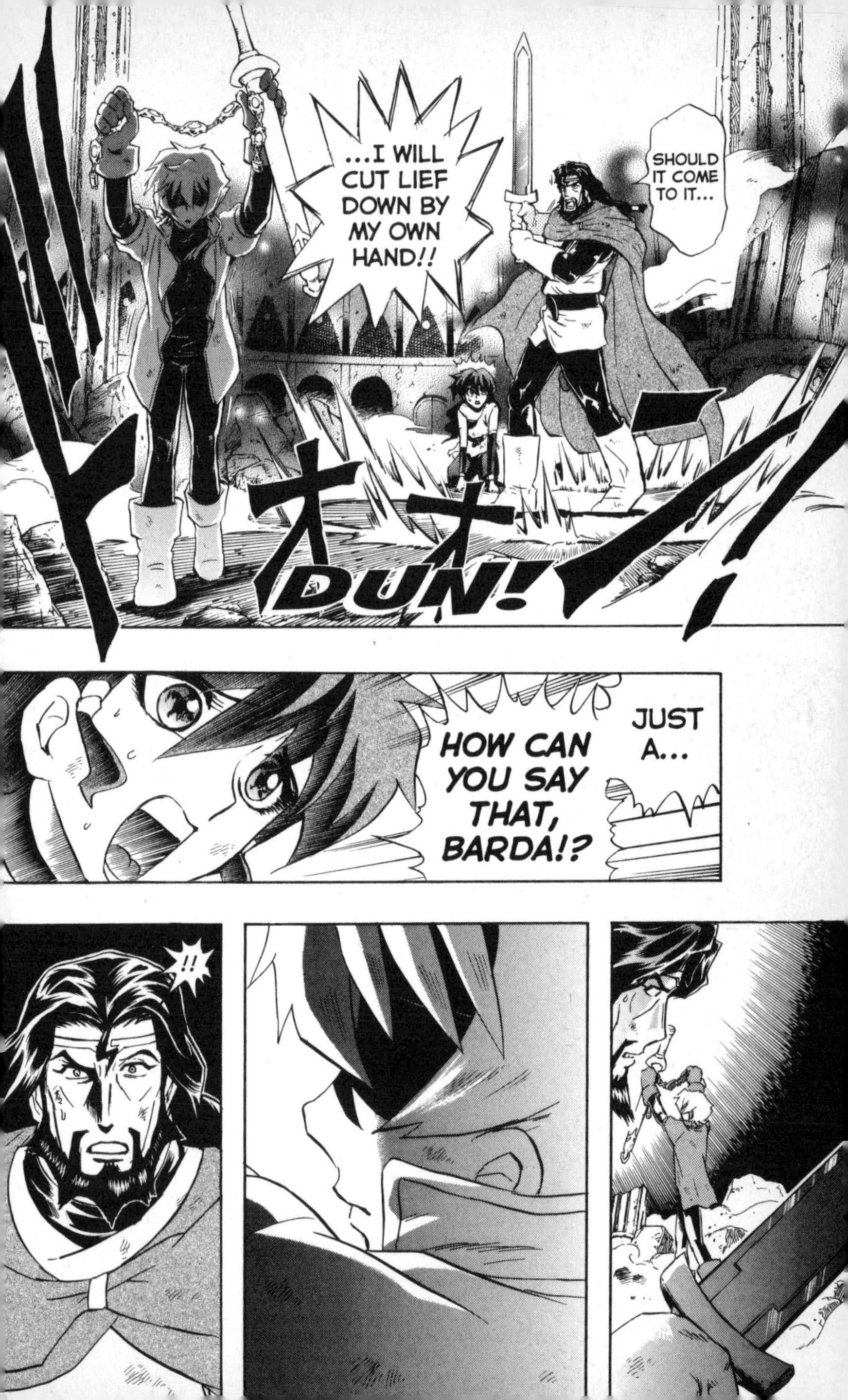
SHOULD IT COME TO IT...
...I WILL CUT LIEF DOWN BY MY OWN HAND!!
DUN!
JUST A...
HOW CAN YOU SAY THAT, BARDA!?
!!

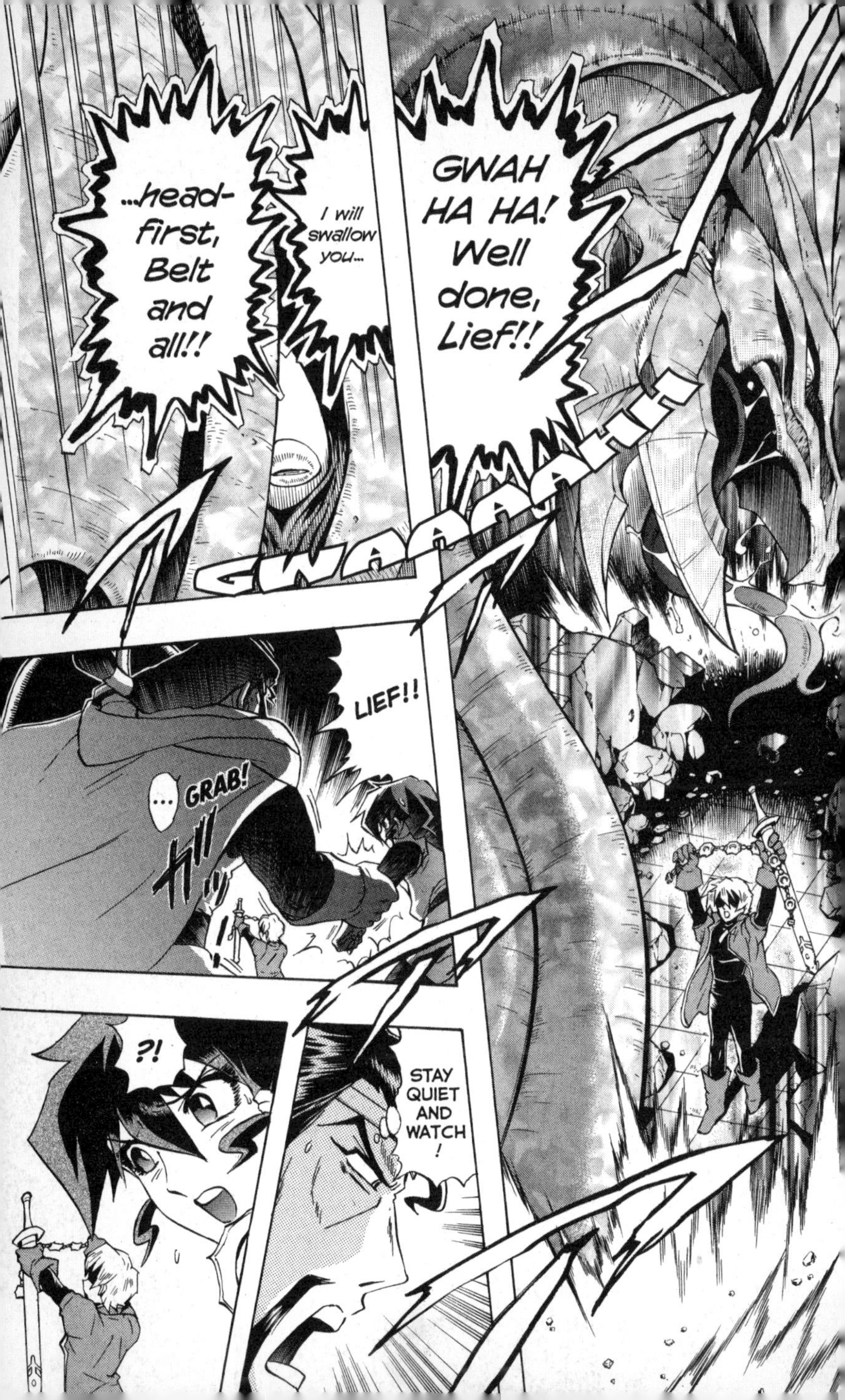
GWAH HA HA! Well done, Lief!!
GWAAAAH!!!
I will swallow you...
...head-first, Belt and all!!
LIEF!!
...
GRAB!
STAY QUIET AND WATCH!
?!

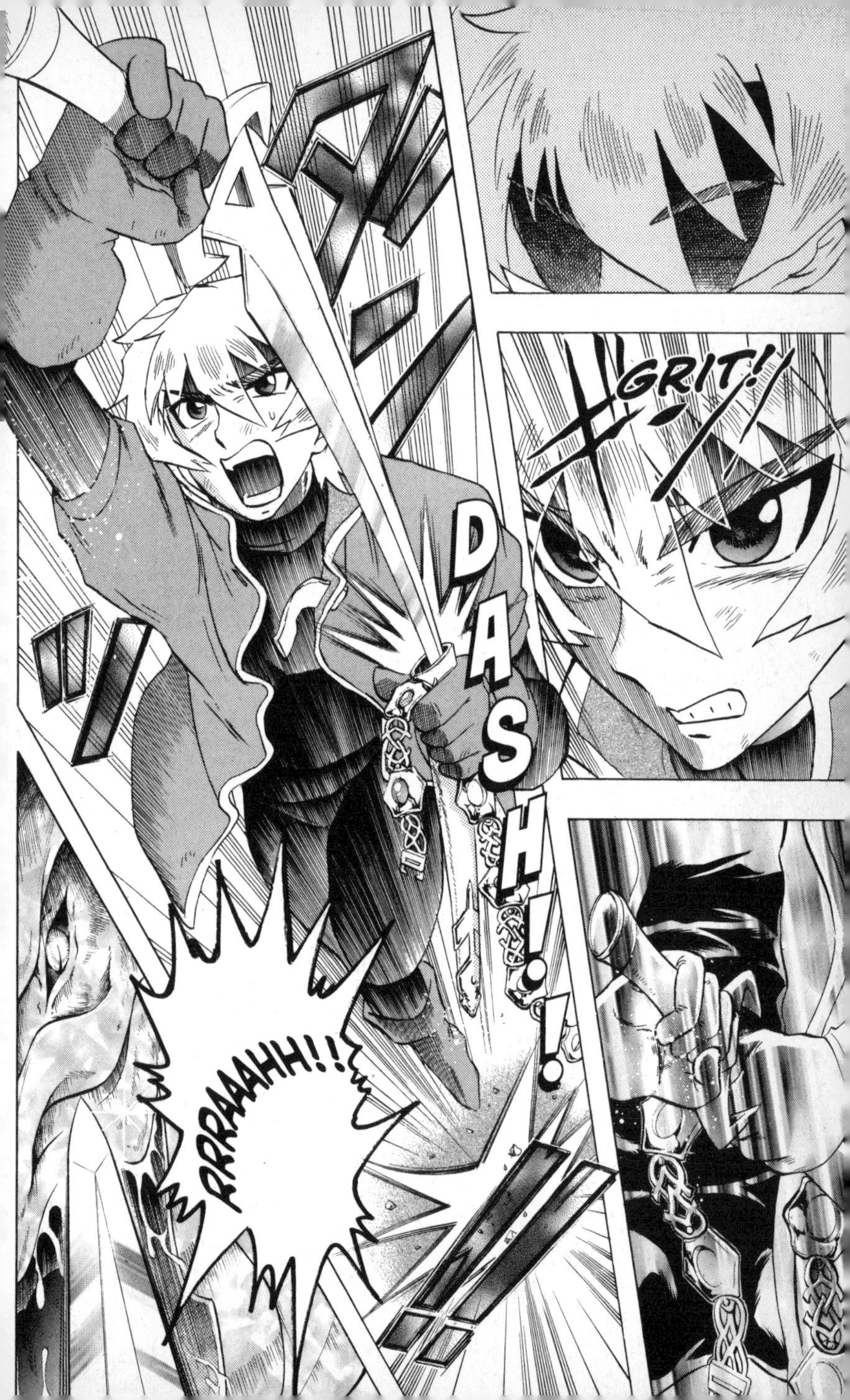
GRIT!
DASH!!
RRRAAAHH!!

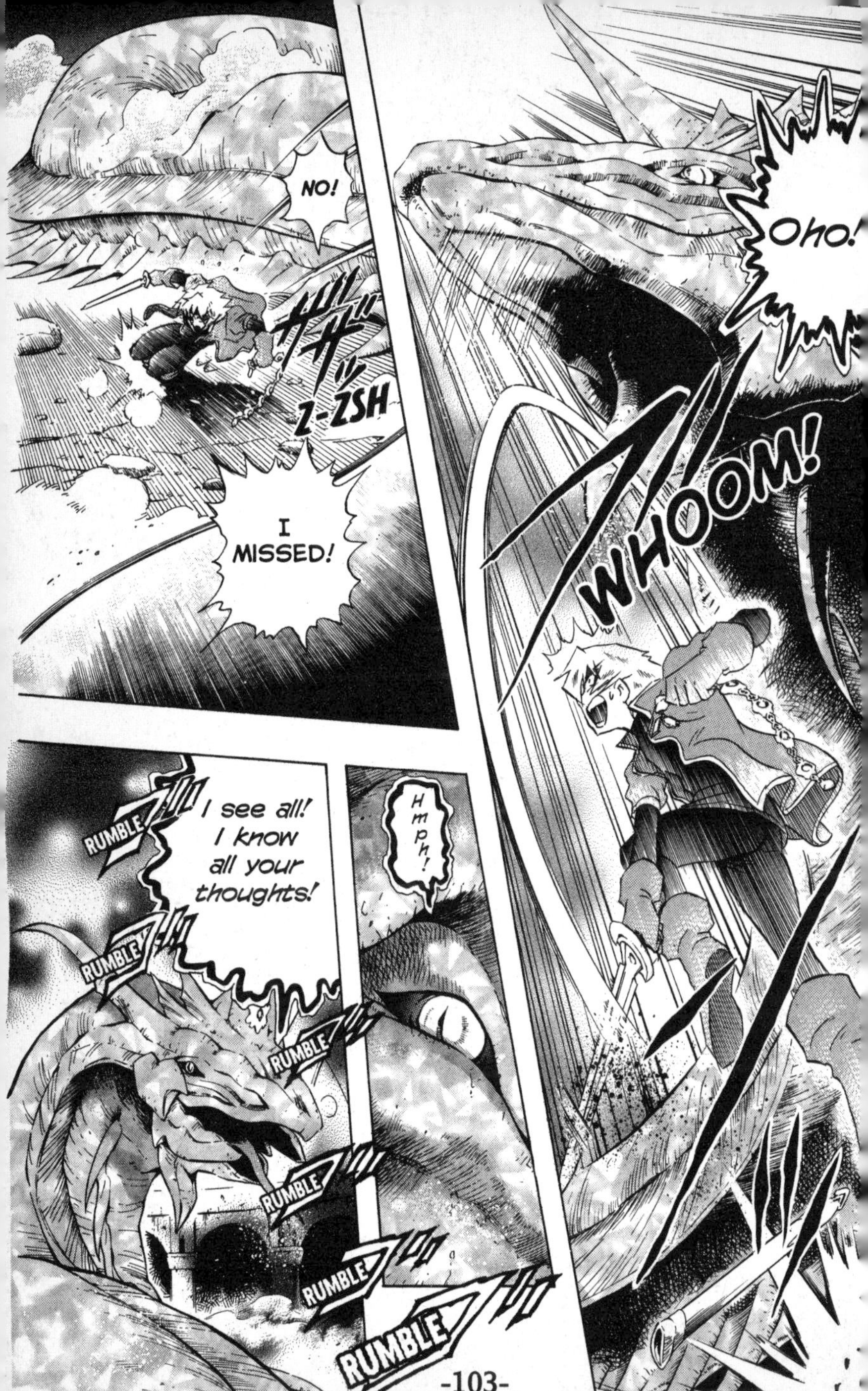
Oho!
WHOOM!
NO!
Z-ZSH
I MISSED!
Hmph!
I see all! I know all your thoughts!
RUMBLE
RUMBLE
RUMBLE
RUMBLE
RUMBLE
RUMBLE

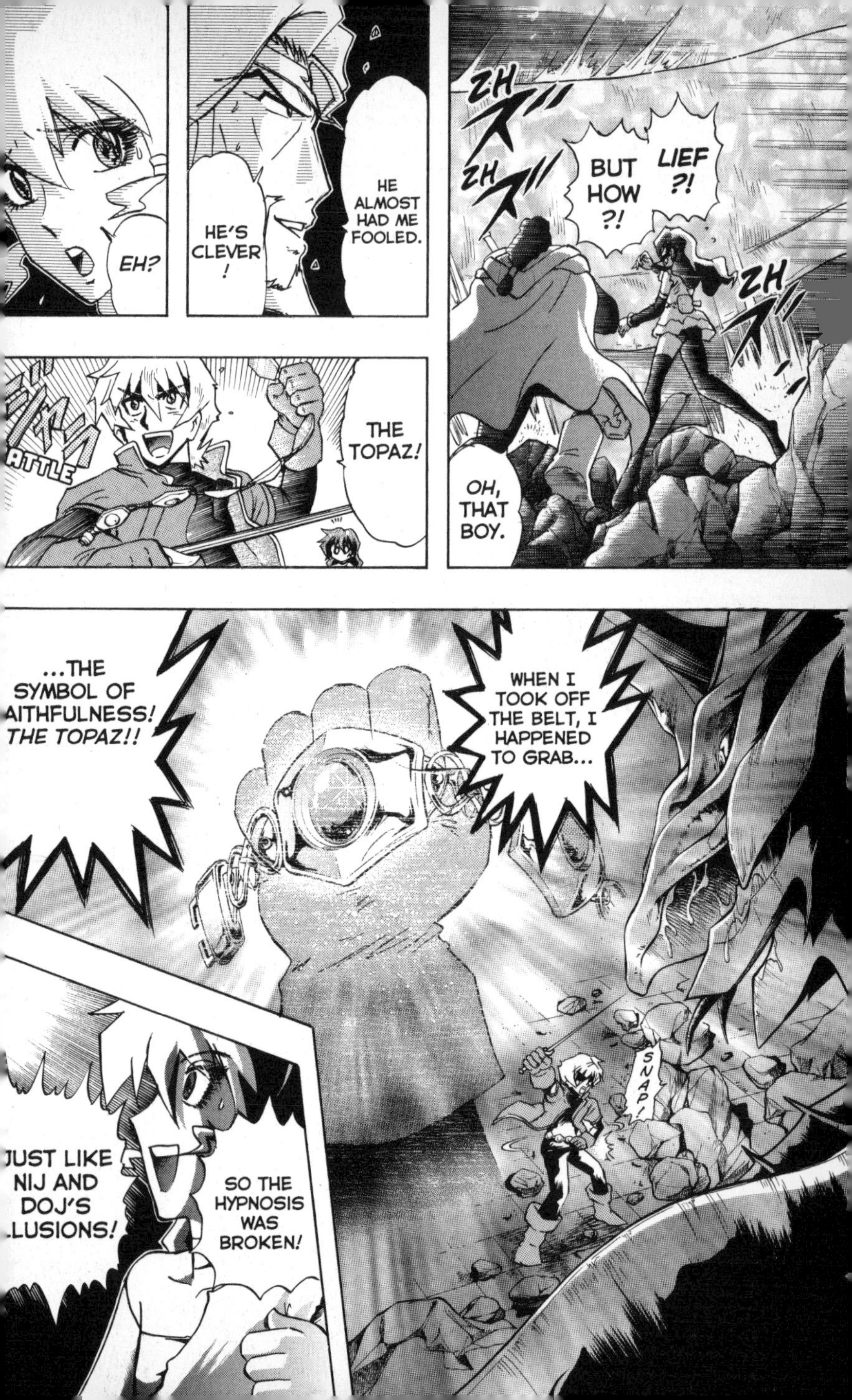

LIEF ?!
BUT HOW ?!
ZH
ZH
ZH
OH, THAT BOY.
HE ALMOST HAD ME FOOLED.
HE'S CLEVER !
EH?
THE TOPAZ!
RATTLE
WHEN I TOOK OFF THE BELT, I HAPPENED TO GRAB...
...THE SYMBOL OF AITHFULNESS! THE TOPAZ!!
SNAP!
SO THE HYPNOSIS WAS BROKEN!
JUST LIKE NIJ AND DOJ'S .LUSIONS!

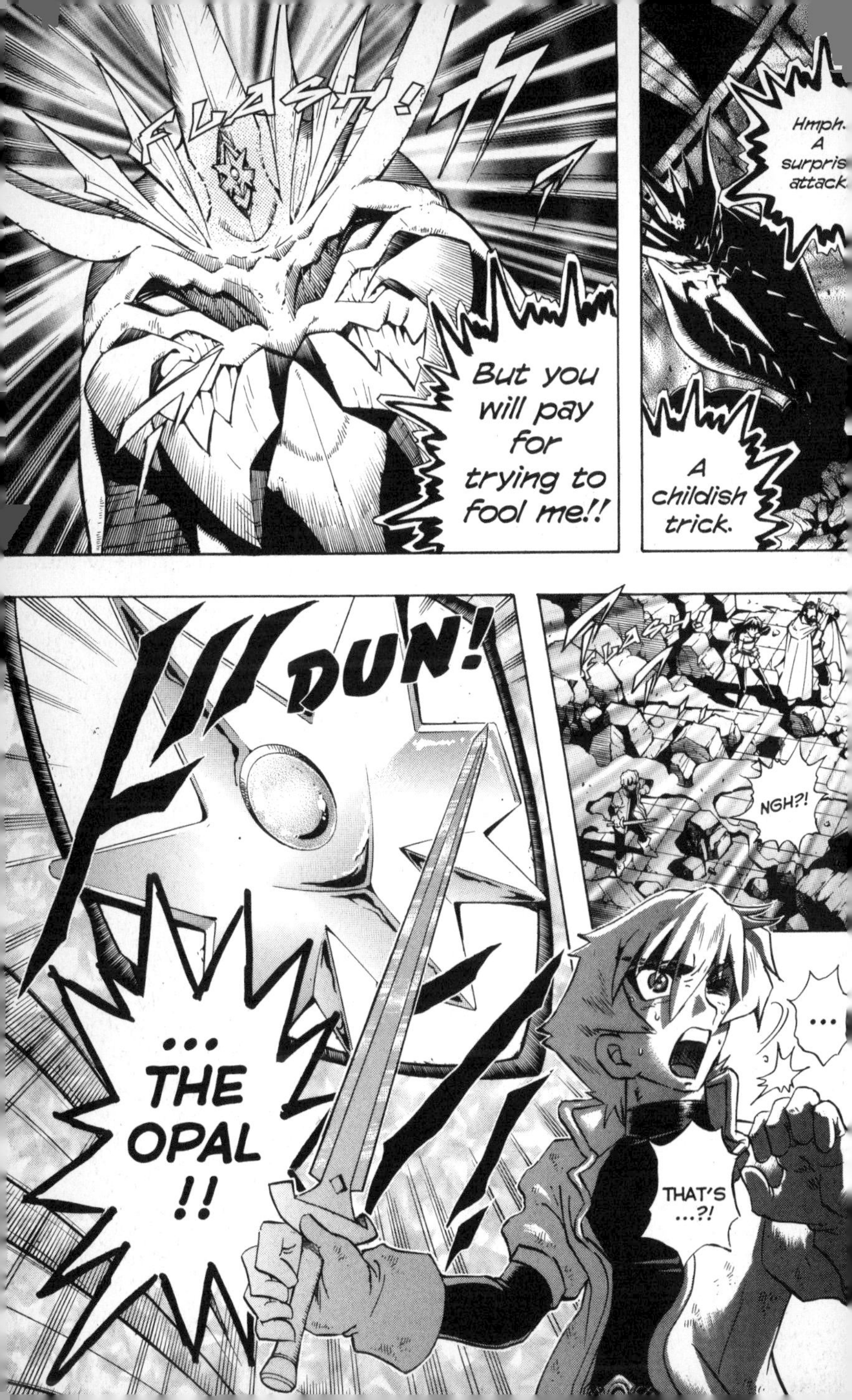
Hmph. A surpris attack
A childish trick.
FLASH!
But you will pay for trying to fool me!!
NGH?!
DUN!
...THE OPAL!!
...
THAT'S ...?!

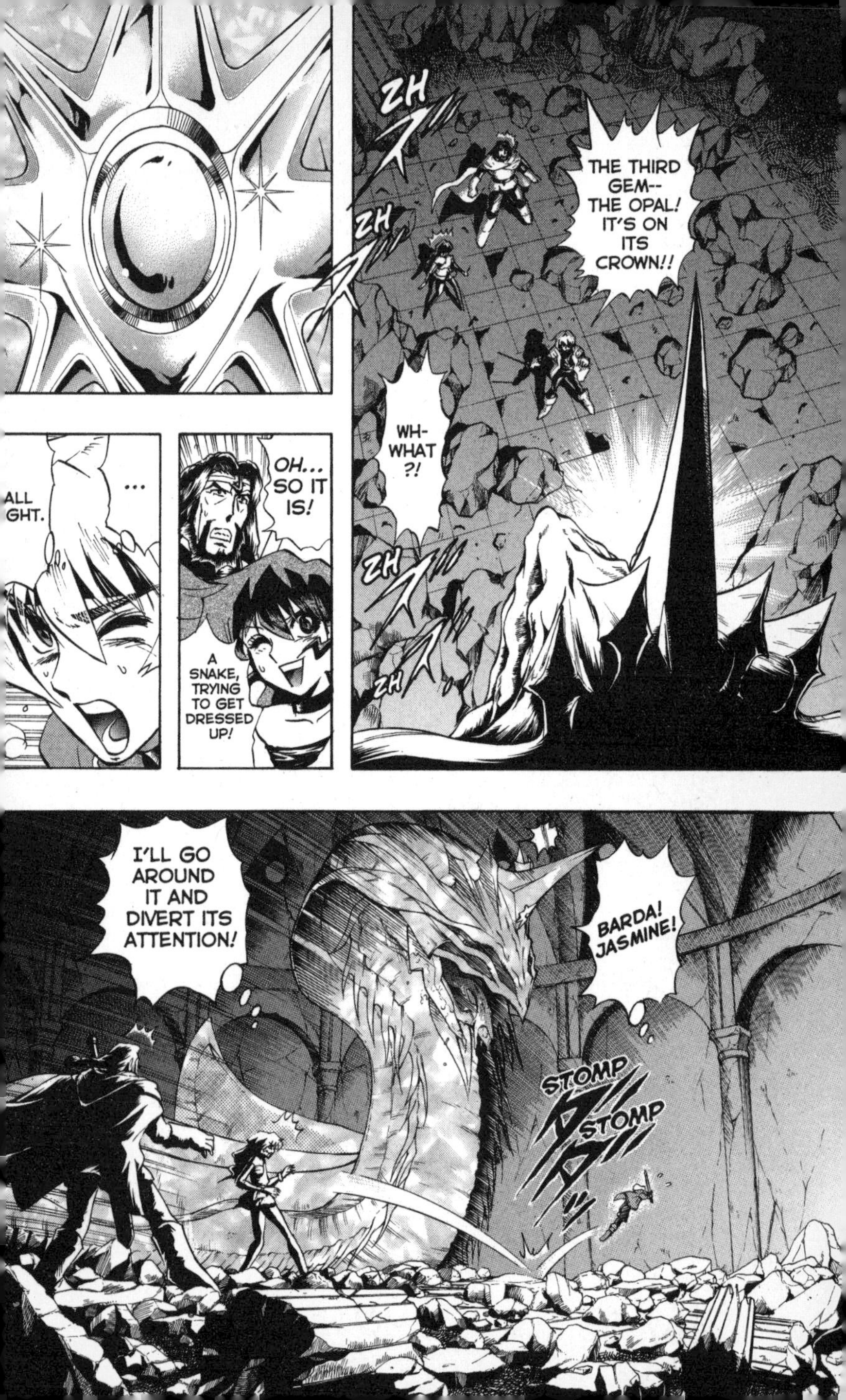
THE THIRD GEM-- THE OPAL! IT'S ON ITS CROWN!!
ZH
ZH
WH-WHAT ?!
ZH
ZH
OH... SO IT IS!
A SNAKE, TRYING TO GET DRESSED UP!
...
ALL
GHT.
BARDA! JASMINE!
STOMP
STOMP
I'LL GO AROUND IT AND DIVERT ITS ATTENTION!

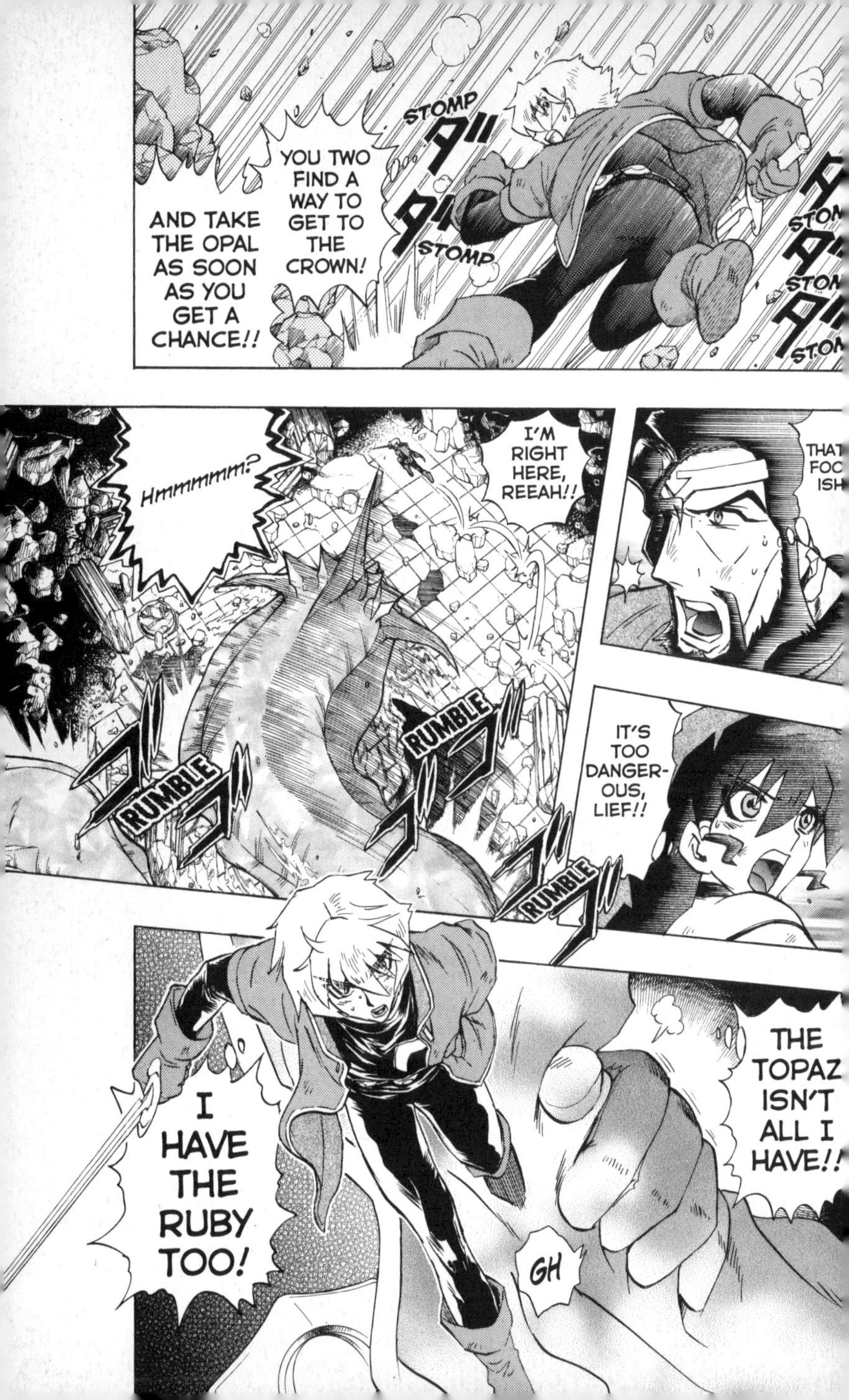
STOMP
STOMP
STOMP
STOMP
STOMP
YOU TWO FIND A WAY TO GET TO THE CROWN!
AND TAKE THE OPAL AS SOON AS YOU GET A CHANCE!!
IT'S TOO DANGER-OUS, LIEF!!
I'M RIGHT HERE, REEAH!!
Hmmmmmm?
RUMBLE
RUMBLE
RUMBLE
THE TOPAZ ISN'T ALL I HAVE!!
GH
I HAVE THE RUBY TOO!

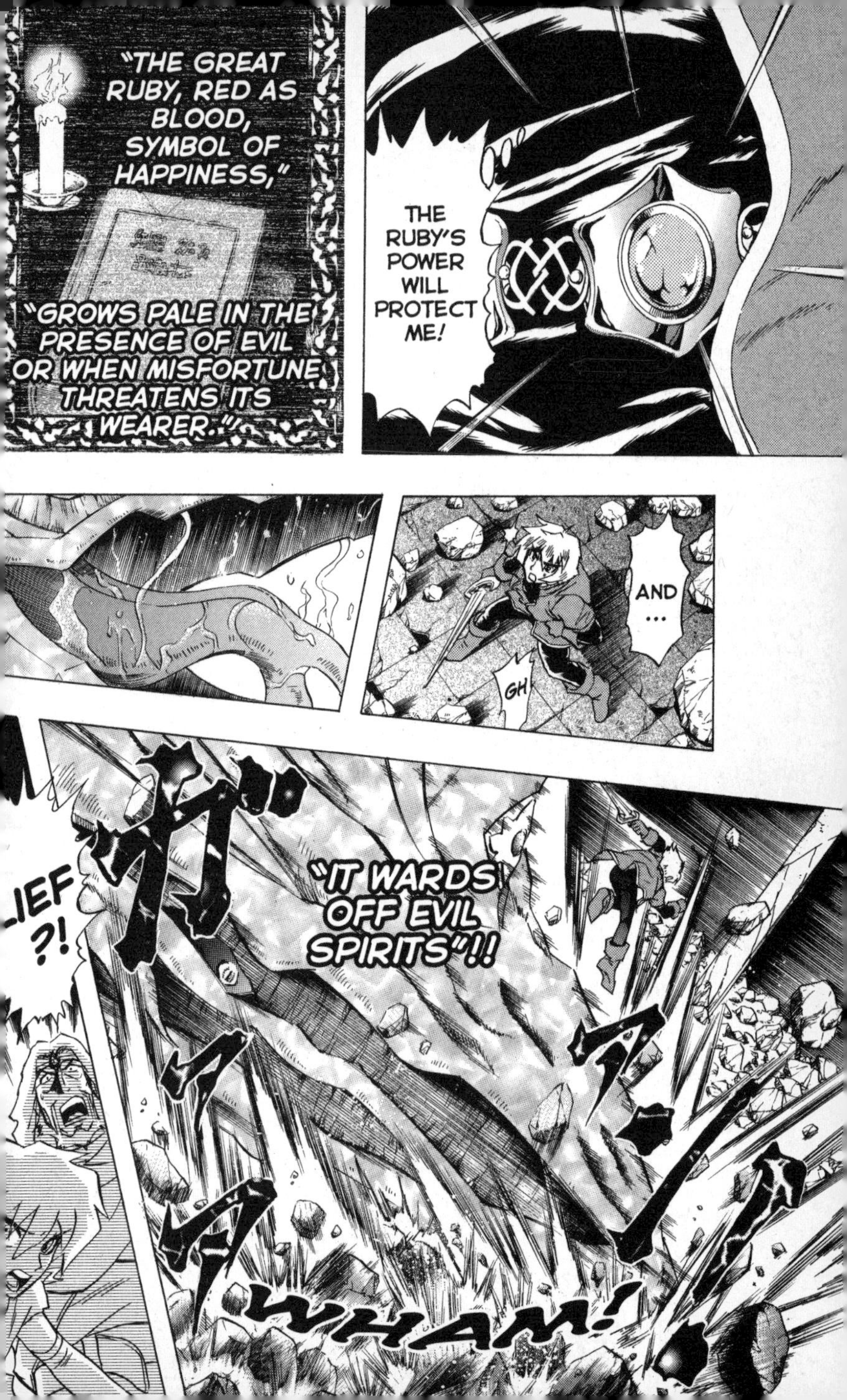
THE RUBY'S POWER WILL PROTECT ME!
"THE GREAT RUBY, RED AS BLOOD, SYMBOL OF HAPPINESS,"
"GROWS PALE IN THE PRESENCE OF EVIL OR WHEN MISFORTUNE THREATENS ITS WEARER."
AND ...
GH
"IT WARDS OFF EVIL SPIRITS"!!
LIEF ?!
WHAM!

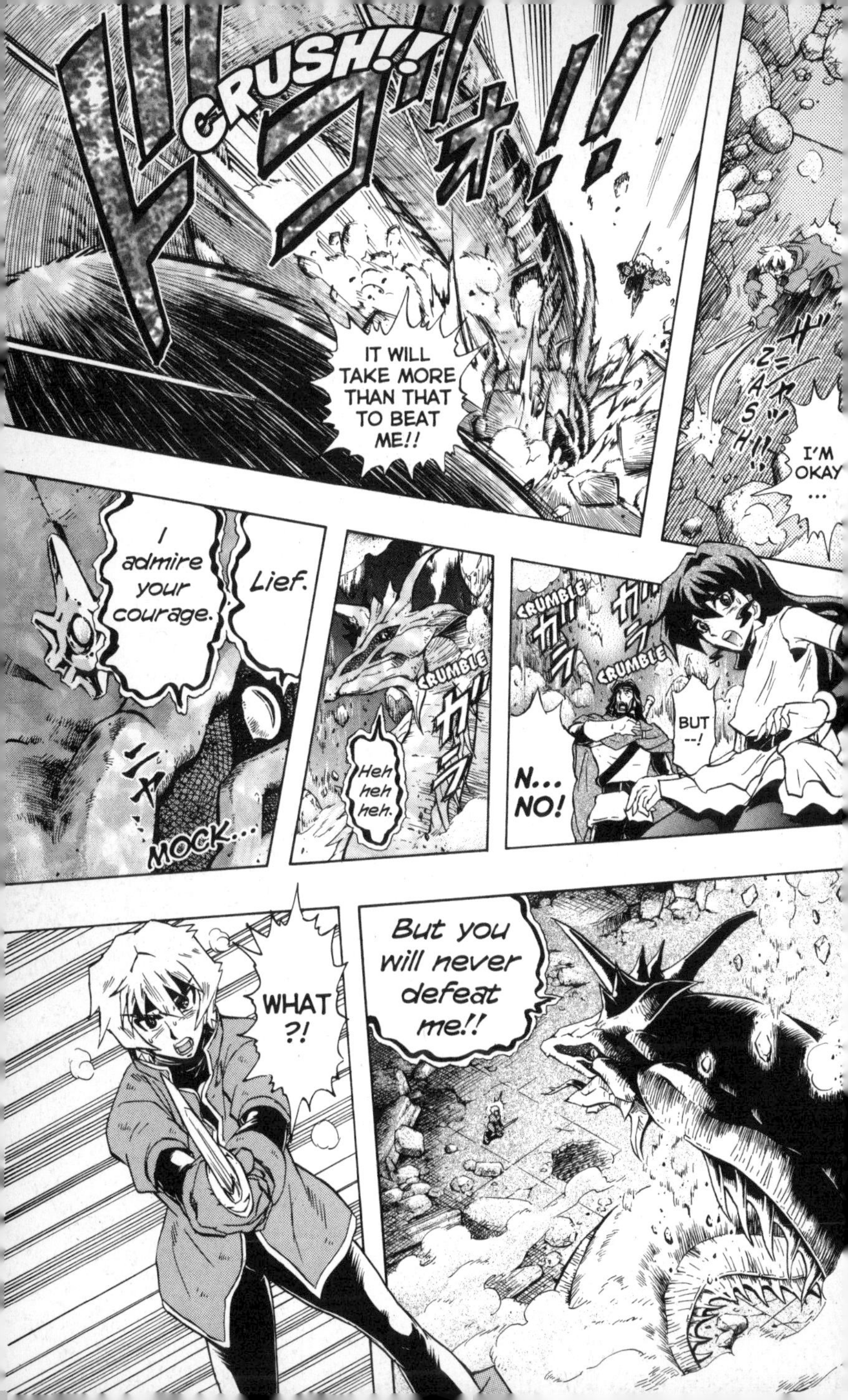
ZASH!!
I'M OKAY ...
CRUSH!!
IT WILL TAKE MORE THAN THAT TO BEAT ME!!
CRUMBLE
CRUMBLE
BUT --!
N... NO!
CRUMBLE
Heh heh heh.
Lief.
I admire your courage.
MOCK...
But you will never defeat me!!
WHAT ?!

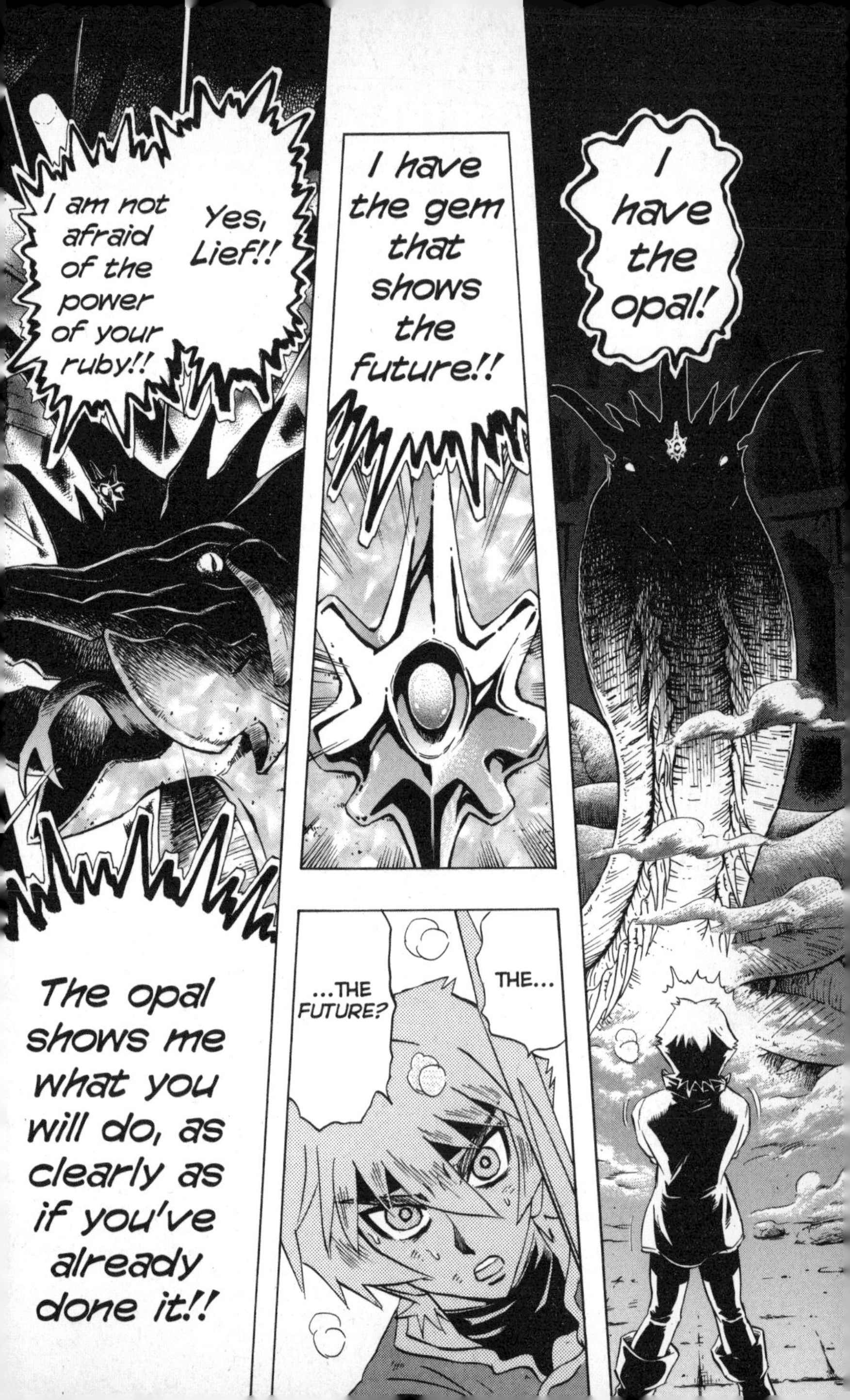
I have the opal!
I have the gem that shows the future!!
THE...
...THE FUTURE?
Yes, Lief!!
I am not afraid of the power of your ruby!!
The opal shows me what you will do, as clearly as if you've already done it!!

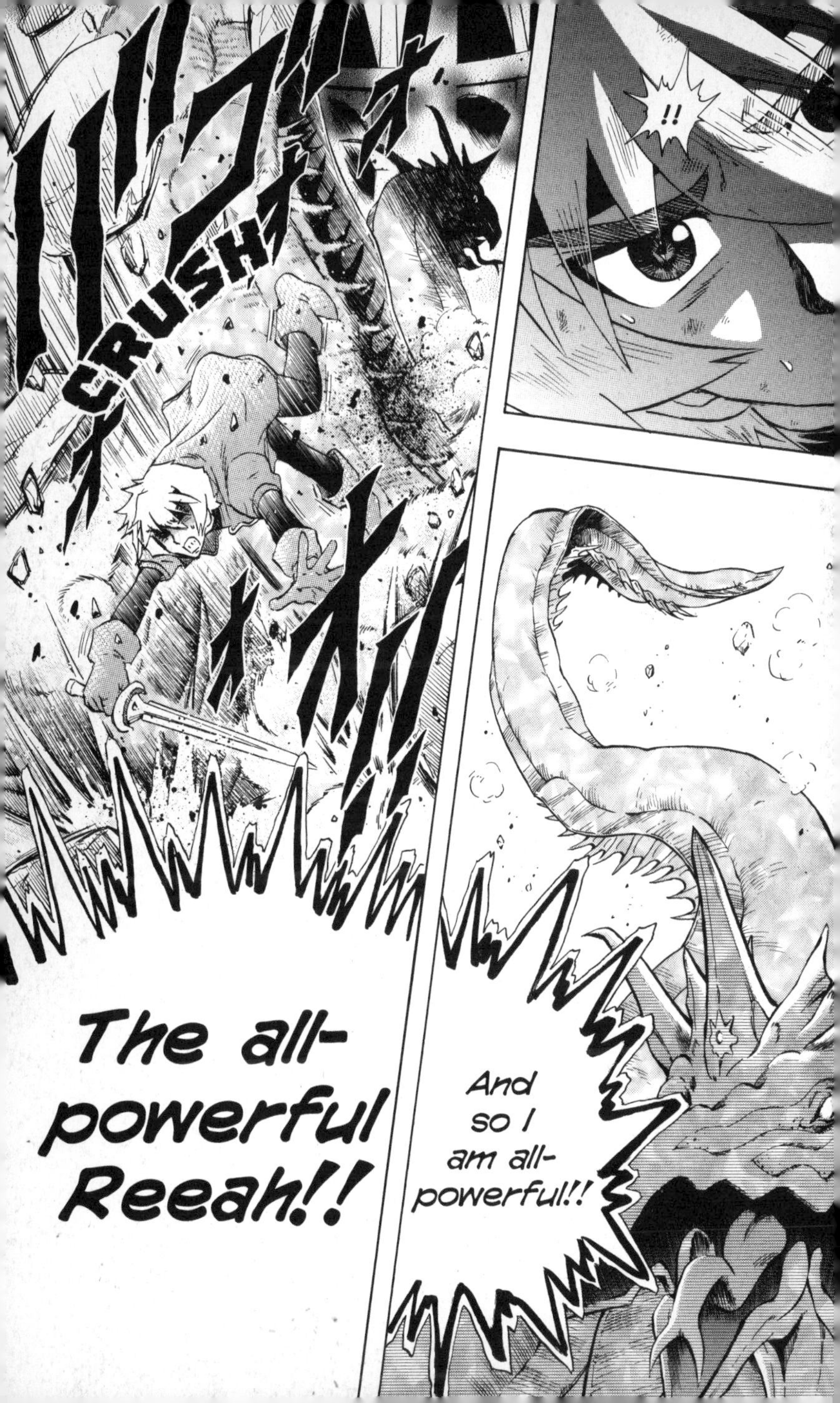
!!
And so I am all-powerful!!
CRUSH
The all-powerful Reeah!!

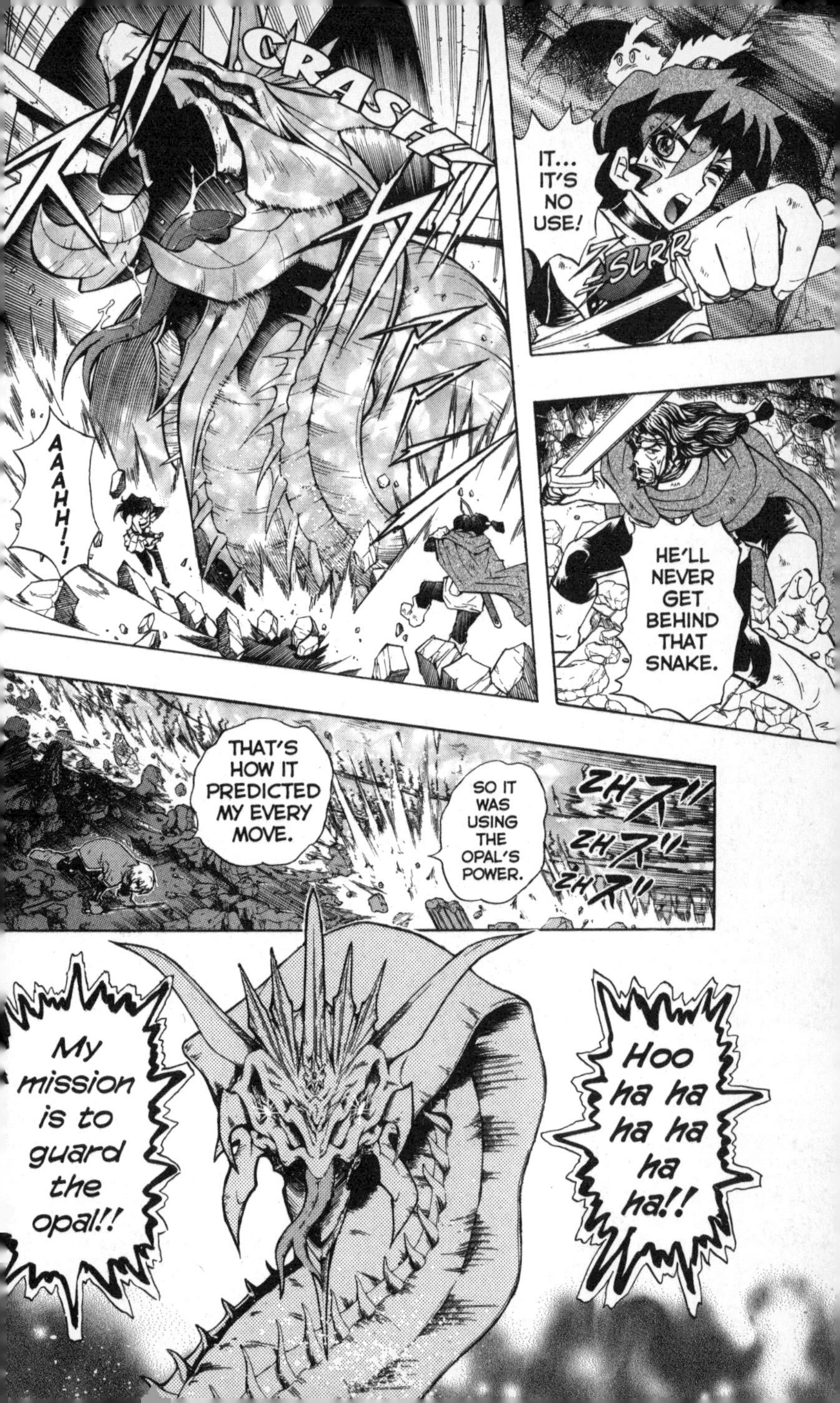
IT... IT'S NO USE!
SLRR
HE'LL NEVER GET BEHIND THAT SNAKE.
CRASH
AAAHH!!
ZH ZH ZH
SO IT WAS USING THE OPAL'S POWER.
THAT'S HOW IT PREDICTED MY EVERY MOVE.
Hoo ha ha ha ha ha ha!!
My mission is to guard the opal!!

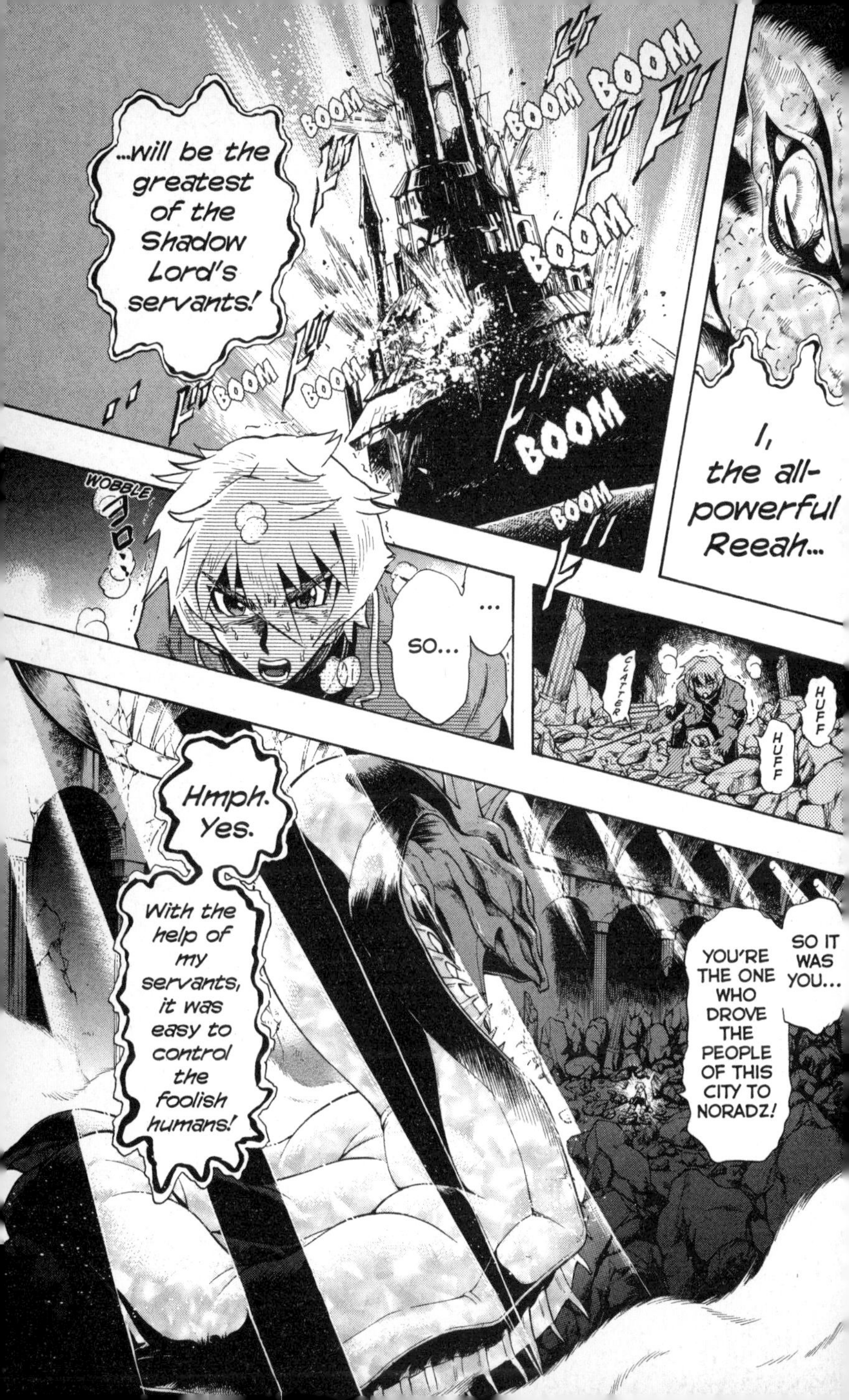
I, the all-powerful Reeah...
...will be the greatest of the Shadow Lord's servants!
BOOM BOOM
BOOM
BOOM
BOOM
BOOM
BOOM
BOOM
BOOM
BOOM
HUFF HUFF
CLATTER
WOBBLE
...
SO...
SO IT WAS YOU...
YOU'RE THE ONE WHO DROVE THE PEOPLE OF THIS CITY TO NORADZ!
Hmph. Yes.
With the help of my servants, it was easy to control the foolish humans!

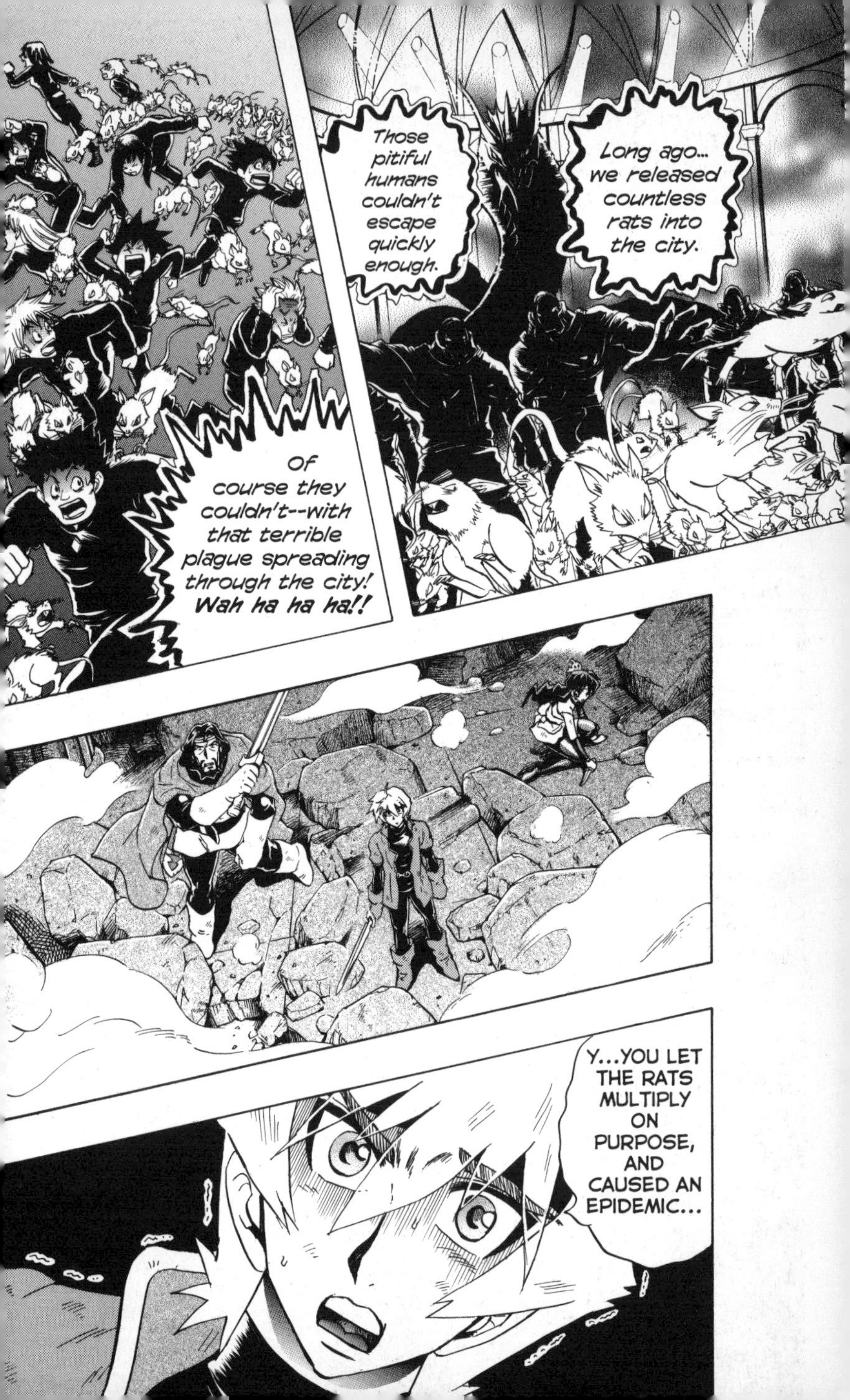
Long ago... we released countless rats into the city.
Those pitiful humans couldn't escape quickly enough.
Of course they couldn't--with that terrible plague spreading through the city! **Wah ha ha ha!!**
Y...YOU LET THE RATS MULTIPLY ON PURPOSE, AND CAUSED AN EPIDEMIC...

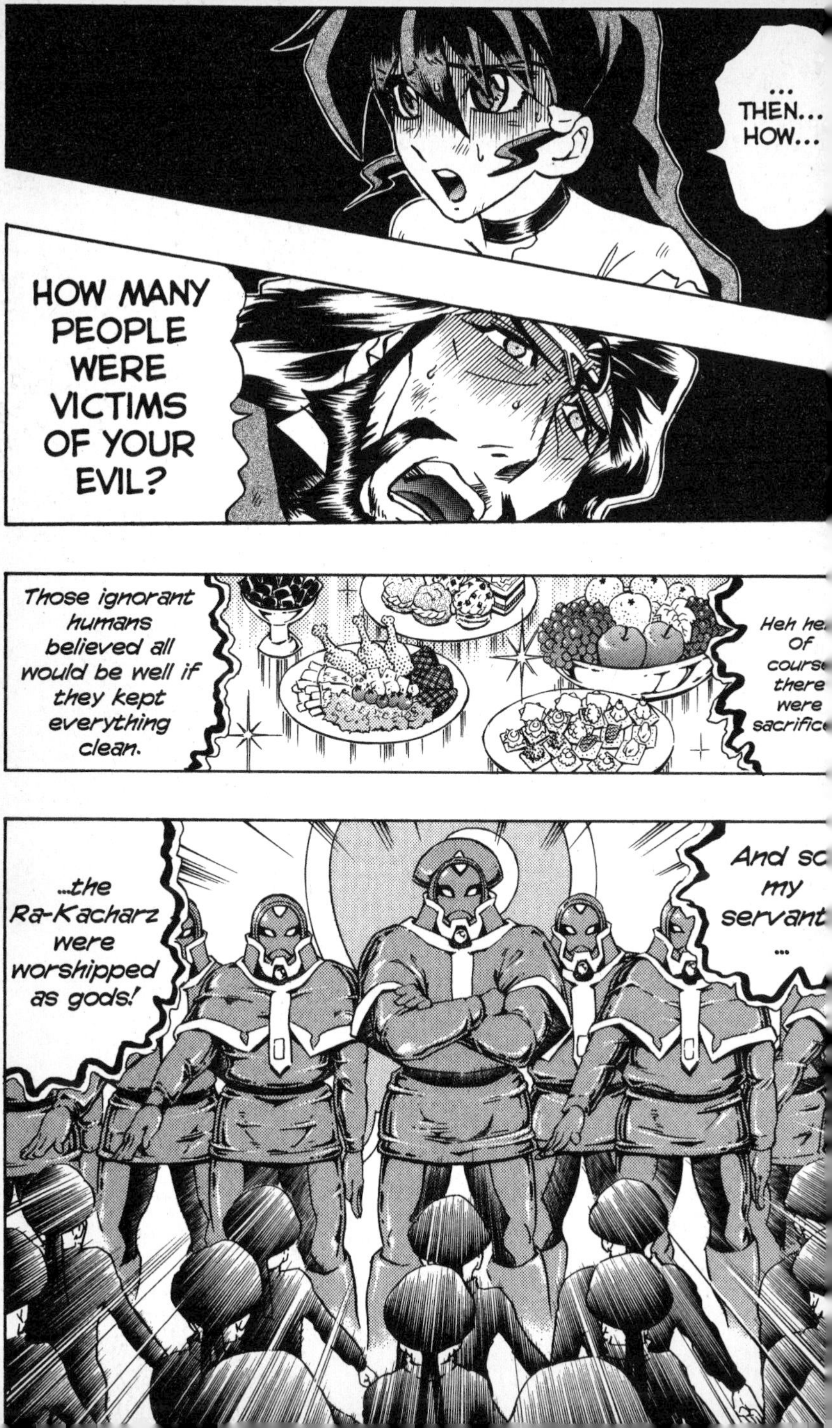
... THEN... HOW...
HOW MANY PEOPLE WERE VICTIMS OF YOUR EVIL?
Heh he Of course there were sacrific
Those ignorant humans believed all would be well if they kept everything clean.
And so my servant ...
...the Ra-Kacharz were worshipped as gods!

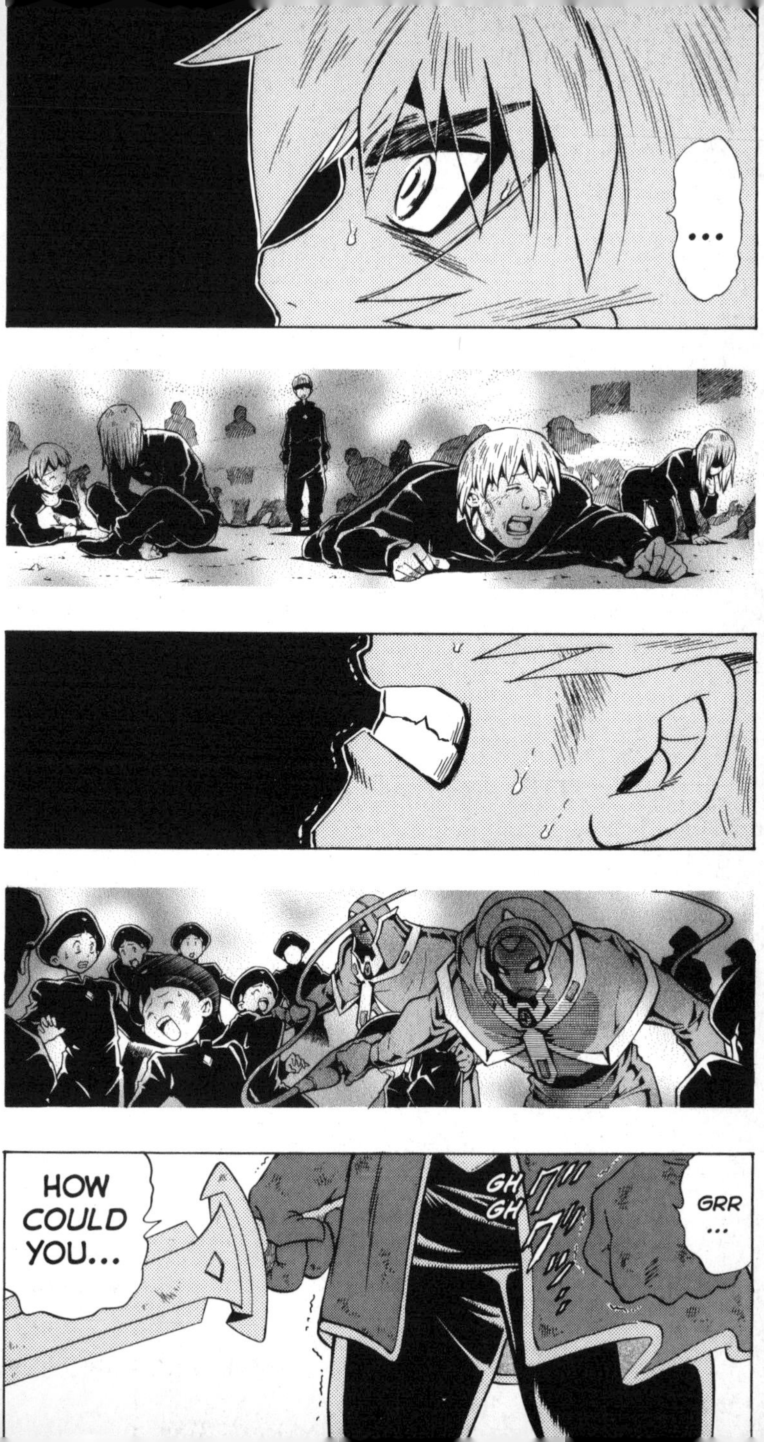
...
GRR ...
GH GH
HOW COULD YOU...

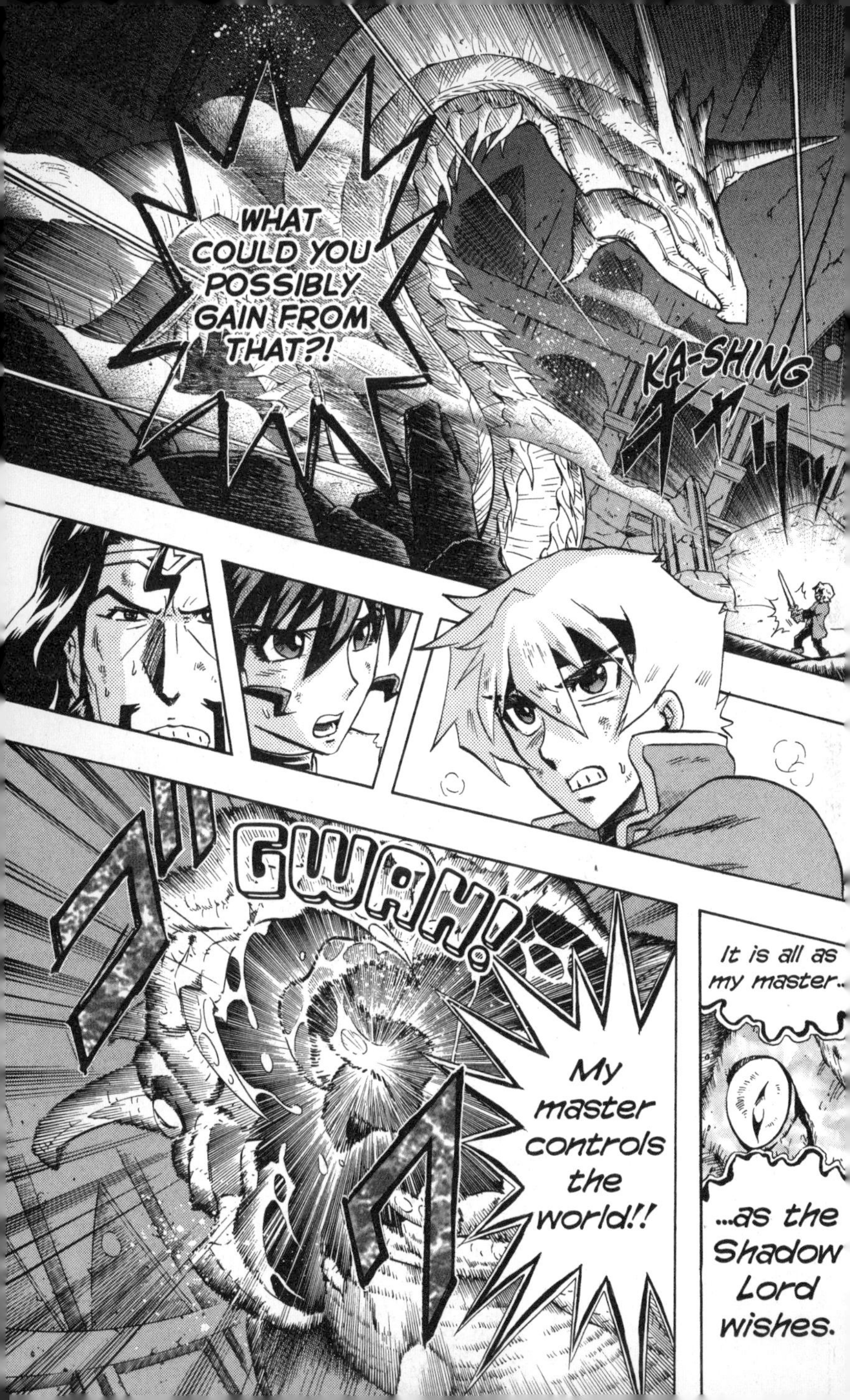
WHAT COULD YOU POSSIBLY GAIN FROM THAT?!
KA-SHING
It is all as my master...
...as the Shadow Lord wishes.
GWAAH!
My master controls the world!!

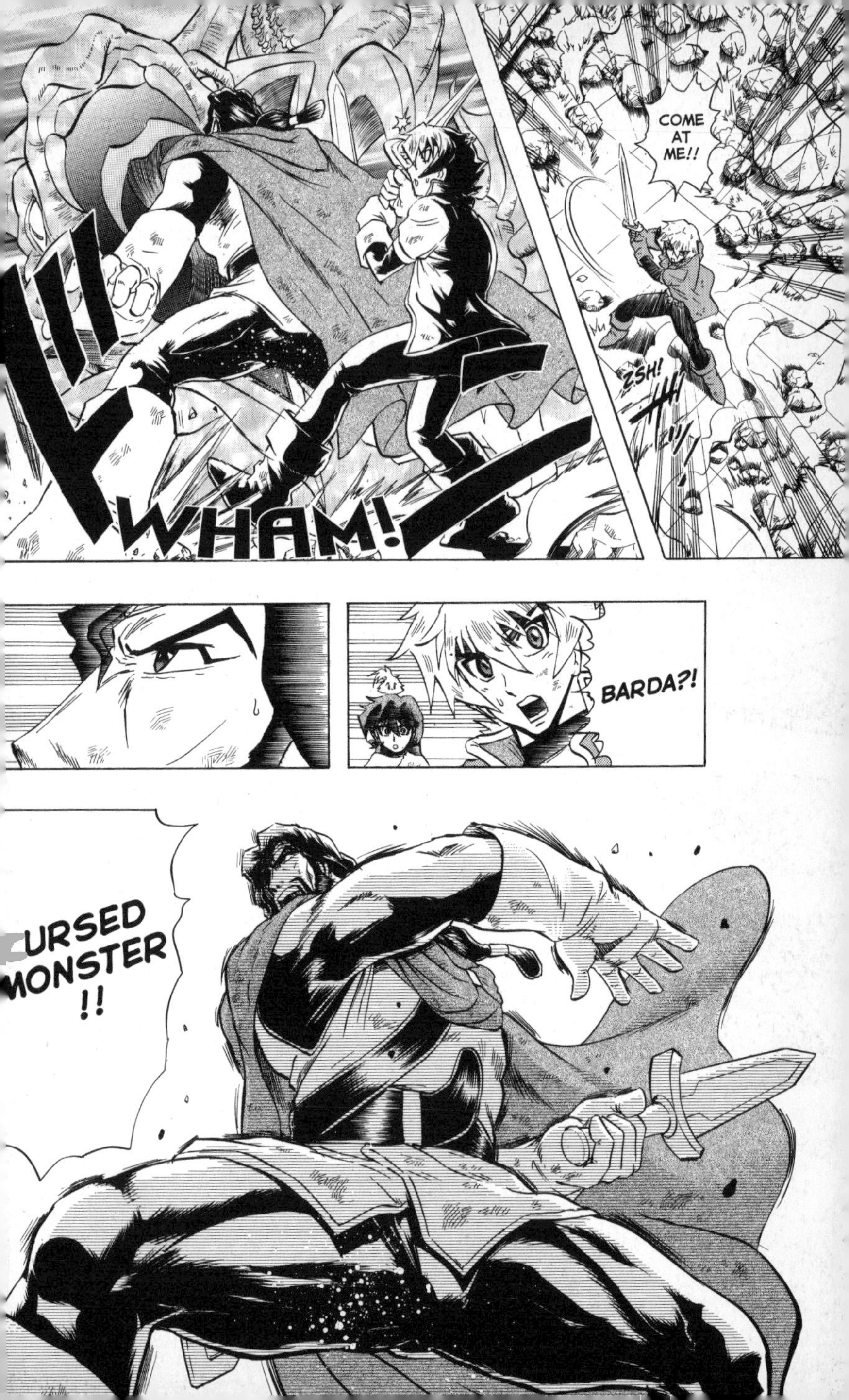
COME AT ME!!
ZSH!
WHAM!
BARDA?!
CURSED MONSTER !!

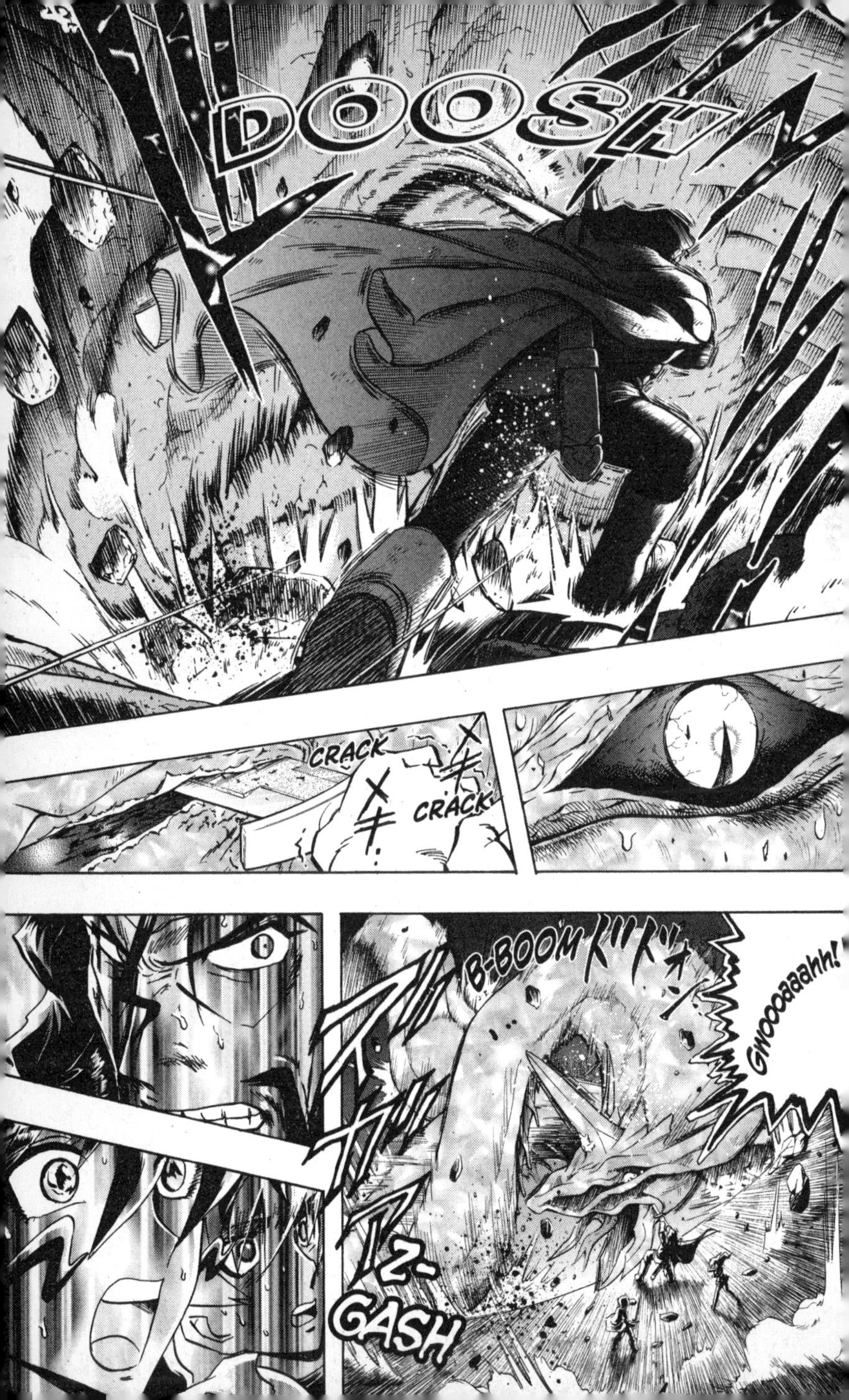
DOOSH
CRACK
CRACK
B-BOOM
GWOOOaaahh!
Z-GASH

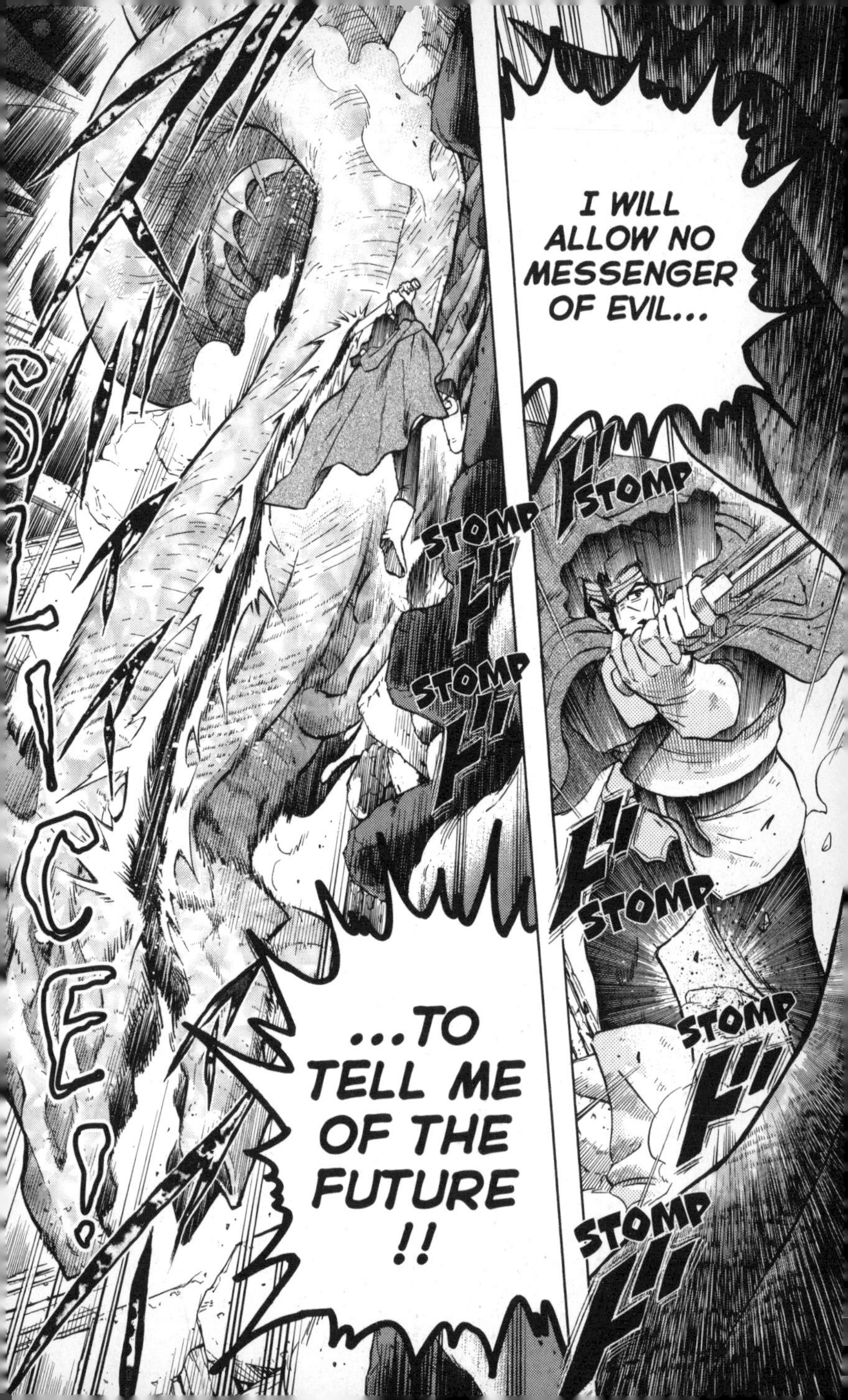
I WILL ALLOW NO MESSENGER OF EVIL...
STOMP
STOMP
STOMP
STOMP
STOMP
STOMP
...TO TELL ME OF THE FUTURE !!
SLICE!

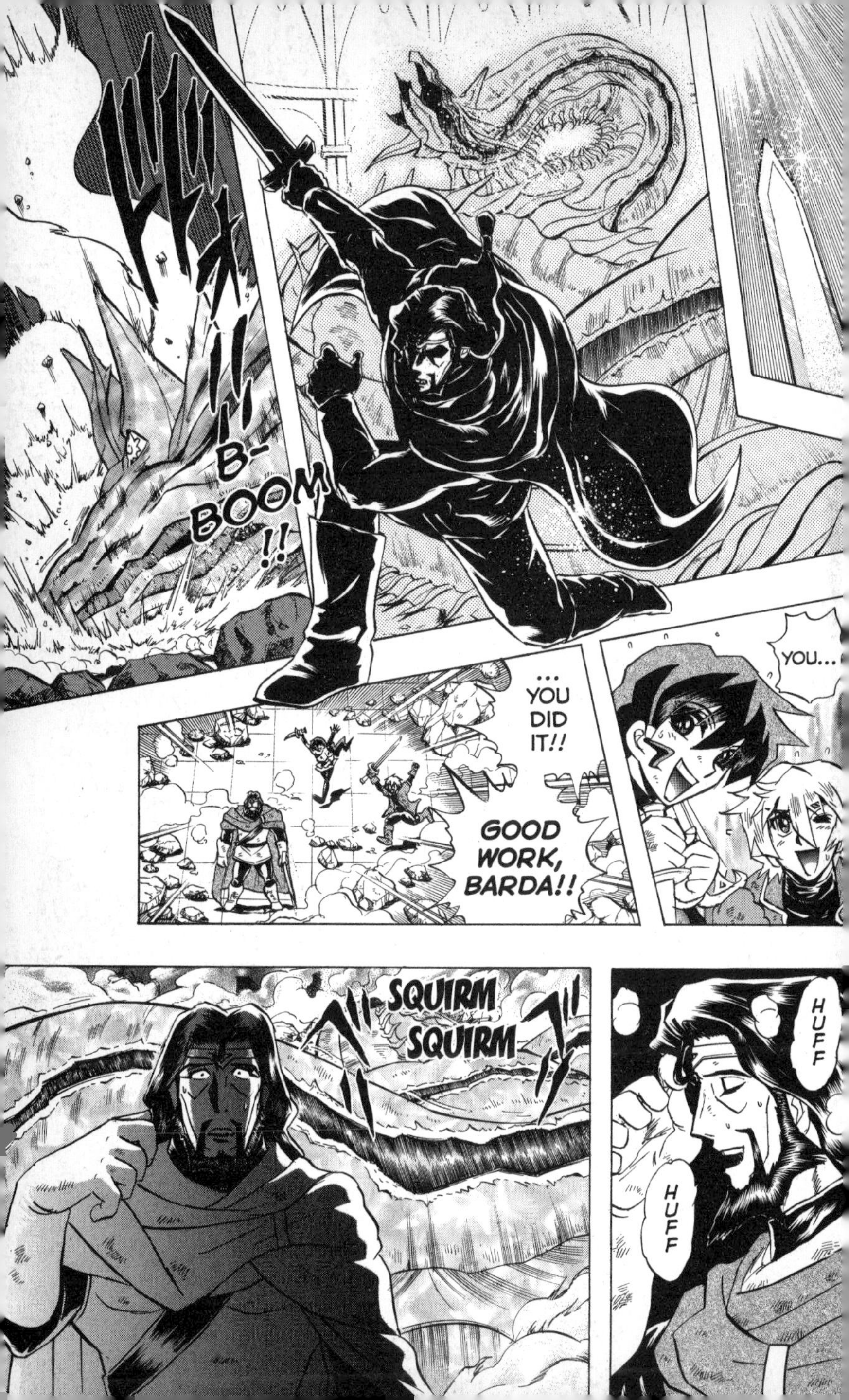
B-BOOM!!
YOU...
...YOU DID IT!!
GOOD WORK, BARDA!!
HUFF
HUFF
SQUIRM SQUIRM

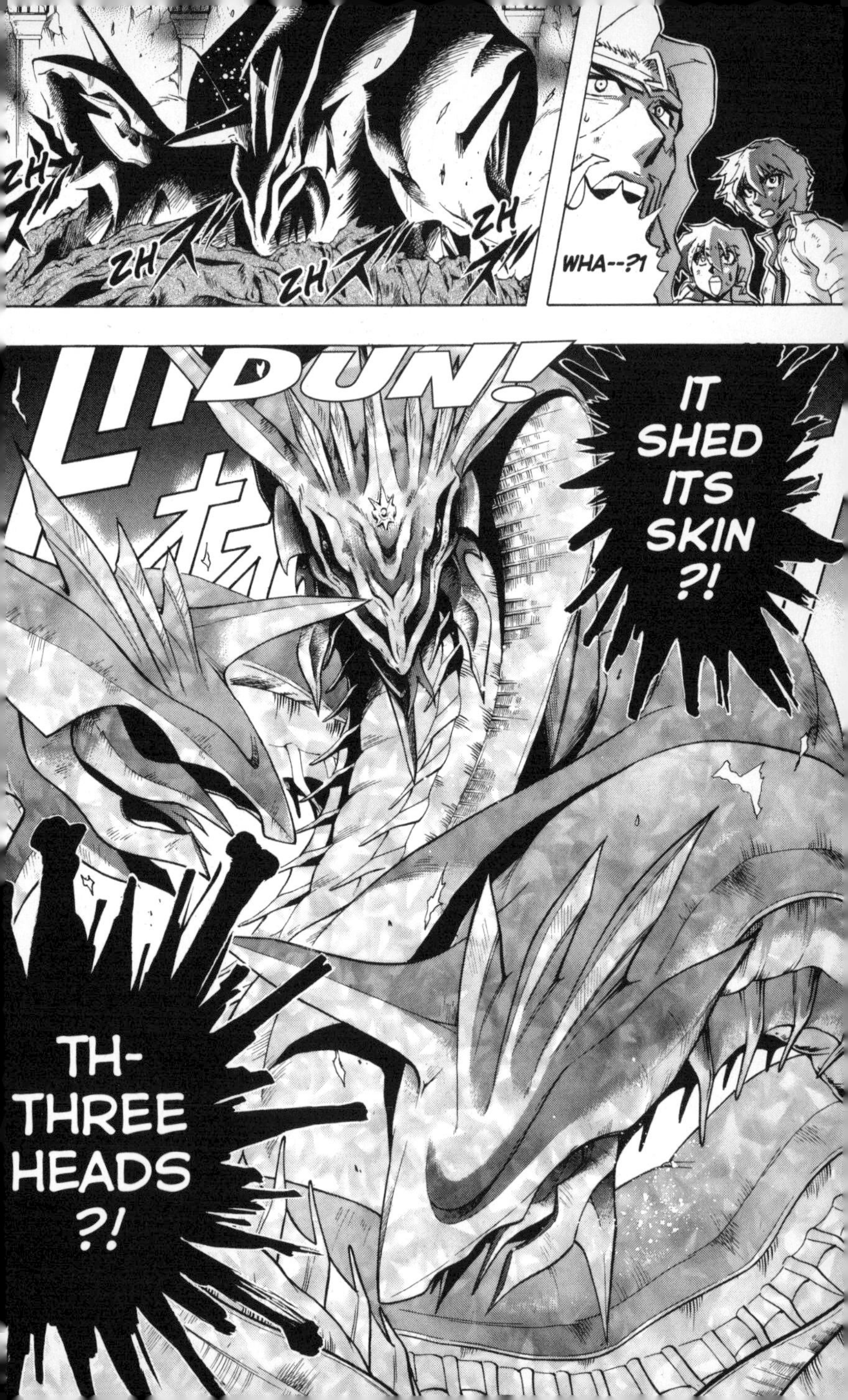
WHA--?!
ZH
ZH
ZH
ZH
DUN!
IT SHED ITS SKIN?!
TH- THREE HEADS?!

DELTORA QUEST
デルトラクエスト

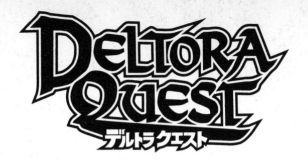

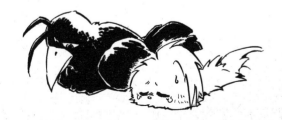

Chapter 28: The Future

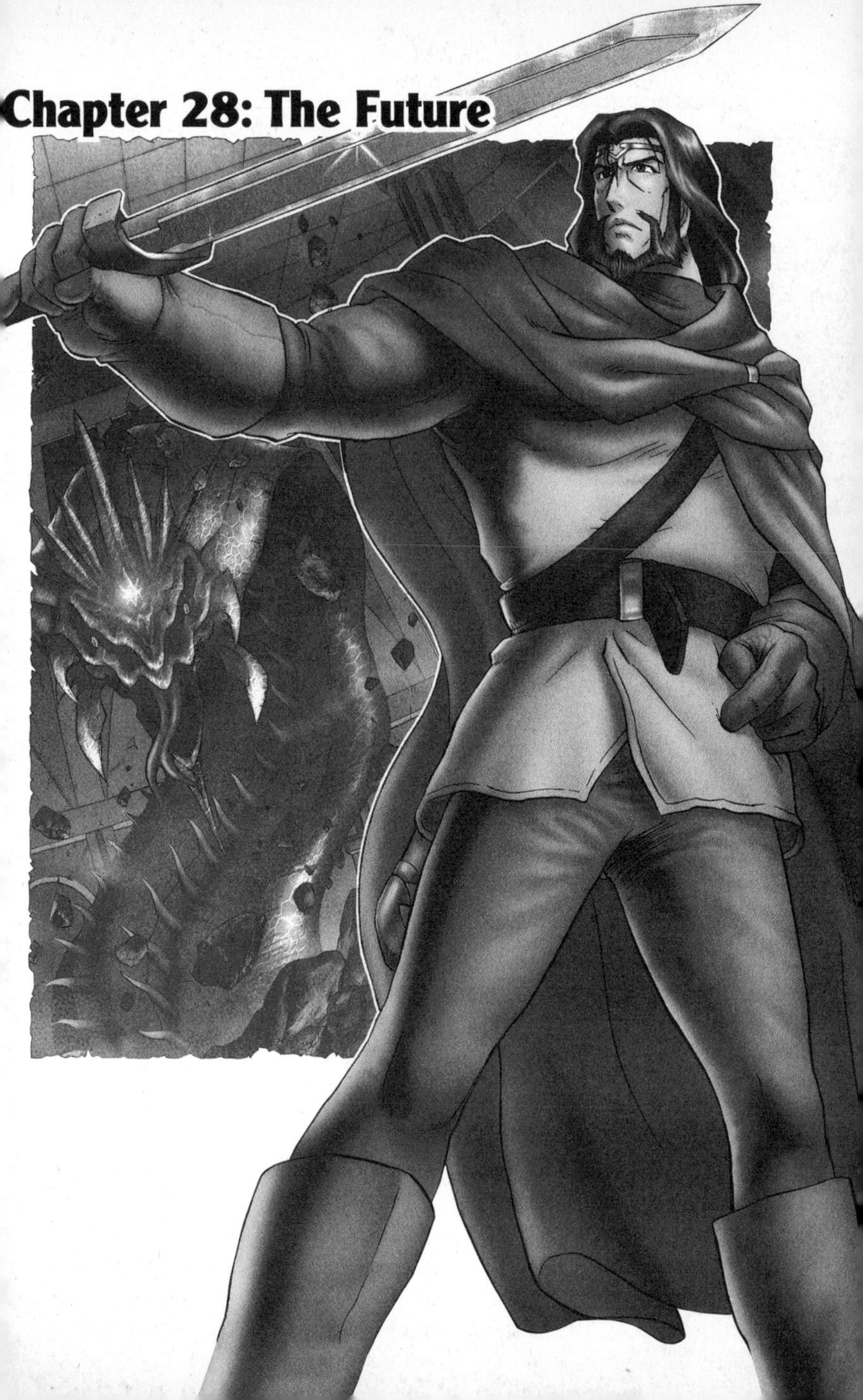

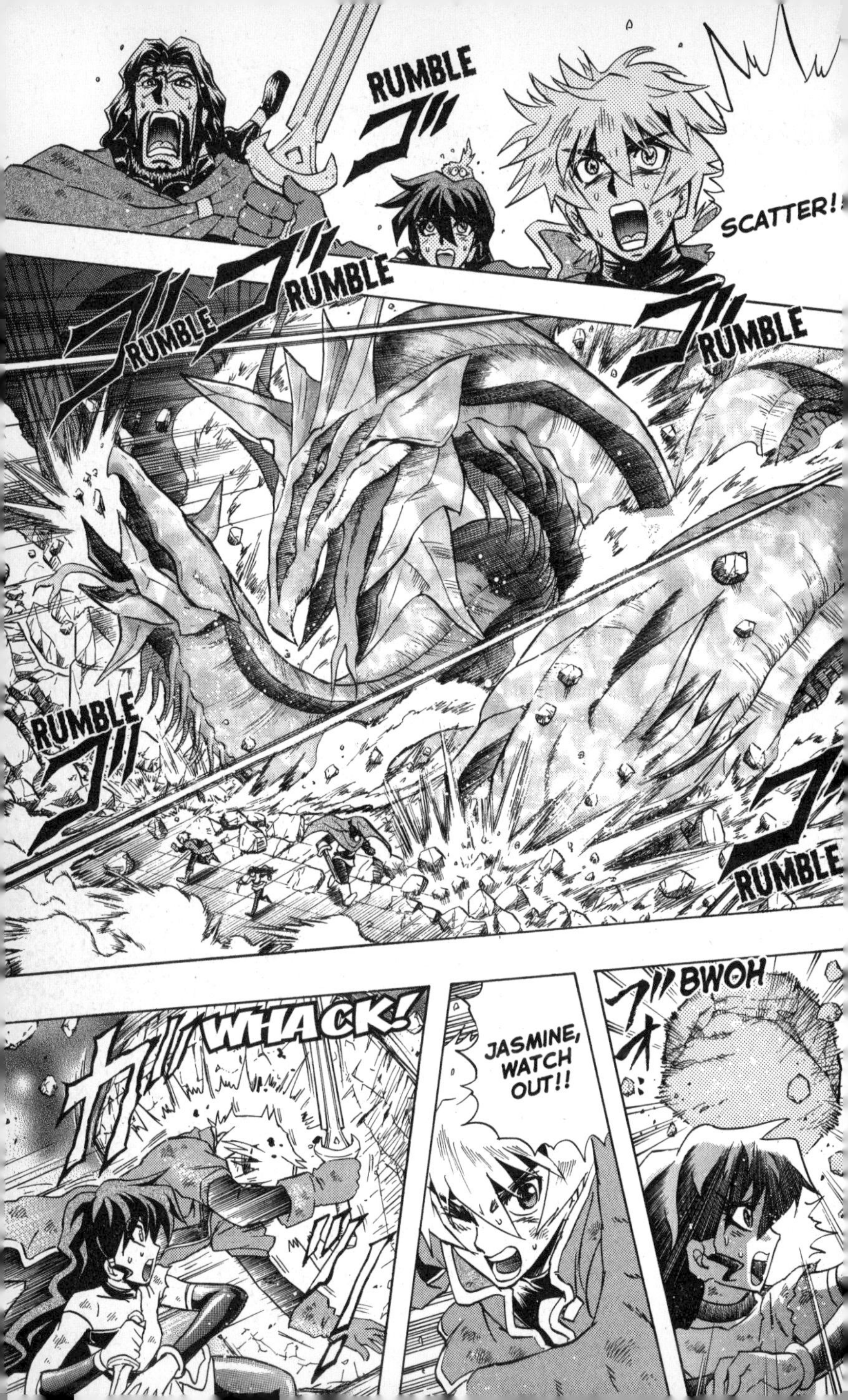
SCATTER!!
RUMBLE
RUMBLE
RUMBLE
RUMBLE
RUMBLE
RUMBLE
BWOH
JASMINE, WATCH OUT!!
WHACK!

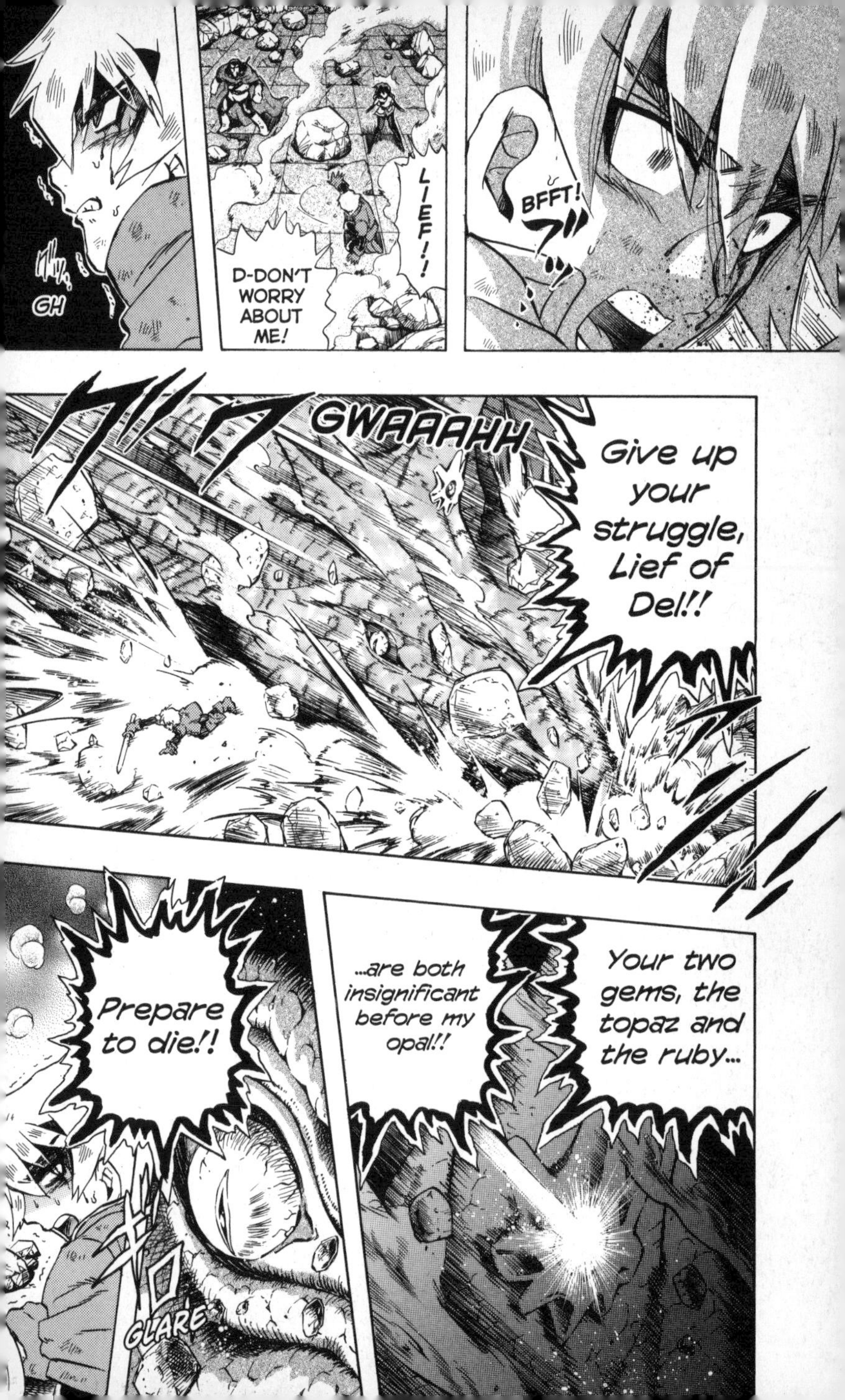
BFFT!
LIEF!!
D-DON'T WORRY ABOUT ME!
GH
GWAAAAHH
Give up your struggle, Lief of Del!!
Your two gems, the topaz and the ruby...
...are both insignificant before my opal!!
Prepare to die!!
GLARE

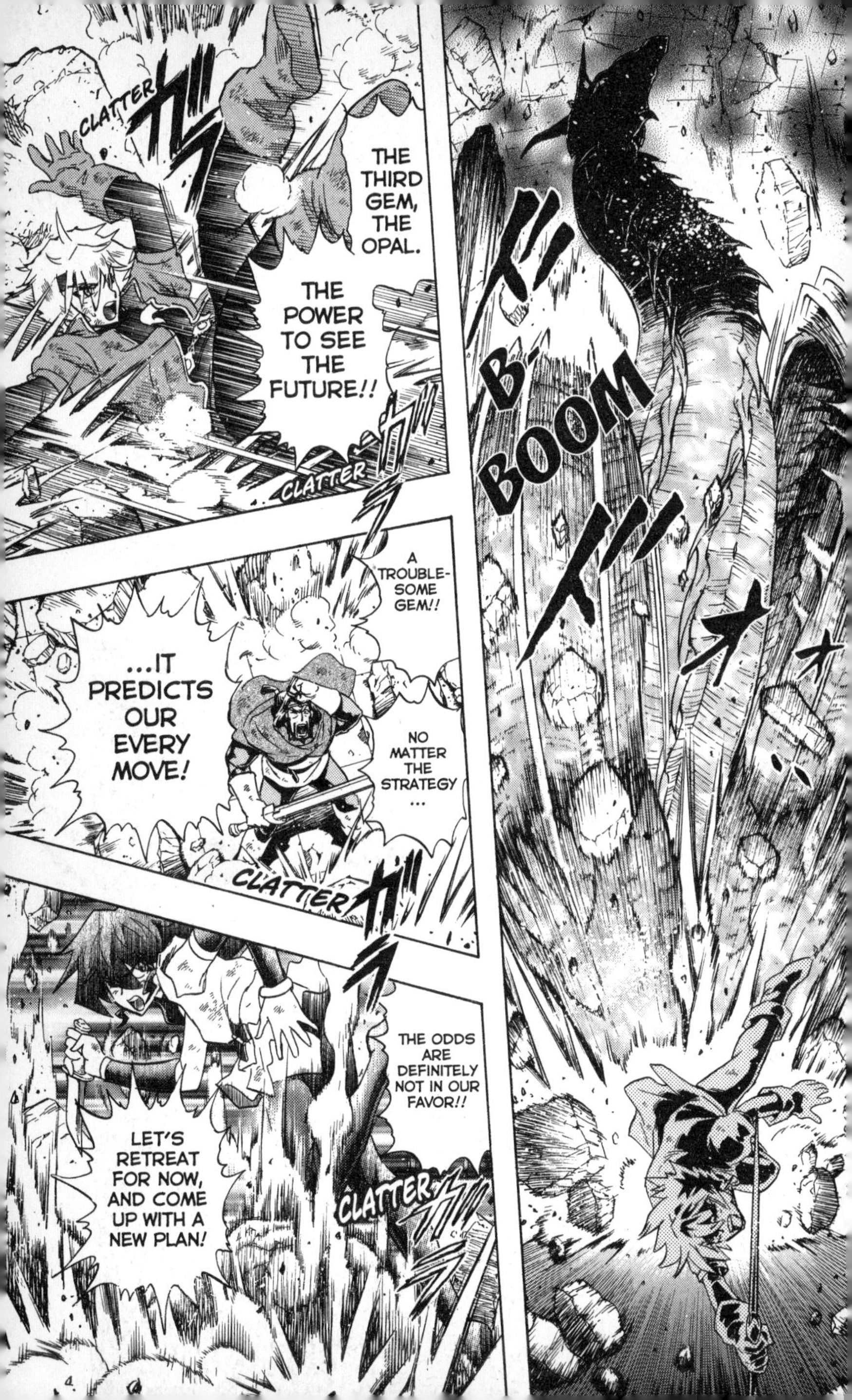
B-BOOM
CLATTER
THE THIRD GEM, THE OPAL.
THE POWER TO SEE THE FUTURE!!
CLATTER
A TROUBLE-SOME GEM!!
NO MATTER THE STRATEGY...
...IT PREDICTS OUR EVERY MOVE!
CLATTER
THE ODDS ARE DEFINITELY NOT IN OUR FAVOR!!
CLATTER
LET'S RETREAT FOR NOW, AND COME UP WITH A NEW PLAN!

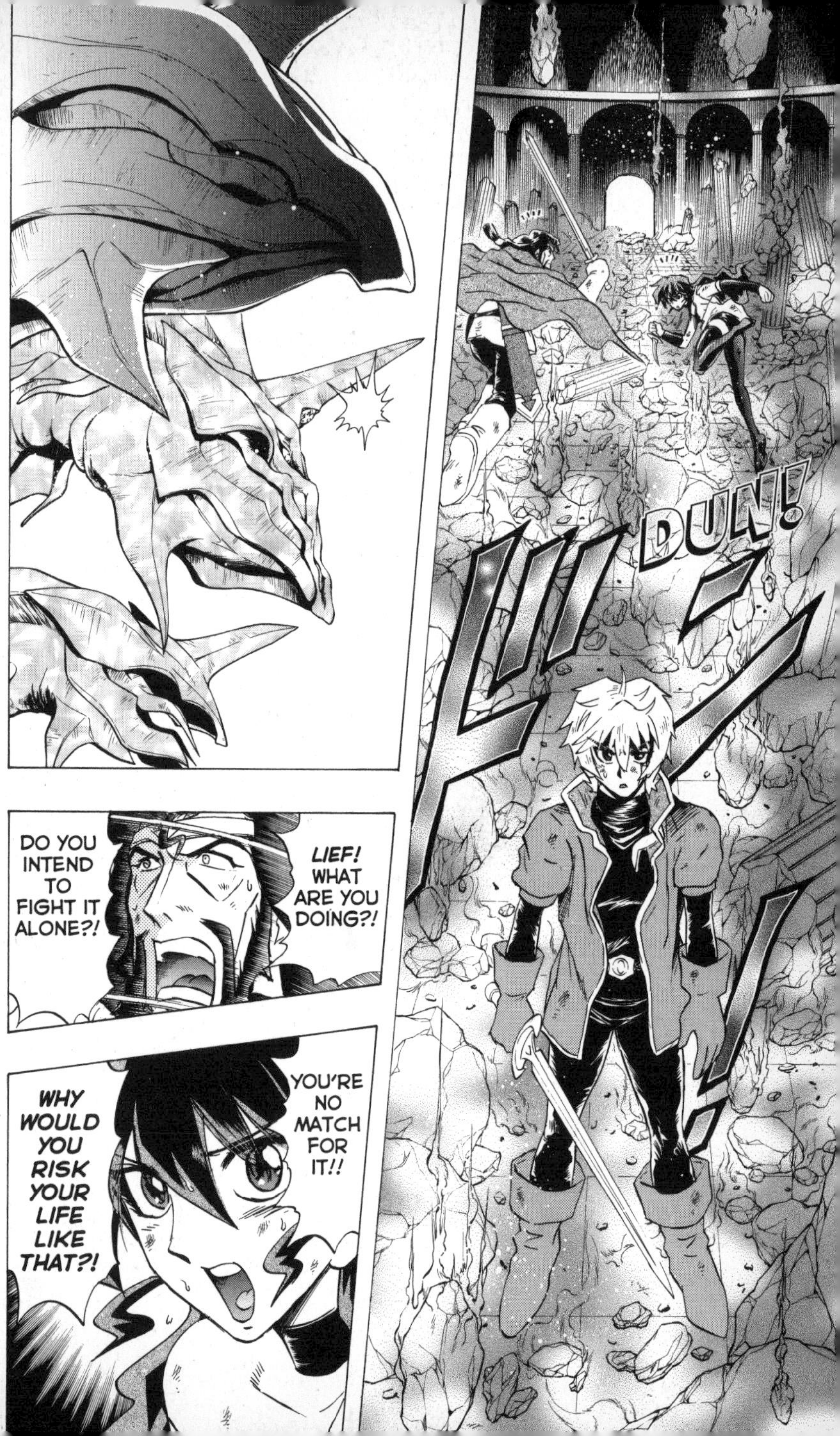
DUN!
LIEF! WHAT ARE YOU DOING?!
DO YOU INTEND TO FIGHT IT ALONE?!
YOU'RE NO MATCH FOR IT!!
WHY WOULD YOU RISK YOUR LIFE LIKE THAT?!

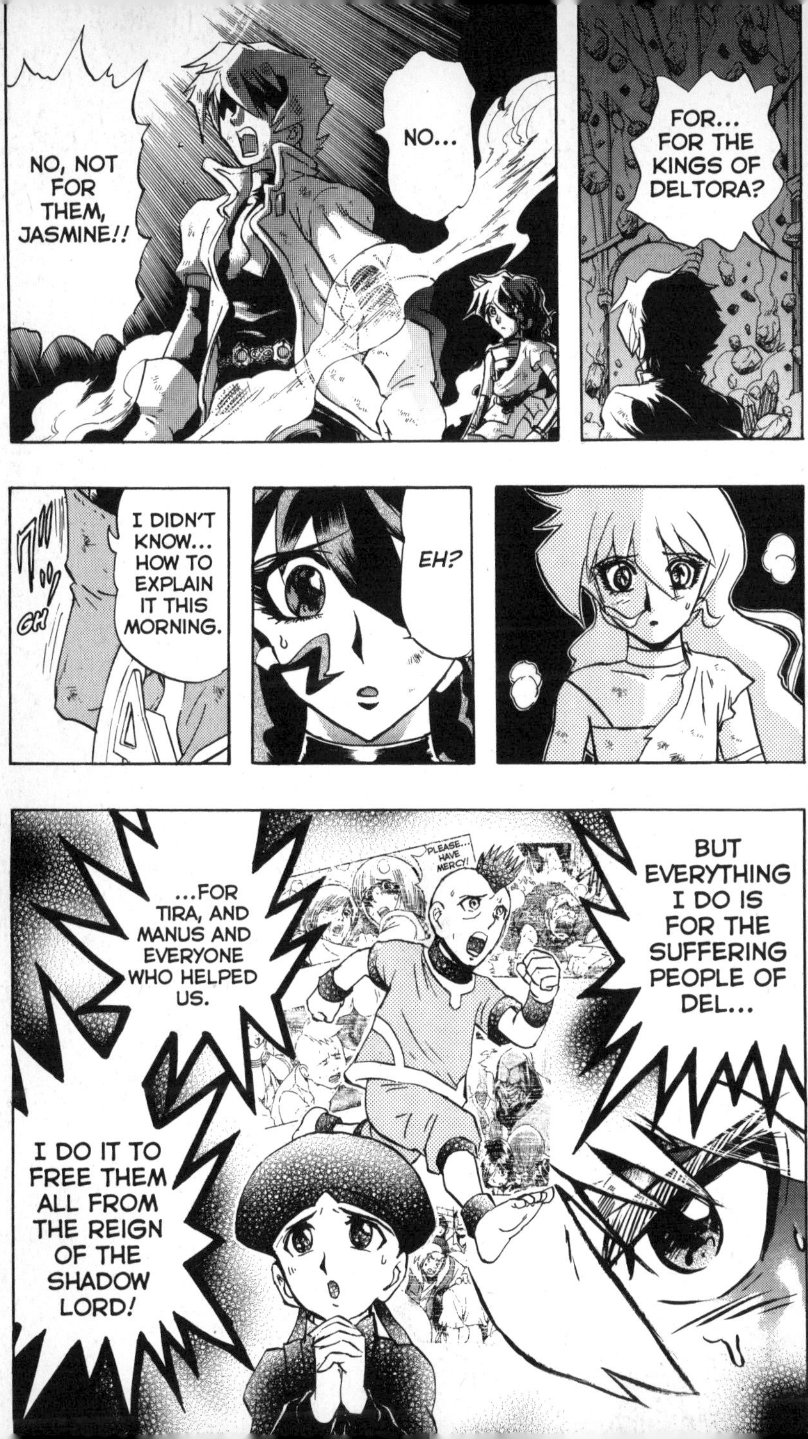
FOR... FOR THE KINGS OF DELTORA?
NO...
NO, NOT FOR THEM, JASMINE!!
EH?
I DIDN'T KNOW... HOW TO EXPLAIN IT THIS MORNING.
GH
BUT EVERYTHING I DO IS FOR THE SUFFERING PEOPLE OF DEL...
PLEASE... HAVE MERCY!
...FOR TIRA, AND MANUS AND EVERYONE WHO HELPED US.
I DO IT TO FREE THEM ALL FROM THE REIGN OF THE SHADOW LORD!

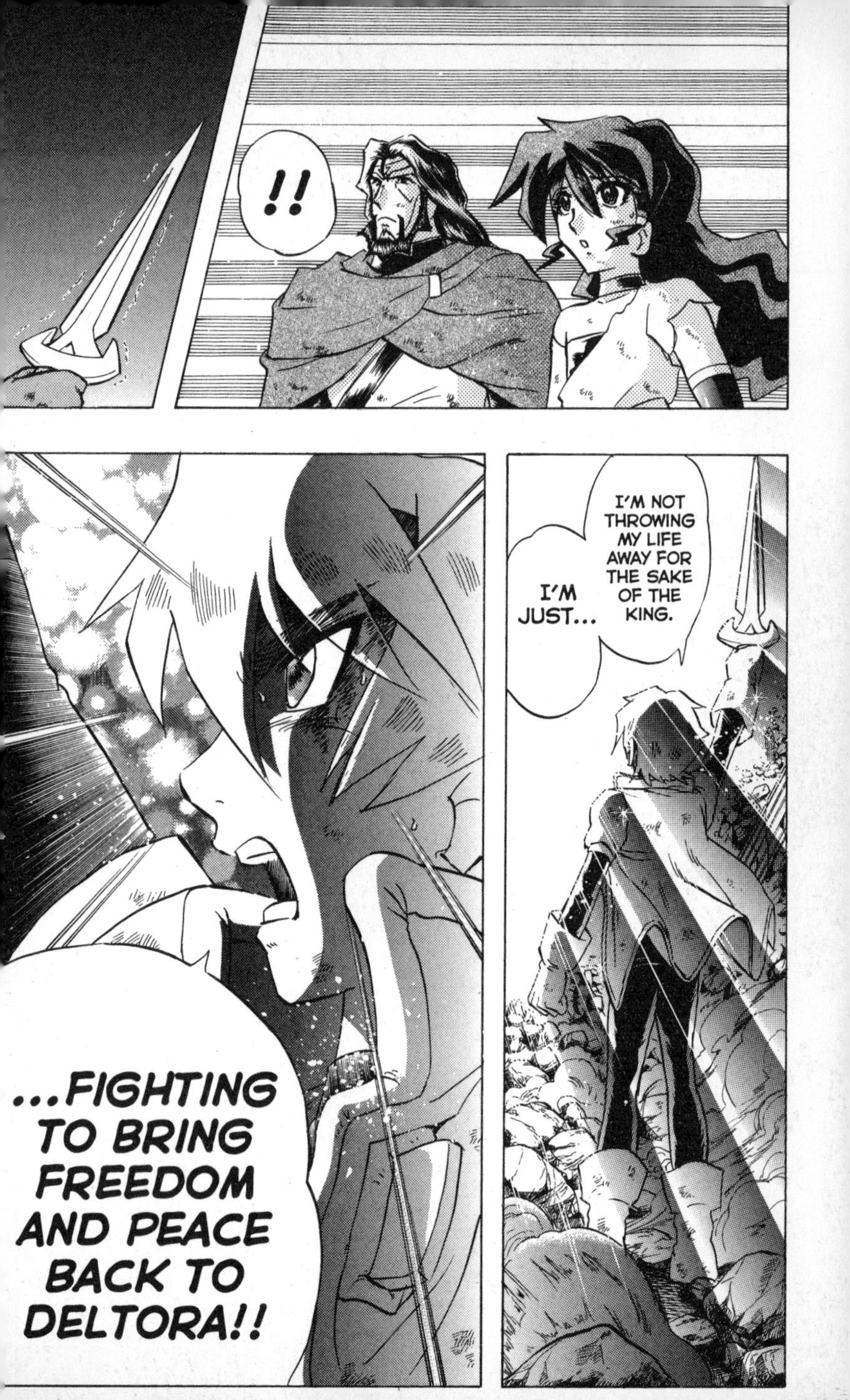
!!
I'M NOT THROWING MY LIFE AWAY FOR THE SAKE OF THE KING.
I'M JUST...
...FIGHTING TO BRING FREEDOM AND PEACE BACK TO DELTORA!!

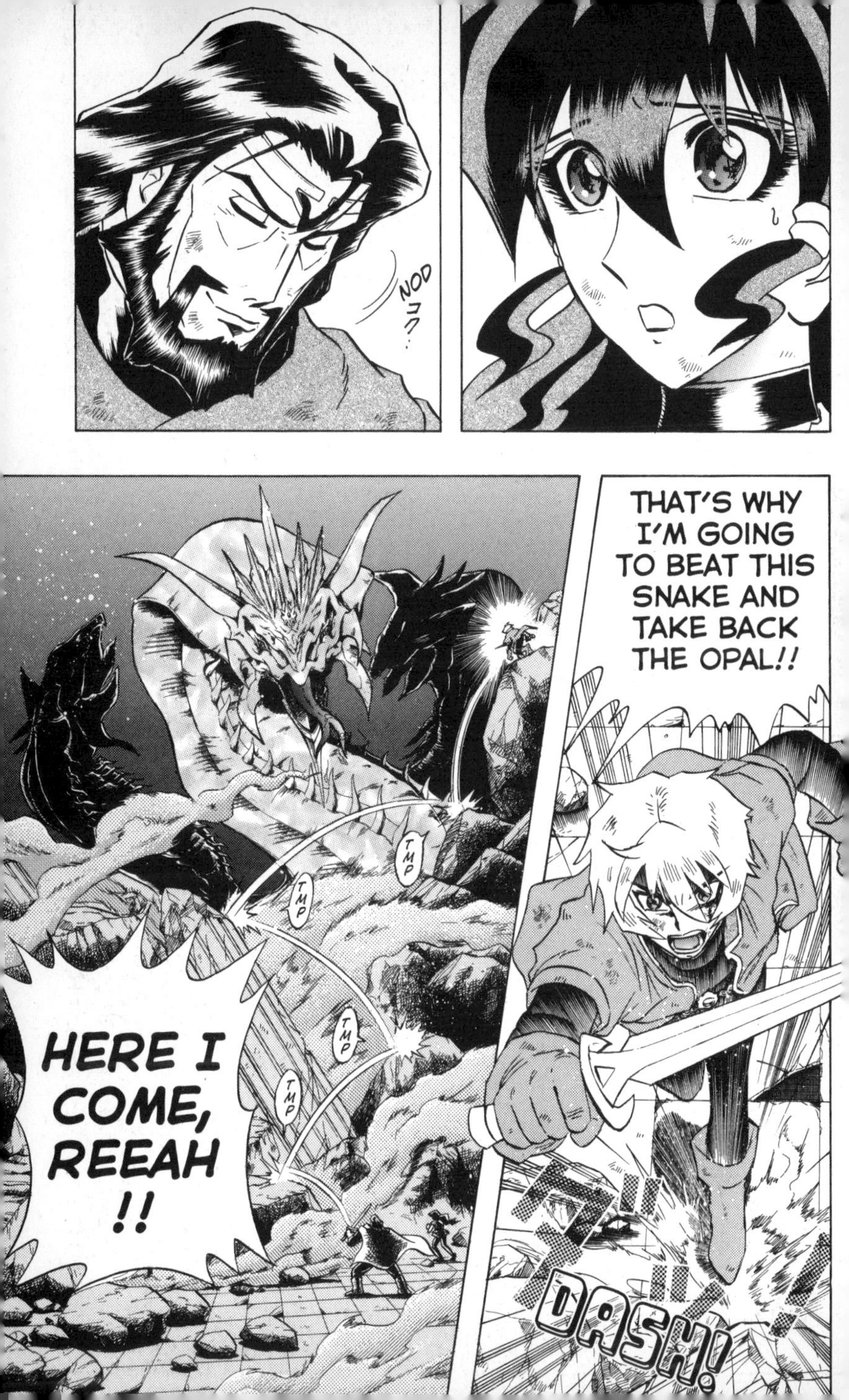
NOD
THAT'S WHY I'M GOING TO BEAT THIS SNAKE AND TAKE BACK THE OPAL!!
DASH!
TMP
TMP
TMP
TMP
HERE I COME, REEAH !!

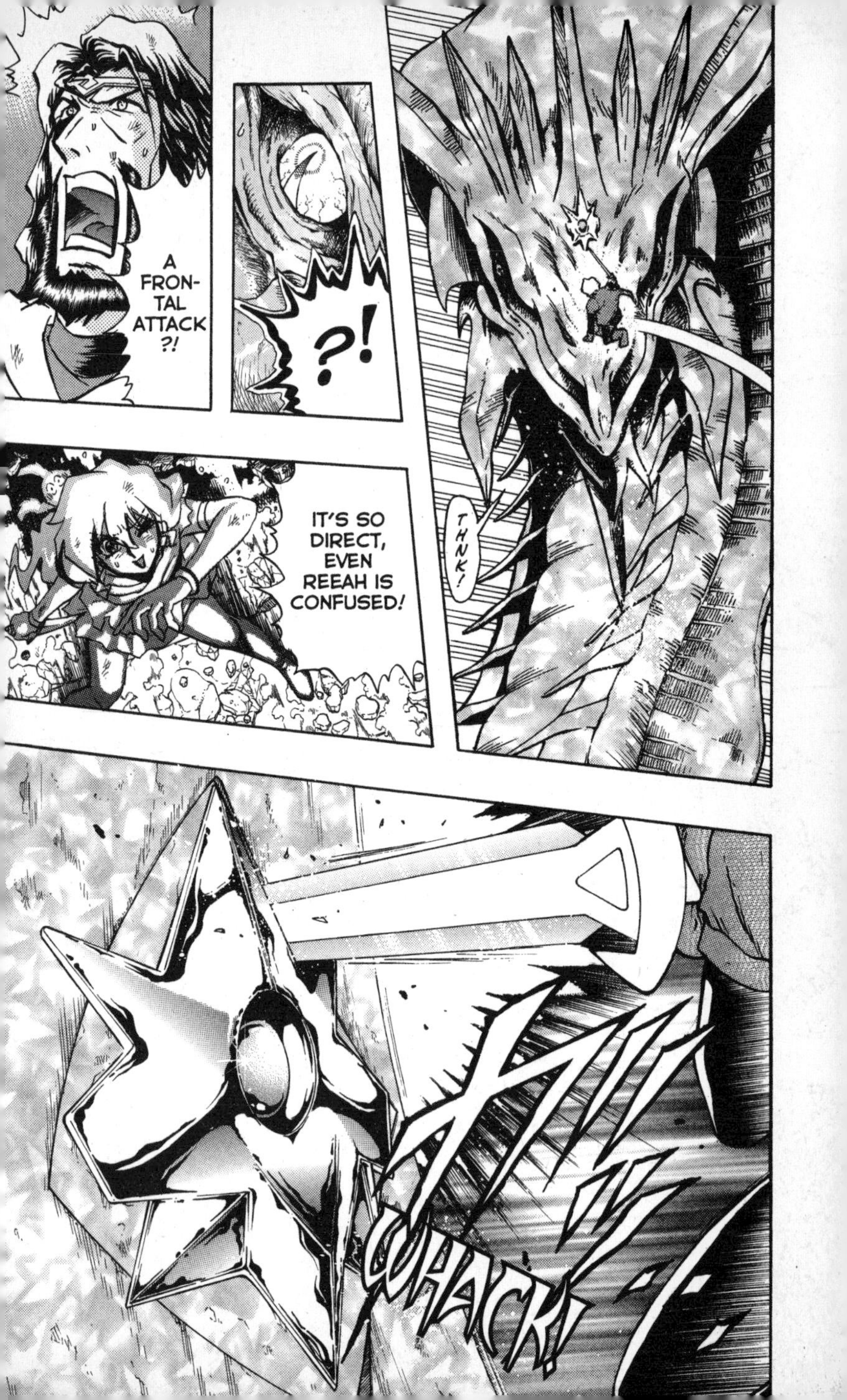
THNK!
?!
A FRONTAL ATTACK?!
IT'S SO DIRECT, EVEN REEAH IS CONFUSED!
GUHACK!

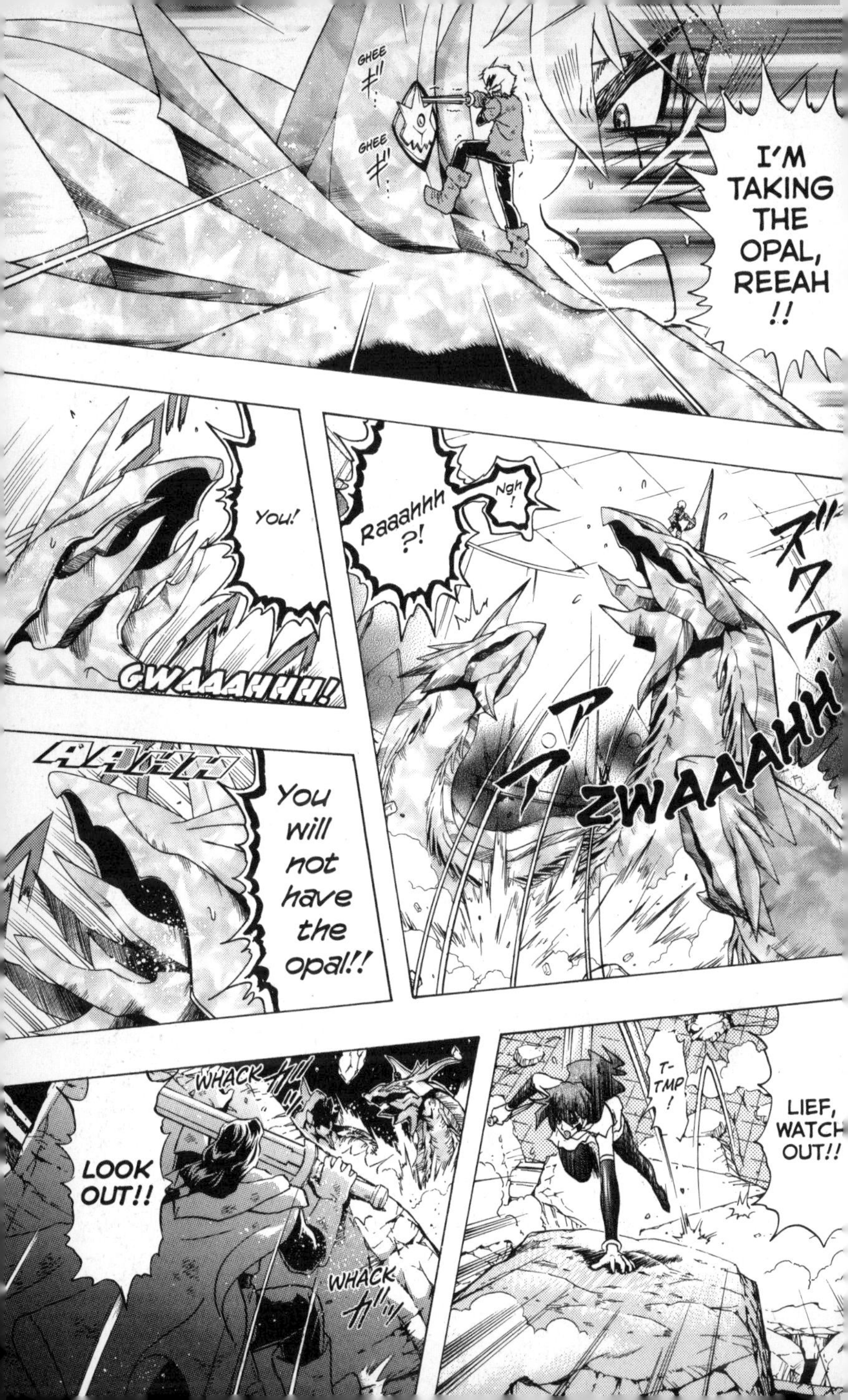
I'M TAKING THE OPAL, REEAH!!
GHEE
GHEE
Ngh!
Raaahhh?!
ZWAAAAHH
You!
GWAAAAHHH!
AAHH
You will not have the opal!!
LIEF, WATCH OUT!!
T-TMP!
WHACK
LOOK OUT!!
WHACK

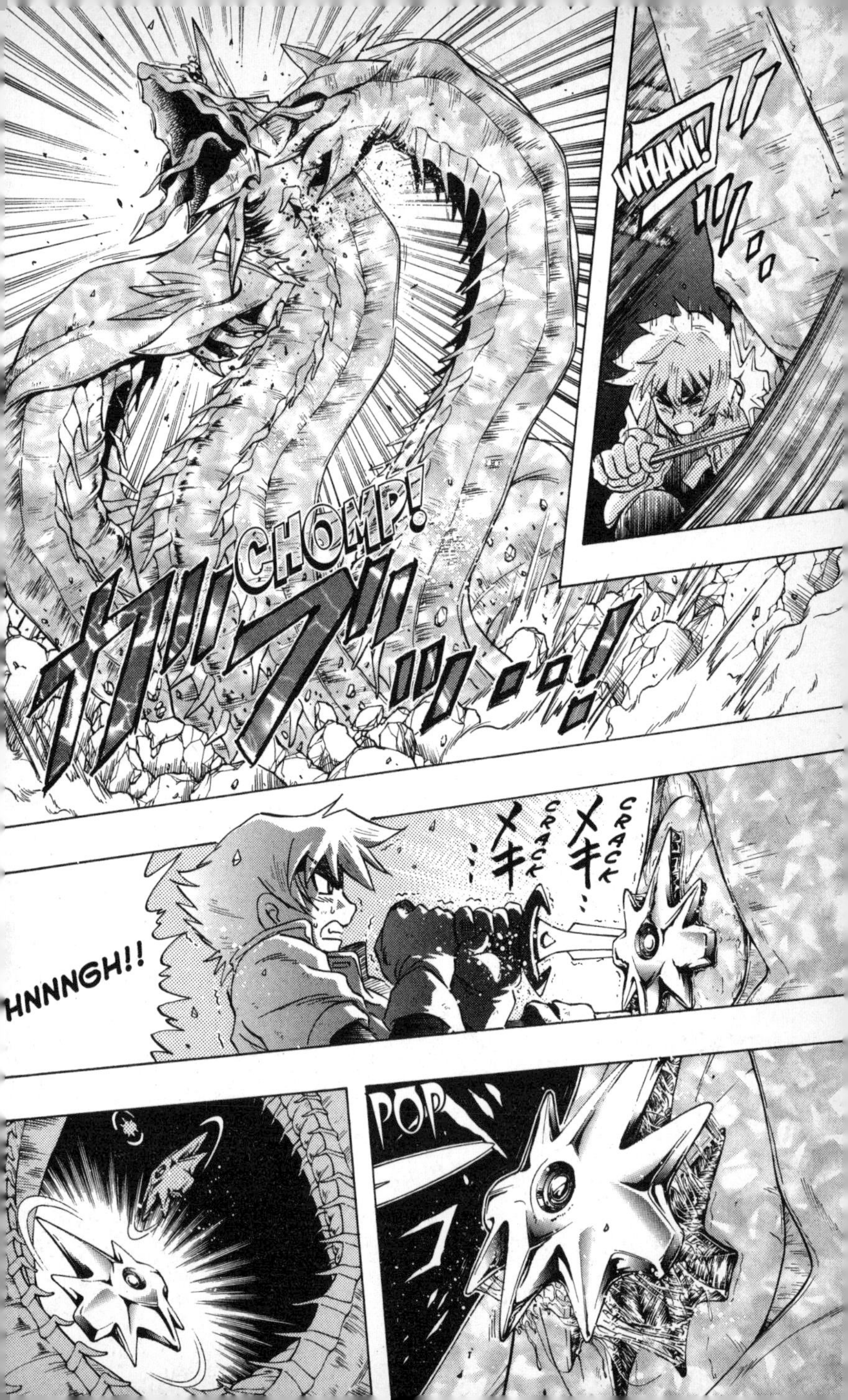
WHAM!
CHOMP!
CRACK
メキ…
CRACK
メキ…
HNNNGH!!
POP

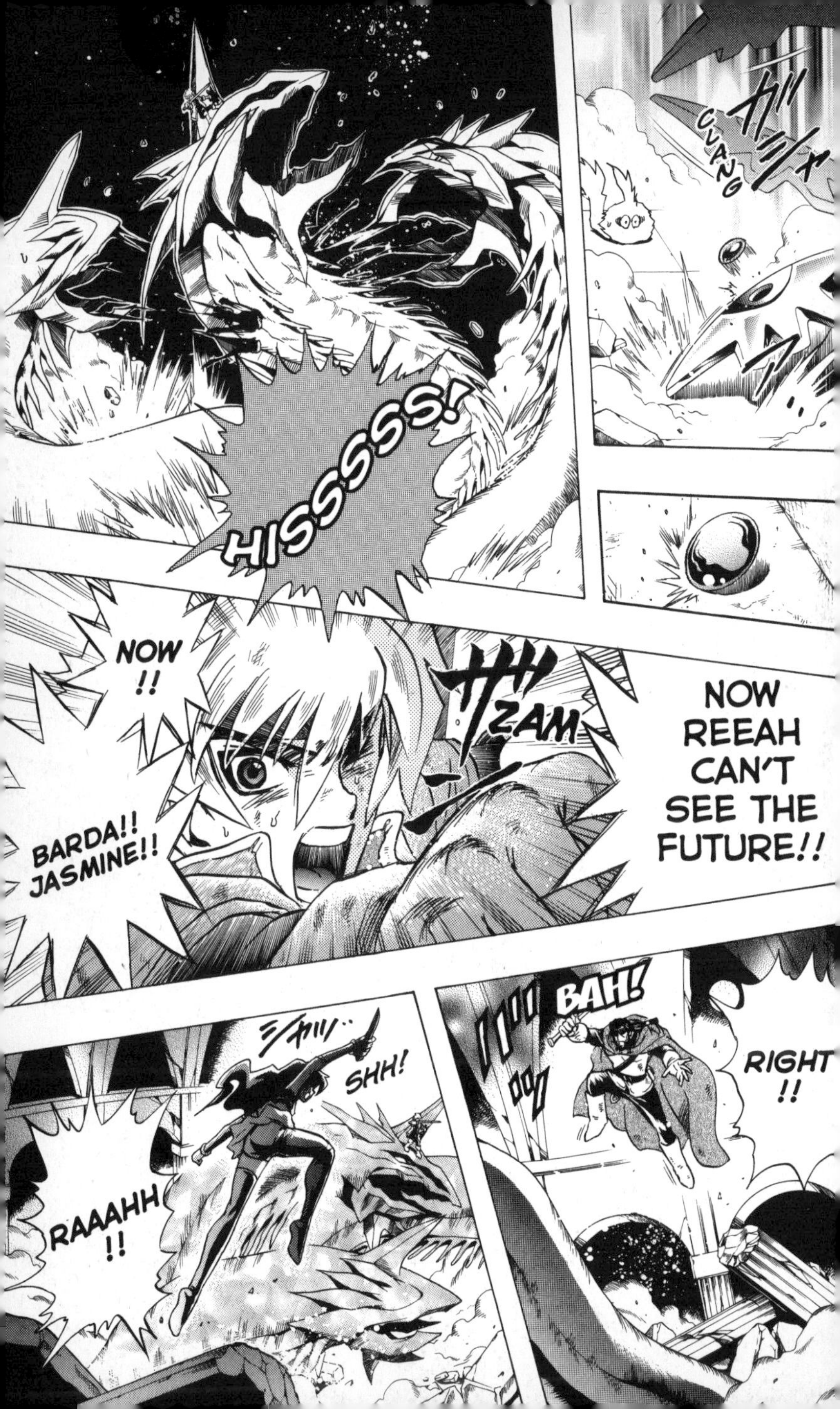
CLANG
HISSSSSS!
NOW REEAH CAN'T SEE THE FUTURE!!
ZAM
NOW !!
BARDA!! JASMINE!!
BAH!
RIGHT !!
SHH!
RAAAHH !!

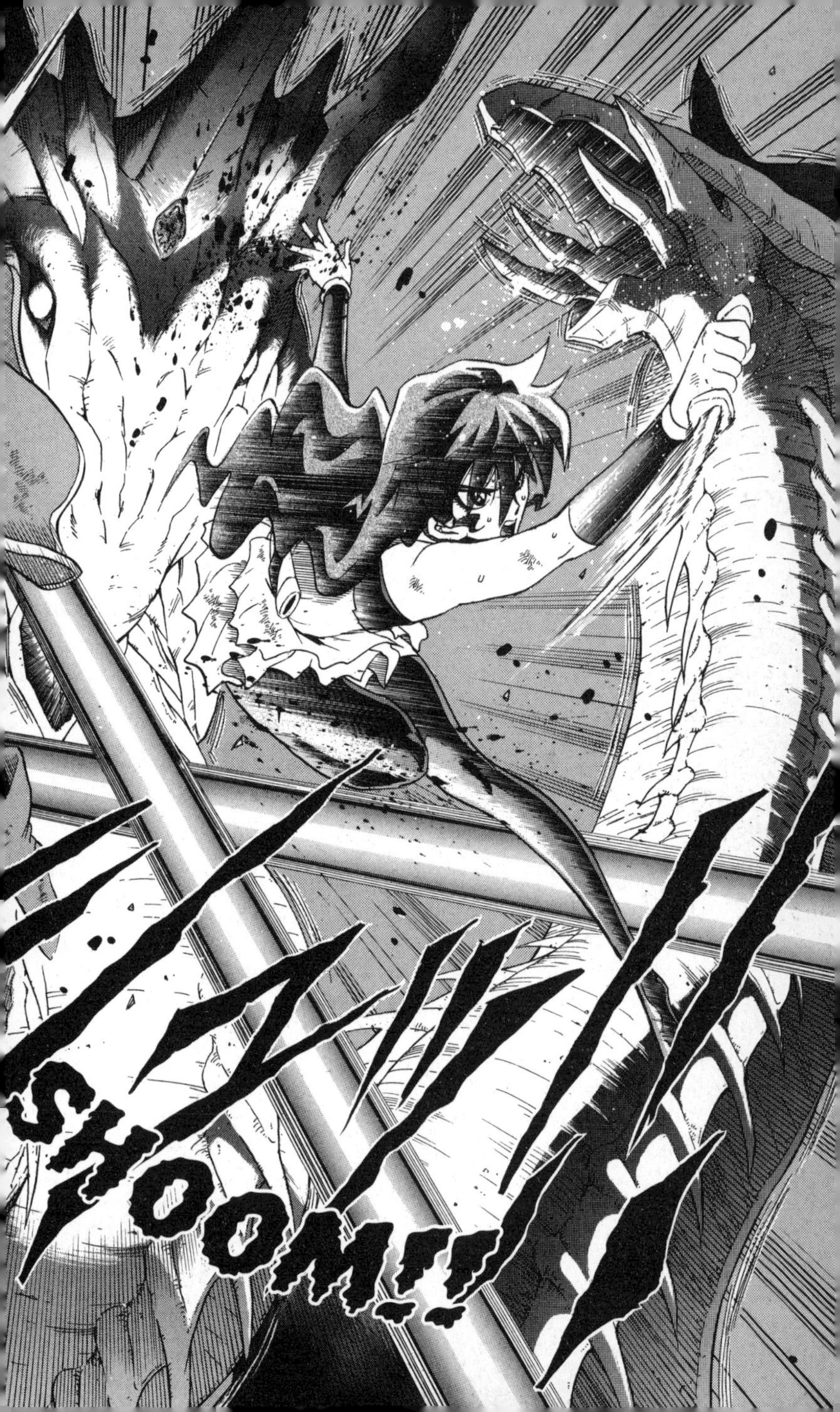
SHOOM!!

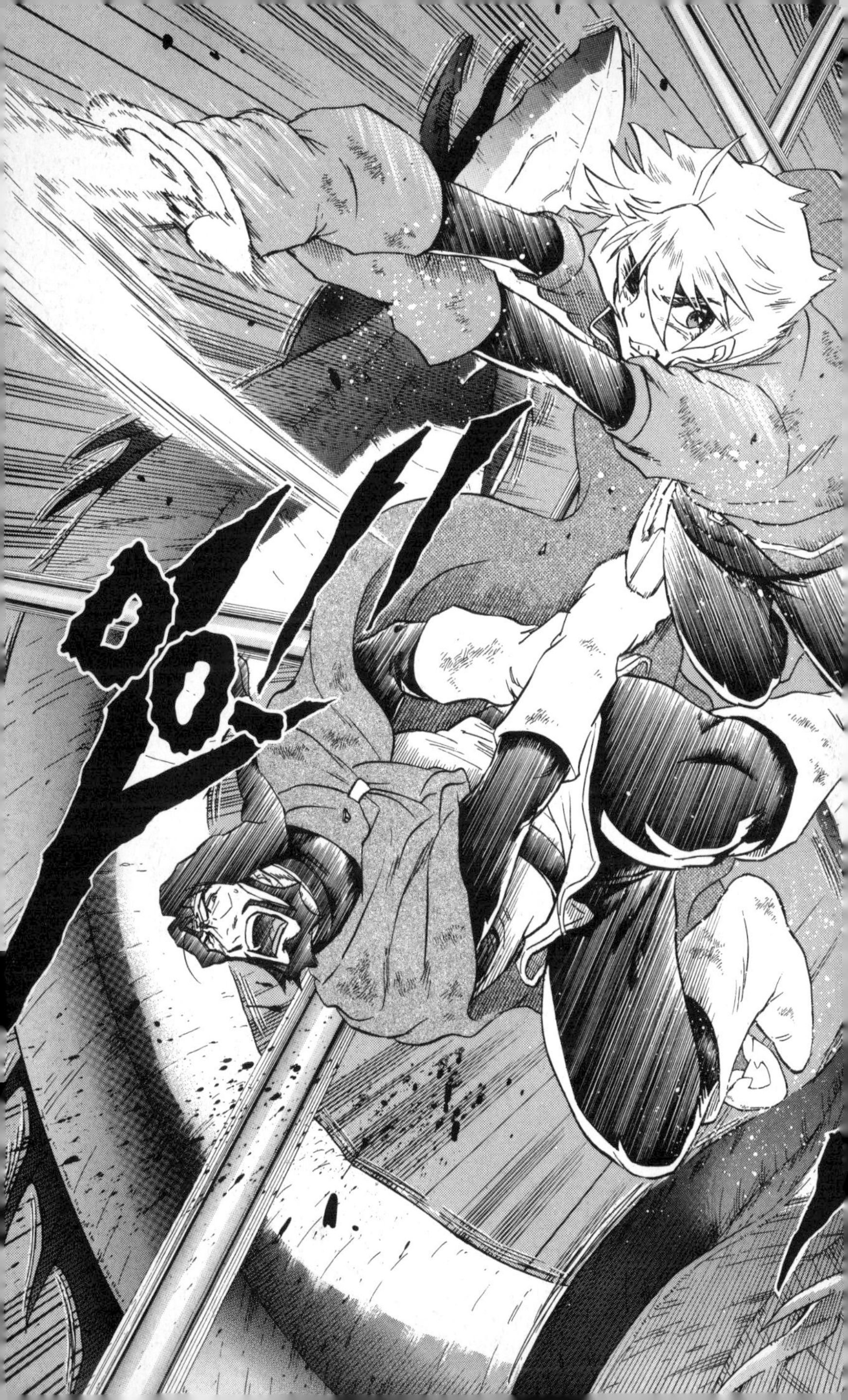

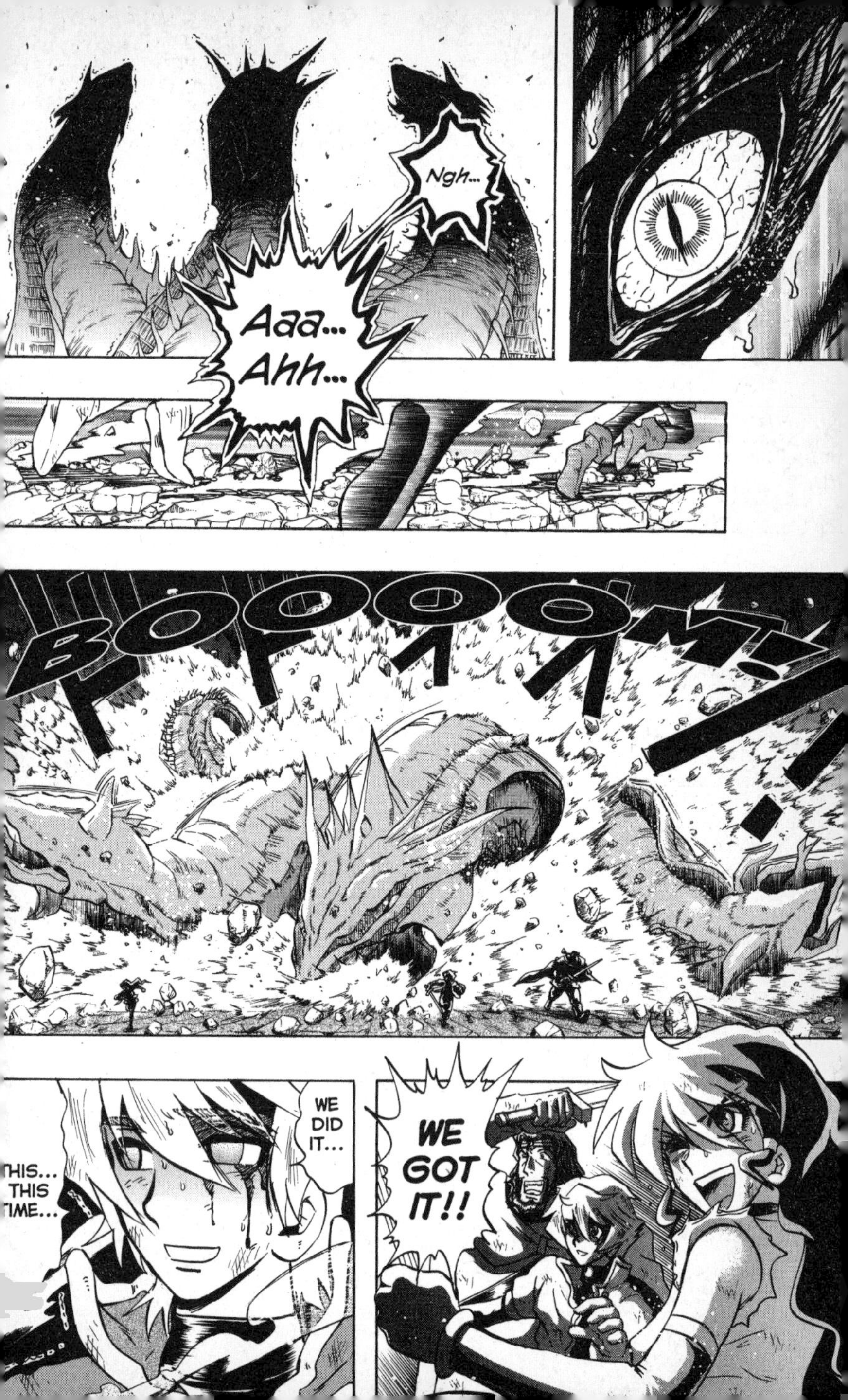
Ngh...
Aaa... Ahh...
BOOOOM!!
WE GOT IT!!
WE DID IT...
THIS... THIS TIME...

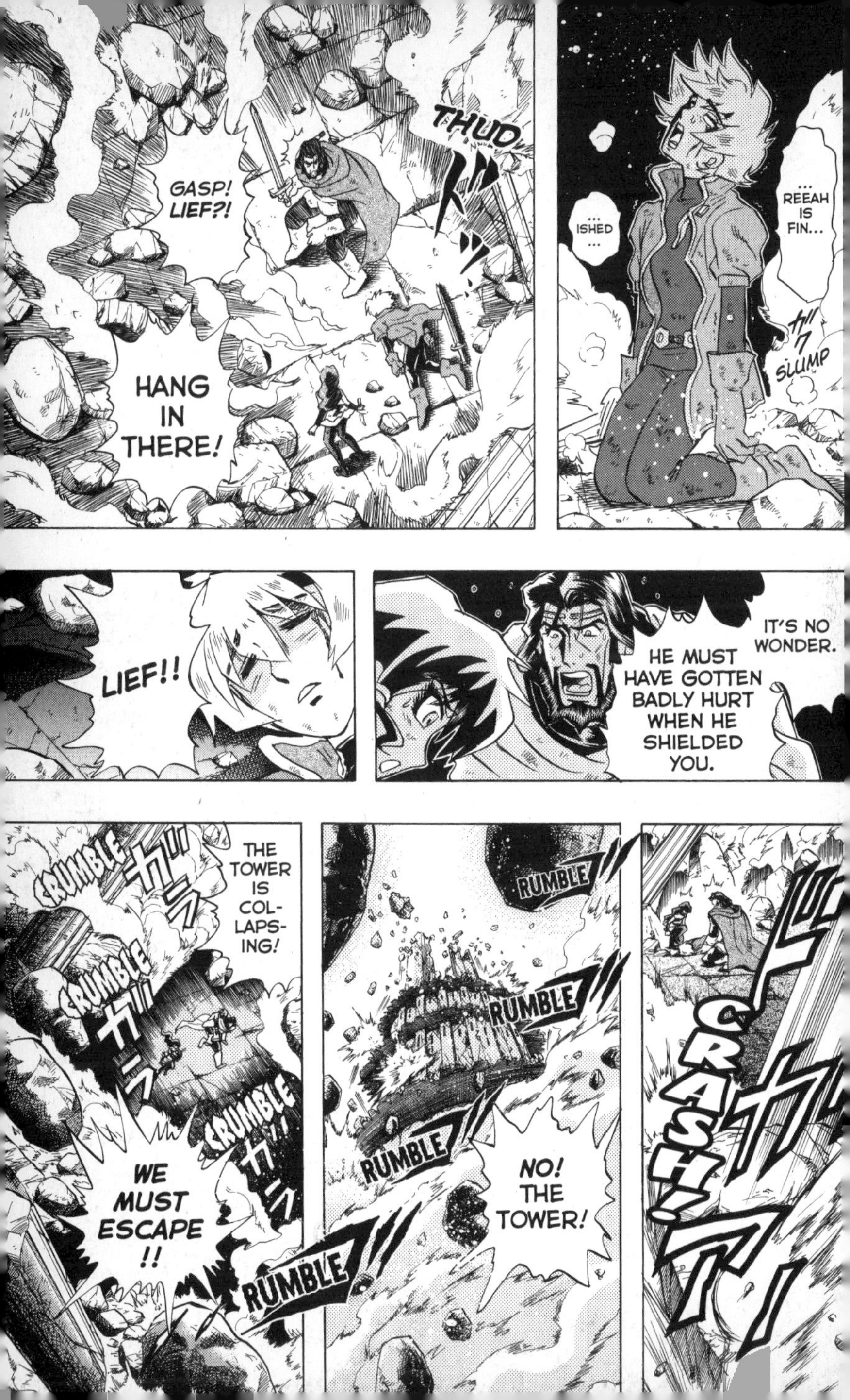
... REEAH IS FIN...
... ISHED ...
SLUMP
THUD
GASP! LIEF?!
HANG IN THERE!
IT'S NO WONDER.
HE MUST HAVE GOTTEN BADLY HURT WHEN HE SHIELDED YOU.
LIEF!!
CRASH!
RUMBLE
RUMBLE
RUMBLE
NO! THE TOWER!
CRUMBLE
THE TOWER IS COL-LAPS-ING!
CRUMBLE
CRUMBLE
WE MUST ESCAPE!!
RUMBLE

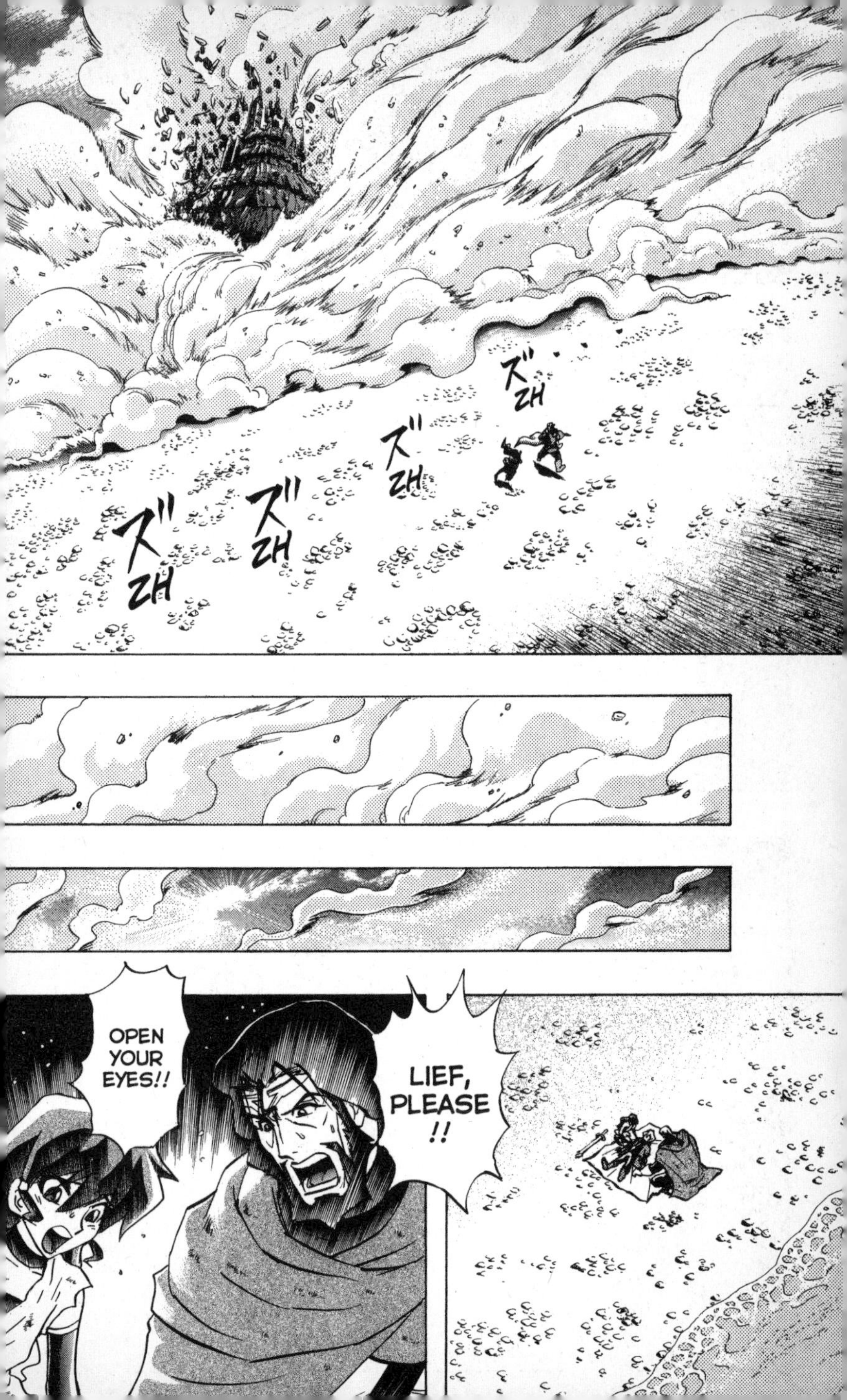
LIEF, PLEASE!!
OPEN YOUR EYES!!

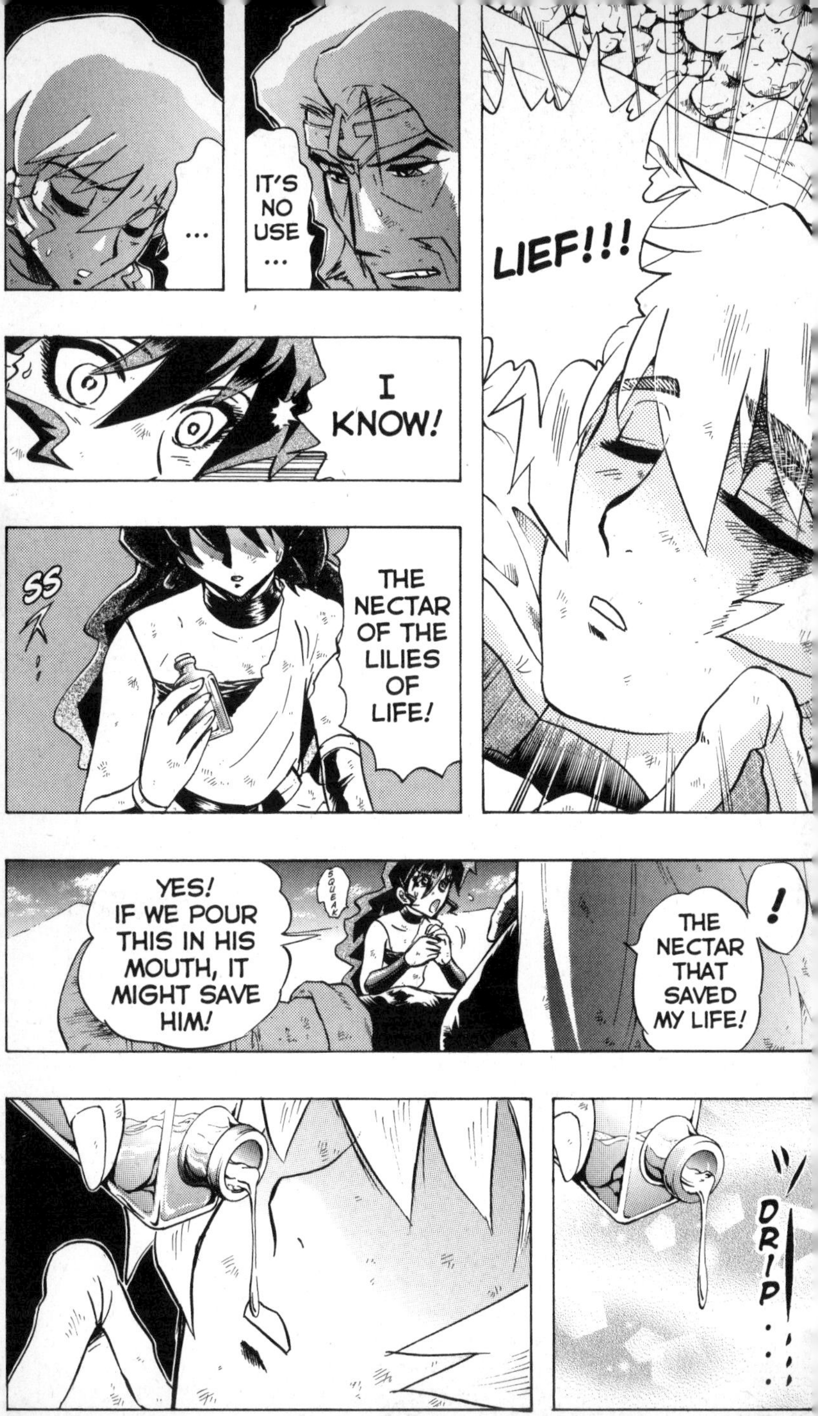
LIEF!!!
IT'S NO USE ...
...
I KNOW!
SS
THE NECTAR OF THE LILIES OF LIFE!
!
THE NECTAR THAT SAVED MY LIFE!
SQUEAK
YES! IF WE POUR THIS IN HIS MOUTH, IT MIGHT SAVE HIM!
DRIP...!!

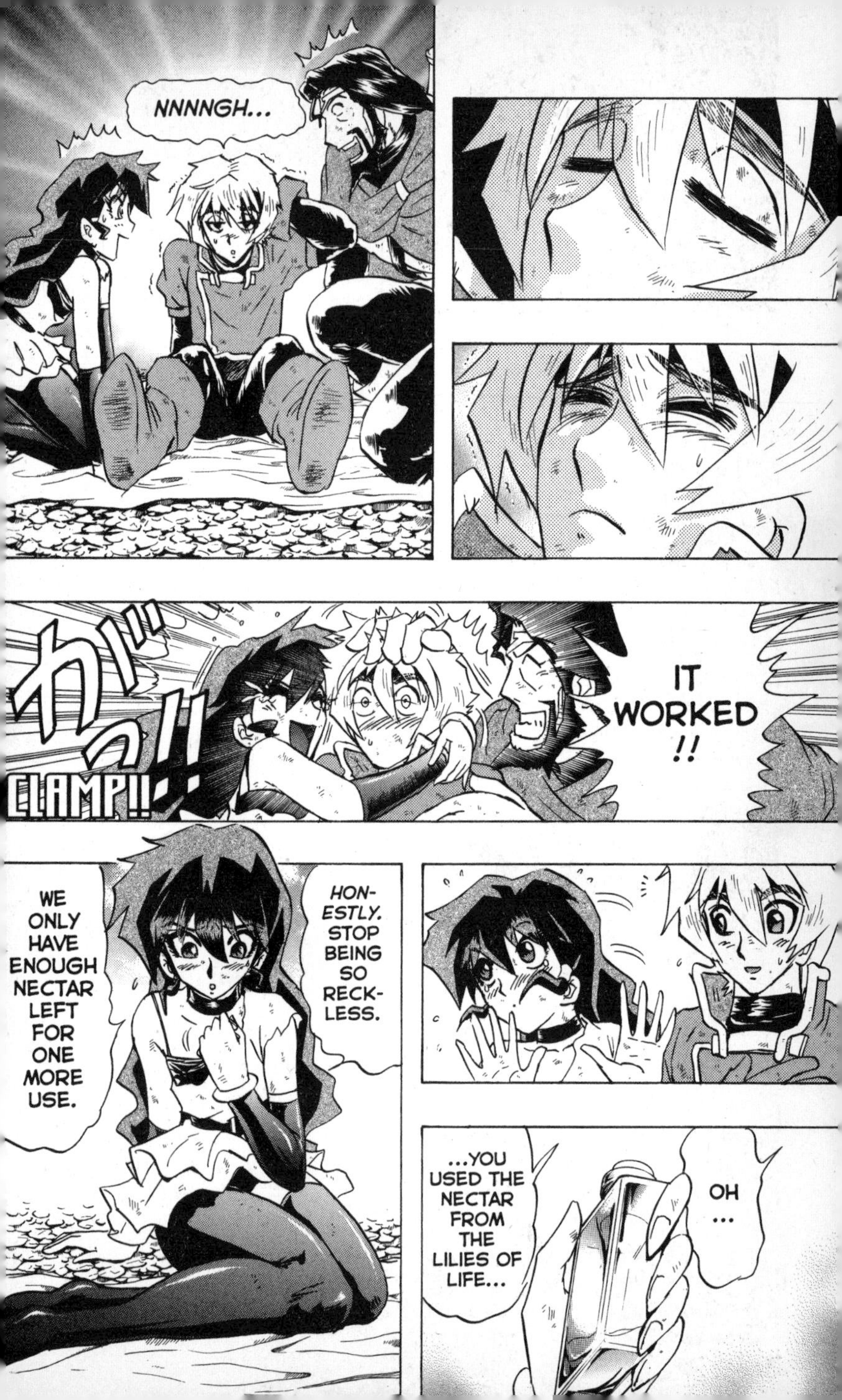
NNNNGH...
IT WORKED!!
がっ!!
CLAMP!!
OH ...
...YOU USED THE NECTAR FROM THE LILIES OF LIFE...
HON-ESTLY. STOP BEING SO RECK-LESS.
WE ONLY HAVE ENOUGH NECTAR LEFT FOR ONE MORE USE.

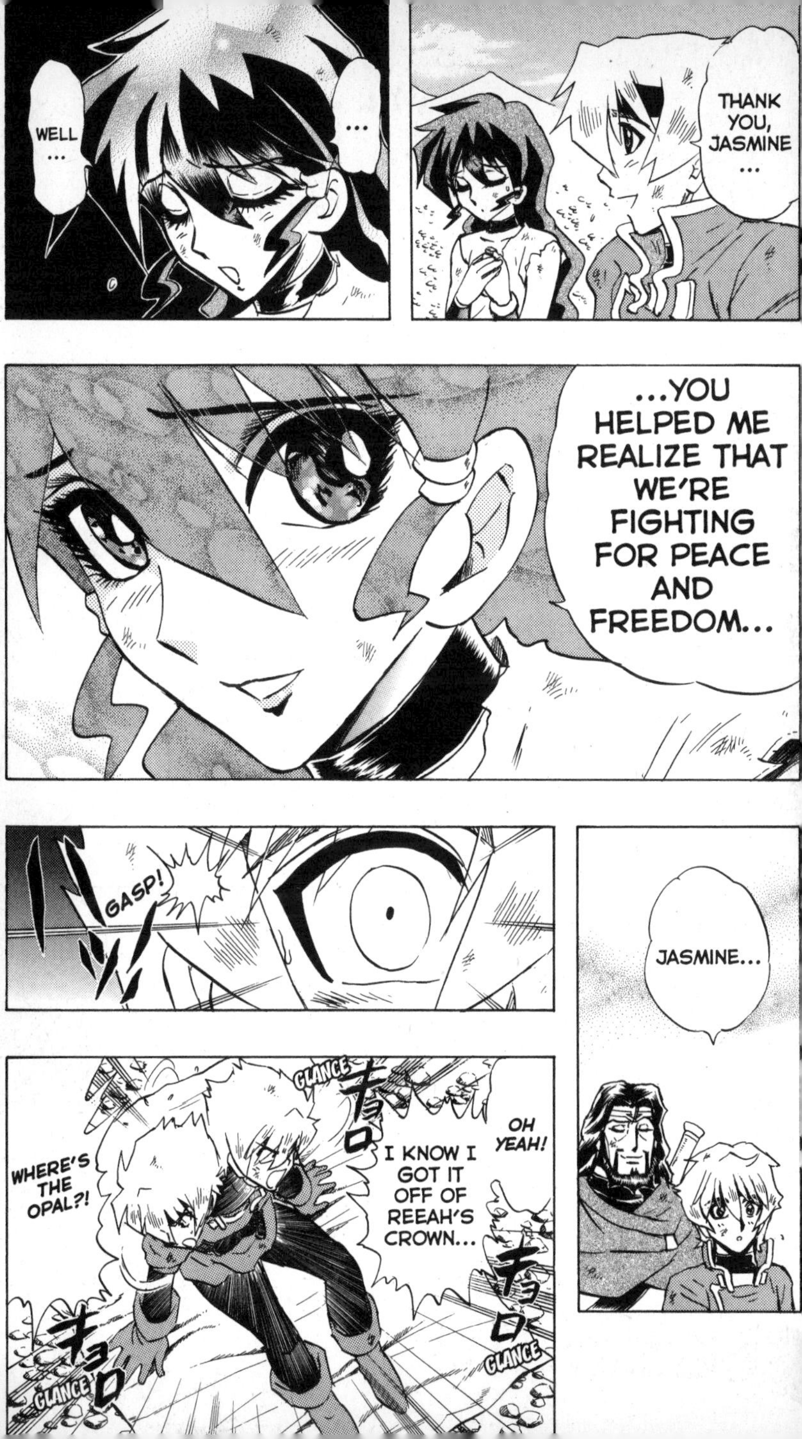
THANK YOU, JASMINE ...
...
WELL ...
...YOU HELPED ME REALIZE THAT WE'RE FIGHTING FOR PEACE AND FREEDOM...
JASMINE...
GASP!
GLANCE
チョロ
OH YEAH!
I KNOW I GOT IT OFF OF REEAH'S CROWN...
WHERE'S THE OPAL?!
チョロ
GLANCE
チョロ
GLANCE

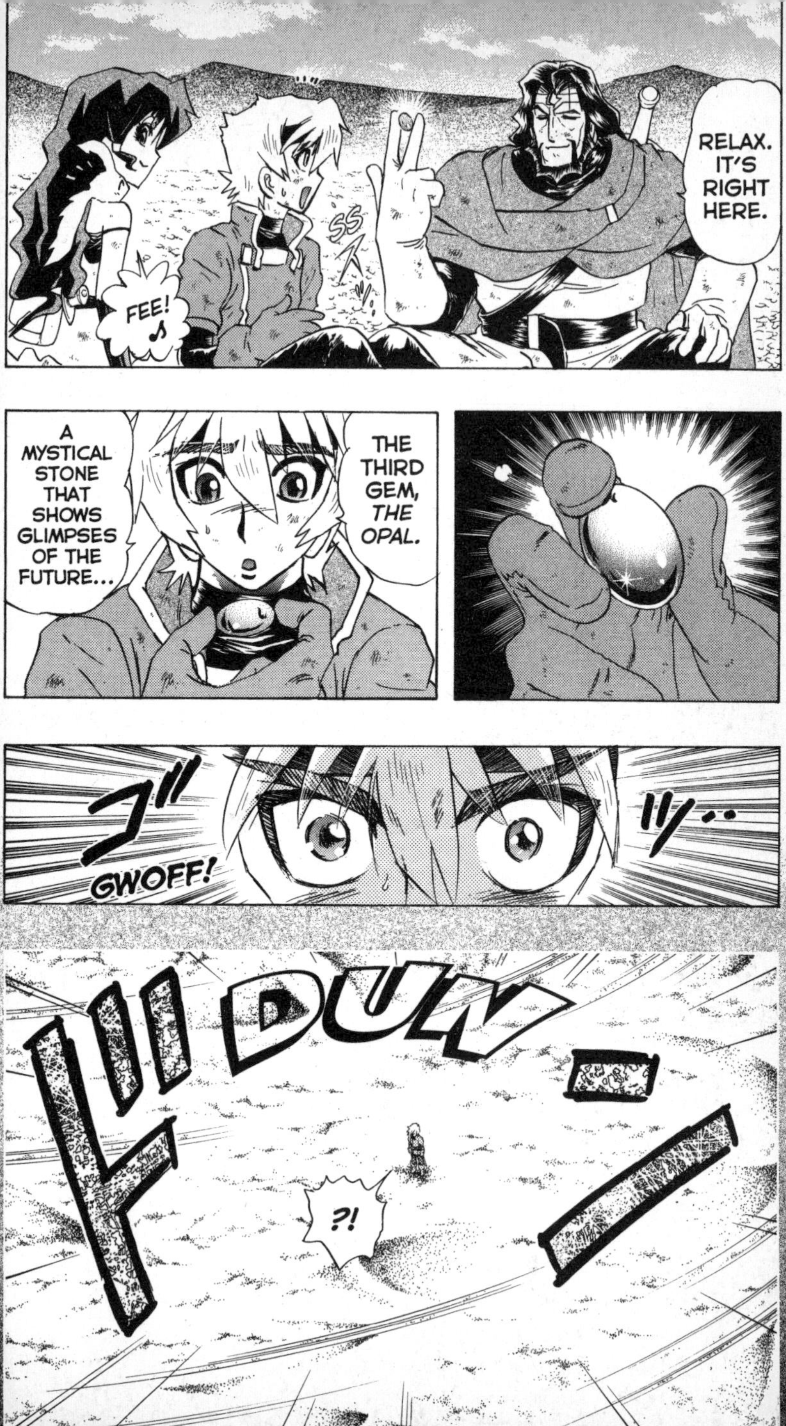
RELAX. IT'S RIGHT HERE.
SS
FEE! ♪
THE THIRD GEM, THE OPAL.
A MYSTICAL STONE THAT SHOWS GLIMPSES OF THE FUTURE...
GWOFF!
DUN
?!

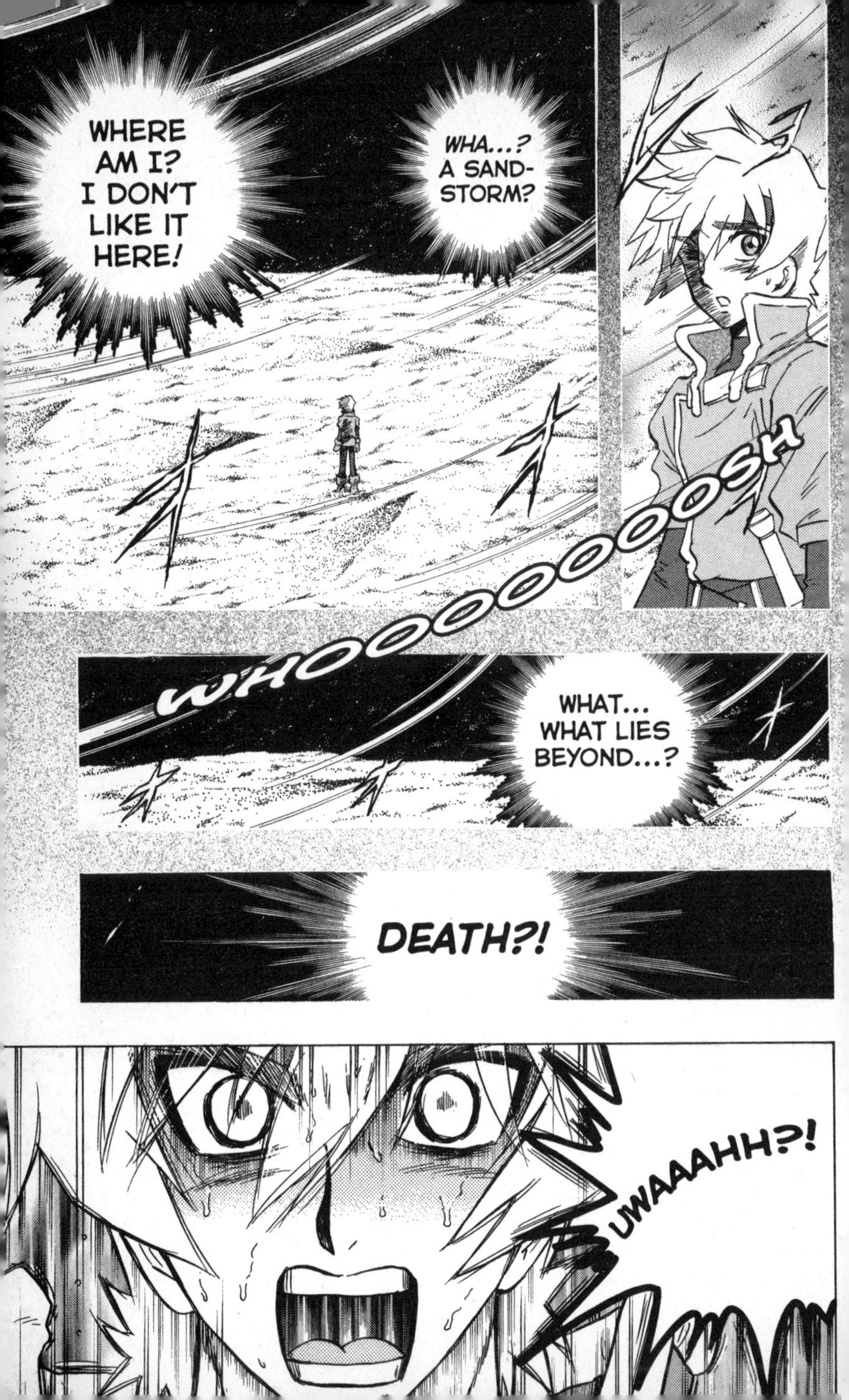
WHA...? A SAND-STORM?
WHERE AM I? I DON'T LIKE IT HERE!
WHOOOOOOOOOOOOSH
WHAT... WHAT LIES BEYOND...?
DEATH?!
UWAAAHH?!

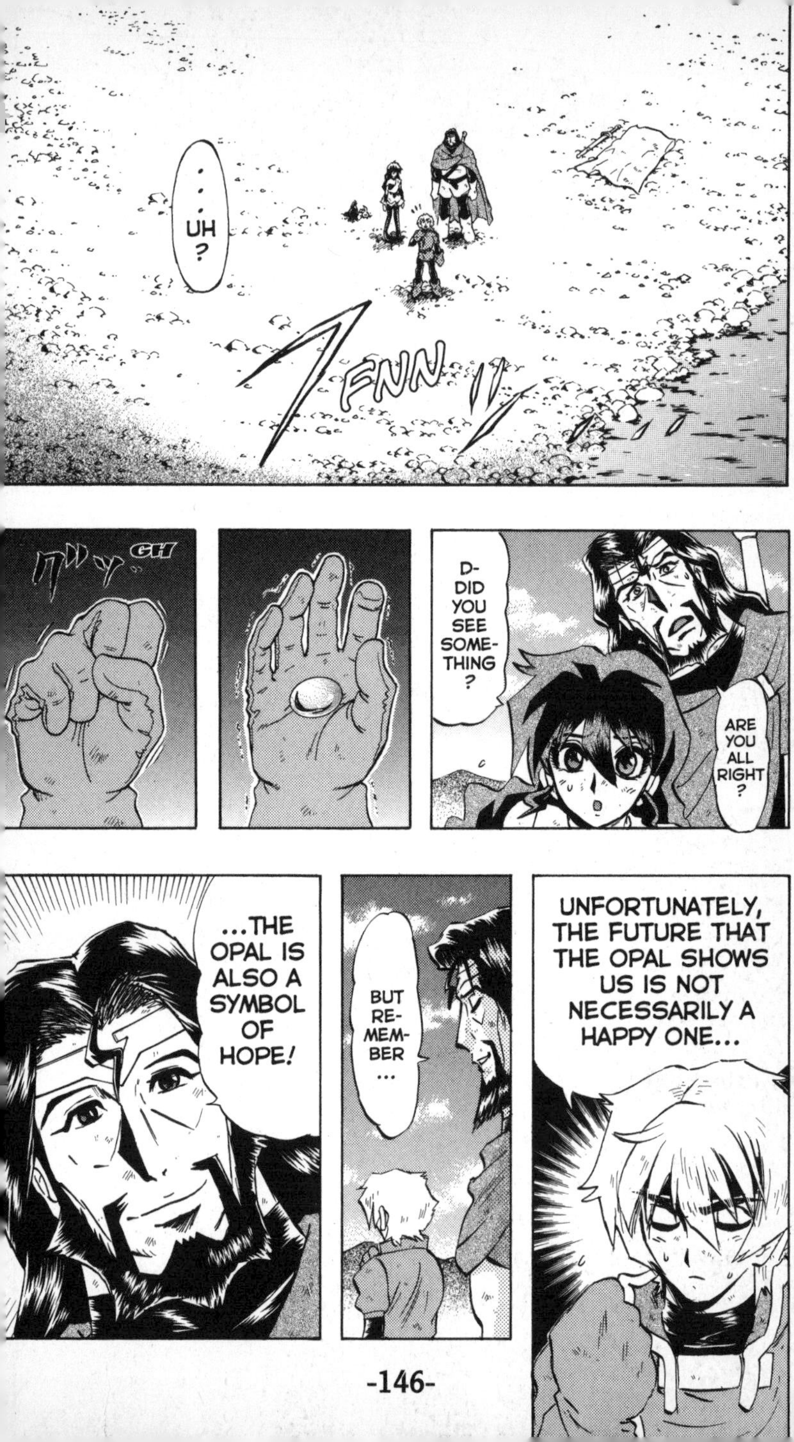
...
UH?
FNN
ARE YOU ALL RIGHT?
D-DID YOU SEE SOMETHING?
GH
UNFORTUNATELY, THE FUTURE THAT THE OPAL SHOWS US IS NOT NECESSARILY A HAPPY ONE...
BUT REMEMBER...
...THE OPAL IS ALSO A SYMBOL OF HOPE!

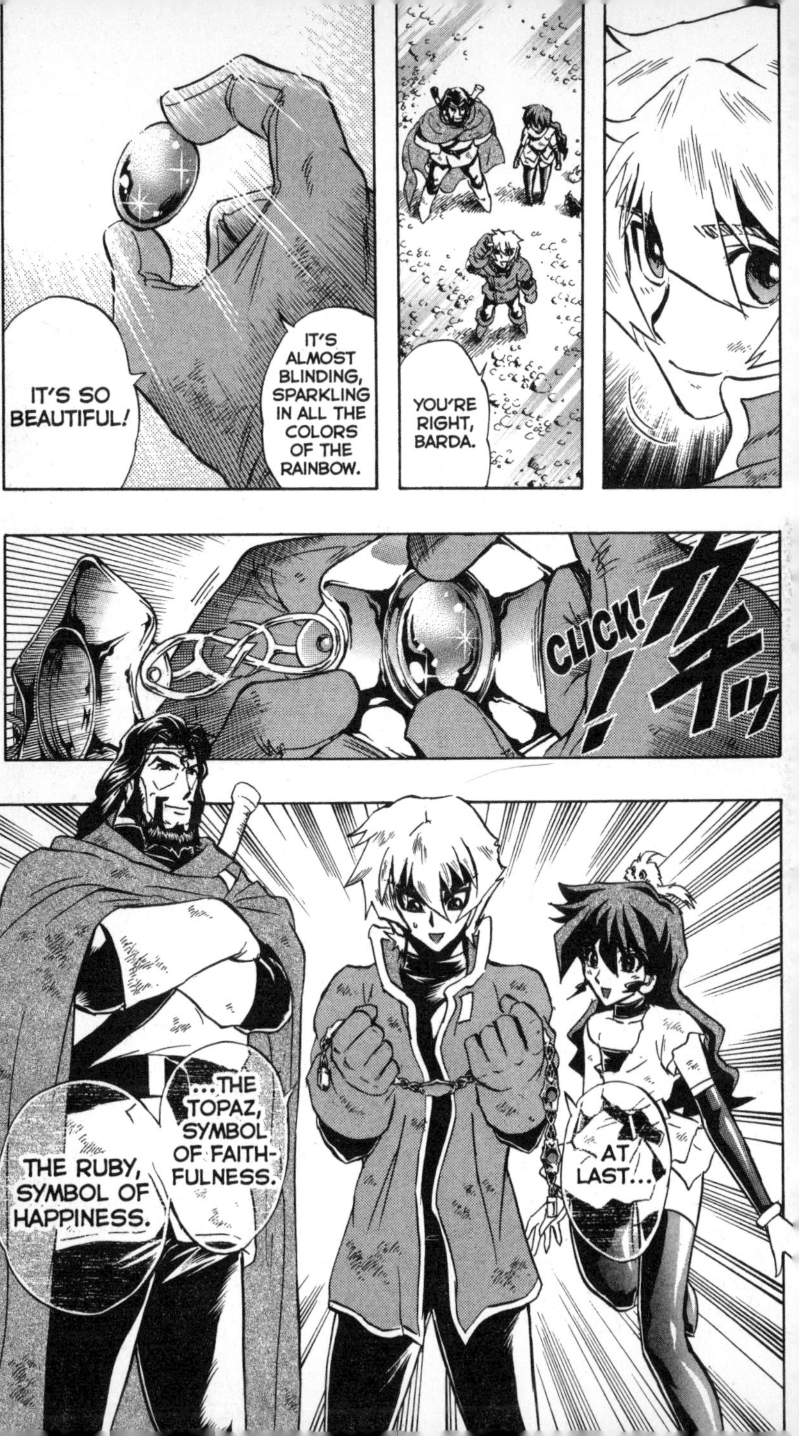
YOU'RE RIGHT, BARDA.
IT'S ALMOST BLINDING, SPARKLING IN ALL THE COLORS OF THE RAINBOW.
IT'S SO BEAUTIFUL!
カチッ!
CLICK!
AT LAST...
...THE TOPAZ, SYMBOL OF FAITH-FULNESS.
THE RUBY, SYMBOL OF HAPPINESS.

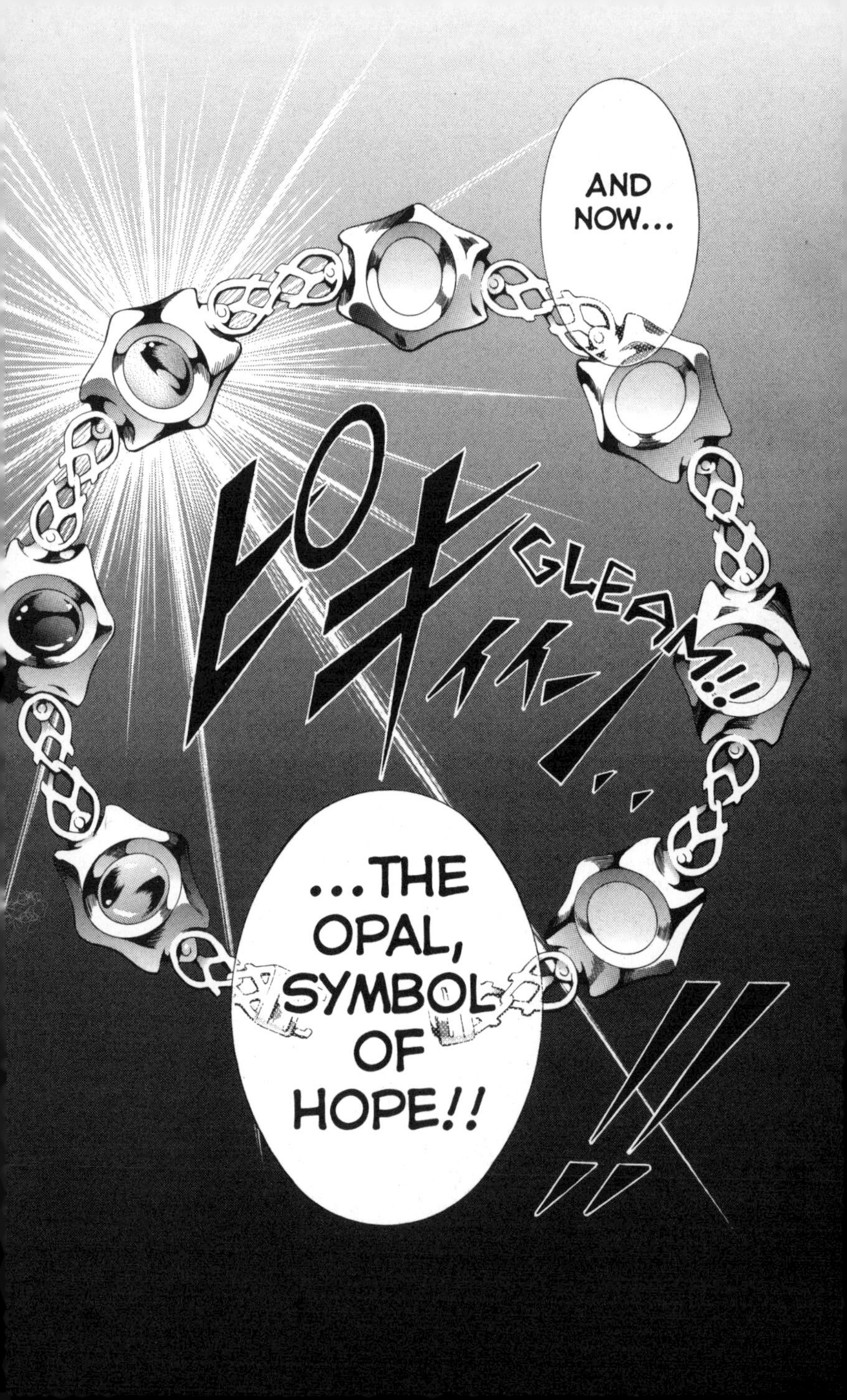
AND NOW...
GLEAM!!
...THE OPAL, SYMBOL OF HOPE!!

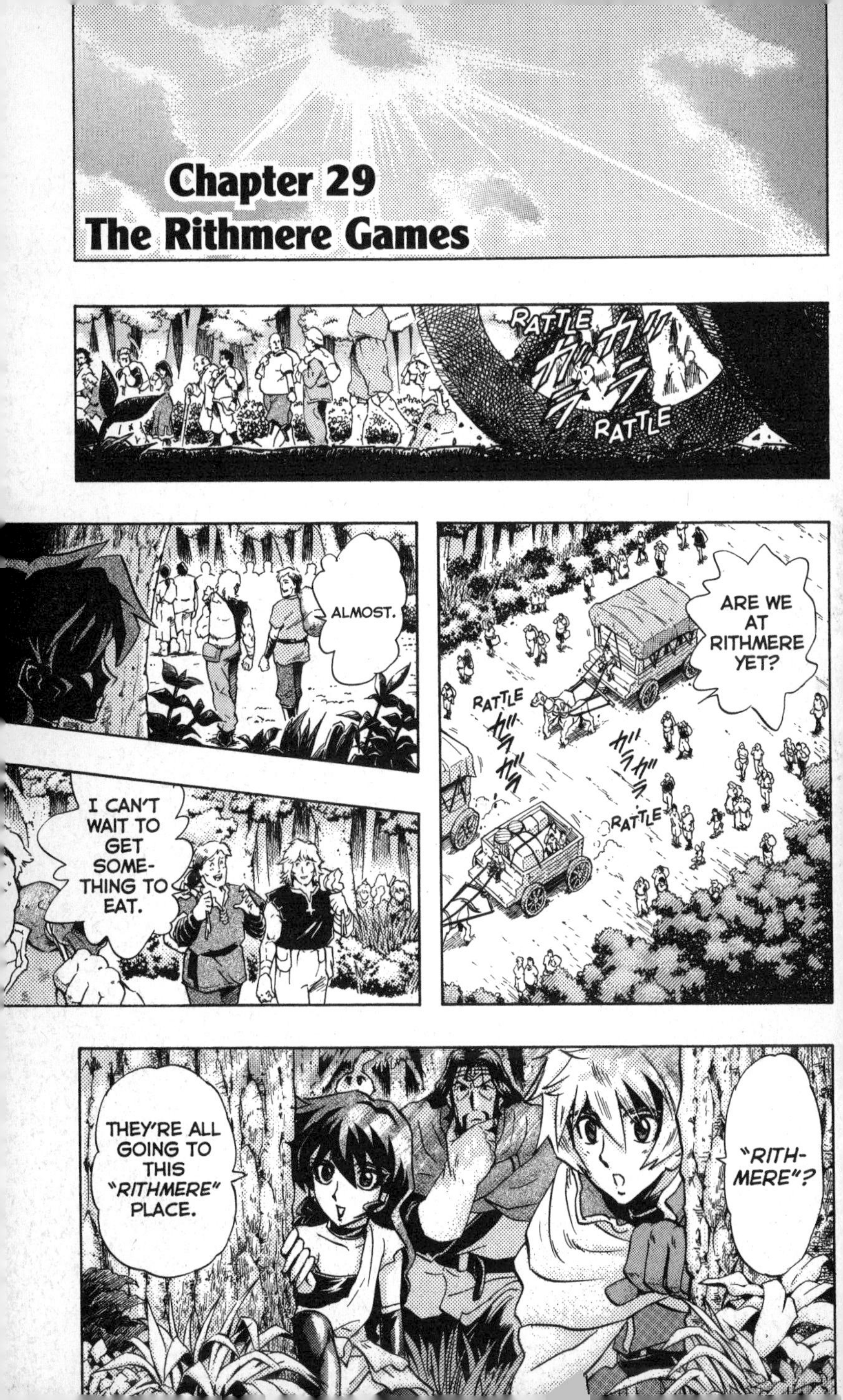
Chapter 29
The Rithmere Games
RATTLE
RATTLE
ARE WE AT RITHMERE YET?
RATTLE
RATTLE
ALMOST.
I CAN'T WAIT TO GET SOME-THING TO EAT.
"RITH-MERE"?
THEY'RE ALL GOING TO THIS "RITHMERE" PLACE.

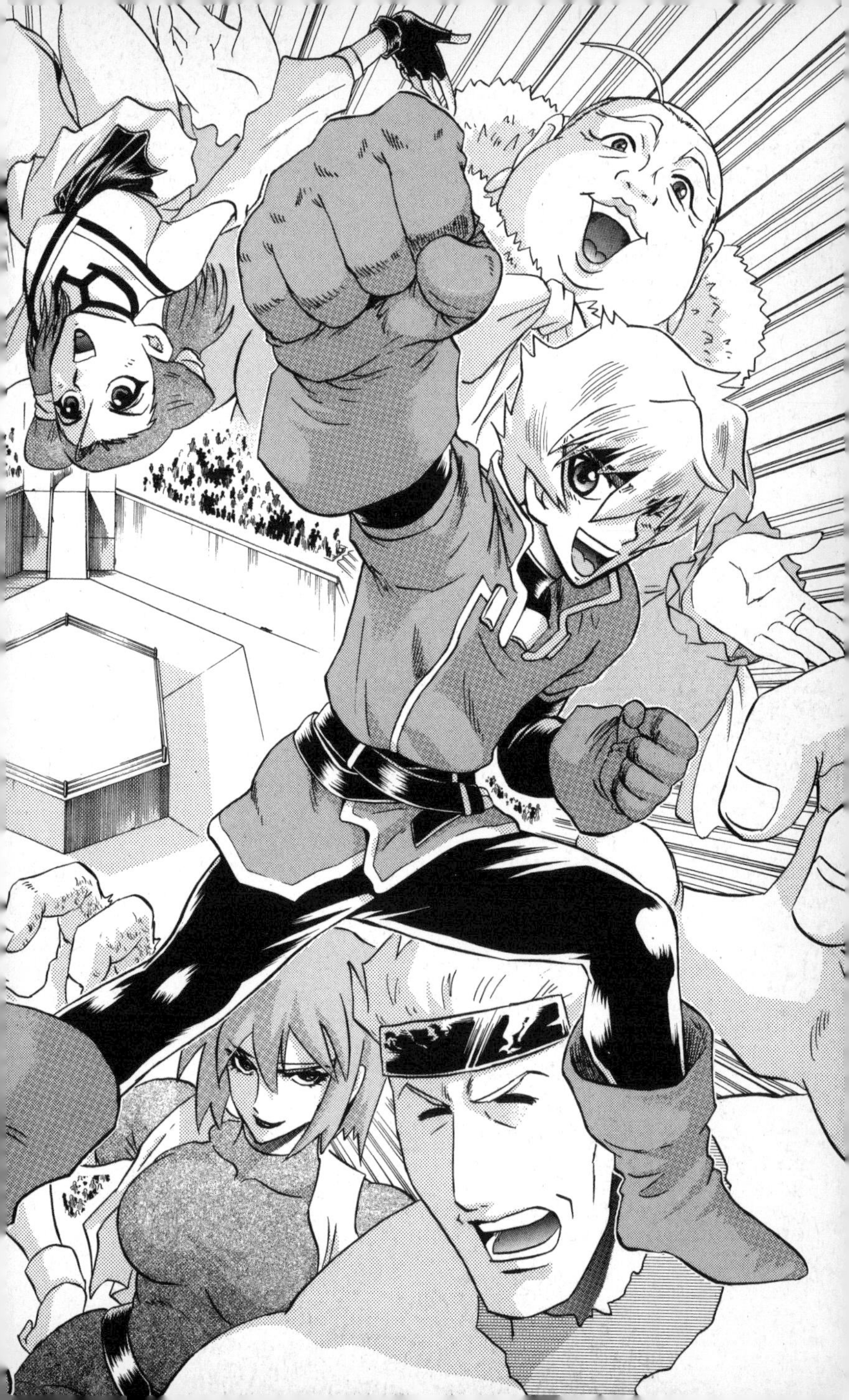

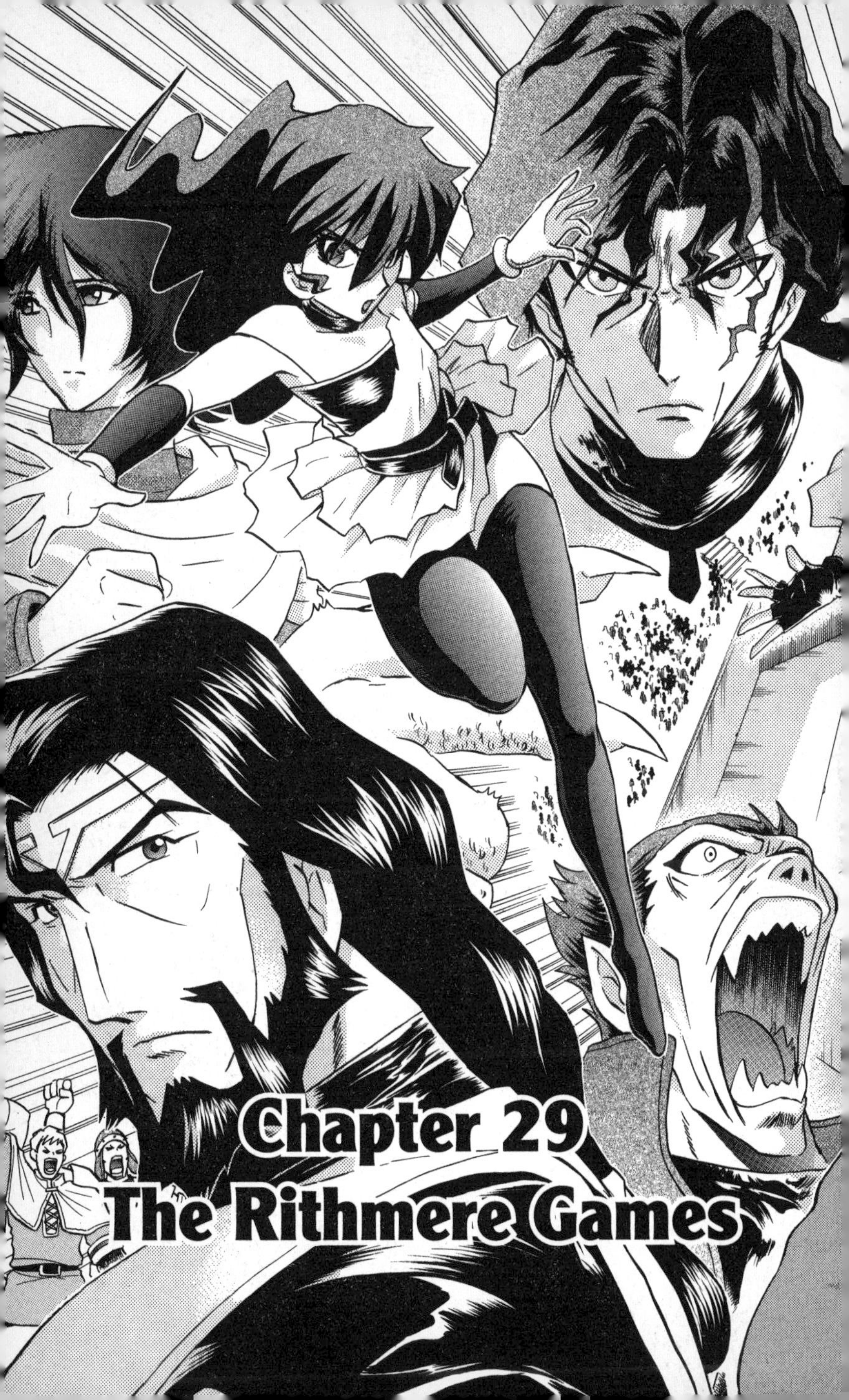
Chapter 29
The Rithmere Games

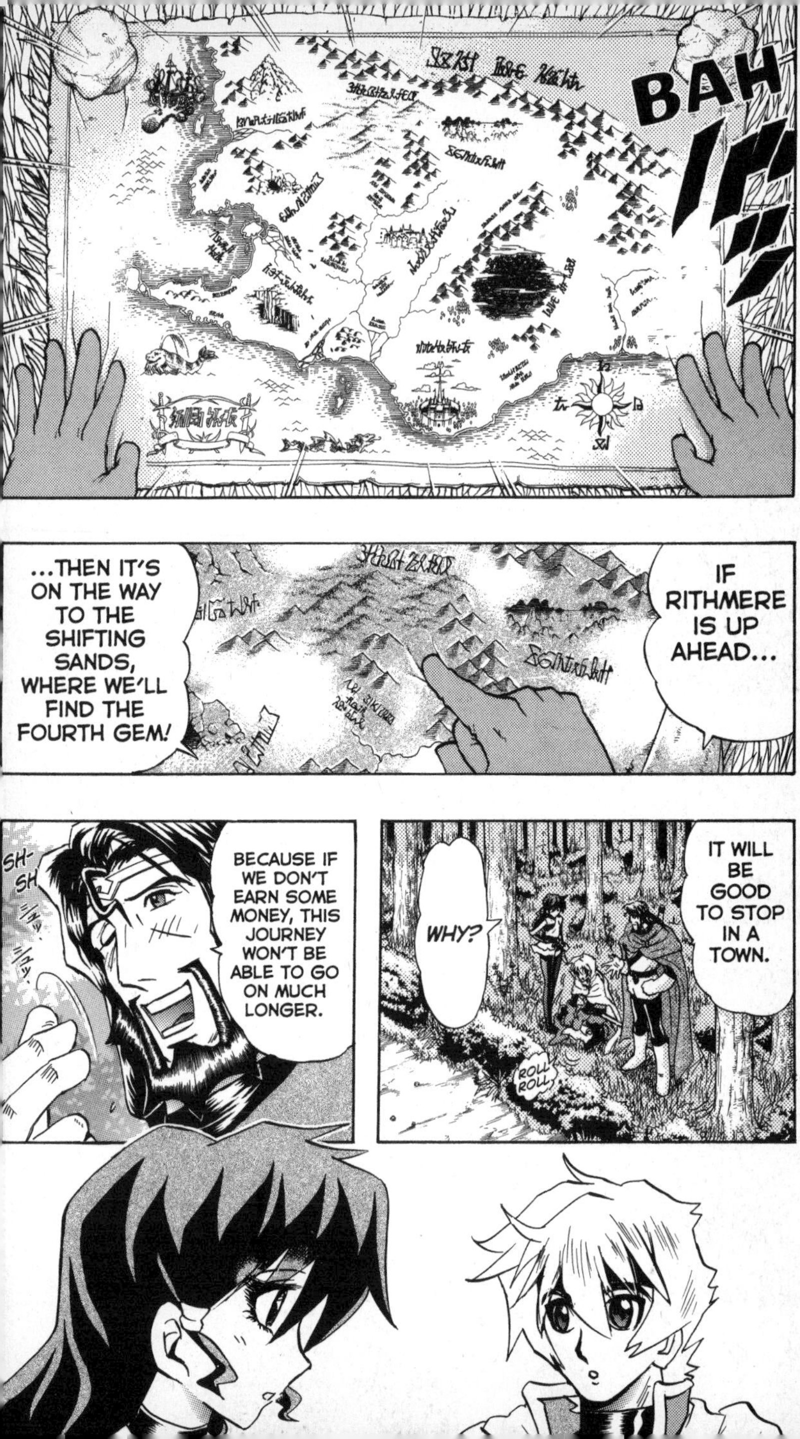
BAH
IF RITHMERE IS UP AHEAD...
...THEN IT'S ON THE WAY TO THE SHIFTING SANDS, WHERE WE'LL FIND THE FOURTH GEM!
IT WILL BE GOOD TO STOP IN A TOWN.
WHY?
ROLL ROLL
BECAUSE IF WE DON'T EARN SOME MONEY, THIS JOURNEY WON'T BE ABLE TO GO ON MUCH LONGER.
SH-SH

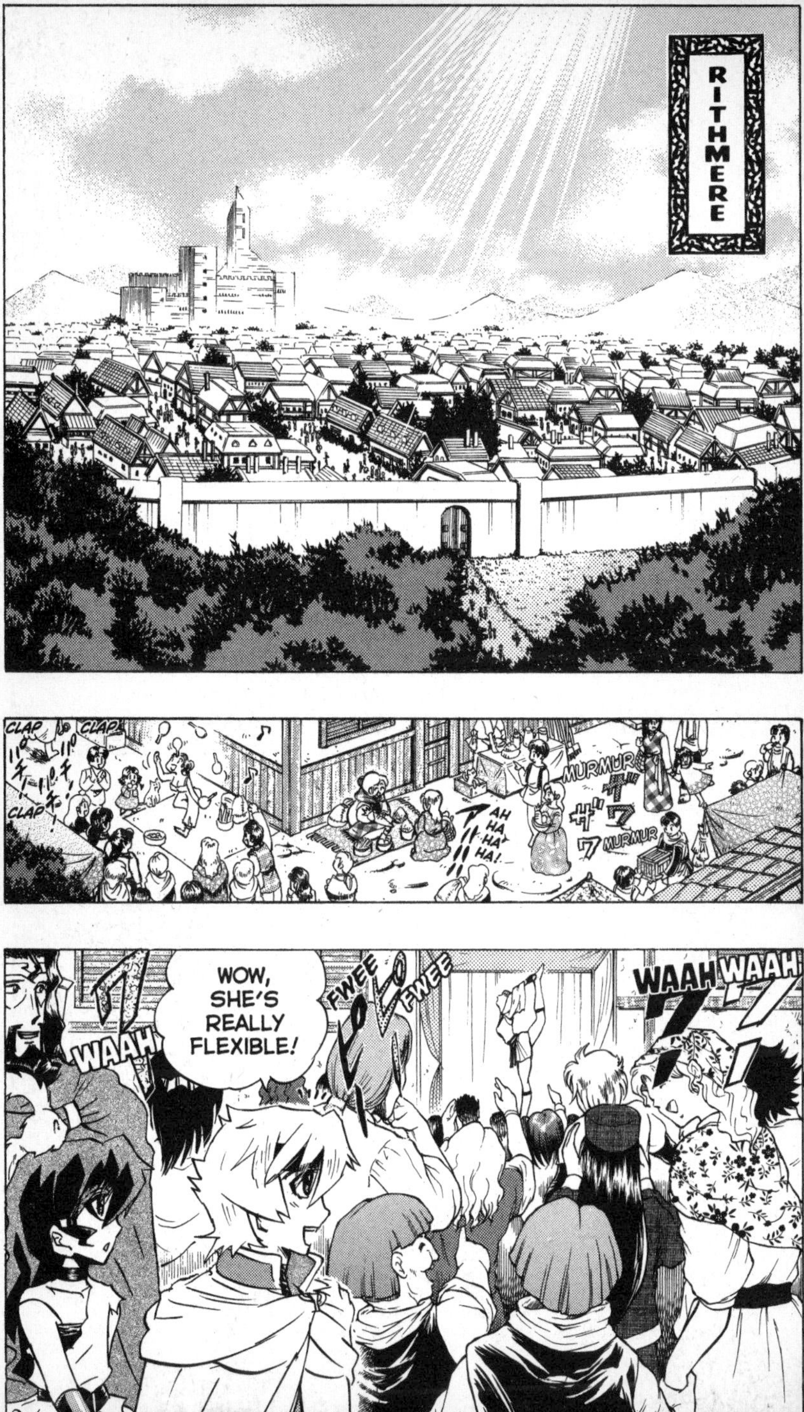
RITHMERE
MURMUR
MURMUR
AH HA HA HA!
CLAP
CLAP
CLAP
WAAH WAAH
FWEE FWEE
WOW, SHE'S REALLY FLEXIBLE!
WAAH

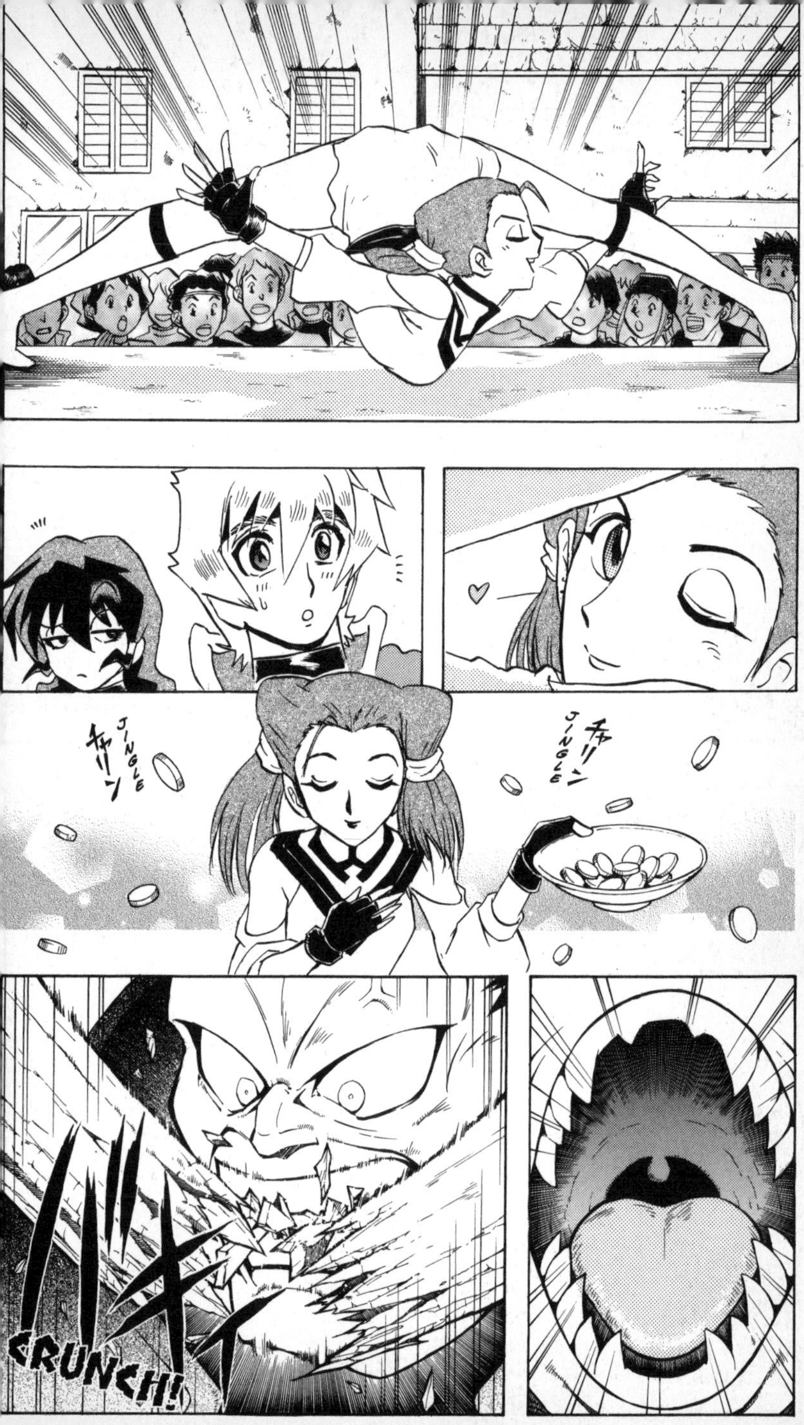
チャリーン
JINGLE
チャリーン
JINGLE
CRUNCH!

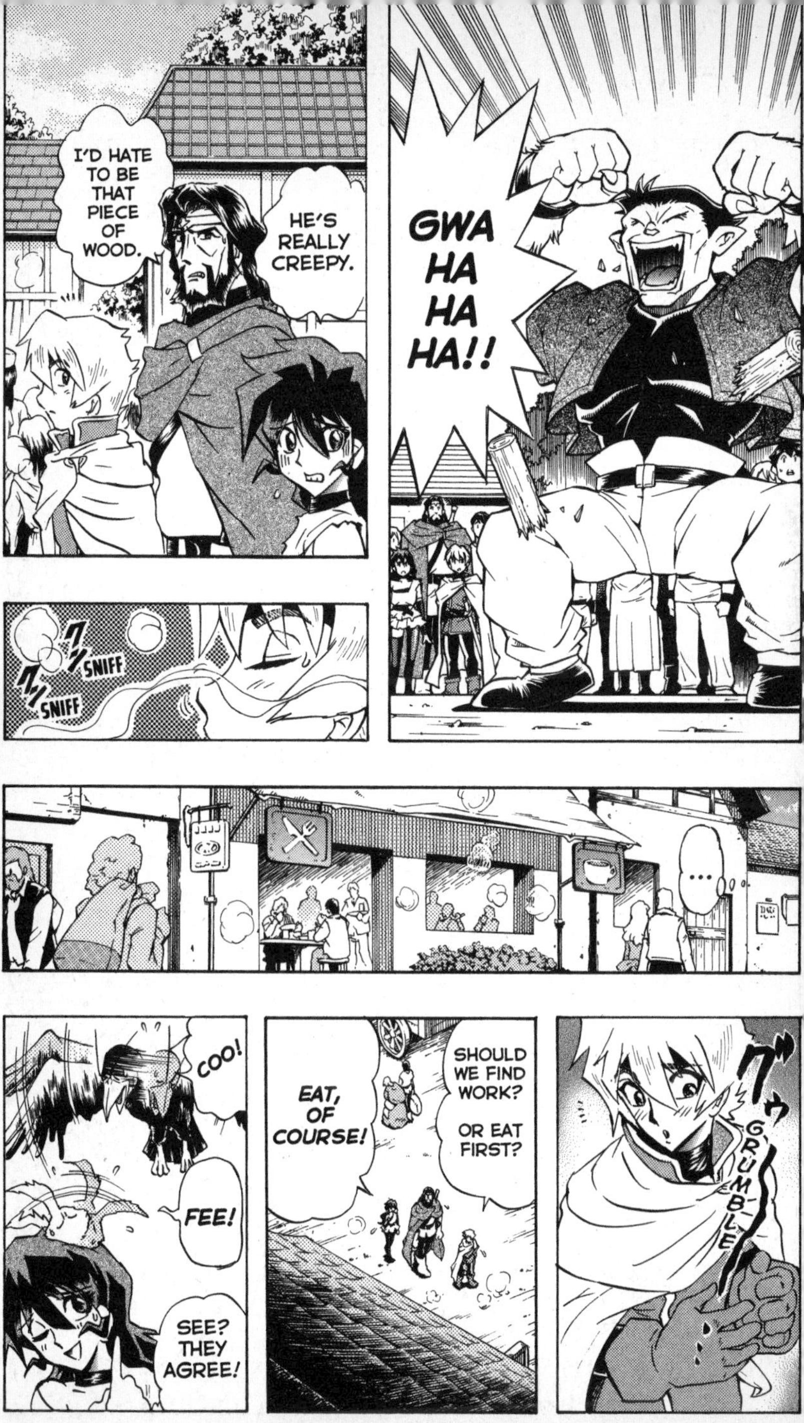
GWA HA HA HA!!
HE'S REALLY CREEPY.
I'D HATE TO BE THAT PIECE OF WOOD.
SNIFF
SNIFF
...
GRUMBLE
SHOULD WE FIND WORK?
OR EAT FIRST?
EAT, OF COURSE!
COO!
FEE!
SEE? THEY AGREE!

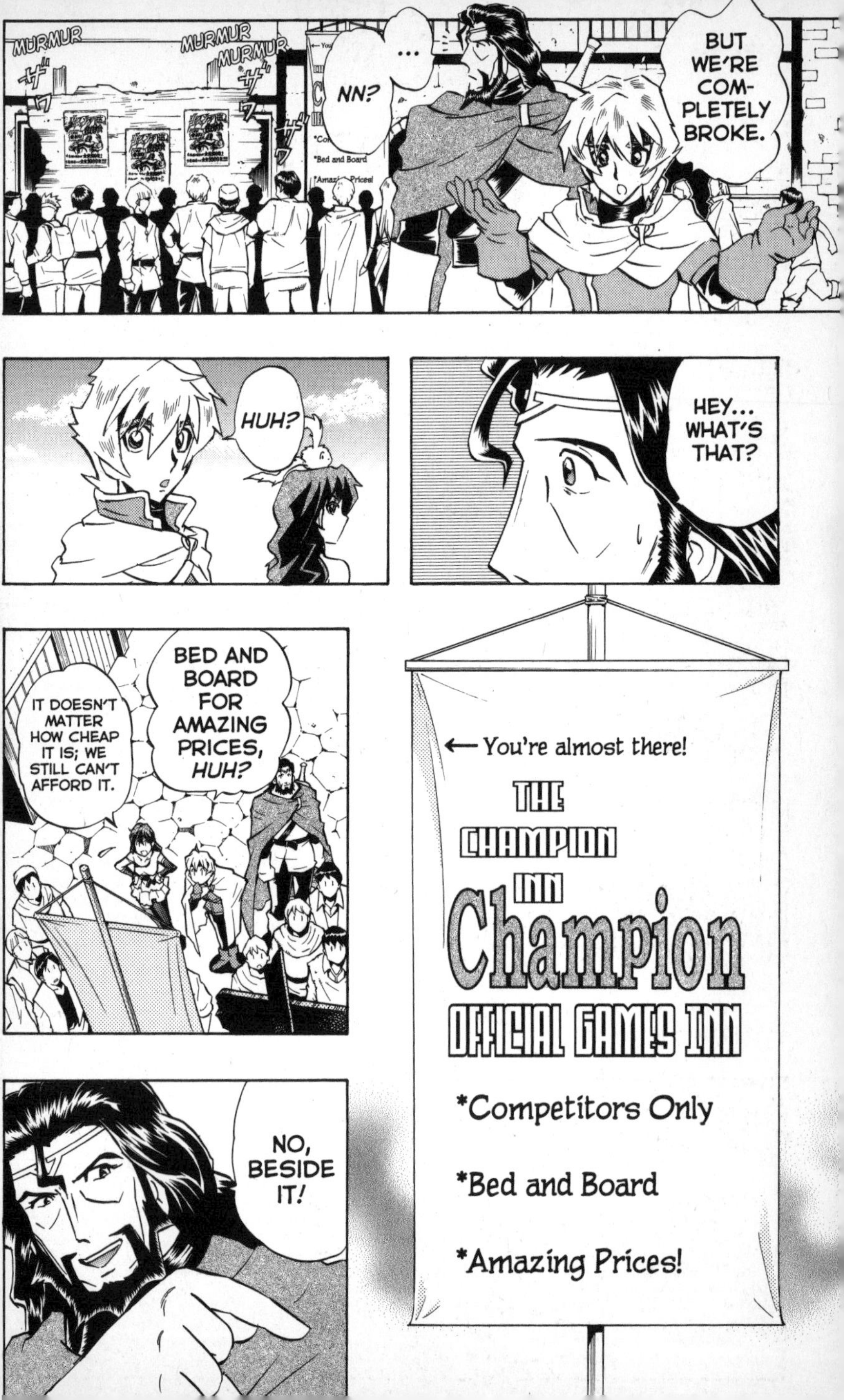
BUT WE'RE COM- PLETELY BROKE.
...
NN?
MURMUR MURMUR
MURMUR
HEY... WHAT'S THAT?
HUH?
← You're almost there!
THE CHAMPION INN
Champion
OFFICIAL GAMES INN
*Competitors Only
*Bed and Board
*Amazing Prices!
BED AND BOARD FOR AMAZING PRICES, HUH?
IT DOESN'T MATTER HOW CHEAP IT IS; WE STILL CAN'T AFFORD IT.
NO, BESIDE IT!

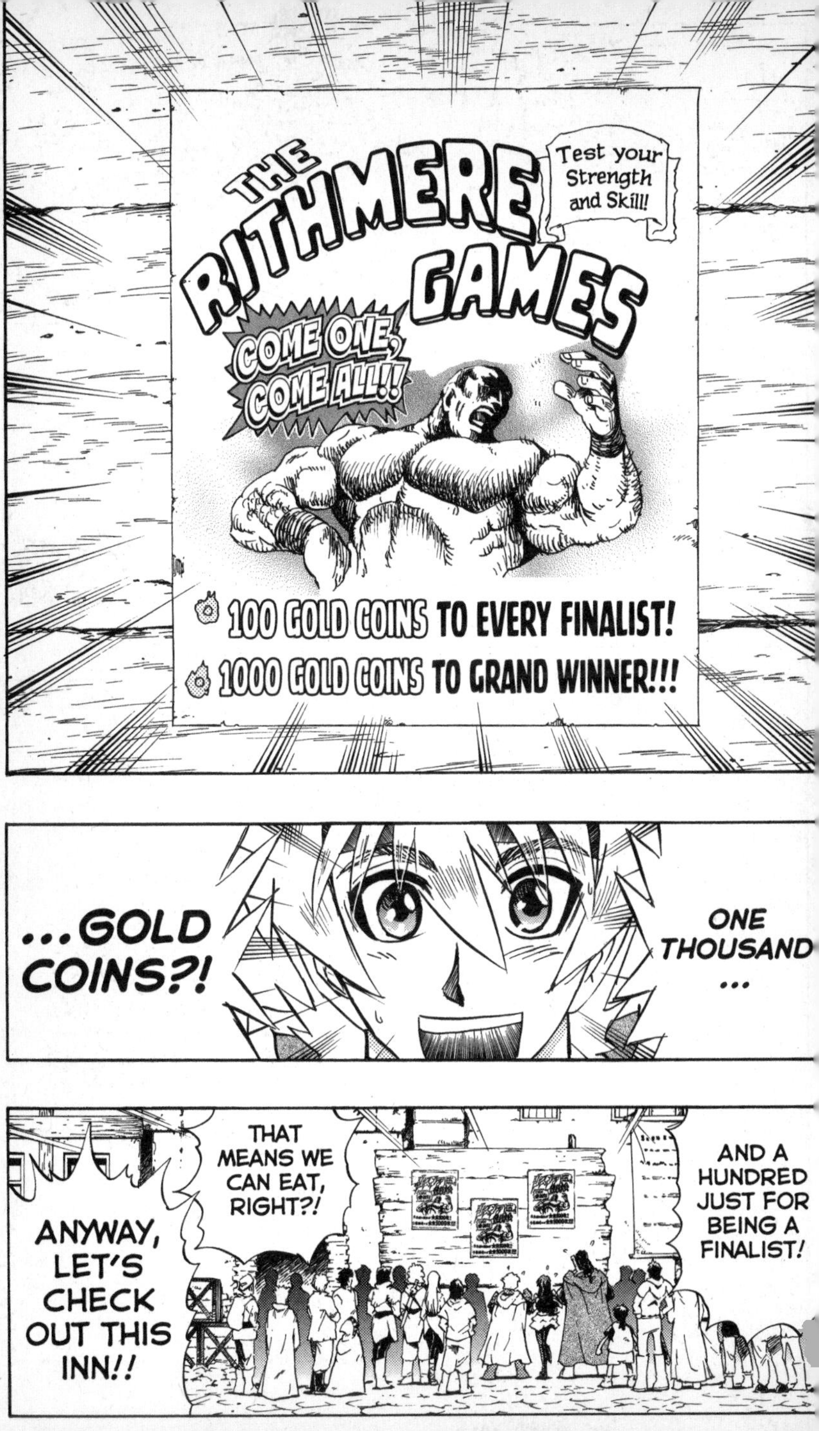
THE RITHMERE GAMES
Test your Strength and Skill!
COME ONE, COME ALL!!
100 GOLD COINS TO EVERY FINALIST!
1000 GOLD COINS TO GRAND WINNER!!!
ONE THOUSAND ...
...GOLD COINS?!
AND A HUNDRED JUST FOR BEING A FINALIST!
THAT MEANS WE CAN EAT, RIGHT?!
ANYWAY, LET'S CHECK OUT THIS INN!!

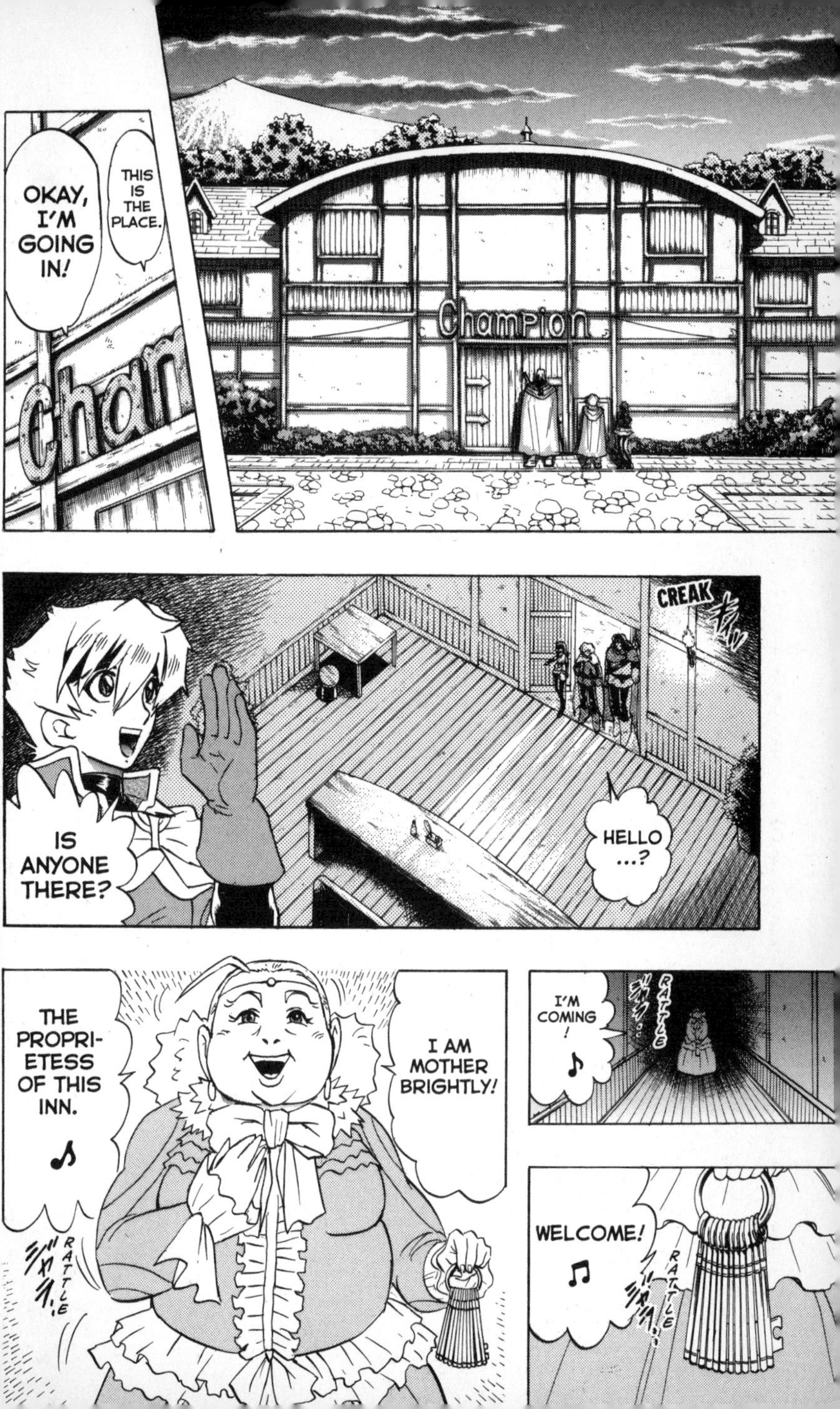

Champion
THIS IS THE PLACE.
OKAY, I'M GOING IN!
CREAK
HELLO ...?
IS ANYONE THERE?
I'M COMING! ♪
RATTLE
WELCOME! ♪
RATTLE
I AM MOTHER BRIGHTLY!
THE PROPRI-ETESS OF THIS INN. ♪
RATTLE

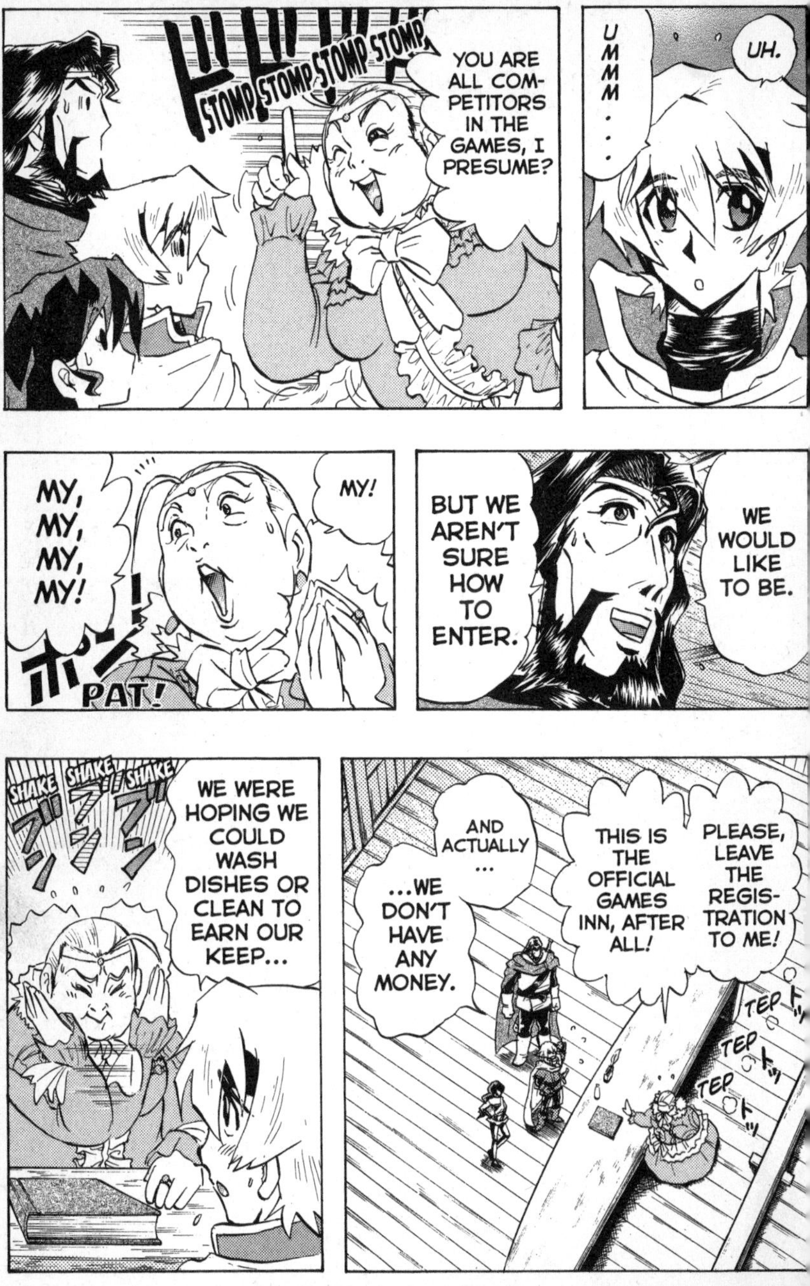
UH.
UMMM...
YOU ARE ALL COMPETITORS IN THE GAMES, I PRESUME?
STOMP STOMP STOMP STOMP
WE WOULD LIKE TO BE.
BUT WE AREN'T SURE HOW TO ENTER.
MY!
MY, MY, MY, MY!
PAT!
PLEASE, LEAVE THE REGISTRATION TO ME!
THIS IS THE OFFICIAL GAMES INN, AFTER ALL!
AND ACTUALLY...
...WE DON'T HAVE ANY MONEY.
TEP
TEP
TEP
WE WERE HOPING WE COULD WASH DISHES OR CLEAN TO EARN OUR KEEP...
SHAKE SHAKE SHAKE

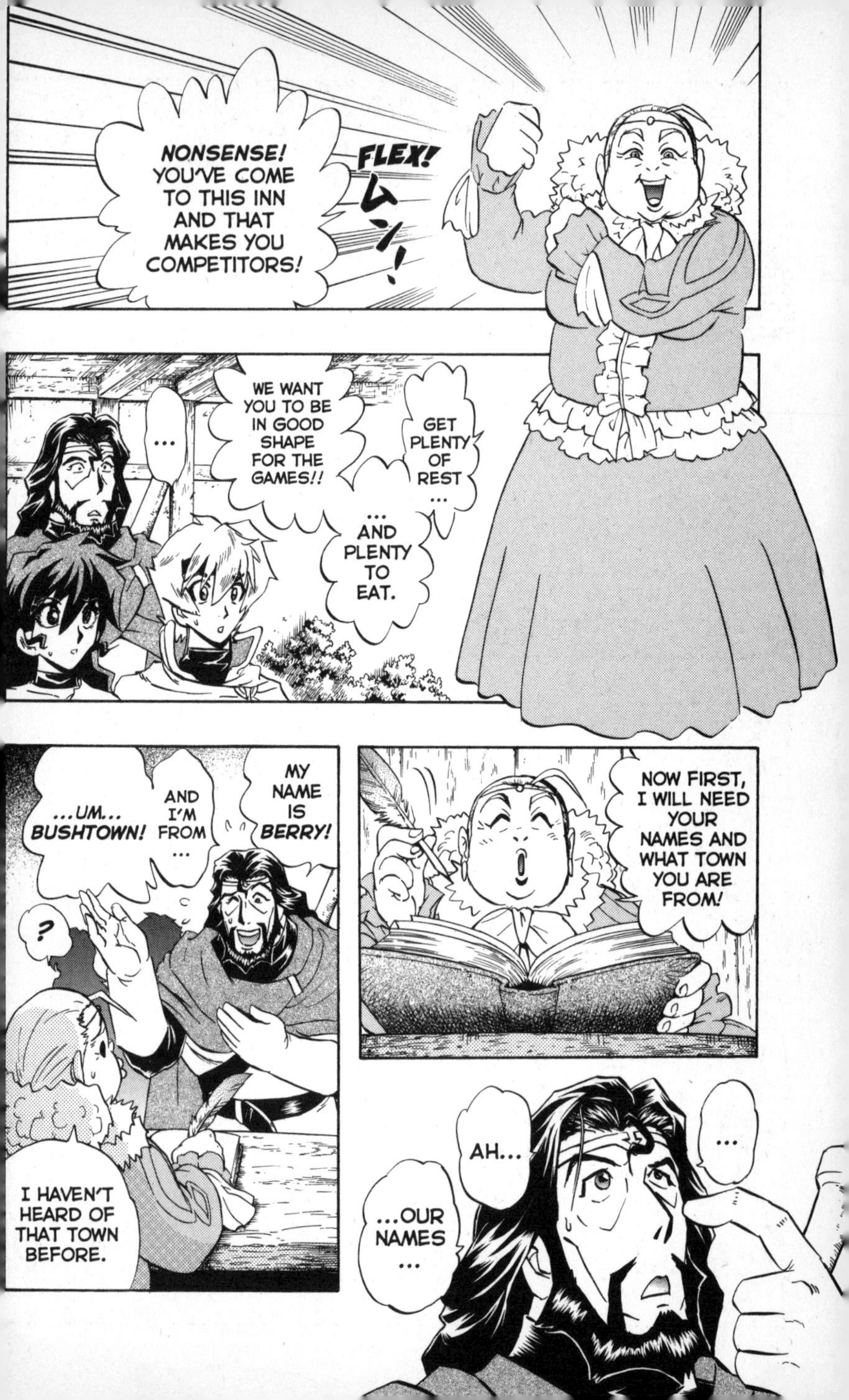
FLEX!
ムン!
NONSENSE! YOU'VE COME TO THIS INN AND THAT MAKES YOU COMPETITORS!
GET PLENTY OF REST ...
... AND PLENTY TO EAT.
WE WANT YOU TO BE IN GOOD SHAPE FOR THE GAMES!!
...
NOW FIRST, I WILL NEED YOUR NAMES AND WHAT TOWN YOU ARE FROM!
...
AH...
...OUR NAMES ...
MY NAME IS BERRY!
AND I'M FROM ...
...UM... BUSHTOWN!
?
I HAVEN'T HEARD OF THAT TOWN BEFORE.

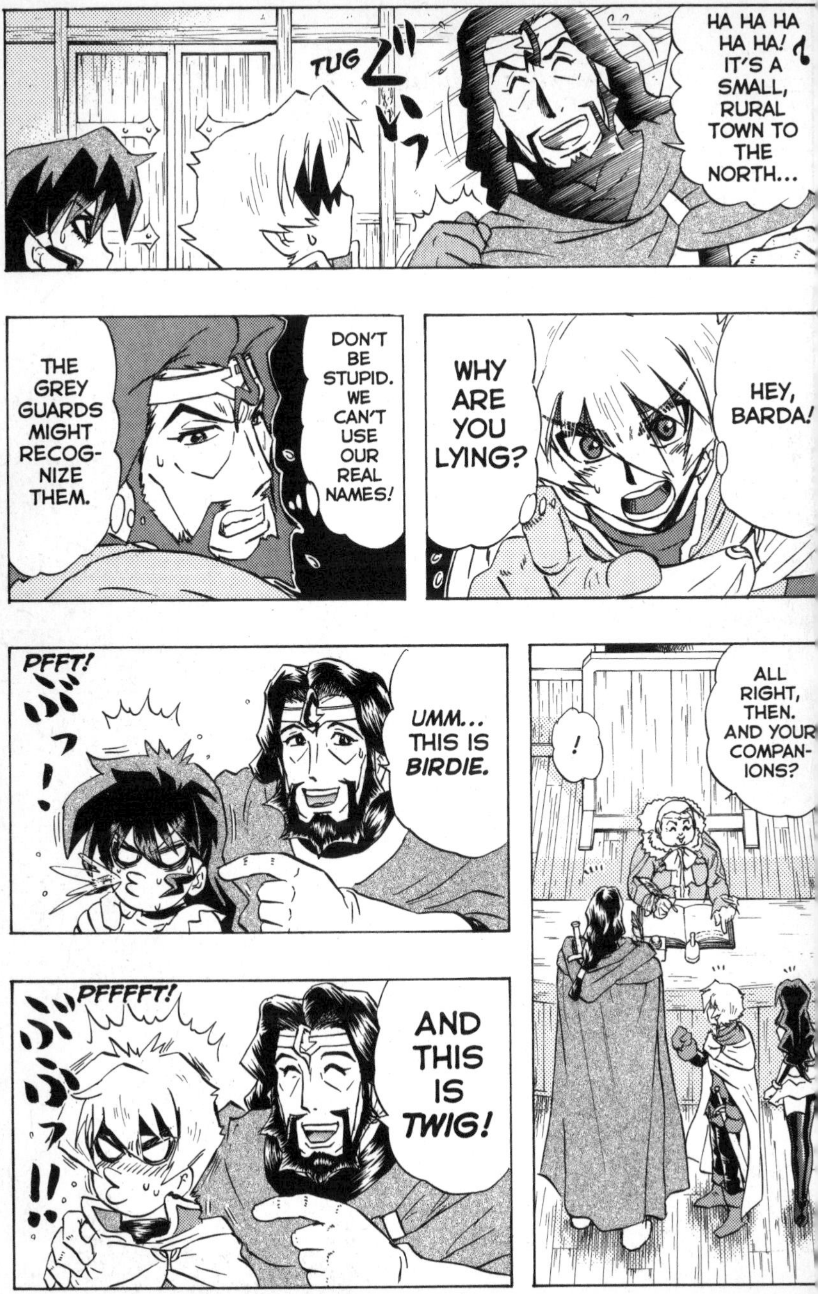
TUG
HA HA HA HA HA! IT'S A SMALL, RURAL TOWN TO THE NORTH...
HEY, BARDA!
WHY ARE YOU LYING?
DON'T BE STUPID. WE CAN'T USE OUR REAL NAMES!
THE GREY GUARDS MIGHT RECOG-NIZE THEM.
ALL RIGHT, THEN. AND YOUR COMPAN-IONS?
!
UMM... THIS IS BIRDIE.
PFFT!
AND THIS IS TWIG!
PFFFFT!

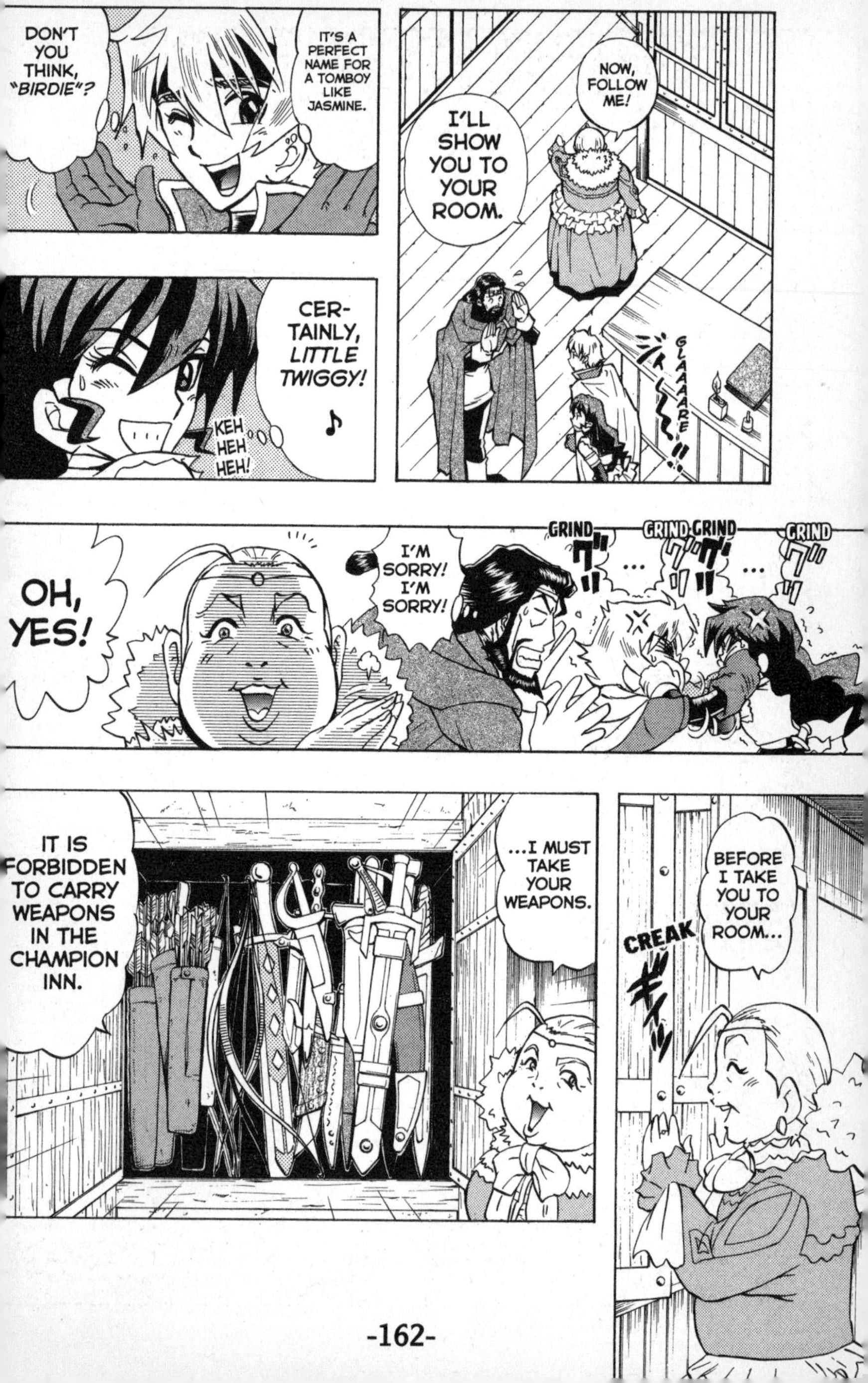
NOW, FOLLOW ME!
I'LL SHOW YOU TO YOUR ROOM.
GLAAAARE!!
IT'S A PERFECT NAME FOR A TOMBOY LIKE JASMINE.
DON'T YOU THINK, "BIRDIE"?
CERTAINLY, LITTLE TWIGGY! ♪
KEH HEH HEH!
GRIND
GRIND GRIND
GRIND
I'M SORRY! I'M SORRY!
OH, YES!
BEFORE I TAKE YOU TO YOUR ROOM...
CREAK
...I MUST TAKE YOUR WEAPONS.
IT IS FORBIDDEN TO CARRY WEAPONS IN THE CHAMPION INN.

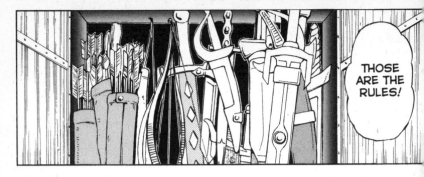

THOSE ARE THE RULES!

CLUNK

WELL, IF THOSE ARE THE RULES.

CHAK

...

I GUESS WE HAVE TO.

GLIN—T!!!

I'LL BE NEEDING *ALL* OF YOUR WEAPONS, YOUNG LADY.

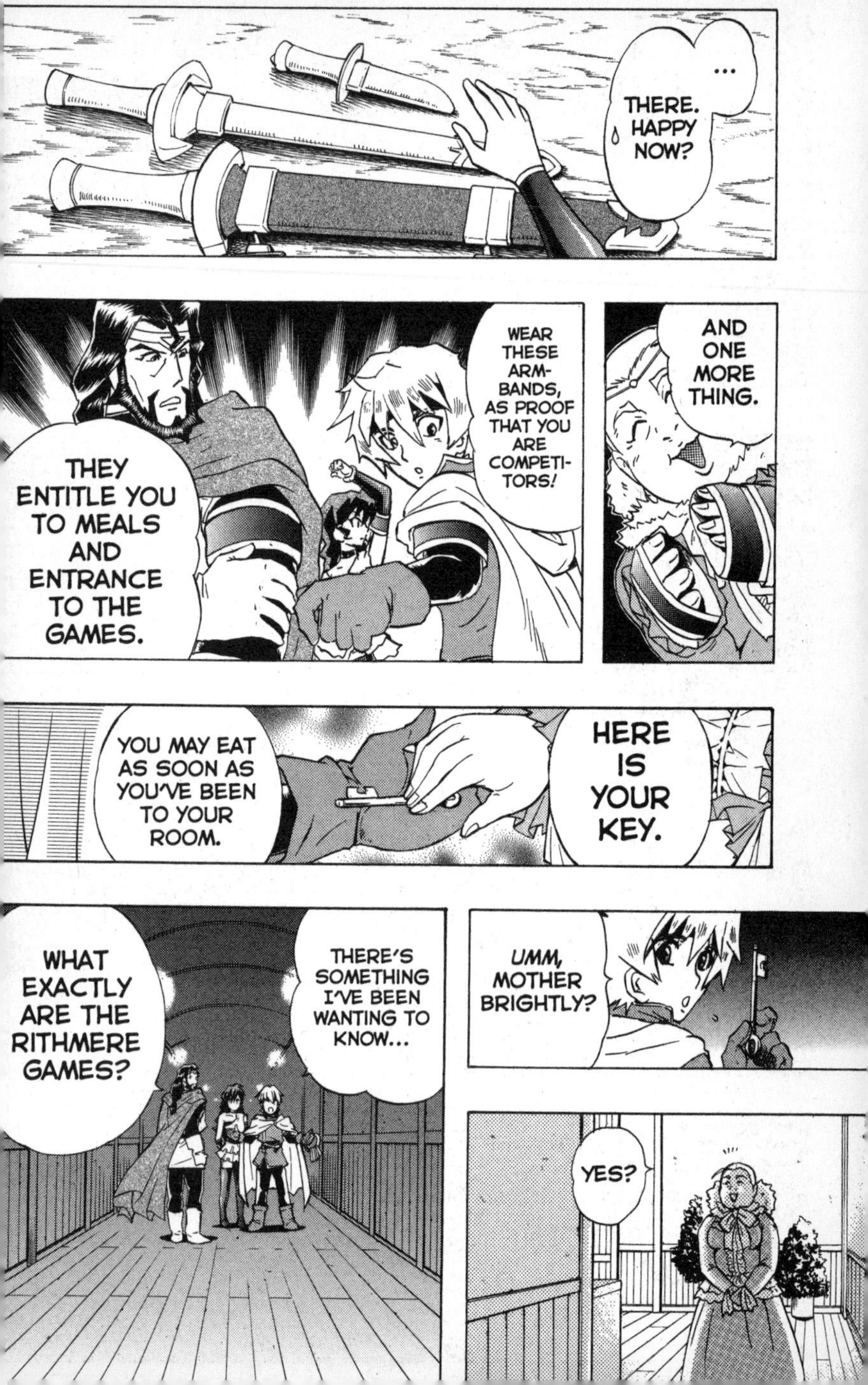
...
THERE. HAPPY NOW?
AND ONE MORE THING.
WEAR THESE ARM-BANDS, AS PROOF THAT YOU ARE COMPETI-TORS!
THEY ENTITLE YOU TO MEALS AND ENTRANCE TO THE GAMES.
HERE IS YOUR KEY.
YOU MAY EAT AS SOON AS YOU'VE BEEN TO YOUR ROOM.
UMM, MOTHER BRIGHTLY?
YES?
THERE'S SOMETHING I'VE BEEN WANTING TO KNOW...
WHAT EXACTLY ARE THE RITHMERE GAMES?

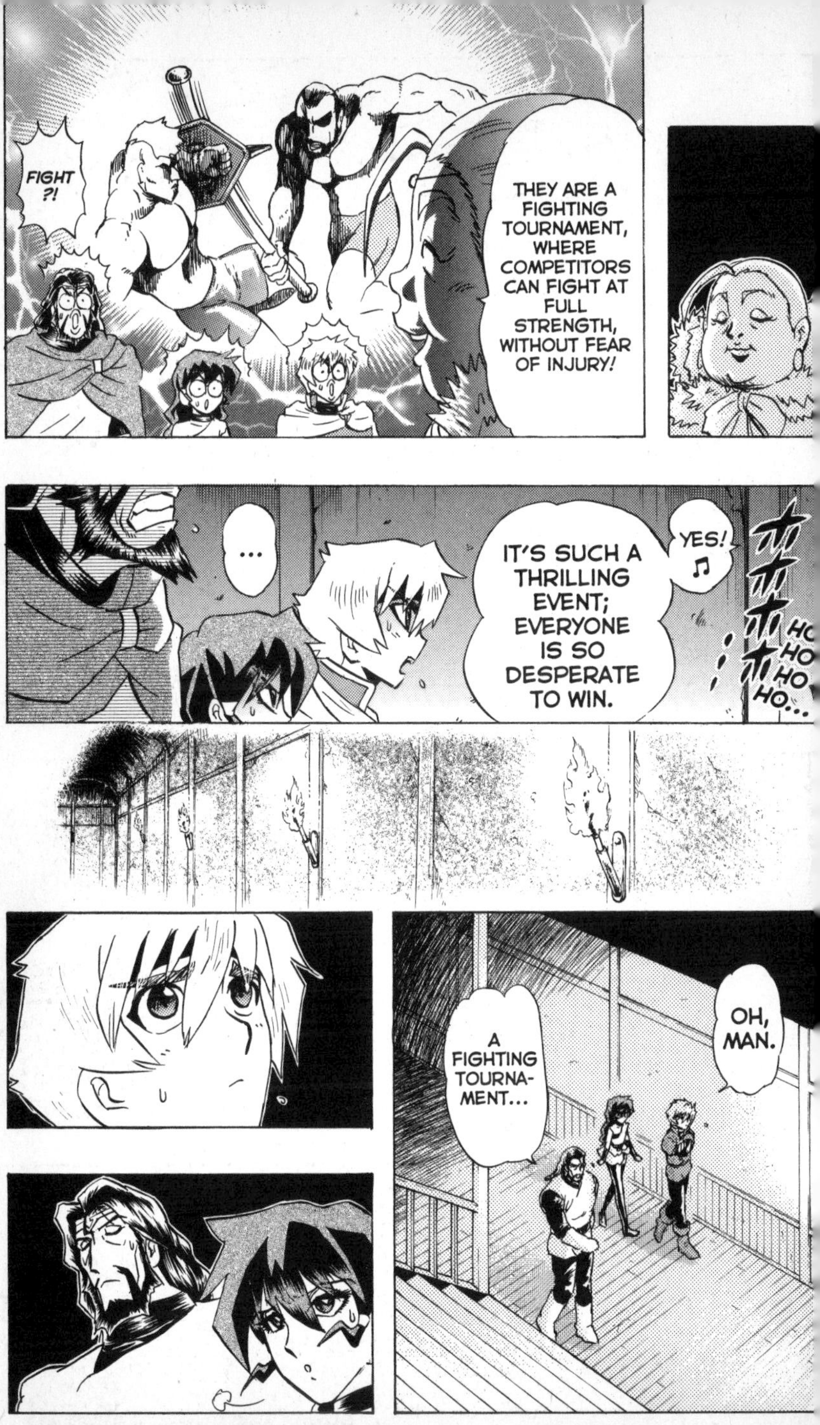
THEY ARE A FIGHTING TOURNAMENT, WHERE COMPETITORS CAN FIGHT AT FULL STRENGTH, WITHOUT FEAR OF INJURY!
FIGHT ?!
HO HO HO HO...
YES! ♫
IT'S SUCH A THRILLING EVENT; EVERYONE IS SO DESPERATE TO WIN.
...
OH, MAN.
A FIGHTING TOURNA- MENT...

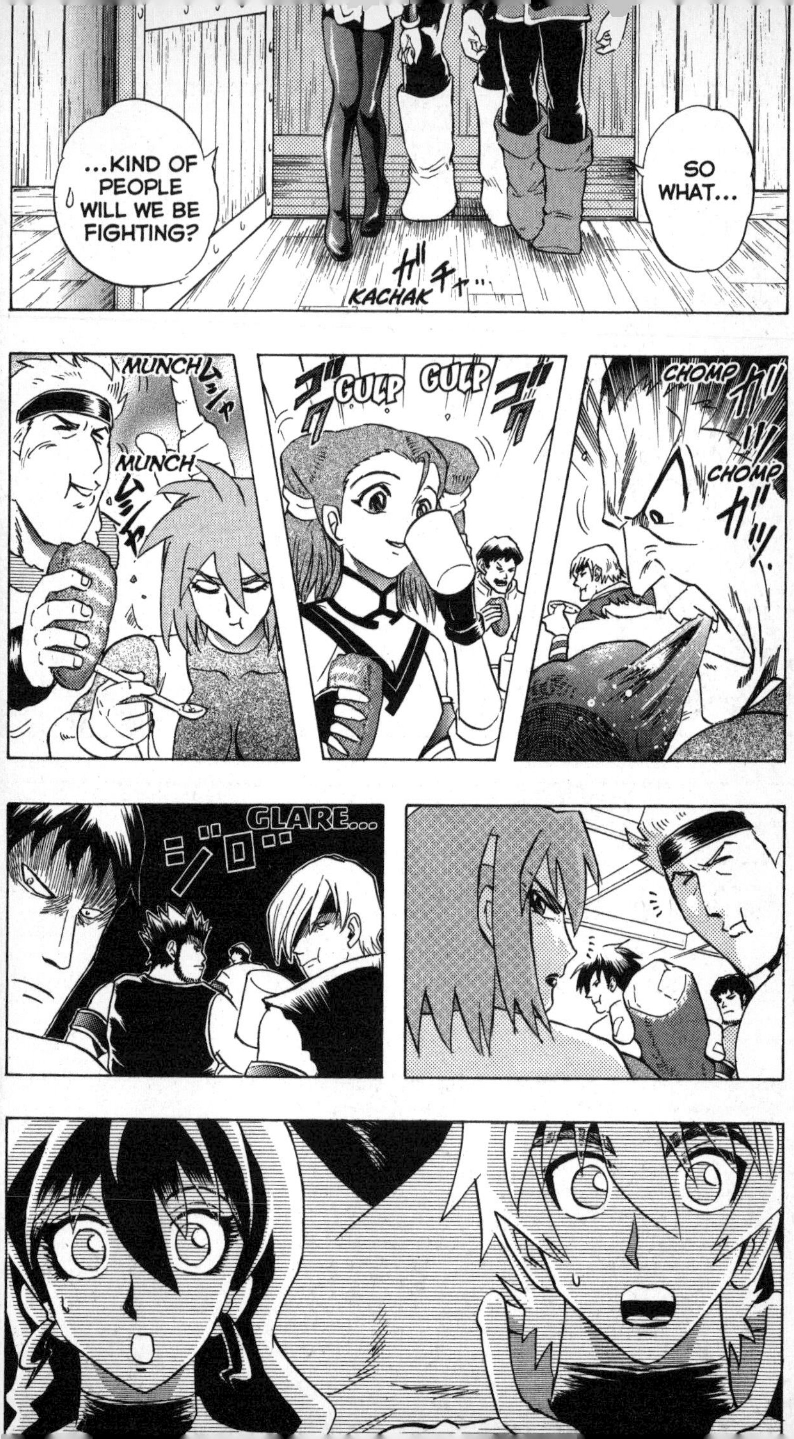
SO WHAT...
...KIND OF PEOPLE WILL WE BE FIGHTING?
ガチャ...
KACHAK
CHOMP
ガリ
CHOMP
ガッ
ゴク
GULP
GULP
ゴク
MUNCH
ムシャ
MUNCH
ムシャ
ジロ...
GLARE...

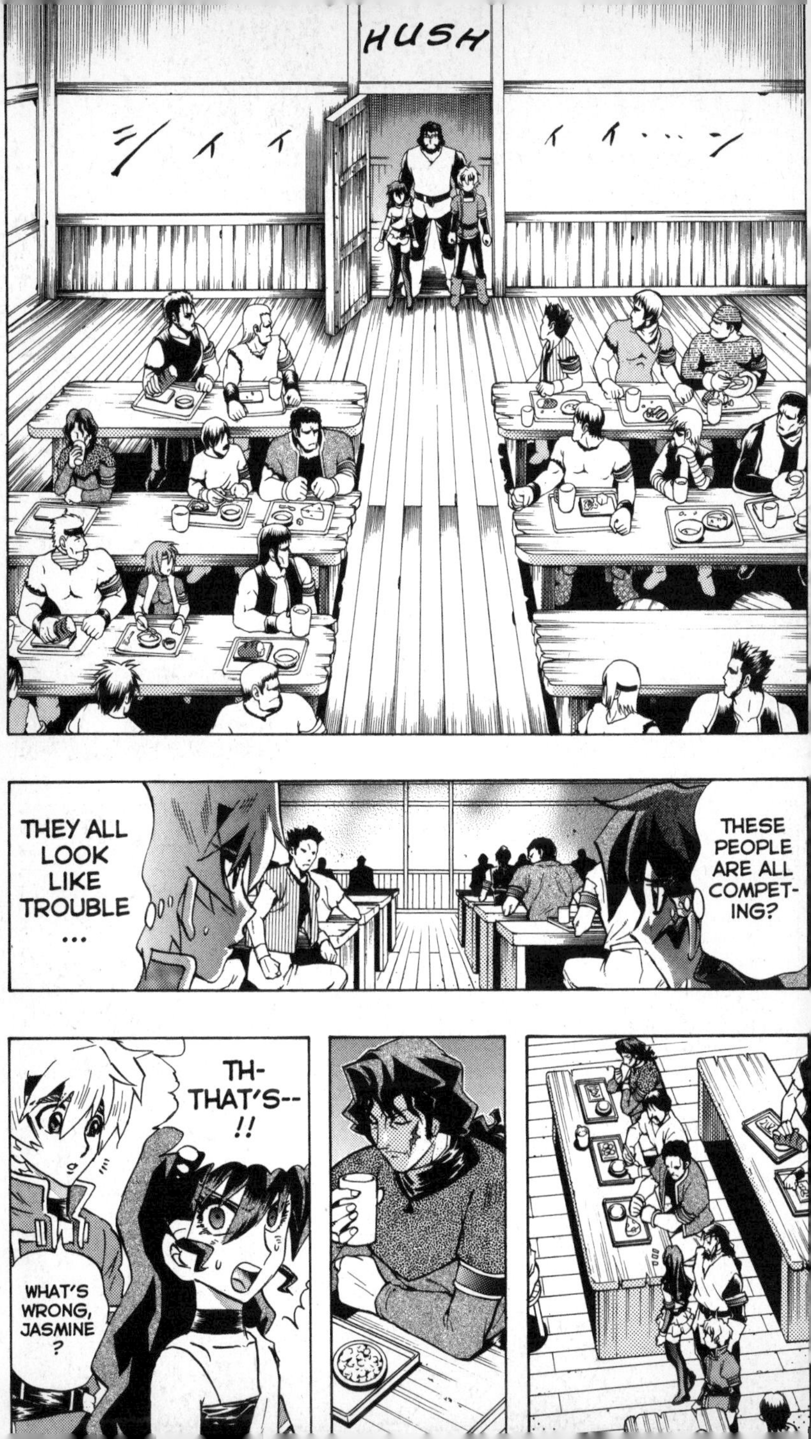
HUSH
シイイ
イイ…ン
THESE PEOPLE ARE ALL COMPET-ING?
THEY ALL LOOK LIKE TROUBLE ...
TH-THAT'S--!!
WHAT'S WRONG, JASMINE ?

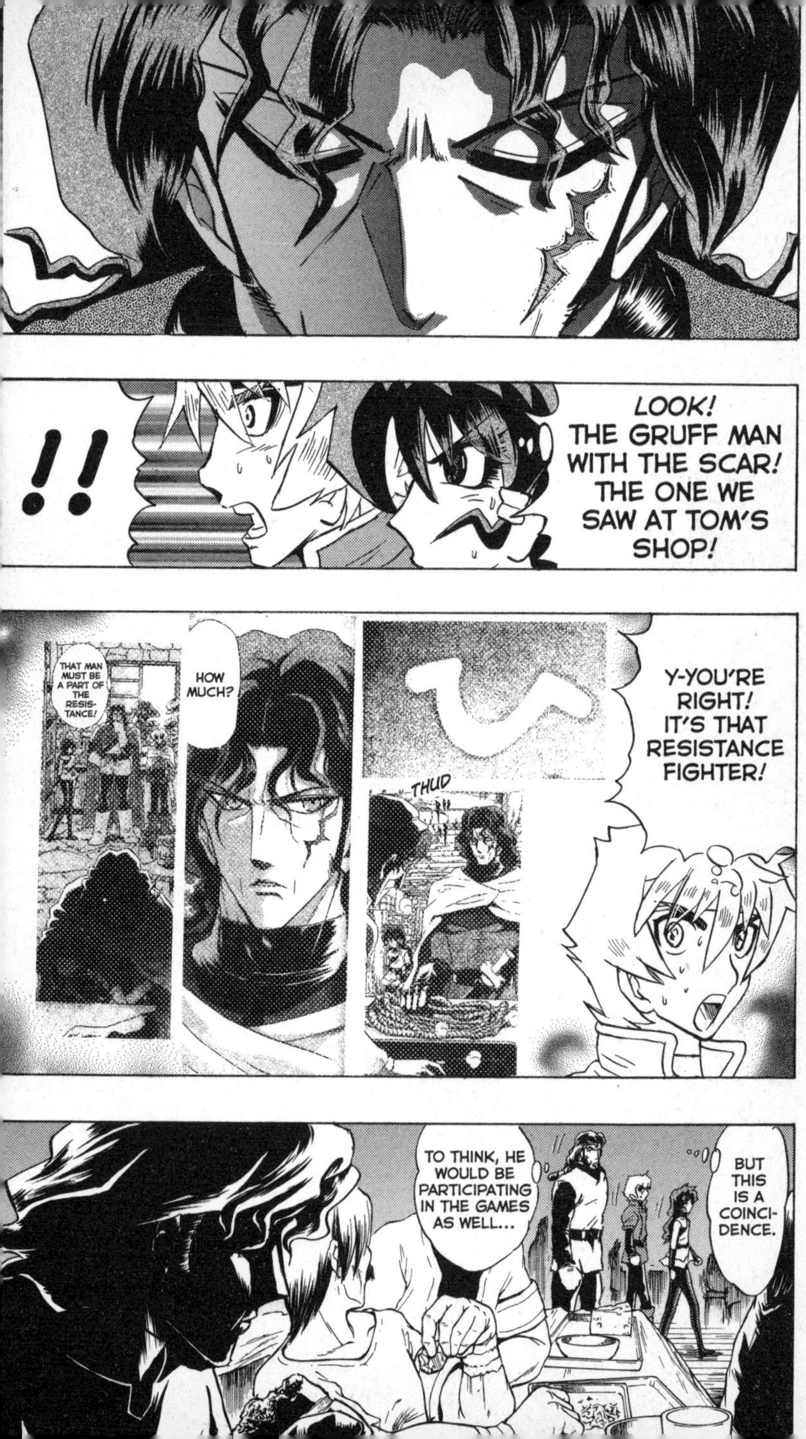
LOOK! THE GRUFF MAN WITH THE SCAR! THE ONE WE SAW AT TOM'S SHOP!
!!
Y-YOU'RE RIGHT! IT'S THAT RESISTANCE FIGHTER!
THUD
HOW MUCH?
THAT MAN MUST BE A PART OF THE RESISTANCE!
BUT THIS IS A COINCIDENCE.
TO THINK, HE WOULD BE PARTICIPATING IN THE GAMES AS WELL...

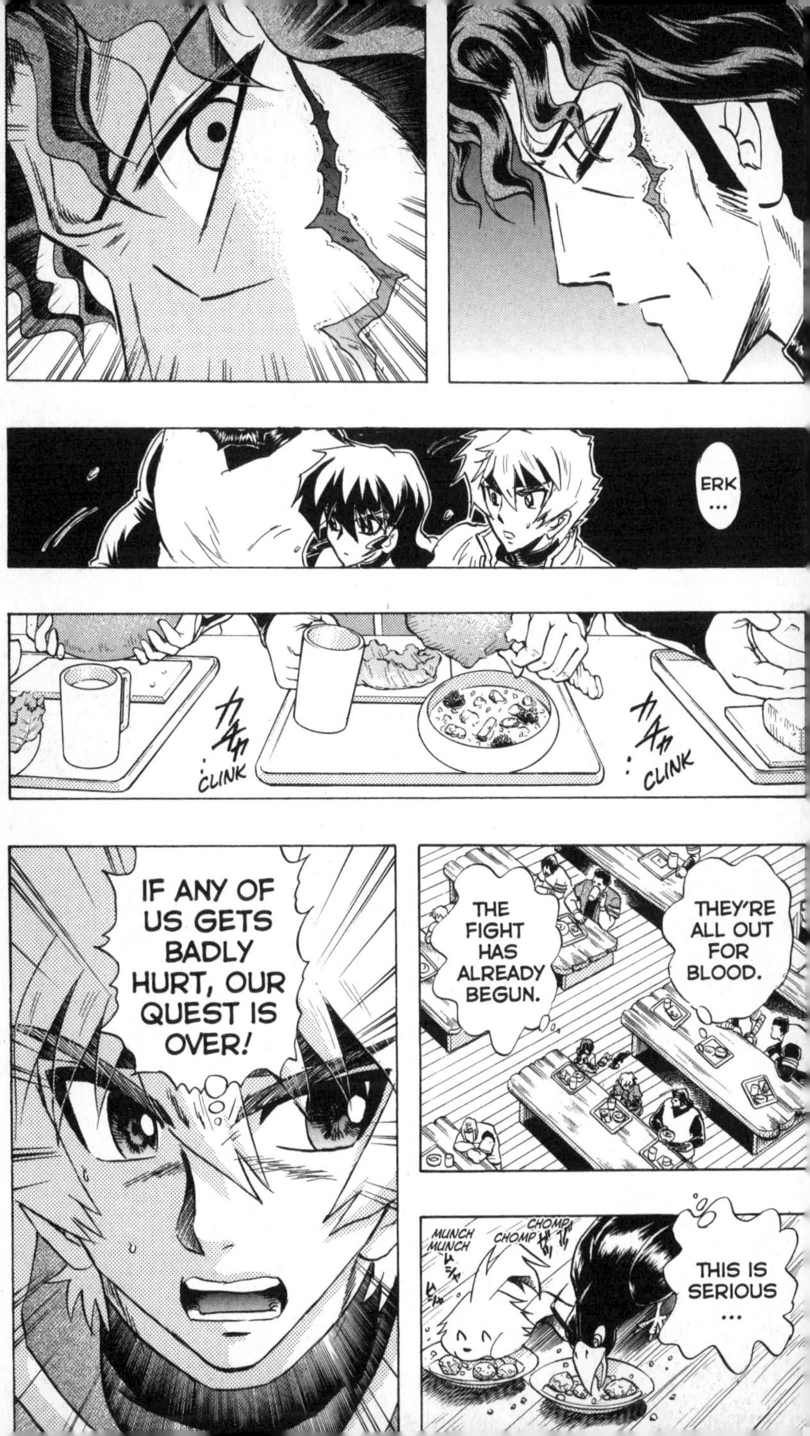
ERK ...
CLINK
CLINK
THEY'RE ALL OUT FOR BLOOD.
THE FIGHT HAS ALREADY BEGUN.
THIS IS SERIOUS ...
CHOMP CHOMP
MUNCH MUNCH
IF ANY OF US GETS BADLY HURT, OUR QUEST IS OVER!

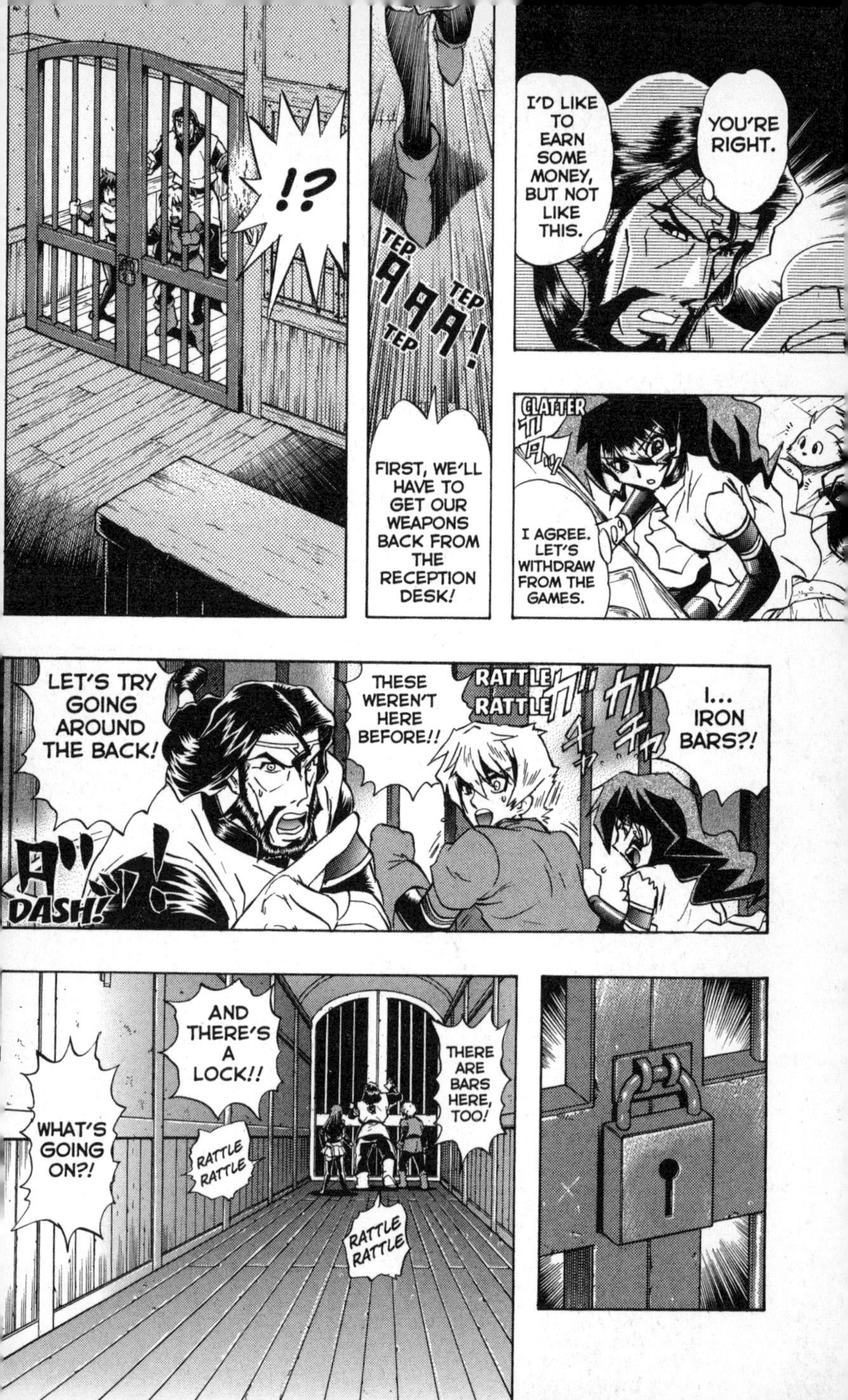
YOU'RE RIGHT.
I'D LIKE TO EARN SOME MONEY, BUT NOT LIKE THIS.
CLATTER
I AGREE. LET'S WITHDRAW FROM THE GAMES.
TEP TEP TEP!
FIRST, WE'LL HAVE TO GET OUR WEAPONS BACK FROM THE RECEPTION DESK!
!?
RATTLE RATTLE
I... IRON BARS?!
THESE WEREN'T HERE BEFORE!!
LET'S TRY GOING AROUND THE BACK!
DASH!
THERE ARE BARS HERE, TOO!
AND THERE'S A LOCK!!
RATTLE RATTLE
RATTLE RATTLE
WHAT'S GOING ON?!

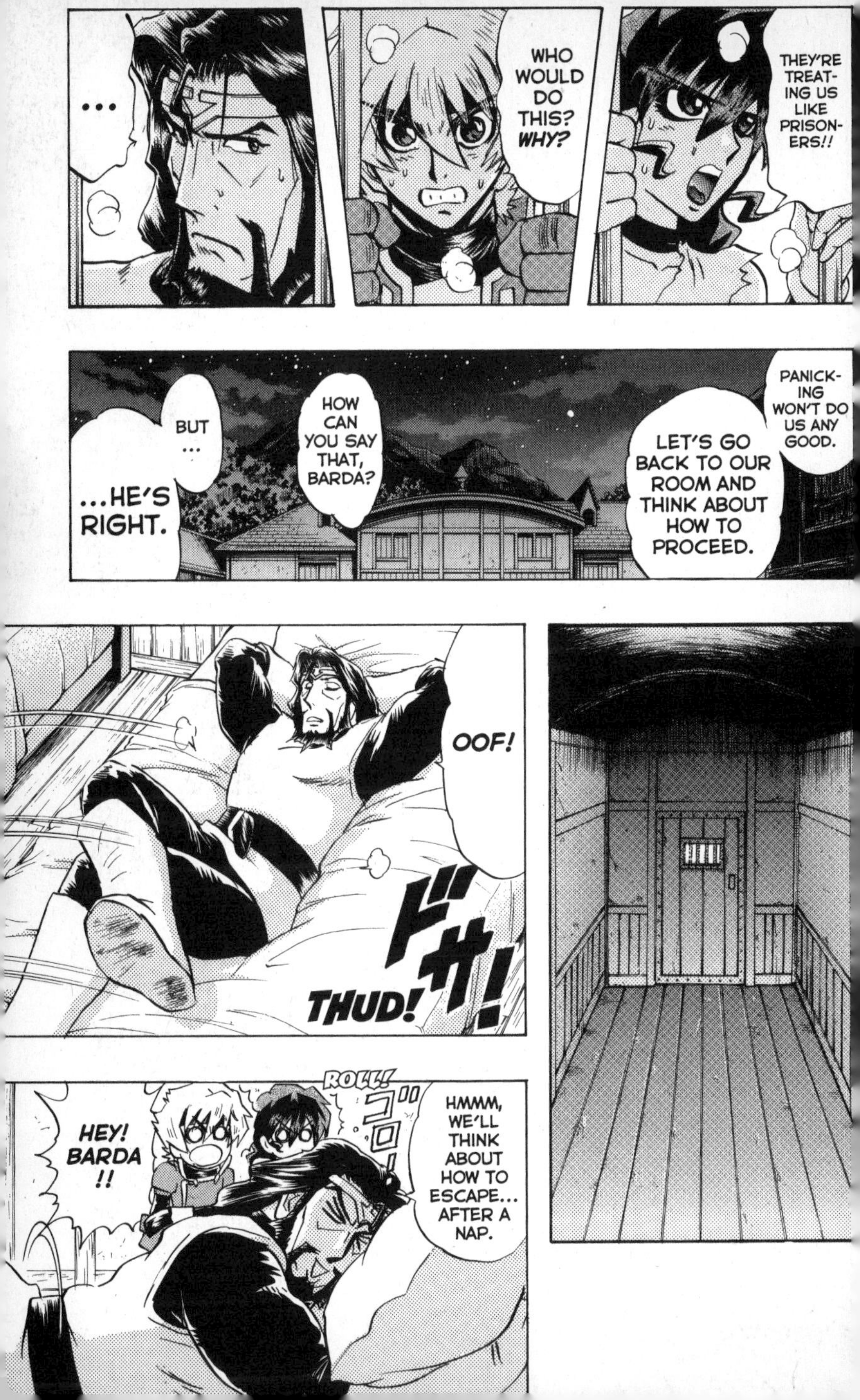
THEY'RE TREATING US LIKE PRISONERS!!
WHO WOULD DO THIS? *WHY?*
...
PANICKING WON'T DO US ANY GOOD.
LET'S GO BACK TO OUR ROOM AND THINK ABOUT HOW TO PROCEED.
HOW CAN YOU SAY THAT, BARDA?
BUT ...
...HE'S RIGHT.
OOF!
ドサ!
THUD!
ROLL!
ゴロー
HMMM, WE'LL THINK ABOUT HOW TO ESCAPE... AFTER A NAP.
HEY! BARDA!!

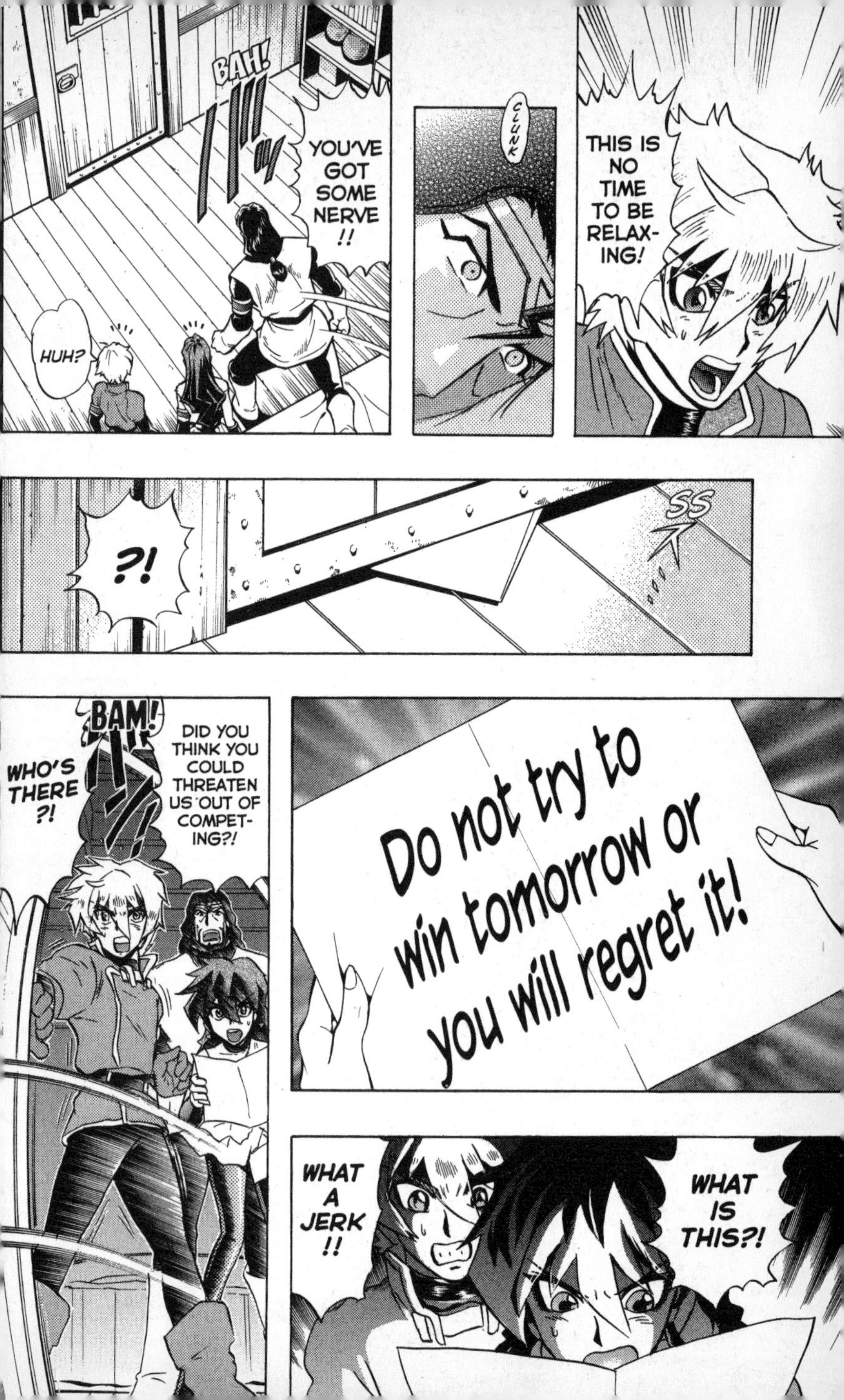
THIS IS NO TIME TO BE RELAX-ING!
CLUNK
YOU'VE GOT SOME NERVE!!
BAH!
HUH?
SS
?!
Do not try to win tomorrow or you will regret it!
WHAT IS THIS?!
WHAT A JERK!!
BAM!
DID YOU THINK YOU COULD THREATEN US OUT OF COMPET-ING?!
WHO'S THERE?!

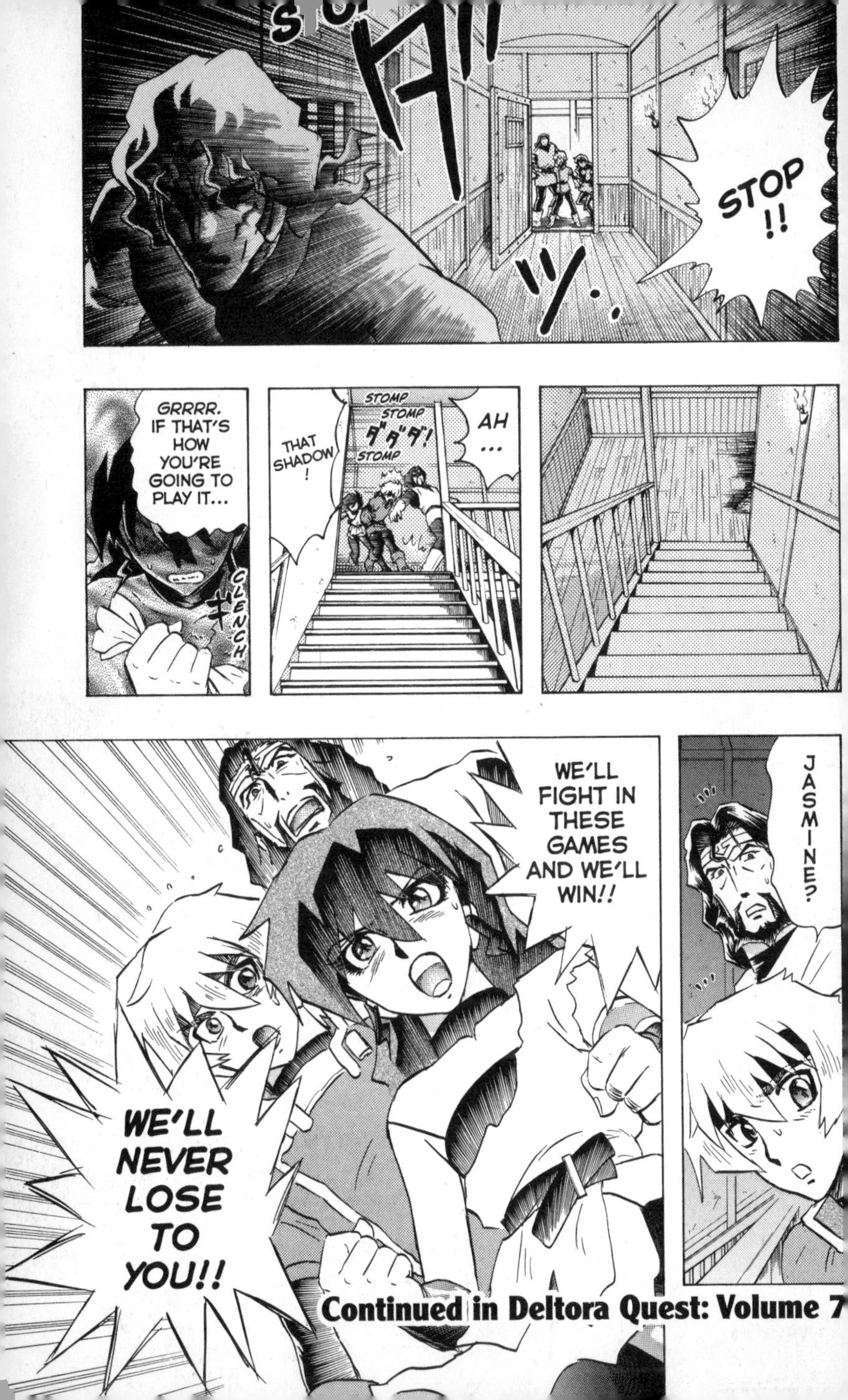
STOP !!
ダダダ!
AH ...
STOMP
STOMP
STOMP
THAT SHADOW !
GRRRR. IF THAT'S HOW YOU'RE GOING TO PLAY IT...
CLENCH
JASMINE?
WE'LL FIGHT IN THESE GAMES AND WE'LL WIN!!
WE'LL NEVER LOSE TO YOU!!

Continued in Deltora Quest: Volume 7

DELTORA QUEST

デルトラクエスト

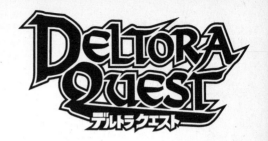

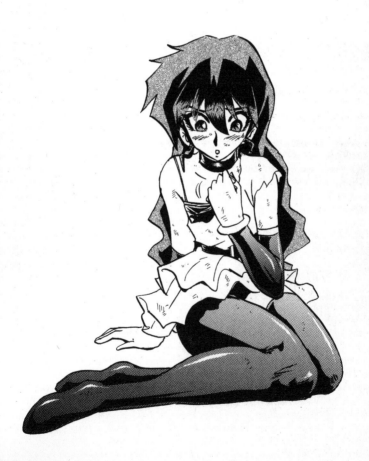

Original story by Emily Rodda

A Kodansha Comics Trade Paperback Original

Deltora Quest volume 6 copyright © 2007 Makoto Niwano © 2007
DELTORA QUEST PARTNERS
English translation copyright © 2012 Makoto Niwano © 2012
DELTORA QUEST PARTNERS

Published in the United States by Kodansha Comics, an imprint of Kodansha USA
Publishing, LLC, New York.

Publication rights arranged through Kodansha Ltd., Tokyo.

First published in Japan in 2007 by Kodansha Ltd., Tokyo.

ISBN 978-1-61262-012-1

Printed in the United States of America

www.kodanshacomics.com

9 8 7 6 5 4 3 2 1

Translator: Mayumi Kobayashi
Lettering: Bobby Timony

TOMARE!

[STOP!]

You are going the wrong way!

Manga is a completely different type of reading experience.

To start at the *beginning*, go to the *end*!

That's right! Authentic manga is read the traditional Japanese way—from right to left, exactly the *opposite* of how American books are read. It's easy to follow: Just go to the other end of the book, and read each page—and each panel—from the right side to the left side, starting at the top right. Now you're experiencing manga as it was meant to be.